Understanding Behaviors for Effective Leadership

PRENTICE HALL BUSINESS PUBLISHING
MANAGEMENT TITLES FOR 2001

Bowin/Harvey: Human Resource Management: An Experiential Approach 2/e
Caproni: Managerial Skills 1/e
Carrell/Heavrin: Labor Relations and Collective Bargaining 6/e
Coulter: Strategic Management in Action 2/e
Coulter: Entrepreneurship in Action 1/e
Daniels/Radebaugh: International Business 9/e
David: Strategic Management 8/e
Dessler: Management 2/e
Ghemawat: Strategy and the Business Landscape: Concepts 1/e
Gomez–Mejia/Balkin/Cardy: Managing Human Resources 3/e
Greer: Strategy and Human Resources 2/e
Harvey/Brown: An Experiential Approach to Organizational Development 6/e
Hersey/Blanchard/Johnson: Managing Organizational Behavior 8/e
Howell/Costley: Understanding Behaviors for Effective Leadership 1/e
Hunger/Wheelen: Essentials of Business Policy and Strategic Management 2/e
Hunsaker: Training in Management Skills 1/e
Jones: Organizational Theory 3/e
Martocchio: Strategic Compensation 2/e
Mische: Strategic Renewal: Becoming a High-Performance Organization 1/e
Osland/Kolb/Rubin: Organizational Behavior Reader 7/e
Osland/Kolb/Rubin: Organizational Behavior: An Experiential Approach 7/e
Robbins/DeCenzo: Fundamentals of Management 3/e
Robbins: Organizational Behavior 9/e
Sanyal: International Management: A Strategic Perspective 1/e
Thompson: The Mind and Heart of the Negotiator 2/e
Tompkins: Cases in Management and Organizational Behavior Vol. 1
Zimmer/Scarbourough: Essentials of Small Business and Entrepreneurship 3/e

OTHER PUBLICATIONS OF INTEREST
Clawson: Level Three Leadership 1/e (1999)
French/Bell: Organizational Development 6/e (2000)
George/Jones: Essentials of Managing Organizational Behavior 1/e (2000)
George/Jones: Understanding and Managing Organizational Behavior 2/e (1999)
Nahavandi: Art and Science of Leadership 2/e (2000)
Pierce/Newstrom: The Manager's Bookshelf 5/e (2000)
Robbins: Essentials of Organizational Behavior 6/e (2000)
Smith: Women at Work 1/e (2000)
Thompson: Making the Team (2000)
Yukl: Leadership 4/e (1998)

Understanding Behaviors for Effective Leadership

Jon P. Howell

New Mexico State University,
College of Business Administration and Economics

Dan L. Costley

New Mexico State University,
College of Business Administration and Economics

Prentice
Hall

Upper Saddle River, New Jersey

Library of Congress Cataloging-in-Publication Data
Howell, Jon P.
  Understanding behaviors for effective leadership / Jon P. Howell, Dan L. Costley.
    p. cm.
  Includes bibliographical references and index.
  ISBN 0-13-028403-3
  1. Organizational behavior. 2. Psychology, Industrial. 3. Supervision of employees. 4.
Leadership. I. Costley, Dan L. II. Title.
  HD58.7 .H684 2000
  158.7—dc21

                                                     99-0870789

VP/Editorial Director: James C. Boyd
Editor-in-Chief: Natalie Anderson
Senior Editor: David Shafer
Editorial Assistant: Kimberly Marsden
Assistant Editor: Michele Foresta
Media Project Manager: Michele Faranda
Executive Marketing Manager: Michael Campbell
Permissions Coordinator: Suzanne Grappi
Director of Production: Michael Weinstein
Production Manager: Gail Steier de Acevedo
Production Coordinator: Kelly Warsak
Manufacturing Buyer: Natacha St. Hill Moore
Senior Prepress/Manufacturing Manager: Vincent Scelta
Cover Design: Kiwi Design
Full Service Composition: Carlisle Communications

10 9 8 7 6 5 4 3 2 1
ISBN 0-13-028403-3

To Julie, Jesse, Matt and Rachel Lee

Brief Contents

Contents

Preface

The basic premise of this book is *we know our leaders by what they do*. Leaders demonstrate their competence by setting worthwhile and challenging goals with followers, by showing confidence in followers and supporting their efforts to perform well and to improve themselves, and by giving recognition to followers when they do a job well. We expect our leaders to perform these and other important leadership behaviors. We may also expect leaders to be intelligent, visionary, inspirational, ethical, fair, and self-confident but we only perceive these personal characteristics by observing and experiencing a leader's behavior. When leaders successfully carry out these behaviors and produce favorable results for their groups and organizations, we view these leaders as effective.

We have been teaching leadership in universities and colleges for over 20 years. We have used existing leadership textbooks as well as academic and popular articles that describe current theories and approaches about what it takes to be an effective leader. Our intent was to convey to our students the richness and breadth of knowledge about leadership that has accumulated during the twentieth century. We finally realized, however, that this approach left most students confused and frustrated. There were simply too many theories and approaches to leadership for most undergraduates (and many MBA students) to absorb and use. They often became lost in the mass of leadership theories and research presented in existing leadership textbooks. By the end of the course, they usually had no idea when or if a given theory was appropriate and often "latched on" to an overly simplistic and poorly supported model of leadership because it was simple enough for them to understand and remember.

We have not emphasized leadership theories in this book. Instead, we organized the book according to a simple common-sense structure that describes current knowledge on *what effective leaders really do*. Most of the leader behaviors described in the chapters that follow have been extensively researched as part of various theoretical models proposed by leadership scholars. In this book, we have presented what is known about each leader behavior without the baggage of many different theories. Although these leader behaviors may overlap to some degree, they are widely recognized and discussed by managers and leadership experts. This structure is designed to minimize confusion, to facilitate understanding, and to provide students with some psychological closure on each leader behavior.

◆ AUDIENCE

This book is intended for use in any college course that focuses on effective leadership. Examples of these courses include Leadership and Motivation, Leadership in Society,

Nursing Leadership, Not-for-Profit Leadership, Leadership in Law Enforcement, or Leadership in Education. The book is also appropriate for a first course in leadership training in business, public, educational, health care, or other organizations.

◆ STRUCTURE AND FEATURES

Part I of the book includes three chapters that introduce the concept of leadership and the approach of the book, and describe and evaluate several currently popular theories of leadership. Part II is composed of ten central chapters that focus on five core leadership behavior patterns that have been studied extensively in different organizational contexts. Two chapters each are devoted to leaders' supportiveness, directiveness, participation, reward and punishment, and charismatic behaviors. These core chapters emphasize *what effective leaders do* by describing in detail each of the core leader behaviors. These chapters also emphasize *how they do it* by identifying leader traits, skills, and sources of power associated with each behavior as well as examples of effective and ineffective leaders carrying out the behaviors. The core chapters also describe *when leaders use each behavior* by identifying situational factors that tell effective leaders when a specific core behavior will be most effective. Part III presents three chapters addressing less-researched leader behavior patterns that will be increasingly important in the new millennium and a concluding chapter that describes popular leadership styles that are combinations of the specific leader behaviors described earlier.

This book also emphasizes the effects of the increasing number of jobs performed by highly educated and professionally oriented employees who use computer technology and/or teams to perform job activities. These individuals and teams are often able to assume more responsibility with less active direction and control by their formal leaders. These emerging workforce and job structure characteristics do not eliminate the need for leadership, but they help organizations economize by reducing the number of middle managers and allowing workers and work groups more freedom to manage their own daily activities.

Examples are provided in each chapter that highlight current and historical leaders who exhibit the leadership behaviors and styles discussed (see the Leadership in Action box on Pat Carrigan, page 4-4). Self-assessment exercises also help the reader understand and apply concepts described in the text (see example on Effective Listening page 4-8). Exercises and short cases are also included to allow students to further understand and apply chapter material (see examples on pages 11-31 entitled Choosing an Appropriate Leadership Style and page 11-37 entitled Move the Supervisors). Numerous illustrations and figures also summarize text material and provide advice on how to apply the material to real leadership situations (see examples on pages 13-26 and 13-27 for charismatic leadership).

◆ INSTRUCTOR'S MATERIAL

- Instructor's Manual/Test Item File
  The Instructor's Manual features Learning Objectives, Lecture Outlines, Answers to Review and Case Questions, and Suggested Activities for each chapter in the text. Included with the Instructor's Manual is a Test Item File

offering a variety of True/False, Multiple/Choice, and Essay questions that facilitate different classroom needs.
- PowerPoint Electronic Transparencies
A comprehensive package of text outlines and figures corresponding to the text, the PowerPoint transparencies are designed to aid the educator and supplement in-class lectures.

◆ ACKNOWLEDGMENTS

During the ten years it took to complete this book, numerous individuals provided valuable assistance by conducting library research, editing, and discussing with us many of the issues we wrote about. Jim Weber, Jennifer Villa, Jim Paul, Michael Clugston, and Lori Paris all provided capable and generous support to our efforts. The College of Business and New Mexico State University provided the library facilities and the environment that allowed us to persist on the project. Our long-time friend and colleague, Peter Dorfman, asked many thought-provoking questions about our project and participated with us on various research projects that produced findings reported in the book. Our families put up with our long hours of work over the years with words of encouragement and they never wavered in their confidence that we would complete the project. The many reviewers who read and commented on earlier versions of the manuscript provided the essential feedback we needed to keep the book relevant to students of leadership as well as true to the leadership literature. These reviewers are listed below:

John Barbuto, University of Nebraska, Lincoln;
Melinda Blackman, California State University, Fullerton;
John Chism, Truckee Meadows Community College;
Samuel Felton, Strategic Management Databases-Maine;
Daron Jones, Franklin-Covey Company;
Tiffany Keller, University of Richmond;
Brenda LeTendre, Pittsburgh State University;
Bronston T. Mayes, California State University, Fullerton;
Leslie Michael, Big Bend Community College;
Lyman Porter, University of California, Irvine;
Josh Powers, Indiana University;
Ron Riggio, Claremont McKenna College;
Bruce Schooling, Point Loma Nazarene University;
Betty Scott, Community College of Southern Nevada;
Paula M. Short, University of Missouri, Columbia;
Judy Turman, Tyler Junior College;
Robert Vecchio, University of Notre Dame;
Jim Weber, St. Cloud State University.

Basic
Leadership
Concepts

CHAPTER

1

Leadership and Its Importance

Learning Objectives
After reading this chapter you should be able to do the following:

1. Define and describe the leadership process.
2. Discuss the similarity of leadership and management in organizations.
3. Describe how power, influence, and authority are related to leadership.
4. Describe the types of power often used by leaders.
5. Describe traits leaders often possess.
6. Discuss how leadership behaviors are critical to a leader's effectiveness.
7. Describe how situational factors can affect a leader's success.
8. Describe the three key tasks leaders must carry out in order to be effective.

Leadership is a fascinating social phenomenon which occurs in all groups of people regardless of geography, culture, or nationality. Ancient Chinese and Greek leaders looked to philosophers for advice, Egyptians attributed specific godlike traits to their leader-kings, and famous writers such as Homer and Machiavelli documented shrewd and cunning strategies of successful leaders. Much of history is recorded through the lives of famous leaders. Names such as George Washington, Abraham Lincoln, Clara Barton, Mahatma Gandhi, Golda Meir, John F. Kennedy, Martin Luther King Jr., and Nelson Mandela symbolize major eras of social upheaval that have had immense repercussions. Most young people today aspire to become leaders in school, athletics, entertainment, politics, industry, military, medicine, or some other area of endeavor. Although Bass (1) has noted that the word "leadership" did not appear in the English language until about 1300, this social phenomenon has been recognized since the beginnings of recorded history.

Careful studies in organizations show that executive leadership can account for 45 percent of an organization's performance (2). Hundreds of surveys show that leadership makes a difference in followers' satisfaction and performance (3,4,5,6). Leadership affects the educational climate in schools, church attendance, job stress, organizational change, and military success. Effective leadership can create shared beliefs, values, and expectations in organizations and in societies and can modify followers' interpretations and understanding of issues and events. Leaders build empires and inspire intense fervor and dedication. Leaders can also bring destruction on followers, organizations, and societies, as shown by Jim Jones, David Koresh, and Adolph Hitler. Thousands of articles and books have been published on leadership. Leadership training is increasingly a topic of university and college courses and programs in industry.

◆ DEFINING LEADERSHIP

Should any person who exerts influence over others be considered a leader? Is the use of coercion and force to gain compliance a part of leadership? Are the processes of management and leadership the same? Numerous definitions of leadership have been offered and discussed over the years (7,8,9,10). Recently experts on the subject have agreed on certain core characteristics of leadership. The following definition contains these characteristics and is intended as a broad but concise explanation of the leadership process to be discussed in the chapters that follow.

Leadership is a process used by an individual to influence group members toward the achievement of group goals, where the group members view the influence as legitimate.

The core characteristics of this definition will be considered one by one.

First, leadership is a process or a reasonably systematic and continuous series of actions directed toward group goals. Leadership is not usually a single act or even a few acts performed only in certain situations. It is a pattern of behaviors that is demonstrated fairly consistently over time with specific objectives. Some writers use the term leadership to represent the individual who carries out these activities. Others define it as the properties or qualities of individuals who carry out this series of actions effectively (11). Because it is the actions of individuals that distinguish them as leaders, most experts today focus on the series of actions or pattern of behaviors that nearly all leaders exhibit.

Second, the actions of leaders are designed to influence people to modify their behavior. Those being influenced are often referred to as followers. Followers play an important role in the leadership process for at least two reasons: without followers, no one can be a leader, and all leaders are followers at times (12,13). Most leaders today do not have total control (absolute power) over followers' behavior. Instead, leaders typically use various behaviors to influence followers.

Third, although at times the series of actions may be carried out by more than one person, a single individual will usually be expected to fulfill the leadership role for a given group. The individual may be appointed to the role by someone outside the group (such as with most managers), he or she may be elected by the group members to serve as leader for a fixed period of time (such as the president of a sorority), or the leader may emerge informally from interaction of the members (such as the leader of a street gang). The rights and obligations vary somewhat for each of these leaders, but the pattern of behaviors they exhibit while fulfilling their leadership roles are remarkably similar.

Fourth, followers view the leader's influence as legitimate; that is, the influence is reasonable and justifiable under the circumstances. This usually means the leader utilizes noncoercive methods to convince followers to comply with requests. In modern societies, leaders often achieve compliance by rewarding or recognizing; displaying their expertise, superior knowledge, and/or moral rightness; emphasizing formal authority; or threatening punishment for noncompliance. When threats of punishment are used, they normally involve a material change such as transfer to a less desirable work threats and attacks. He attended to his followers by directing their activities and serving as a role model for them. His support for followers was shown through encouragement and declarations of the righteousness of their cause. He sought followers' advice on decisions about strategies and tactics. King represented their cause by working frequently with leaders outside the civil rights movement. Activities such as outlining an appealing future vision for followers, clarifying their identities, providing a historical perspective, expressing constant dissatisfaction with the status quo, and using symbolism to develop public appeal were examples of King's charismatic behaviors. Such leadership behaviors and traits are the subject of much of this book and will be discussed in detail in the following chapters. Although King was a master at many of these behaviors, the beginning of mastery is understanding. We have dedicated this book to providing an understanding of these effective leadership traits and behaviors.

◆ LEADERSHIP VERSUS MANAGEMENT

Many writers have attempted to distinguish between management and leadership. From early classical writers to modern researchers, the distinction between management and leadership has often been based on viewing management as "doing things right" and viewing leadership as "doing the right things." Management is seen as a mechanical and administrative activity, while leadership involves changing and developing more effective organizations. Managers are often viewed as "organizational engineers," who apply rational problem solving, use objective technical criteria, and manipulate standardized building blocks in organizations to achieve well-known goals. Leadership, however, is viewed as the process of creating a social organism or "living enterprise" that is active, capable of changing, and responsive to the environment. Finding an environmental niche in which an organization can function and grow is a leadership role (14,15).

Each of these views is incomplete in its description of the leadership/management role in real organizations. Each perspective emphasizes certain aspects of the leadership/management role while ignoring other interpretations. These incomplete views have inhibited our ability to understand the increasingly complex leadership/management process.

Today's complex organizations and increasingly complicated environments require a more well-rounded view of the leadership/management process. The process must include rational analysis and problem solving while also encouraging organizational growth, identification of environmental niches, and development of a mission to guide the organization in adapting to its surroundings. In modern organizations, leadership and management roles are seldom separable. At times a leader/manager may need to "charge up" followers, creating commitment, inspiration, growth, and adaptation. Here the individual is clearly exerting leadership. At other times, the same person must attend to mundane administrative matters such as modifying rules and regulations, allocating resources, and assigning tasks. Here the individual is generally viewed as managing. In this book, we acknowledge that management and leadership are closely related and that the same individuals usually perform both activities. It therefore is not realistic to separate leadership activities from management activities when both are designed to influence followers to accomplish goals. The behaviors described in this book are useful for any person who attempts to influence a group of people toward achievement of group goals.

◆ POWER, INFLUENCE, AUTHORITY, AND LEADERSHIP

In discussions of leadership, power is usually considered the ability of one person to cause another person to do something. Influence is often defined as the use of power or power in action. Power and influence are clearly related and both play a major role in the leadership process. As mentioned earlier, leaders use a variety of methods to exert influence on followers—offering rewards, threatening punishment, demonstrating expertise or formal authority, and using moral persuasion. The major sources or types of influence leaders use can be classified according to whether they emanate primarily from characteristics of the individual leader, from the position the leader holds in the group or organization, or from both these sources. Table 1–1, which defines these types of influence, is partially based on early work by French and Raven (16,17,18).

Some writers believe that leaders rely most heavily (or exclusively) on person-based types of influence. But the research shows that leaders also utilize rewards, punishments, and formal authority to influence followers (19,20,21,22). Leaders in any formal organization also use connections or networks to obtain resources that they use to encourage followers to comply with requests. The role of position-based types of influence in leadership is often underestimated (23). This is probably because followers prefer to attribute their own compliance to the leader's referent or expert power than to admit they were primarily influenced out of fear or a hope for personal gain. It seems safe to conclude that most effective leaders use various types of power, including formal authority, to influence followers (24). Some evidence indicates that the type of influence a leader uses also depends on the situation (25,26). The following chapters will address behavior patterns common to most leaders, and specific types of influence appropriate for each situation. The following example demonstrates how leadership and power were viewed in Nazi Germany prior to World War II.

TABLE 1–1 Types of Power Used by Leaders

Person-Based Power
Expert Power—The followers comply because they believe the leader has special knowledge about the best way to do something.
Referent Power—The followers comply because they admire or identify with the leader and want to gain the leader's approval.

Position-Based Power
Legitimate Power—The followers comply because they believe the leader has the right to make requests and followers have the obligation to comply.

Position-and/or Person-Based Power
Reward Power—The followers comply in order to obtain rewards (e.g. a raise or a compliment) from the leader.
Coercive Power—The followers comply in order to avoid punishments from the leader.
Connection/Resource Power—The followers comply because the leader provides needed resources or has close ties with another powerful person who can influence followers' status.

Adapted from G. Yukl, *Leadership in Organizations* (3rd ed.) (Upper Saddle River, NJ: Prentice Hall, 1994) p. 197.

LEADERSHIP SELF-ASSESSMENT: EVALUATING LEADERSHIP TRAITS

Objective: To help the reader think about how personal traits of leaders may help or hinder the leader's effectiveness.

Instructions: The following leader traits or personal characteristics have been the subject of research on leaders' effectiveness. Some of these traits have contributed to successful performance of leaders, while others have been detrimental to leadership performance, although the effectiveness of a leader trait usually depends on the situation and followers involved. Mark an X next to each trait you believe generally helps a leader to be effective and that hinders leadership effectiveness.

Leader Traits	*Usually Makes Leaders:*	
	More Effective	Less Effective
1. Persistence	_____	_____
2. Good speaking ability	_____	_____
3. Perfectionist	_____	_____
4. Sociable	_____	_____
5. Arrogant	_____	_____
6. Cooperative	_____	_____
7. Afraid of failure	_____	_____
8. Impulsive	_____	_____
9. Task oriented	_____	_____
10. Argumentative	_____	_____
11. Self confident	_____	_____
12. Adaptable	_____	_____

Now turn to the end of the chapter to compare your answers with research results on leader traits.

Source: Based on R. T. Hogan, G. T. Curphy, and J. Hogan, "What Do We Know About Leadership?: Effectiveness and Personality," *American Psychologist,* 49 (1994), pp. 493–504 and B. M. Bass, *Bass and Stogdills Handbook of Leadership* (3rd ed.) (New York: The Free Press, 1990).

◆ TRAITS OF LEADERS

Early attempts to understand why some individuals were effective leaders focused on their personal characteristics or traits as the most critical determinant. A leadership trait is a relatively permanent characteristic that does not change as the individual moves from situation to situation. The first published article on leadership traits appeared in the United States in 1904 and focused on intelligence. Examples

---

LEADERSHIP IN PERSPECTIVE

In Nazi Germany during the 1930s and early 1940s, the idea of *fuhrer princip* required complete obedience and loyalty to leaders. This type of absolute command was believed to result in order and prosperity for those members of society who were the favored race. Others were imprisoned and many were executed. After the destruction of the Nazi war machine during World War II, the German people rejected this principle of leadership. This resulted in the current practice in most German organizations of consulting with workers about management decisions.

---

of other leader traits that were studied include height, energy, socioeconomic status, education, age, alertness, aggressiveness, and popularity. Between 1904 and 1970, hundreds of leadership trait studies were published with apparently significant findings regarding leaders' physical and social characteristics, psychological and background traits, as well as task and ability variables. Table 1–2 summarizes findings of these trait studies. At first, the leadership trait research seemed to support the notion that effective leaders had some inherent general characteristics which enabled them to influence people toward group goals—that good leaders were born, not made. Summaries of this research, however, uncovered several problems with the findings (1).

First, researchers did not agree on which leader traits were most important. Second, much of the trait research distinguished leaders from nonleaders rather than effective from ineffective leaders. Third, researchers often disagreed on how to define and measure certain traits. Finally, the research findings showed little or nothing about how much of a given trait was needed for leadership effectiveness. When individuals who apparently possessed important leadership traits were selected for leadership positions, their performance was usually no more effective than leaders who did not have the traits. Based on these observations, in the early 1950s, leadership traits became less popular as a topic of leadership research, and most leadership researchers changed their focus to study how leaders actually behaved.

Recently, however, there has been a renewal of interest in personal traits of leaders (27). Though many years of research showed no one set of traits as essential for leader-

TABLE 1–2 Important Traits of Leaders from Early Research

Physical or Background Traits	*Personality or Ability Traits*	*Task or Social Traits*
Activity or energy	Assertiveness	Motivation to achieve
Education	Dominance	Responsibility
Social status	Independence/Originality	Initiative
	Self-confidence	Persistence
	Administrative ability	Task orientation
	Fluency of speech	Cooperativeness
	Social perceptiveness	Sociability
	Adaptability	

ship effectiveness, the decrease in popularity of the trait approach among researchers may have been premature. Certain traits can certainly help a leader to be effective in specific situations, although most important traits vary with the situation. Still, a few traits, such as fluency of speech, self confidence, social perceptiveness, and adaptability appear to help leaders be effective in a broad spectrum of situations.

Another look at Table 1–2 reveals that some of the so-called traits of leaders are learned abilities and skills, not inherited physical or personal characteristics a leader possesses at birth. Fluency of speech and administrative ability are obvious examples, and training programs exist to increase participants' assertiveness skills and achievement motivation. Also, during the 1950s, a high level of interest was developing in group dynamics. How groups perform and develop, and how key roles emerge, including leadership roles, were topics from social psychology that leadership researchers began to address. These two developments helped support the trend toward the study of how leaders behave.

◆ LEADERSHIP BEHAVIORS

During the 1950s and 1960s, researchers sought an ideal pattern of leadership behavior that would produce satisfaction and high performance among followers regardless of the leadership situation or type of followers. For some time it appeared that the ideal pattern had been found in leaders who were very considerate of their followers' personal feelings and concerns and were very active in structuring, guiding, and monitoring followers' work activities. Several studies showed increased group cohesion, improved performance, and increased effectiveness ratings when leaders demonstrated this pattern of behavior with followers (28,29,30,31). By the mid 1970s, however, it became clear that the notion of an ideal pattern of leadership behavior was as much a myth as the idea that a single set of personal traits would characterize all effective leaders (32). Comparative studies using multiple samples from different organizations showed that the most effective leadership behavior pattern varied, depending on the situation and the type of followers involved.

Nearly all current leadership experts agree that effective leadership behavior depends on situational and follower characteristics. This means that a leadership behavior pattern that is effective in one situation is not necessarily effective in another situation. For a leader to be continuously effective over time and in different situations, the leader's behavior must vary with the situation. In order to vary leadership behavior correctly, the leader must be able to diagnose the situation and follower characteristics, determine the pattern of leader behaviors that will result in high performance, and then provide the appropriate leadership behaviors. Several writers have proposed theoretical models to explain which leadership behaviors are needed in which situations. The Path-Goal Theory (33), the Situational Leadership Theory (34), and the Multiple Linkage Model (35) are three well-known models of this type. These models are generally known as "contingency" or "situational" leadership theories, meaning that the most effective leadership behavior depends on the situation.

A factor common to contingency models of leadership is that behaviors which make leaders effective can be learned. Thus, they depart from the original impetus for research on leadership traits, which assumed leaders were naturally gifted individuals who possessed certain "magical" traits that gave them influence over followers. (This

LEADERSHIP IN ACTION: EFFECTIVE LEADER BEHAVIORS

The following are specific examples of leader behaviors that many leaders use to influence followers:

- Explaining methods and techniques for followers to use in completing tasks
- Being friendly and informative and encouraging two-way communication
- Consulting with followers to obtain information and opinions before making important decisions
- Praising followers for a job well done
- Expressing high expectations and confidence in followers' performance

These and other behaviors by the leader help followers to work efficiently, to feel they are part of a productive team where good work is recognized, and to have confidence in their own abilities. Leaders who effectively demonstrate these behaviors are not born with the knowledge and experience needed to carry them out. They must develop this type of leadership expertise over time, usually through interaction with followers, peers, and higher level leaders. However, certain traits and skills may assist a knowledgeable leader in providing specific leader behaviors effectively, such as fluency of speech, self-confidence, sociability, or a desire for influence over others. Each of the major behavior patterns used by leaders will be described in detail in the following chapters.

---

philosophy was often summarized in the statement, "Leaders are born, not made.") Contingency models of leadership behavior maintain that much effective leadership can be learned, and therefore leadership training can be a key factor in effective leadership. This is not to say that anyone can learn to be a Lee Iacocca or a Martin Luther King Jr. People learn at different rates, some learn more than others, some put forth extra effort to enhance their learning, and some are able to apply their learning more effectively than others. But people can learn about how effective leaders behave and how they diagnose situations. With effort, many people can learn to exhibit leader behaviors with varying degrees of expertise. Several leader behaviors often used by highly effective leaders are described in the box titled Leadership Behaviors.

It should be clear from this brief discussion that leader behaviors differ from leadership traits or skills. Moreover, behaviors and traits or skills interact to determine a leader's effectiveness. For example, a leader who has considerable expertise at the employees' tasks, is self-confident, enjoys influencing others, and is articulate (all traits and skills) will likely enjoy assigning followers to specific tasks and explaining appropriate work methods (leadership behaviors). The leader will have the verbal and task skills to make this guidance meaningful and easily understandable. Leaders who lack several of these characteristics may be reserved, uncertain of their task or verbal skills, and unwilling to take the initiative necessary to provide this type of guidance. Another example is the leader who is naturally sociable and agreeable and enjoys friendly and informative interactions with followers (leadership traits). This person will probably be effective involving followers in decision making (leadership behaviors).

◆ SITUATIONAL FACTORS AND LEADERSHIP

Situational factors are often extremely important to effective leadership. Some situational factors actually increase a leader's impact on followers (36). An example is when a leader is given control over important rewards, such as bonuses, promotions, or desirable job assignments. When followers know a leader controls these rewards, they are more responsive to the leader's efforts to influence them. Other situational factors that increase a leader's influence may be the followers' lack of experience or unclear work tasks, which often cause followers to look to the leader for guidance.

Other situational factors decrease a leader's impact on followers (37). Specific follower characteristics are often important aspects of the leader's situation. An example is a follower who has an unusually strong desire for independence and autonomy. This type of individual may resent being told how to do a task and refuse to comply with a leader's directions even though guidance may be needed to do the task well. Another situational factor that can decrease a leader's impact is a cohesive but uncooperative work group that may conspire to make the leader look bad. These factors make followers less responsive to a leader's behavior.

Finally, certain situational factors replace followers' needs for specific leader behaviors (38). In these situations, other factors often provide followers with guidance, motivation, and satisfaction. Examples of these factors include:

- Redesigned job tasks that are inherently interesting and motivating
- Self-managed work groups that structure and control their members' activities
- Reward systems, such as bonus programs based on company profits, that guide and motivate follower efforts with little or no leader involvement
- Follower self-leadership, where followers are encouraged to become increasingly responsible for planning, monitoring, and controlling their own activities
- Participative goal setting programs, where key motivating factors are the goals followers establish for themselves (often in conjunction with the leader) to guide and control task behavior

Each of these situational factors can motivate, guide, and influence employees toward higher performance and improved attitudes. They also replace the need for many leader actions. Leaders should obviously consider implementing these types of situational factors. In the following chapters we will explain when and how leaders should adjust their behavior to make the most of these factors. The Leadership in Action box describing Margaret Thatcher demonstrates how a leader's traits and behaviors can fit the situation at one time, resulting in success for the leader. Later, when the situation changes, the leader's behavior may no longer fit and, as with Thatcher, she can lose the consent of her followers to lead.

LEADERSHIP IN ACTION: MARGARET THATCHER

Margaret Thatcher served three terms as prime minister of Great Britain and was highly influential in changing the course of post-World War II British society. She responded to a change in British sentiment away from socialistic institutions, heavy public spending, and repeated concessions to unions, and toward privatization of industry, conservative spending, and curbing union power. The daughter of a middle-class grocer and local politician, she demonstrated her intelligence, self-confidence, energy, and skills at public speaking, debating, and networking early in her career. These skills and traits helped her move successfully among the male-dominated government elite in Britain. When she became prime minister, she was so firm in her views that she became divisive—she viewed people as either on the "right side or the wrong side." She liked to direct her personnel but also seemed to enjoy browbeating and humiliating her political opponents. She ignored criticism and preferred to make her own decisions over participation and consensus in decision making. Her exclusionary and decisive style and another shift in public sentiment resulted in her resignation in 1990 under pressure from her own party.

◆ THE LEADERSHIP PROCESS: THREE KEY TASKS

The discussion of leadership behaviors and situational factors thus far leads us to three key tasks effective leaders must carry out to fulfill their role in increasingly complex organizations. These three tasks are shown in Figure 1–2. The first task in the leadership process is *diagnosing situational and follower characteristics.* Effective leaders must carefully evaluate their followers, the tasks followers perform, and the organizations in which they work to determine the extent to which followers need a particular leader behavior. Diagnosing situations also requires an understanding of the followers and situational factors that may prevent certain types of leadership from being effective or that allow individuals to function on their own. Leaders need this diagnostic information so they can make informed decisions about appropriate types of leadership behavior.

If the leader's diagnosis indicates that a follower's ability, experience, and motivation are adequate to permit the follower to make all necessary task decisions, then the leader should refrain from providing task guidance and allow the follower to work independently. Attempts by the leader to provide guidance in this situation will likely be viewed as a lack of trust and may lead to follower resentment. If, on the other hand, the leader's diagnosis indicates that a follower needs guidance on a specific task, then the leader must provide it or see that someone else provides it. This is the second task in the leadership process: *providing the leadership behavior needed by followers.* In this second leadership task the leader matches leadership behaviors with situational and follower needs. Some followers deserve to be complimented for outstanding performance; others may need a sympathetic ear for a personal problem that affects their work. Providing the appropriate leader behavior requires that the leader be familiar with the needed leader behavior and have the necessary traits and skills to demonstrate it. The third leadership task requires the leader to be familiar with methods or programs for developing followers and modifying their situations to make them more productive. As the effective leader diagnoses the situation and provides the needed leadership behav-

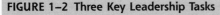

FIGURE 1–2 Three Key Leadership Tasks

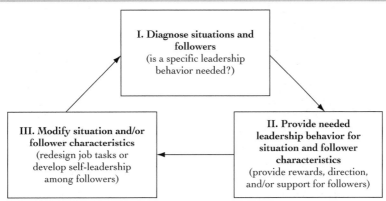

ior, the leader is also thinking about what could be done to develop the follower or change the environmental situation to permit more independent follower action in the future. The final task in the leadership process is *developing followers and/or modifying their tasks or environment* to allow them to act more effectively and/or independently of the leader. Here the leader may actually promote self-leadership by followers. However, some followers need or prefer more direction and personal involvement with the leader than others. For these individuals, the leader can often modify the situation to make the follower more responsive to the leader's behavior. This book provides information to enable a leader to effectively carry out this leadership process.

Summary ▪

Leadership is a process an individual uses to influence group members toward the achievement of group goals, where the group members view the influence as legitimate. The processes of leadership and management are complex and interconnected, with both being focused on influencing groups of people toward achievement of goals. Leaders use both position-based and person-based sources of power to influence followers. Early leadership researchers focused on personal characteristics of leaders in explaining who emerged as a leader and who became an effective leader. Most later researchers, however, have emphasized leaders' behavior as key to leader effectiveness. Certain situational or follower characteristics can increase or decrease the effectiveness of a leader's behavior. Other characteristics can cause followers to perform effectively or to have positive attitudes with little or no need for a leader's influence. Still, leaders have important roles to play in organizations, and effective leaders need to be aware of the three tasks in the effective leadership process: diagnosing situations to determine the need for a specific leader behavior, providing the needed leader behavior(s), and modifying situations and followers to increase their ability to work effectively and/or independently of the leader in attaining high performance and positive attitudes. Chapter 2 will describe the leader behaviors that have been the primary focus of leadership researchers. The model of leadership to be utilized throughout this book is described in detail in chapter 2.

Research Results for Leadership Self-Assessment: Evaluating Leadership Traits ▪▪▪▪▪▪▪▪▪▪▪▪▪▪▪▪▪▪▪▪▪▪▪▪▪▪▪▪▪▪▪▪

Items 1, 2, 4, 6, 9, 11, and 12 have usually been related to effective performance as a leader. These traits are helpful for gaining followers' support, dealing with new situations, and overcoming obstacles. Items 3, 5, 7, 8, and 10 can often decrease a leader's performance by making the leader less helpful, intolerant of mistakes, unreactive, self-centered, and unpredictable. These tendencies often eliminate followers' trust and confidence in their leader and decrease their willingness to support and communicate important information the leader often needs.

Key Terms and Concepts in this Chapter ▪▪▪▪▪▪▪▪▪▪▪▪▪▪▪▪▪▪▪▪▪▪▪▪▪

- authority
- coercive power
- connection/resource power
- expert power
- influence
- key leadership tasks
- leadership behaviors
- leadership traits
- power
- reward power
- role
- referent power
- situational factors and leadership

Review and Discussion Questions ▪▪▪▪▪▪▪▪▪▪▪▪▪▪▪▪▪▪▪▪▪▪▪▪▪▪▪▪▪▪▪

1. Identify a leader you think has had a major impact on society. What characteristics did this leader have that contributed to his or her effectiveness?
2. What are some examples of legitimate and not legitimate methods of influence which leaders might use? How could the perception of legitimacy change from one group to another?
3. Think of a powerful leader you have known, heard of, or read about. Describe the sources of power that the leader used to influenced the behavior of followers.
4. What are the traits you have most frequently observed in effective leaders? What could you do to develop these traits yourself?
5. What leader behaviors have been effective in influencing your behavior toward group goals? How could you develop these behaviors?
6. What situational or task factors could increase followers' needs for certain types of behavior by the leader?
7. What situational or task factors could decrease followers' needs for certain types of behavior by the leader?

Exercise: Leaders You Have Observed ▪▪▪▪▪▪▪▪▪▪▪▪▪▪▪▪▪▪▪▪▪▪▪▪▪▪▪▪▪▪

Review the definition of leadership in this chapter. Think of at least five or six individuals you have observed who carried out the process of leadership. These people may have been leaders in school, your family, your community, religious organizations, sports teams, student groups, political groups, service organizations, or other situations you observed. The only requirement is that they influenced followers to achieve group goals in a reasonable or legitimate manner.

Select one of these leaders and describe how the leader influenced followers. Was the influence effective? Why or why not?

Keep the list of leaders you have made for this exercise. You will use this list in later exercises that ask for specific examples of leader behaviors and characteristics of the situation where the leader was functioning.

Exercise: Rating a Manager's Power ▪▪▪▪▪▪▪▪▪▪▪▪▪▪▪▪▪▪▪▪▪▪▪▪▪▪▪

Directions: If you currently have a supervisor or can clearly recall one from the past, rate him or her. Circle the appropriate number of your answer, using the following scale: 5 = strongly agree, 4 = agree, 3 = neither agree or disagree, 2 = disagree, 1 = strongly disagree.

My manager (or former manager could) . . .	Strongly Agree				Strongly Disagree
Reward Power					
1. increase my pay level	5	4	3	2	1
2. influence my getting a pay raise	5	4	3	2	1
3. provide me with specific benefits	5	4	3	2	1
4. influence my getting a promotion	5	4	3	2	1
Coercive Power					
5. give me undesirable job assignments	5	4	3	2	1
6. make my work difficult for me	5	4	3	2	1
7. make things unpleasant here	5	4	3	2	1
8. make being at work distasteful	5	4	3	2	1
Legitimate Power					
9. make me aware that I have commitments to meet	5	4	3	2	1
10. make me feel like I should satisfy my job requirements	5	4	3	2	1
11. give me the feeling that I have responsibilities to fulfill	5	4	3	2	1
12. make me recognize that I have tasks to accomplish	5	4	3	2	1
Expert Power					
13. give me good technical suggestions	5	4	3	2	1
14. share with me his or her considerable experience and /or training	5	4	3	2	1
15. provide me with sound job-related advice	5	4	3	2	1
16. provide me with needed technical knowledge	5	4	3	2	1
Referent Power					
17. make me feel valued	5	4	3	2	1
18. make me feel that he or she approves of me	5	4	3	2	1
19. make me feel personally accepted	5	4	3	2	1
20. make me feel important	5	4	3	2	1

Connection/Resource Power

21. give me the physical resources I need to accomplish my tasks	5	4	3	2	1
22. obtain information I need about important organizational issues	5	4	3	2	1
23. gain needed cooperation from other departments	5	4	3	2	1
24. obtain approval from upper management for our budget	5	4	3	2	1

Scoring and interpretation: Add all the circled numbers to calculate how powerful you perceive your supervisor to be. You can make a tentative interpretation of the score as follows:

95+:   high power
80–94:   moderate power
below 80: low power

Also, see if you rated your manager much higher on one type of power than on the others.

Source: Adapted from Thomas R. Hinkin and Chester A. Schriesheim, "Development and Application of New Scales to Measure the French and Raven (1959) Bases of Social Power," *Journal of Applied Psychology,* August 1989, p. 567. Copyright© 1989 by the American Psychological Association. Adapted with permission.

◆◆◆ **Case Incident**

Don't Baby Them

Ann was relieved. The report was completed and it looked good. She thought it was the best market analysis the research section she supervised had ever done. She was especially proud because several members of her section were fairly new to their jobs and they had been pushed by upper management to rush completion of the report. The market analysis involved analyzing complex and detailed data. Since the report was completed ahead of schedule, she thanked each person in the section. Not only did she express her appreciation to the employees for knocking themselves out, she invited them to her house for pizza and drinks after work.

She could not wait to give the report to Tom Benson, the marketing director. When she put the report on Tom's desk, his first comment was, "So you finally got it done." Ann responded with, "Look, Tom, my section really went all out on this one. They worked overtime to beat the schedule and did an outstanding job. Maybe some appreciation from you is in order."

"Now Ann," Tom replied, "why baby them? They are paid to do their jobs and they did it. I do not see anything special about employees doing what they are assigned."

QUESTIONS

1. How would you describe the leadership approaches of Ann and Tom?
2. What situational characteristics were important for a leader to consider in this case?
3. What sources of power did Ann and Tom use?
4. If you were Tom, would you have handled the situation differently? If so, how?
5. Do you think Ann's or Tom's leader behaviors were the most appropriate for the employees and the situation? Why?

Endnotes ▪▪▪

1. Bass, B. (1990).*Bass & Stogdill's Handbook of Leadership.* New York: The Free Press.
2. Day, D. V. and Lord, R. G. (1988). Executive leadership and organizational performance: Suggestions for a new theory and methodology. *Journal of Management,* 14, 453–464.
3. Bass, *Bass & Stogdill's Handbook of Leadership.*
4. Katzell, R. A. and Guzzo, R. A. (1983). Psychological approaches to productivity improvement. *American Psychologist,* 38, 468–472.
5. Virany, B. and Tushman, M. L. (1986). Executive succession: The changing characteristics of top management teams. Paper, Academy of Management Meeting, Chicago.
6. Schriesheim, C. A. and Neider, L. L. (1996). Leadership theory and development: The coming "new phase." *Organizational Behavior and Human Performance,* 22, 374–403.
7. Bass, *Bass & Stogdill's Handbook of Leadership.*
8. Yukl, G. (1998). *Leadership in Organizations* (4th ed.), Upper Saddle River, NJ: Prentice Hall.
9. Zaleznik, A. (1990). The leadership gap. *Academy of Management Executive,* 4 (1), 1–22.
10. Kouzes, J. M. and Posner, B. Z. (1993). *Credibility: How Leaders Gain and Lose It, Why People Demand It.* San Francisco: Jossey-Bass.
11. Jago, A. G. (1982). Leadership: Perspectives in theory and research. *Management Science,* 28 (3), 315–336.
12. Yukl, *Leadership in Organizations,* (4th ed.).
13. Hollander, E. P. (1993). Legitimacy, power and influence: A perspective on relational features of leadership. In M. M. Chemers and R. Ayman, *Leadership Theory and Research.* San Diego: Academic Press, 29–44.
14. Terry, L. D. (1995). The leadership-management distinction: The domination and displacement of mechanistic and organismic theories. *Leadership Quarterly,* 6 (4), 515–527.
15. Bennis, W. and Nanus, B. (1985). *Leaders: The Strategies for Taking Charge.* New York: Harper and Row.
16. French, J. R. P. and Raven, B. (1959). The basis of social power. In D. Cartwright (Ed.), *Studies in Social Power.* Ann Arbor: University of Michigan, Institute for Social Research.
17. Pfeffer, J. (1992). *Managing With Power.* Boston: Harvard Business School Press.
18. Whetten, D. A. and Cameron, K. S. (1998). *Developing Management Skills* (4th ed.). Reading, MA: Addison-Wesley.
19. Podsakoff, P. M., Todor, W. D. and Skov, R. (1982). Effects of leader contingent and noncontingent reward and punishment behaviors on subordinate performance and satisfaction. *Academy of Management Journal,* 25, 810–821.
20. Warren, D. I. (1968). Power, visibility, and conformity in formal organizations. *American Sociological Review,* 6, 951–970.
21. Podsakoff, P. M., Todor, W. D., Grover, R. A. and Huber, V. L. (1984). Situational moderators of leader reward and punishment behavior: fact or fiction? *Organizational Behavior and Human Performance,* 34, 21–63.
22. Yukl, G. and Falbe, C. M. (1991). The importance of different power sources in downward and lateral relations. *Journal of Applied Psychology,* 76, 416–423.
23. Yukl, *Leadership in Organizations,* (4th ed.).
24. Ibid.
25. Yukl and Falbe, The importance of different power sources in downward and lateral relations.
26. Kipnis, D., Schmidt, S. M. and Wilkinson D. (1980). Intra-organizational influence tactics. *Journal of Applied Psychology,* 65, 440–452.
27. Lord, R. G., DeVader, C. L. and Alliger, G. M. (1996). A meta-analysis of the relations between personality traits and leadership perceptions: An application of

validity generalization procedures. *Journal of Applied Psychology,* 71 (3), 402–410.

28. Hemphill, J. K. and Coons, A. E. (1957). Development of the leader behavior description questionnaire. In R. M. Stogdill and A. E. Coons (Eds.), *Leader Behavior: Its Description and Measurement.* Columbus, OH: Ohio State University, Bureau of Business Research.

29. Hemphill, J. K. (1955). Leadership behaviors associated with the administrative reputation of college departments. *Journal of Educational Psychology,* 46, 385–401.

30. House, R. J. and Filly, A. C. (1971). Leadership style, hierarchical influence, and the satisfaction of subordinate role expectations: A test of Likert's influence propositions. *Journal of Applied Psychology,* 55, 422–432.

31. Keller, B. T. and Andrews, J. H. M. (1963). Leader behavior of principles, staff morale, and productivity. *Alberta Journal of Educational Research,* 9, 179–191.

32. Larson, L. L., Hunt, J. G. and Osborn, R. N. (1976). The great hi-hi leader behavior myth: A lesson from Occam's razor. *Academy of Management Journal,* 19, 628–639.

33. House, R. J., and Mitchell, T. R. (1974). Path-goal theory of leadership. *Journal of Contemporary Business,* 3, 81–97.

34. Hersey, D. and Blanchard, K. (1982). *Management of Organizational Behavior* (4th ed.). Upper Saddle River, NJ: Prentice Hall.

35. Yukl, *Leadership in Organizations* (4th ed.).

36. Howell, J. P., Dorfman, P. W. and Kerr, S. (1986). Moderator variables in leadership research. *Academy of Management Journal,* 11, 88–102.

37. Ibid.

38. Kerr, S. and Jermier, J. (1978). Substitutes for leadership: Their meaning and measurement. *Organizational Behavior and Human Performance,* 22, 374–403.

CHAPTER 2

Leadership Behaviors and Processes

Learning Objectives
After reading this chapter, you should be able to do the following:

1. Describe patterns of behavior that leaders frequently exhibit.
2. Identify the effects of specific leader behaviors on followers' psychological reactions and performance.
3. Discuss the impact of situational and follower characteristics on leader effectiveness.
4. Explain how leaders can utilize specific types of situational and follower characteristics to increase their effectiveness.
5. Describe the Leadership Process Model for influencing followers' behavior.

At one time or another leaders typically exhibit different kinds of behavior patterns to influence followers to achieve group goals. The following are examples of leader behaviors.

- Explaining to a follower the level of performance that is expected
- Showing respect and concern for the personal feelings of a follower
- Asking a follower for suggestions on how to solve a problem
- Complimenting a follower for doing outstanding work
- Coordinating the activities of the group with those of other groups
- Communicating displeasure when a follower's work is below acceptable levels
- Insisting that followers comply with policies and procedures of the organization
- Making sure that followers have adequate resources to complete assigned work
- Communicating ideas about the future of the organization
- Taking high personal risks to benefit the organization
- Providing information that helps a follower perform effectively

To positively influence followers, the leader must use these behavior patterns in an effective manner (1,2). When leaders fail to use needed behaviors or use behaviors in an inappropriate way, followers are not influenced to achieve group goals (3). This chapter introduces the major behavior patterns most leaders use to influence

FIGURE 2–1 Core Behavior Patterns of Leaders

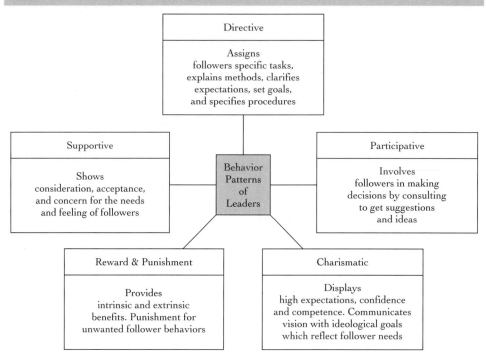

followers. Factors that may increase or decrease the effectiveness of leader behaviors and overall impacts that leaders have on followers are also described in this chapter. Types of situational and follower characteristics that leaders must consider in selecting an appropriate behavior are identified.

Figure 2–1 presents the five core leader behavior patterns that will be focused on in Part II of this book. The chapters in Part II will identify how and when to effectively use each of the behavior patterns.

◆ BEHAVIOR PATTERNS OF LEADERS

Each behavior pattern in Figure 2–1 is described in more detail below:

1. **Supportive leadership behavior:** This behavior pattern refers to the leader's role in showing concern for the comfort and well-being of followers; demonstrating a considerate, kind, and understanding attitude in dealing with followers; being friendly and informative, and encouraging open two-way communication and follower development. Familiar terms associated with supportive leadership are consideration, relationship-orientation, or concern for people leadership.

2. **Directive leadership behavior:** This pattern refers to the leader's behaviors in assigning followers to specific tasks, explaining the methods to be used in completing the tasks, clarifying expectations regarding quantity

and quality of follower performance, setting goals for followers, planning and coordinating followers' work, and specifying rules and procedures to be followed. This behavior pattern has also been known as or is closely related to initiating structure, instrumental leadership, or task-oriented leadership.

3. **Participative leadership behavior:** The leader who uses this approach involves followers in the decision-making processes. Participative leader behaviors may include holding one-on-one meetings with individuals or groups of followers to gather input for decisions; it may involve a group decision-making effort initiated by the leader; or it may involve assigning a particular problem to a follower to resolve. Each of these options represents different degrees or types of participative leader behavior. Participative leadership is sometimes referred to as consultative, democratic, or delegatory leadership.

4. **Leader reward and punishment behavior:** With this leader behavior, when followers provide services to the organization, the leader rewards them with tangible and intangible benefits. The rewards may be monetary or they may consist of praise. Punishments may come in the form of a reduction in pay or a notice to the follower that work needs improvement. Rewards and punishments may be provided based on follower performance (contingently) or based on the leader's whim (noncontingently). Rewards and punishments based on performance are usually the most effective.

5. **Charismatic leadership behavior:** This pattern of behavior involves the leader communicating a vision of the future that has ideological significance to followers (often through use of powerful imagery and metaphors), arousing follower needs which are relevant to goal accomplishment, serving as a role model, expressing high expectations and confidence in followers' capabilities, and projecting a high degree of self-confidence.

Although there are other ways to describe and classify leader behaviors, these five have been extensively researched and they have been found useful in describing specific behaviors that improve leader effectiveness. These patterns of behavior are not as independent of each other as they might at first appear. For example, a specific behavior by a leader, such as providing information, may serve different leadership functions depending on the situation and therefore may be considered an aspect of more than one leader behavior pattern. If the information is intended to show the leader's concern for followers' anxieties over possible layoffs, then it is an aspect of supportive leader behavior. If the information is to help in a group problem-solving effort, it may be part of participative leadership. If the information clarifies management expectations of follower performance, then it is directive leadership. Although the leadership behavior patterns are described as distinct from one another, they are not mutually exclusive, and a given activity may occasionally be included in more than one leader behavior category.

Three other leader behavior patterns are emerging as especially important in organizations in 2000 and beyond. These behaviors have not been studied as extensively as the five core leader behaviors, but they warrant attention by leaders and will be described in detail in Part III of this book. These emerging leader behaviors include the leader's role in boundary spanning, which is representing the group, protecting members from outsiders, obtaining resources, and resolving conflicts among members and with other groups. Developing exchange relationships with followers is another emerging leader behavior. It includes identifying and developing follower potential, delegating and helping with challenging assignments, and providing additional time for particular followers. A final behavior pattern of leaders that is becoming increasingly important is followership. This involves leaders building a close exchange with their own leader, being proactive in attacking problems without the leader's request, developing one's own competencies, and role modeling followership behaviors for followers. In today's complex and highly technological organizations these behavior patterns will become critical to a leader's success.

Leaders use these behavior patterns to influence followers to accomplish group goals. At times, however, different leader behaviors may be used to achieve the same influence objective. For example, in order to motivate followers to put forth added effort, a leader might engage in inspirational speeches (an aspect of charismatic leader behavior) or simply offer followers a special reward for a certain level of performance. Some leaders rely heavily on a limited set of behavioral strategies. However, those leaders who use a variety of behaviors are most likely to obtain desired outcomes with followers (4).

A leader may demonstrate all of the behavior patterns or any subset of them with any group of followers. For example, because a leader participates extensively with one group does not mean the leader should do so with all groups or with the same group in

FIGURE 2–2 Leadership Model for Influencing Follower Behaviors

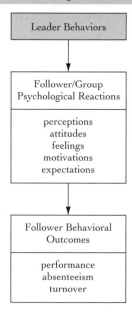

all situations. As another example, a leader may be directive in some situations and participative or supportive in others. A leader may demonstrate a combination of two or three leader behaviors in one five-minute exchange with a group of followers. Different combinations of behaviors are called leadership styles. Several popular styles are described in the final chapter of this book. Most effective leaders demonstrate all of these behavior patterns at one time or another as required by the situation.

Figure 2–2 represents the basic elements in the leadership process to influence followers. As indicated in the figure, leader behaviors influence followers' psychological reactions, which in turn result in followers' behavioral outcomes. Future chapters will cover these psychological reactions and behavioral outcomes in connection with each of the leader behavior patterns.

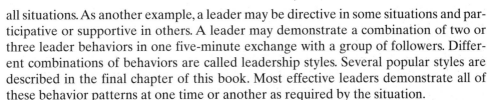

◆ EFFECTS OF A LEADER'S BEHAVIOR ON FOLLOWERS

A leader's behavior has its most direct impact on the psychological reactions of individual followers and groups of followers (see Figure 2–2). These reactions include followers' attitudes, feelings, perceptions, motivations, and expectations. More specific examples of these factors include followers' satisfaction with supervision, general job satisfaction, organizational commitment, job stress, role clarity, motivation, and group cohesion. Followers' psychological reactions are important to organizations because they indicate the quality of the work environment by demonstrating how satisfied or frustrated people are on the job. Psychological reactions indicate whether the workplace is seen as a pleasant or unpleasant place to spend one's time. A leader's behavior can produce positive or negative psychological reactions. Positive effects make the workplace more pleasant and can help individuals cope with the frustrating or unpleasant aspects of their jobs. In addition, in a pleasant work place leaders more easily obtain group cooperation. Negative effects reduce satisfaction and can result in resentful and uncooperative followers.

The real objective of effective leadership is to influence followers' behaviors and outcomes. As shown in Figure 2–2, followers' behaviors and outcomes result from psychological reactions. For example, a follower who is motivated to excel (a favorable psychological reaction) exhibits high effort on the job and often performs effectively (a favorable behavioral outcome). Important outcomes include high individual and group performance; low turnover, absenteeism, lateness, and grievance rates; and high quality levels, all of which result in a productive organization (5). To maintain high levels of productivity, it is necessary to have a stable workforce without overspending on training and recruitment; low grievance rates and high quality result in money saved from costly grievance procedures and errors. A supportive leader (who frequently shows concern and consideration for the personal welfare of followers) tends to increase followers' job satisfaction (a psychological reaction), and a high level of job satisfaction among workers typically results in lower turnover, absenteeism, and grievance rates. Here it is the leader's behavior that increases employees' job satisfaction, which in turn reduces employee turnover, absenteeism, and grievances.

One purpose of Figure 2–2 is to explain the process by which leaders influence organizational outcomes. By understanding which psychological reactions are affected by

LEADERSHIP IN ACTION: DWIGHT D. EISENHOWER

Dwight D. Eisenhower played a role in shaping history for almost twenty years. He was supreme commander of the Allied forces in Europe during World War II, commander of the North Atlantic Treaty Alliance, and president of the United States from 1953 to 1961.

Eisenhower's great test as a leader was as supreme commander of the Allied Expeditionary Forces in World War II. He was able to weld together a team of British and American officers unequaled in the annals of warfare for its cooperation. Eisenhower's leadership style was in dramatic contrast to the flamboyant, colorful egotists who were the other Allied leaders during World War II. Eisenhower's calm, participative style was well suited to developing the Allies into an effective military force capable of the largest amphibious invasion in history at Normandy.

Eisenhower led with the great and powerful and was challenged by leaders who were accustomed to having their own way. The issues were always critical when Eisenhower had discussions with men like Churchill, De Gaulle, Montgomery, Patton, and Bradley. They did everything they could to convince Eisenhower of their point of view, and he could not insult any of them while still maintaining their cooperation. He gave each person the opportunity to fully state his case and used great patience to hold the alliance together. Eisenhower was convinced that victory depended on making the alliance work, and he was constantly focused on that purpose.

The basic method of Eisenhower's leadership was to approach problems objectively and to convince others that he was objective. He had the ability to see issues from the other person's point of view. He was also known for getting the best out of people by adapting his leadership behaviors to their unique personalities, habits, and motivations. And no matter how bitter the disagreements over an issue, Eisenhower always maintained good interpersonal relations.

Eisenhower liked to emphasize his Kansas childhood and express amazement at his good fortune. He was known for being a modest person. He could be directive when it was necessary, tolerant to promote cooperation, and participative and conciliatory to obtain commitment to objectives. World War II was a "people's war," and Eisenhower's qualities of moderation and natural good sense appealed to the people. He was able to communicate his ordinariness in an extraordinary manner by projecting human warmth in talking with the troops.

It was General Eisenhower who captured the imagination of the public as he led the assault on Hitler's European fortress, the invasion of Normandy, the drive through France, the battles on the German border, and the final victory over the Third Reich. Eisenhower was certainly one of the greatest generals of this century. Contributing to his greatness was his breadth of view, his unmatched strategic vision, and his ability to involve others to obtain commitment to a common purpose.

a specific leader behavior and how those reactions affect outcomes, leaders can make better choices of behaviors for specific situations. Choosing an effective behavior is critical in achieving leader effectiveness.

Figure 2–3 provides an example of the application of the leadership model from Figure 2–2 in analyzing the leader behaviors of Eisenhower.

FIGURE 2–3 Leadership Model Applied to Eisenhower's Leader Behavior

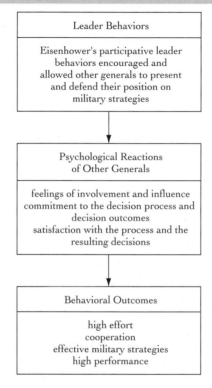

DETERMINING AN APPROPRIATE BEHAVIOR PATTERN: SITUATIONAL AND FOLLOWER CHARACTERISTICS

In addition to the leader's influence on followers' psychological reactions and behaviors, situational and follower characteristics also affect followers (6). For example, situational characteristics such as aspects of the follower's work task—its challenge, complexity, or danger; the follower's work group—its cohesiveness, norms, or size; and the organization's structure—its rules and procedures or overall mission—all affect followers' reactions and behaviors. Important followers' characteristics include abilities—their skills, education, and training; needs—for achievement or power for example; and value orientation—work ethic, culture, and self esteem. These situational and follower characteristics affect followers' attitudes, motivation, and performance.

The leader can manipulate many situational and follower characteristics to effectively influence followers. This is one reason why leaders often use a wide range of approaches in dealing with a follower problem and still obtain effective results. As one alternative, the leader may modify the follower's task to make it more interesting and challenging or transfer an individual to a new work group whose members are especially helpful. A leader may implement rules and procedures to decrease the danger associated with a task or see that a follower obtains additional training to help deal with task-related problems. Both the leader's behavior vis-à-vis the follower and the follower's individual and situational characteristics influence follower reactions and behaviors. Leaders must consider their own behavior, the followers' characteristics, and the situational factors to be effective in influencing followers to achieve group goals. Any one or a combination of situation and follower characteristics can often be modified to obtain the desired effect on followers. Figure 2–4 summarizes factors that interact to influence leader effectiveness. The boxed quote by Sandy Alderson emphasizes the importance of situational factors for leadership effectiveness.

> Sandy Alderson
>
> Vice President for Operations in Professional Baseball
>
> "Managers aren't fired because they are incompetent.
>
> They're fired because leadership situations change."

SITUATIONAL FACTORS THAT INCREASE LEADERSHIP EFFECTIVENESS

Leadership enhancers are situational or follower characteristics that increase the leader's influence on followers. A highly cohesive work group is an important leadership enhancer. When cohesive groups have "strong norms in support of cooperation with management [they] can crystallize ambiguous goals and role definitions, amplify overly subtle leader provided feedback, and otherwise increase the power of weak, inconsistent leaders" (7). In a study of leadership in four large hospitals, it was found that the development of a culture with strong performance norms greatly enhanced the impact of the head nurse's directive leadership behavior (8). Enhancers are clearly something that most leaders would like to create. Creating situational or follower char-

FIGURE 2–4 Factors that Influence Leader Effectiveness

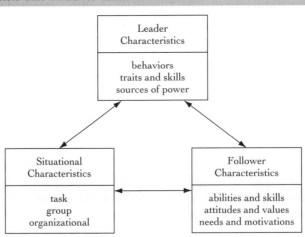

acteristics that increase leader effectiveness can require the cooperation of upper-level management. Several enhancers that suit specific leadership behaviors are summarized below.

- Members of cohesive work groups with strong norms to cooperate with leaders are highly responsive to participative leader behaviors.
- Workers on stressful, dangerous, or dissatisfying job tasks are especially appreciative of a supportive leader who shows concern for their difficulties.
- Directive leadership is needed to organize a large number of followers and prevent their working at cross purposes with one another.

SITUATIONAL FACTORS THAT DECREASE LEADERSHIP EFFECTIVENESS

Leadership neutralizers are situational or follower characteristics that can decrease the effectiveness of the leader's influence on followers. Spatial/geographic distance between a leader and subordinate is a typical example of a condition that decreases leadership effectiveness. Kinko's, which provides professional copying services at many widely dispersed locations nationwide, has reported the neutralizing effect of geographic distance as a major leadership problem for its regional managers. The managers are constantly frustrated because they are unable to provide enough personal direction, guidance, and support for new store managers due to the great distances involved. Telephone calls, memos, and occasional visits are just not enough. Continuous personal interaction is needed, but it is impossible with their current management structure. Other factors that can decrease the effectiveness of leaders include organizational reward systems based on seniority, union contracts or civil service policies that limit a leader's freedom in motivating followers, or a senior manager who continually countermands a leader's directions and instructions.

These factors and the leader behaviors they neutralize are summarized below.

- A large spatial/geographic distance between leaders and followers inhibits leaders from effectively directing followers.
- Organizational reward systems based on seniority, union contracts, or civil service policies prevent leaders from adequately rewarding the best performers.
- Senior managers who countermand or modify effective directions by a lower-level manager prevent leaders from having the influence that is needed.

Although neutralizers are usually dysfunctional, they can also be used to the followers' advantage. When an incompetent manager cannot be replaced because of political factors or seniority, a neutralizer such as a large spatial distance between the manager and followers can be implemented to minimize the damage this individual may cause.

SITUATIONAL FACTORS THAT REPLACE THE NEED FOR LEADERSHIP BEHAVIORS

Another group of factors that can provide important benefits to leaders are situational and follower characteristics that replace the need for specific leadership behaviors. Characteristics of followers, their work tasks, or the organization can provide task guidance and incentives to such an extent that they replace certain leader behaviors. To the

extent that powerful factors replace the need for leadership, certain types of leader behavior may be unnecessary. The following example demonstrates two factors that replace the need for directive leadership:

> Todd LaPorte, Gene Rochlin, and Karlene Roberts are three researchers
> studying highly stressful work such as landing jet fighters on a nuclear carrier
> or directing air traffic into San Francisco's main airport. They have found that
> in such situations, directive leadership is relatively unimportant compared to
> the experience and training of these workers and their closely knit work
> groups. These influences become particularly evident "... in the white heat of
> danger, when the whole system threatens to collapse. ... The stress creates a
> need for competence among colleagues who by necessity develop close
> working relationships with each other." All individuals are trained
> extensively and daily, regardless of their position in the hierarchy, to redirect
> operations or to bring them to an abrupt halt. This can involve ignoring
> orders from managers who are removed from the front line of action. Here
> the experience and continuous training of individuals along with the close
> working relationships with members of their work group replace the need for
> the manager's directive leadership (9).

Many models of leadership suggest that leadership effectiveness can be improved
in one of three ways: (1) by finding a leader who is better suited to deal with the problem and challenges posed by situational and follower characteristics; (2) by coaching or
training the existing leader to more effectively influence the followers and cope with
the situational factors; or (3) by modifying situational and/or follower characteristics to
increase the leader's influence and effectiveness. Situational factors can also be created
that replace the need for specific leadership behaviors. These factors focus on assuring
that subordinates are receiving needed task guidance and incentives without assuming
that the formal leader is the only supplier. Leadership scholars recently noted that:

> ... strong leaders understand and are comfortable with the idea that effective
> results can be achieved when task guidance and incentives to perform
> emanate from sources other than themselves. When other sources are
> deficient, the hierarchical superior is in a position to play a dominant role;
> when strong incentives and guidance derive from other sources, the
> hierarchical superior has less opportunity, but also less need, to exert
> influence (10).

Other factors that effectively replace the need for specific leadership behaviors include work tasks that are intrinsically satisfying to subordinates, computer-integrated
manufacturing combined with networked computer systems, and the existence of a
highly trained, competent, and professional work force. Each of these factors has effectively decreased the need for certain types of leadership influence and has replaced that
influence with guidance or incentives of its own, resulting in very favorable outcomes
for the organization and the people involved. These situational factors and the specific
types of leadership behaviors they replace are summarized below.

- A high degree of training and experience by followers can enable them to
  perform well without the leader's direction and guidance.

- Work tasks that followers find intrinsically satisfying can result in positive follower attitudes and alleviate the need for a leader's supportive leader behaviors.
- Networked computer systems and computer-integrated manufacturing can make needed knowledge, information, and feedback available to followers and alleviate the need for much direction by the leader.

These situational factors replace the need for leadership because (1) their purpose is to attain the same results leaders strive to attain, (2) they create situations where followers receive guidance, motivation, and good feelings on the job from sources other than the leader, and (3) they can therefore make certain types of leadership behavior unnecessary in achieving individual and group goals. To say that these situational factors can replace the need for leadership does not mean that leadership is no longer needed. Some followers are not secure without personal leader-follower interaction. Leaders must also attend to many other activities in addition to direct task guidance and attitude improvement. For example, they create visions to inspire followers, they model desired values for followers to emulate, they obtain resources and buffer the group against unreasonable requests, and they monitor the group environment to keep members apprised of important developments. Situational factors that replace the need

LEADERSHIP IN PERSPECTIVE

When leaders choose appropriate behavior patterns to help achieve group goals, they sometimes face ethical dilemmas. In these situations, the leader's choice is difficult because each alternative may have possible undesirable consequences. The following are examples of possible ethical dilemmas that confront leaders:

1. The leader's superior insists that the leader's followers work overtime to complete an important and dangerous job, when they are already exhausted from overtime work during the past week.

2. A college coach is expected to help players stay academically eligible in order to field a competitive team by providing tutors who not only instruct, but sometimes write term papers for the athletes to assure passing grades.

3. A college professor assigns a group of students to research a topic and present their findings to the class. Noncontributing members are to be reported to the professor. A group member who is a close friend of the elected leader never attends the group meetings and makes no contribution to the project, but asks the leader not to inform the instructor.

4. A very competent employee who is having personal problems asks his supervisor to make an exception to a company rule that specifies disciplinary action for too many absences. The rule has been strictly enforced in the past with other employees.

Leaders may use one or more of the major leader behaviors to address these situations, but choosing the appropriate action involves ethical issues and consequences. Choices like these are almost never clear cut and leaders need to carefully assess the consequences of their action in each situation. Ethical dilemmas like these will be described in connection with several leader behavior patterns throughout this book.

for specific leader behaviors can support leadership effectiveness. For one thing, the leader does not have to be continuously present and ever mindful of the day-to-day monitoring and control of follower activities. Thus, situational factors can give the leader more time to devote to other important matters such as vision creation, modeling, and obtaining resources. Situational factors can also positively contribute to the leader's effectiveness in handling large numbers of followers, thus reducing managerial costs. Finally, situational factors can benefit organizations by making leadership influence consistent across organizational units. This is especially important in organizations where leaders are frequently transferred, such as the military or multinational corporations. When situational or follower characteristics are stable sources of guidance and motivation for followers, a change in leadership is less upsetting for the unit's performance. Because situational factors that replace the need for leadership can be created by leaders, they are actually an indirect form of leader influence.

Summary ■

Figure 2–5 summarizes this discussion in a Leadership Process Model that will be used throughout this book to describe important leader behaviors. Leadership behaviors (such as directiveness or supportiveness) are a major focus of the model in Figure 2–5. A leader

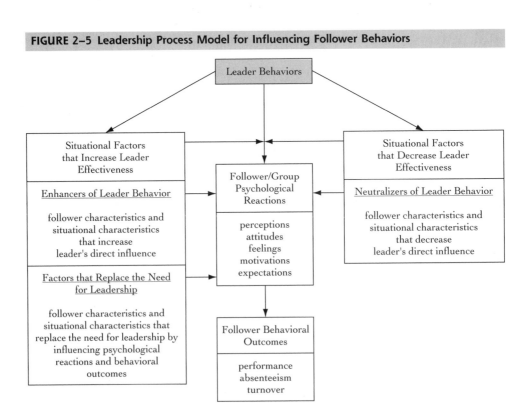

FIGURE 2–5 Leadership Process Model for Influencing Follower Behaviors

selects a behavior pattern based on an assessment of situational and follower characteristics. Then, as noted earlier, the leader's behavior most immediately affects the psychological reactions of followers and groups of followers, such as their perceptions and attitudes. These follower reactions then affect follower behaviors and outcomes, such as absenteeism and group performance. This process is also affected by situational and follower characteristics that may neutralize, enhance, or replace a leader's influence and/or directly affect follower reactions that influence behavioral outcomes. Followers' behavioral outcomes also affect the leader's choice of leadership behavior. However, the model shows that leaders may influence followers directly through their own leadership behavior or indirectly by modifying situational or follower characteristics. Leaders are thus the primary source of influence in the leadership process model, and their behavior is the focus of the remainder of this book.

Key Terms and Concepts in this Chapter ▪▪▪▪▪▪▪▪▪▪▪▪▪▪▪▪▪▪▪▪

- boundary spanning
- charismatic leadership behaviors
- directive leadership behaviors
- exchange relationships
- factors that replace the need for leadership

- follower characteristics
- followership
- leader reward and punishment behavior
- leadership enhancers
- leadership neutralizers
- leadership styles

- participative leadership behaviors
- psychological reactions
- situational characteristics
- supportive leadership behaviors

Review and Discussion Questions ▪▪▪▪▪▪▪▪▪▪▪▪▪▪▪▪▪▪▪▪▪▪▪▪▪

1. Give a specific example of each of the five core patterns of leader behaviors that were exhibited by a leader you have observed.
2. Describe three leader behaviors that had great influence (impact) on your behavior. Which of the five core leader behavior patterns were involved?
3. Which follower reactions are likely to be most important where you have worked or plan to work?
4. Discuss how a specific situational characteristic (task, group, or organization) has affected your reactions to a leader.
5. Discuss how one of your own characteristics (abilities, needs, or values) has affected your reactions to a leader.
6. Identify several leader behaviors that could produce a high level of satisfaction among followers you have known. Identify leader behaviors that could produce high follower performance.
7. Describe situational and/or follower characteristics you have observed that neutralized or enhanced a leader's impact on followers.
8. Analyze a situation you experienced as a leader or follower using the concepts contained in the model in Figure 2–5 (the leadership process model).

Exercise: Self-assessment of Important Leader Behaviors ■ ■ ■ ■ ■ ■ ■ ■ ■ ■

Objective: To help the reader identify patterns of leader behavior that may be used when leading a task group.

Directions: Circle the number on the 1-to-5 scale that best indicates how you would normally behave as leader of a group which is responsible for completing some task.

	Almost Never				*Almost Always*
1. I assign specific tasks to others.	1	2	3	4	5
2. I explain methods and set goals for the group.	1	2	3	4	5
3. I explain what each group member needs to accomplish.	1	2	3	4	5
4. I show consideration and acceptance of others.	1	2	3	4	5
5. I show concern for the feelings of others.	1	2	3	4	5
6. I help develop the abilities of others to contribute to the task.	1	2	3	4	5
7. I get others involved in making decisions.	1	2	3	4	5
8. I consult others to get their ideas and suggestions.	1	2	3	4	5
9. I encourage subgroups to handle certain aspects of the group's task.	1	2	3	4	5
10. I provide others with benefits and rewards.	1	2	3	4	5
11. I punish others for undesirable behavior.	1	2	3	4	5
12. I compliment those who do a good job.	1	2	3	4	5
13. I display high expectations and confidence.	1	2	3	4	5
14. I communicate a vision for the group.	1	2	3	4	5
15. I attempt to inspire others by pointing out the importance of the group's task and their part in accomplishing it.	1	2	3	4	5

If you rated items 1, 2, and 3 highly (by giving them a rating of 4 or 5), then you normally would tend to be directive with followers. If you rated items 4, 5, and 6 highly, you tend to be supportive. High ratings on items 7, 8, and 9 indicate participative leadership. High on items 10, 11, and 12 indicates reward and punishment type of leader behavior. High ratings on items 13, 14, and 15 indicate a charismatic approach with followers. These behavior patterns are important in different situations, and most effective leaders vary their behavior patterns with different situations and followers.

Source: The items for this exercise are based on research instruments used in an empirical study of leadership effectiveness by P. W. Dorfman, J. P. Howell, B. G. Cotton and U. Tate, "Leadership Within the Discontinuous Hierarchy Structure of the Military: Are Effective Leadership Behaviors Similar Within and Across Command Structures," in Clark, K. E., Clark, M. B. and Campbell, D. P. (1992) *Impact of Leadership,* Center for Creative Leadership, Greensboro, North Carolina.

◆◆◆ **Case Incident**

The "Informal" Leader

Mike Thomas is the manager of a branch bank for a large West Coast bank corporation. The employees in the branch are beginning to depend heavily on Betty Dale, who was recently transferred to the branch from the bank's corporate headquarters. Betty has been with the bank longer than any of the branch employees. No other employee at the branch has ever worked in the bank's corporate headquarters. Betty is respected by the branch employees because she has been recognized as an effective community leader in youth activities. Mike Thomas is concerned about his ability to exert managerial leadership because the branch employees look to Betty for advice on how to do their jobs and ask her what bank rules they should and should not be concerned about.

The branch employees have told Mike Thomas that "everything will run effectively without him because Betty can help them when there are any problems or questions about bank policies or procedures." When executives from corporate headquarters come to visit the branch, they always make a point to see Betty and get her input on how the branch could increase business. Mike Thomas believes these conversations between Betty and bank executives are putting him in a difficult position because the branch employees may think Betty is in line for his job.

When Betty was transferred to the branch, Mike Thomas felt she was a competent individual who would exert informal leadership. Now Mike is beginning to feel that he is losing the ability to manage the branch because the employees are becoming totally dependent on Betty for leadership.

QUESTIONS

1. Do the characteristics of the situation favor Mike Thomas or Betty in their attempts to influence employee behavior? Why?
2. What factors in the situation could be functioning as neutralizers and enhancers for Mike's leadership?
3. What factors could be functioning as neutralizers and enhancers for Betty's leadership?
4. What could Mike Thomas do that would increase his influence as a leader?

Endnotes ■■■■■■■■■■■■■■■■■■■■■■■■■■■■■■■■■■■■■■■

1. House, R. J. (1996). Path-goal theory of leadership: Lessons, legacy and a reformulated theory. *The Leadership Quarterly,* 7 (3), 323–352.
2. Yukl, G. (1998). *Leadership in Organizations,* (4th ed.), Upper Saddle River, NJ: Prentice Hall.
3. Huntington, A. S. (1997). A ship with no captain. *HRMagazine,* November, 94–99.
4. Zaccaro, S. J., Foti, R. J. and Kenny, K. A. (1991). Self-monitoring and trait based variance in leadership: An investigation of leader flexibility across multiple group situations. *Journal of Applied Psychology,* 76, 308–315.
5. Bass, B. (1990). *Bass and Stogdill's Handbook of Leadership.* New York: The Free Press.
6. Howell, J. P., Dorfman, P. W. and Kerr, S. (1986). Moderator variables in leadership research. *Academy of Management Review,* 11 (1), 88–102.
7. Howell, J. P., Bowen, D., Dorfman, P. W., Kerr, S. and Podsakoff, P. M. (1990). Substitutes for leadership: Effective

alternatives for ineffective leadership. *Organizational Dynamics,* Summer Issue.

8. Sheridan, J. E., Vredenburgh, D. J. and Abelson, M. A. (1984). Contextual model of leadership influence in hospital units. *Academy of Management Journal, 27,* 57–78.

9. LaPorte, T., Rochlin, E. and Roberts, K. (1989). The secret of life at the limits: Cogs become big wheels. *Smithsonian Magazine,* July.

10. Howell, Bowen, Dorfman, Kerr & Podsakoff, Substitutes for leadership: Effective alternatives for ineffective leadership.

CHAPTER 3 # Contingency Models of Leadership

Learning Objectives
After reading this chapter, you should be able to do the following:

1. Describe the concept of contingency theories of leadership.

2. Explain the two leadership styles used in Fiedler's Contingency Model of leadership.

3. Use Fiedler's Contingency Model to predict the leadership style that will be most effective.

4. Describe the four leadership styles of the Hersey and Blanchard Situational Leadership Model.

5. Explain the relationship described by the Situational Leadership Model between leadership styles and followers' competence and commitment.

6. Describe the four leader behaviors of Path-Goal Theory of leadership and their motivational effects.

7. Discuss the recommendations of Path-Goal Theory for effective leader behaviors.

8. Describe the Multiple Linkage Model of leadership and its recommendations for leader behavior to improve group performance.

There are numerous theories of leadership effectiveness and many of these theories imply that one leadership style can be effective in all situations. Examples include Blake and Mouton's 9–9 Leadership style, Ouchi's Theory Z, Bass's Transformational Leadership, House's Charismatic Leadership, and Steven Covey's Principle Centered Leadership. Most of these theories recommend an approach involving extensive participation, delegation, and group involvement, or a visionary style involving inspirational rhetoric and a value-oriented mission with strong moral dimensions. Specific situational factors are seldom considered in detail in these models. When situational factors are mentioned, the leader is usually expected to make only minor adjustments in leadership behaviors. Little guidance is given in these models as to how the leader's approach should be modified under different organizational conditions or with different types of followers.

Other leadership theories incorporate aspects of the organization and/or characteristics of followers as key elements of the leader's effectiveness. These theories are referred to as contingency or situational theories of leadership because a leader's impact on followers depends on (is contingent on) both the leader's behavior and the characteristics of the organizational situation. An effective leader in one situation is not assumed to be effective in all situations. Effectiveness depends on the match between the leader's characteristics and behavior, and the situational and follower characteristics (1).

These contingency theories of leadership are more realistic than the "one best style approach" because they include characteristics of leadership situations that can be vastly different. The type of followers, work tasks, resources, technology, legal, and economic environments all vary from organization to organization. Effective leaders recognize these differences and adapt their leader behaviors to fit the situational characteristics (2).

Four contingency theories of leadership are described in this chapter to provide a background for the remainder of this book. Two early models that have been very popular for more than twenty years are described first. The last two models that are described have evolved over the years into very sophisticated, complex, and current contingency theories of leadership. These four theories are representative of contingency models available today. Each has strengths and weaknesses that are described, and their implications for the approach taken in this book are discussed.

◆ FIEDLER'S CONTINGENCY MODEL OF LEADERSHIP

Fred Fiedler's Contingency Model of leadership is a situational theory that focuses on the match between the leader's predisposition or style and the characteristics of the situation. In the early 1950s, Fiedler noted that the style of the leader and the leader's acceptance by subordinates had a strong effect on the performance of the group. This and other observations led to the development of the Least Preferred Coworker (LPC) scale (a questionnaire), and a situational theory of leadership based on the LPC score of the leader and the "favorableness" or "control" of the situation (3).

A leader's LPC score is determined by asking the leader to indicate characteristics of a person with whom it is most difficult to work. Thus, the LPC is a description of the leader's emotional reaction to a person who obstructs goal attainment. A low LPC score indicates that a leader would reject an unsatisfactory worker and that the leader has a high need for task accomplishment, recognition, and reward. This type of leader is described by Fiedler as "task oriented." A high LPC score reveals a more tolerant attitude toward the difficult worker and a high need by the leader for positive social interaction. This type of leader is described by Fiedler as "relationship oriented" (4,5,6). A medium LPC score implies a style that Fiedler calls socioindependent. The self assessment shows the LPC scale that Fiedler uses to measure a leader's predisposition or style.

The situational "favorableness" or "situational control" depends upon (1) the quality of leader-member relations—high quality relations indicate liking and trust between the leader and group members, which is a favorable situation for the leader; (2) task structure—highly structured tasks can be effectively performed according to a standard set of procedures, which the leader can explain to followers—a favorable situation; and (3) the leader's position power—the leader's authority and control over rewards and punishments which are favorable for the leader's influence attempts (7). Leadership situations are classified in this model as either high or low on each of these three characteristics: good/poor leader-member relations, high/low task structure, high/low position power. This results in eight possible combinations (called octants) of situational control. The most favorable situation (high control) is good leader-member relations, a struc-

LEADERSHIP SELF-ASSESSMENT:
LEAST PREFERRED COWORKER

Instructions: Think of the person with whom you can work least well. This may be someone you work with now or someone you knew in the past. It does not have to be the person you like least well, but should be the person with whom you had the most difficulty in getting a job done. Describe this person as he or she appears to you, by circling a number for each scale. There are no right or wrong answers.

Pleasant	8	7	6	5	4	3	2	1	Unpleasant
Friendly	8	7	6	5	4	3	2	1	Unfriendly
Rejecting	1	2	3	4	5	6	7	8	Accepting
Helpful	8	7	6	5	4	3	2	1	Frustrating
Unenthusiastic	1	2	3	4	5	6	7	8	Enthusiastic
Tense	1	2	3	4	5	6	7	8	Relaxed
Distant	1	2	3	4	5	6	7	8	Close
Cold	1	2	3	4	5	6	7	8	Warm
Cooperative	8	7	6	5	4	3	2	1	Uncooperative
Supportive	8	7	6	5	4	3	2	1	Hostile
Boring	1	2	3	4	5	6	7	8	Interesting
Quarrelsome	1	2	3	4	5	6	7	8	Harmonious
Self-Assured	8	7	6	5	4	3	2	1	Hesitant
Efficient	8	7	6	5	4	3	2	1	Inefficient
Gloomy	1	2	3	4	5	6	7	8	Cheerful
Open	8	7	6	5	4	3	2	1	Guarded

Scoring and Interpretation: Your LPC score is the sum of the answers to these 16 items. According to Fiedler's Contingency Model a score greater than 76 indicates a relationship orientation and a score of less than 62 indicates a task orientation. A score of 58 to 63 places you in the intermediate range, which indicates socioindependent leadership orientation. Relationship-oriented leaders tend to function best in situations that are moderately favorable for exercising control (explained below). Task-oriented leaders tend to function best in situations that are either highly favorable or highly unfavorable for exercising control. Socioindependent leaders tend to be more effective in situations that are highly favorable for exercising control.

Source: Adapted from F. E. Fiedler, M. M. Chemers and L. Mahar, *Improving Leadership Effectiveness.* Copyright 1976. Reprinted by permission of John Wiley & Sons, Inc.

tured task and strong leader position power. A very unfavorable situation (low control) is poor leader-member relations, an unstructured task and weak position power. An example of a moderately favorable situation (moderate control) would be poor leader-member relations, a structured task, and strong position power.

Fiedler's theory predicts that task-oriented leaders are expected to produce high group performance in either very favorable or very unfavorable situations. Relationship-oriented leaders will produce high group performance when the situation is only moderately favorable. Socioindependent leaders (who are midway between task oriented and relationship oriented) tend to perform best in situations that are very favorable. Table 3–1 summarizes Fiedler's situation classifications and recommended leader type (8).

RECOMMENDATIONS OF THE CONTINGENCY MODEL

Fiedler and associates believe that the LPC score reflects a stable characteristic of the leader and that a consistent leadership style results from the LPC score. They therefore suggest it is ineffective to try to change a person's leadership style (9). Fiedler advocates that an effective leadership approach is to assess the situation and then select leaders with the appropriate style to match the situational characteristics. When choosing or changing the leader is not an option, the situation should be reengineered to match the leader's style. The favorableness of the situation is altered (engineered) by changing one or more of the three elements of situational control—leader-member relations, task structure, or position power. The *Leader Match* training program is used to teach managers how to determine their LPC score, assess their situation, and engineer the situation to better match their leadership style (10).

HOW VALID AND USEFUL IS THE MODEL?

Fiedler's Contingency Model has been examined, criticized, and defended by many writers, and detractors have called LPC "a measure in search of a meaning" (11). Fiedler has redefined the LPC several times, and some researchers find a leader's LPC to be fairly stable over time while others find the score for a leader to vary dramatically at different times. If LPC does vary for a leader, then engineering situations to fit a leader's LPC score may be like trying to hit a moving target and an expensive and ineffective strategy to improve group performance. Research shows that a leader's behavior does not always directly reflect the leader's LPC score. There is also some evidence that the leader's LPC score and leader-member relations may be affected by group performance rather than the other way around (12).

Recent reviews of much research on Fiedler's Contingency Model show that both high LPC and low LPC leaders can be effective in different situations (13). High LPC leaders are sometimes more effective in situations where low LPC leaders are supposed to be best. The reviews also found statistical evidence that other situational factors can have important effects on a leader's performance (14).

TABLE 3–1 Fiedler's Contingency Model for Leadership

	Situation Classification and Leader Type							
Octant	I	II	III	IV	V	VI	VII	VIII
Leader-member relations	Good				Poor			
Task structure	Structured		Unstructured		Structured		Unstructured	
Position power	High	Low	High	Low	High	Low	High	Low
Recommended leader type	Task motivated (low LPC) Socioindependent (medium LPC)				Relationship motivated (high LPC)			Task motivated (low LPC)

Paul Hersey and Ken Blanchard developed a contingency model of leader effectiveness that recommends four possible combinations of task-oriented and relationship-oriented behavior depending on a subordinate's readiness to perform a particular task. Leader behavior is described as consisting of two factors that are similar to those in Fielder's model: task-oriented or directive behavior, which focuses on assuring that followers complete their work tasks efficiently and effectively, and relationship-oriented or supportive behavior, which focuses on listening, encouraging, supporting, and caring about followers' welfare. The terms directive and supportive behavior are used in current versions of this model and are therefore used in this description. These factors are represented in this theory by a two-dimensional graph with four quadrants that describe different combinations of high and low levels of directive and supportive behavior. Quadrant 1 ("telling") represents a high task, low relationship style of leader behavior, while Quadrant 2 ("selling") represents a high task, high relationship style of leader behavior. Quadrant 3 ("participating") represents a low task, high relationship leadership style, and Quadrant 4 ("delegating") is characterized by a low task, low relationship style of leader behavior. These four styles of leadership are said to be effective for different levels of follower readiness (15).

The follower's readiness level reflects the stages or levels an employee might go through in learning new tasks. Level 1 is described as unable and unwilling, reflecting low follower ability and lack of confidence or commitment when trying something new. Level 2 is described as unable but willing, where the follower is low in ability but motivated and is making an effort. Level 3 is characterized as able but unwilling, where followers have the ability to perform the task, but are insecure or apprehensive about doing it on their own. Level 4 is described as able and willing, where followers have the ability to perform and are confident and commited to the task. Readiness level is specific to the task. For example, an employee would be considered highly ready if able and willing and working at a task that is liked. The same employee would be considered less ready when doing an unfamiliar task that is disliked. Table 3–2 shows the leader behavior combinations that Hersey and Blanchard recommend for followers at different readiness levels.

RECOMMENDATIONS OF THE SITUATIONAL LEADERSHIP MODEL

Leaders are advised to use a telling style of leader behavior (high direction, low support) with employees who lack the ability to complete the task without guidance (level 1—low readiness). That is, the leader needs to set goals, organize the work, set time deadlines for completing the work, and direct and observe the performance of the employee.

TABLE 3–2 Hersey and Blanchard's Behavioral Recommendations for Leaders

Subordinate Readiness Level	Leader behavior		Leadership Style
	Supportiveness	Directiveness	
Low ability & low willingness	Low	High	Telling
Low ability & high willingness	High	High	Selling
High ability & low willingness	High	Low	Participating
High ability & high willingness	Low	Low	Delegating

Employees who still have low ability but are willing and motivated to perform the task (level 2 readiness) require a selling style from the leader (high direction, high support). The leader is expected to provide encouragement, listen to the subordinate's opinions, and provide feedback on the employee's performance in addition to closely supervising the work.

For employees who have the ability, skills, and knowledge to complete the task, but are unwilling or insecure about doing it on their own (level 3 readiness), a participating style is recommended (low direction, high support). The leader should share ideas with employees and facilitate their decision making, but the amount of direct supervisory involvement in organizing and directing the work is reduced.

A delegating style of leader behavior (low direction and low support) is recommended for those employees who are both able and willing to perform their assigned tasks on their own (level 4 readiness). The leader should entrust such employees with the implementation and completion of their projects.

HOW VALID AND USEFUL IS THE MODEL?

The research evidence for Hersey and Blanchard's Situational Leadership Model is mixed and generally weak. One researcher studied high school teachers and found some support for the model in the low-readiness conditions, but not for high-readiness level followers (16). A later study found follower performance and satisfaction were not significantly higher when leaders' behavior fit the model's recommendations (17). Another study of retail employees also found little support for the model (18). For these individuals, the delegating and telling styles produced low levels of satisfaction and commitment for both high and low readiness employees. Supportive behaviors produced high satisfaction for all employees. These findings do not match the model's predictions. However, the participating style did fit well for high readiness employees and the selling style fit employees who were low on readiness.

Although the model has not been well supported by researchers, it remains widely accepted by managers and management trainers. Part of the reason for this acceptance is the ease with which the model and its behavioral recommendations are learned. The emphasis on adapting the leader's behavior to match subordinate levels of ability and willingness (readiness) is reasonable. The readiness level of the subordinate is assessed by the manager. It is likely that few employees will be completely lacking in ability or so able and willing that they will require no supervision. This means the most common leadership style will be either a selling or participating style. It appears that the leadership process in real organizations is more complex than these simple recommendations.

◆ PATH-GOAL THEORY OF LEADERSHIP

The Path-Goal Theory of leadership is a contingency theory that addresses a leader's interaction with individual followers. The theory suggests that a leader's behavior is motivating or satisfying to the follower if the behavior increases the attractiveness of goals and increases followers' confidence in achieving them. Path-Goal Theory also suggests that effective leaders help followers achieve task goals and make followers' efforts satisfying and rewarding. With this model, the leader is very active in coaching, guiding, encouraging, motivating, and rewarding followers for their efforts and achievements (19).

Four types of leader behavior are usually included in this model: directive, supportive, participative, and achievement-oriented. Directive leader behavior is nonauthoritarian and nonpunitive guidance by the leader. The leader organizes and schedules the work and tells the followers in a nonthreatening manner what, when, and how the work is to be done. Supportive leader behavior involves being concerned and considerate of the well-being and needs of followers. The supportive leader creates a "friendly and psychologically supportive work environment" (20). Participative leader behavior involves encouraging subordinates to contribute to the decision-making process. Participative behaviors consist of asking followers for suggestions and opinions, and using their input when making decisions. Achievement-oriented leader behavior includes setting challenging goals, encouraging followers to perform at high levels, and showing confidence in their ability to do so. The model states that these four leader behaviors will result in improved follower attitudes and expectations, such as satisfaction with work, acceptance of the leader, and follower beliefs that their effort will lead to effective performance and rewards (see Table 3–3).

Path-Goal Theory predicts that situational factors will influence the effectiveness of the four types of leader behavior as follows:

1. Nonauthoritarian and nonpunitive directive leader behavior will increase follower satisfaction and performance when followers are engaged in unstructured or ambiguous tasks.
2. Supportive leader behavior will increase the satisfaction of followers engaged in frustrating, stressful, or dissatisfying tasks. When supportive leader behavior is provided primarily for followers who show high effort, it will increase the performance of those followers.
3. Participative leader behavior will increase follower satisfaction and motivation when tasks are ambiguous, nonrepetitive, and challenging. Participative leader behavior will also increase satisfaction of nonauthoritarian followers who have a high need for independence when tasks are clearly specified in advance.
4. Achievement-oriented leader behavior will increase follower effort and confidence in goal achievement when tasks are ambiguous, nonrepetitive, and challenging.

TABLE 3–3 Predicted Effects of Path-Goal Leader Behaviors

Leader Behavior	*Predicted Motivational Effects*
Directive	Reduces role ambiguity; increases follower beliefs that effort will result in good performance and performance will be rewarded
Supportive	Increases self-confidence; increases the personal value of job-related effort
Participative	Reduces ambiguity, clarifies expectations, increases consistency of subordinate and organizational goals, increases involvement with and commitment to organizational goals
Achievement-oriented	Increases subordinate confidence and the personal value of goal-directed effort

LEADERSHIP RECOMMENDATIONS OF PATH-GOAL THEORY

The main recommendation of Path-Goal Theory is that the leader should consider the existing follower characteristics and task and organizational factors and choose a leader behavior that is appropriate for the situation. If the leader demonstrates the appropriate behavior, followers will be highly satisfied and accepting of the leader. They will put forth considerable effort and will utilize effective work methods to achieve their task-related goals. These effects should result in low levels of follower grievances and turnover and high levels of overall performance.

HOW VALID AND USEFUL IS THE MODEL?

Portions of the Path-Goal Theory have been widely tested with varying results. One comprehensive review of research on Path-Goal Theory (21) demonstrated considerable support for some aspects of the theory. Directive leader behavior improved the satisfaction of subordinates whose tasks were ambiguous. However, contrary to Path-Goal Theory, directive leadership improved follower performance even when followers' tasks were repetitive and unambiguous. As predicted by the theory, supportive behavior had a strong positive effect on the satisfaction and performance of followers doing highly repetitive, unambiguous, and stressful tasks. However, support also had positive effects on satisfaction, performance, and job clarity in jobs that were ambiguous and nonrepetitive. Supportive leader behavior also improved the job clarity of lower level employees more than that of higher level employees. Another recent review of Path-Goal Theory research supports some of these findings but not others (22). A limited amount of research data on participative leader behavior indicates some support for its positive effects when followers' tasks are ambiguous and nonrepetitive (23). There is almost no published research on achievement-oriented leader behavior.

The overall proposition of Path-Goal Theory, that the effects of leadership behavior are contingent on situational factors, is generally supported. Furthermore, although some specific predictions of Path-Goal Theory have not been supported, researchers point to faulty testing methods as the potential culprit. In response to the mixed research results and methodological problems, Bob House (the originator of Path-Goal Theory) recently introduced a new version of the theory (24). The reformulated theory expands the focus from the effects of four leader behaviors on the work satisfaction, motivation, and performance of individual subordinates to include the effects of ten types of leader behaviors on subordinate empowerment, satisfaction, ability, performance, and work unit performance. The revised model also includes the immediate (short term) effects of leader behaviors on followers as well as longer term outcomes. Twenty-six propositions are presented relating different types of leader behaviors and situational characteristics to individual and work unit outcomes. The theory now includes charismatic leadership as well as a broader emphasis on shared decision making, representation, and networking behaviors of managers. The newest version of Path-Goal Theory is very complex and has not been tested by research in organizations. Table 3–4 presents the ten types of leader behaviors in the revised Path-Goal Theory as well as specific examples of each type.

As House stated, "all theories, no matter how good at explaining a set of phenomena, are ultimately incorrect and consequently will undergo modification over time."(25) It appears that the original Path-Goal Theory has produced enough research

TABLE 3–4 Revised Path-Goal Theory Leader Behaviors

General leader behaviors	Specific leader behaviors
Clarifying	Clarifying performance goals, standards, and means to achieve them
	Clarifying who subordinates should respond to
	Implementing contingency rewards and punishments
Participative	Consulting with subordinates
	Incorporating subordinate opinions in decision making
Achievement-oriented	Setting high goals and seek improvement
	Emphasizing excellence and showing confidence in subordinates
	Stressing pride in work
Work facilitation	Planning, scheduling, and organizing work
	Coordinating subordinates' work
	Guiding, coaching, counseling, and giving feedback
	Eliminating roadblocks and bottlenecks
	Providing resources
	Delegating authority to subordinates
Supportive	Creating a friendly and psychologically supportive environment
	Displaying concern for subordinates' welfare
Interaction facilitation	Resolving disputes and facilitating communication
	Giving minority views a hearing
	Emphasizing collaboration and teamwork
	Encouraging close relationships among team members
Group-oriented decision processes	Posing problems to the group
	Searching for mutual interests in problem solving
	Encouraging participation by all group members
	Searching for and displaying alternatives
	Delaying evaluation until all alternatives are found
	Encouraging evaluation of all alternatives
	Combining advantages of alternatives to create solutions
Representing and networking	Representing the group in a favorable way
	Communicating the importance of the group's work
	Maintaining positive relations with influential others
	Being an effective trading partner
	Keeping in touch with network members
	Participating in social functions and ceremonies
	Doing favors for others
	Showing positive regard for others
Charismatic	Articulating a vision of a better future
	Displaying a passion for the vision
	Displaying self-sacrifice in the interest of the vision
	Demonstrating self-confidence, confidence in the attainment of the vision, and determination and persistence in the interest of the vision
	Selectively arousing nonconscious motives of followers
	Taking extraordinary personal and organizational risks
	Communicating high performance expectations
	Using symbolic behaviors to emphasize values
	Providing frequent positive evaluation of followers
Shared leadership	Encouraging subordinates to behave as leaders
	Setting an example for subordinates to follow

and insight into the leadership process to produce another generation of leadership theories. The new version of Path-Goal Theory and the model described next are examples of these new generation theories.

◆ MULTIPLE LINKAGE MODEL OF LEADERSHIP

The Multiple Linkage Model of leadership presents four broad categories of leadership behavior that are then broken down into eleven mid-range behaviors, which in turn comprise numerous specific behaviors (see Table 3–5). This model, developed by Gary Yukl, proposes that the overall impact of specific leader behaviors on work group performance is complex and is influenced by two sets of factors. One set is the immediate effects of the leader's behavior on follower effort, job knowledge, resources, organization of the work, cooperation, cohesion, and coordination with other individuals and groups. These immediate effects are called intervening variables in this model, and when they are improved by the leader, group performance is usually high. The second set of factors that influence the leader's impact on group performance is situational characteristics, such as the formal organizational reward system, the type of work task performed by followers, the organization's policies and procedures, and the technology of the workplace. These situational factors may affect group performance, they may

TABLE 3–5 Leadership Behaviors in Yukl's Multiple Linkage Model

Broad Behavior	*Mid-range Behaviors*	*Specific Behaviors*
Building relationships	Supporting	Being friendly, showing concern, listening to problems, giving advice and support
	Networking	Developing and maintaining positive relationships with influential others
	Managing conflict and team building	Reducing and resolving disputes, facilitating communication, encouraging teamwork and cooperation
Influencing People	Motivating	Influencing subordinates to achieve work goals, setting good behavioral examples
	Rewarding and recognizing	Providing valued rewards, praise, and recognition for performance; expressing appreciation, respect, and admiration for achievement
Making decisions	Problem solving	Identifying and analyzing problems and solutions, implementing and evaluating solutions
	Planning and organizing	Determining objectives, strategies, and actions needed to improve efficiency and productivity
	Consulting and delegating	Discussing decision options with subordinates, asking for input from subordinates, and allowing subordinates some autonomy in decision making
Giving-seeking information	Monitoring	Collecting information on work progress and quality, determining opportunities, threats, and needs
	Clarifying	Providing direction, telling subordinates what, how, and when to do certain tasks
	Informing	Providing information subordinates need to do their work and to understand the importance of their work

constrain leaders from using certain behaviors, or they may affect the type of impact the leader has on group performance (26).

In this model, intervening variables may also be directly affected by situational characteristics. For example, the formal reward system and aspects of the tasks (situational characteristics) can affect the degree of effort subordinates will exhibit (intervening variables). Recruitment and selection procedures (situational characteristics) also affect the level of job knowledge in the subordinates' work group (intervening variable). Other organizational policies and procedures, as well as the technology of the workplace (situational characteristics), can affect how efficiently the work is organized and the adequacy of available resources (intervening variable). The Multiple Linkage Model clearly allows for many sources of influence on followers.

RECOMMENDATIONS OF THE MULTIPLE LINKAGE MODEL

The model makes two general recommendations in the form of propositions to improve group performance:

> Proposition 1: In the short term, group effectiveness is determined by the degree to which the leader uses the leader behaviors shown in Table 3–5 to correct deficiencies in the intervening variables.
>
> Proposition 2: In the long term, group effectiveness is determined by the degree to which the leader improves situational factors (27).

Proposition 1 of the Multiple Linkage Model addresses the short-term motivational needs of subordinates. Leaders need to set challenging goals; provide direction, recognition, and support; organize the work; reduce conflict; and encourage cooperation. Proposition 2 addresses longer-term strategic actions that modify situational influences in such a way as to decrease negative effects and increase the positive effects of situational factors. For example, leaders can increase demand for the unit's products by finding new customers; upgrade the skill level of the work unit through training programs and personnel changes; and expand output by replacing old equipment, simplifying procedures, and improving sources of supplies.

HOW VALID AND USEFUL IS THE MODEL?

The model is not specific about the effects individual leader behaviors have on the intervening variables. It also fails to specify when certain situational factors affect intervening variables or group performance, or how the situational factors influence the impacts of specific leader behaviors. This lack of specific predictions makes it very difficult to test the model, and very few tests have been conducted (28). However, the linkages between leader behaviors and their impacts on followers are grounded in prior research in the field of leadership. Yukl recognizes the limitations of the model and suggests that it is a general framework for describing the leadership process rather than a formal theory with precise predictions for effective leadership.

Table 3–6 provides a summary of the elements in each of the four major contingency theories of leadership described in this chapter. The reader will notice these models often share some of the same elements, although there are differences in the recommendations made to improve leaders' effectiveness. These models are compared and evaluated in the concluding section of this chapter.

TABLE 3–6 Summary of Leader Behaviors, Situational Factors, and Leader Effects in Four Major Contingency Theories of Leadership

Contingency Theories	Leader Behaviors or Predispositions	Situational Characteristics	Follower's Psychological Reactions	Follower & Group Outcomes
Fiedler's Contingency Model	Task oriented Relationship oriented	Leader-member relations Task structure Leader's position power		High group performance
Hershey & Blanchard's Situational Leadership Model	Task oriented/ directive Relationship oriented/ supportive	Follower readiness (ability and willingness to perform a task)	Satisfaction Commitment	High follower performance
House's Path-Goal Theory	Directive Supportive Participative Achievement oriented Work facilitation(e) Interaction facilitation(e) Group oriented(e) Representative(e) Charismatic(e) Shared leadership(e)	Task structure or ambiguity Frustrating, stressful or dissatisfying task Challenging tasks Low follower authoritarianism or high need for independence	Satisfaction Motivation Acceptance of the leader Job clarity High effort	High follower performance Low levels of grievances & turnover High group performance(e)
Yukl's Multiple Linkage Model	Supporting Networking Managing conflict Team building Motivating Rewarding & recognizing Problem solving Planning & organizing Consulting & delegating Monitoring Clarifying Informing	Organization's reward system Follower's tasks Policies & procedures Technology of the workplace Organizational crises or major change Follower's characteristics Economic conditions	Job Knowledge High effort Organization of the work Adequate resources Cooperation & group cohesion Role clarity Coordination with other groups	High group performance

(e)-Indicates items that are part of a recently expanded version of this model with no research support.

Summary ■

All the contingency leadership theories presented in this chapter describe the leadership situation as a key aspect of leadership effectiveness. Some models focus on the leader's effect on individuals' attitudes and performance, and others focus on group performance. Three of the models describe specific leader behaviors, and one model describes an aspect of the leader's personality or predisposition. All the models indicate that some type of adaptation is required between the leader and the situation. Most of the contingency theories recommend that the leader modify behavior to fit the situation. One model suggests that either the situation should be changed to fit the leader's style or the leader should be transferred to a different situation in order to be effective.

Fiedler's Contingency Model and Hersey and Blanchard's Situational Leadership Model were both proposed more than twenty years ago and have remained largely unchanged. Although they can be helpful, research evidence indicates that these models are too simple to provide adequate guidance for effective leadership in today's complex organizational environments. The Path-Goal Theory and the Multiple Linkage Model have both evolved over several years to be more comprehensive and realistic in their description of the leader's behavior and the situational factors important to leadership effectiveness. However, the newly revised Path-Goal Theory is untested and the Multiple Linkage Model is very general, with no specific recommendations about when certain leader behaviors are most appropriate. Consequently, these models also are lacking in the amount of guidance they provide for practicing leaders.

The approach of this book is to build on these contingency theories by describing key leadership behaviors that have been proposed and researched in conjunction with the various leadership models. In coming chapters, we address leader characteristics that help leaders exhibit each behavior effectively; we identify sources of power for leaders that tend to facilitate these leader behaviors; we examine situational factors that increase or decrease the impact of the behaviors; and we describe the effects of the behaviors on followers and their groups. We will also expand on the suggestion contained in some of the contingency models, that leaders should modify the situations facing their groups to make followers more effective with or without the leader (29). We also describe several newer and less researched leadership behaviors and issues along with their implications for leadership effectiveness in organizations of the future.

The Leadership Process Model described in chapter 2 is a general way of describing the leader behaviors detailed in this book. The model's basic structure incorporates features of several earlier contingency models.

Key Terms and Concepts in this Chapter ■

- achievement-oriented leader behaviors
- contingency theories of leadership
- directive leader behaviors
- Fiedler's Contingency Model of leadership
- Hersey and Blanchard's Situational Leadership Model
- intervening variables
- leader's position power
- Multiple Linkage Model of leadership
- participative leader behaviors
- Path-Goal Theory of leadership
- relationship-oriented leader behaviors
- situational characteristics
- situational favorableness or control
- supportive leader behaviors
- task-oriented leader behaviors
- task structure

Review and Discussion Questions ■

1. Which of the four contingency models described in this chapter would be the most useful to you as a leader? Why?
2. Which of the elements of situational favorableness or situation control in Fiedler's Contingency Model do you think is the most important for a leader? Why?
3. According to Fiedler's Contingency Model, how does changing the situation influence the effectiveness of the leader?
4. Using the Hersey and Blanchard Situational Leadership Model, describe the four leadership styles that result from combining directive and supportive leadership behaviors.
5. How does the Hersey and Blanchard Situational Leadership Model define the readiness level of followers? How could a leader determine the readiness level of specific followers?
6. What do you think are the most valid criticisms of the Hersey and Blanchard Situational Leadership Model?
7. Think of a job you have had or may have in the future. Using Path-Goal Theory, identify the task and organizational factors a leader should consider. Given the factors you have identified, which of the four types of leader behavior would be most effective?
8. According to Path-Goal Theory, what are the contingency or situational factors that most impact each of the four types of leader behavior?
9. How does the Multiple Linkage Model of leadership expand our understanding of the leadership process?

Exercise: Changing Situational Favorableness or Control ■ ■ ■ ■ ■ ■ ■ ■ ■ ■ ■ ■

Using the concepts in Fiedler's Contingency Model, how could a leader increase or decrease the situational favorableness or situational control by increasing or decreasing each of the three situation characteristics used in the model? Indicate specific actions a leader could take to increase and decrease each characteristic. Try to be innovative and creative in identifying possible leader actions.

Quality of leader-member relations (high quality results from liking and trusting the leader)
    Leader actions to increase the quality of leader-member relations
    Leader actions to decrease the quality of leader-member relations

Task structure (highly structured tasks can be performed using a standard set of procedures)
    Leader actions to increase the task structure
    Leader actions to decrease the task structure

Leader's position power (leader's authority and control over rewards and punishments)
    Leader actions to increase position power
    Leader actions to decrease position power

◆◆◆ **Case Incident**

Tough Assignment

Ted Wills has been hired as the new supervisor for the parts department of an automobile dealership. His first day on the job his manager, Linda Dunn, tells him, "You have a tough assignment. In the group you supervise there is an active trouble maker who has managed to keep from getting fired because he is the only employee who knows the inventory system. Three other employees follow his lead in consistently finding things to complain about, and the other four employees stay out of trouble by doing only what they are told." Linda handed the personnel files for the department employees to Ted. "The most important thing," Linda continued, "is that you change the sloppy way work is being done in the department and improve the accuracy in filling parts orders."

After hesitating a moment, Ted asked, "What was the former supervisor like?" "Well," replied Linda, "He had semiretired on the job and let the employees do what they wanted. He was not concerned about accuracy in filling orders or maintaining the inventory. As I said before, it is a tough assignment, especially since all your employees have been with the dealership for more than five years, and most are friends with the owner."

Ted smiled, "I guess I have my work cut out for me."

QUESTIONS

1. How would you define the leadership problems in this situation?
2. What situational factors should Ted take into account before deciding on what leadership actions to take?
3. What leader behaviors would you recommend to Ted? Why?

Endnotes ▪▪▪▪▪▪▪▪▪▪▪▪▪▪▪▪▪▪▪▪▪▪▪▪▪▪▪▪▪▪▪▪▪▪▪▪▪▪▪

1. House, R. J. and Aditya, R. N. (1997). The scientific study of leadership: Quo vadis? *Journal of Management, 23* (3), 409–473.
2. Wofford, J. C. and Liska, L. Z. (1993). Path-goal theories of leadership: A meta-analysis, *Journal of Management, 19* (4), 857–876.
3. Jacobs, T. O. (1970). *Leadership and Exchange in Formal Organizations.* Alexandria, VA: Office of Naval Research.
4. Schriesheim, C. A. and Kerr, S. (1977). Theories and measures of leadership: A critical appraisal of current and future directions. In J. G. Hunt & L. L. Larson (Eds.), *Leadership: The Cutting Edge.* (pp. 9–45). Carbondale: Southern Illinois University Press.
5. Fiedler, F. E. and Garcia, J. E. (1987). *New Approaches to Effective Leadership: Cognitive Resources and Organizational Performance.* New York: John Wiley & Sons.
6. Jacobs, *Leadership and Exchange in Formal Organizations.*
7. Schriesheim and Kerr, Theories and measures of leadership: A critical appraisal of current and future directions.
8. Fiedler, F. E., Chemers, M. H. and Mahar, L. (1994). *Improving Leadership Effectiveness: The Leader Match Concept* (2nd ed.) New York: John Wiley & Sons.
9. Fiedler and Garcia, *New Approaches to Effective Leadership: Cognitive resources and Organizational Performance.*

10. Fiedler, Chemers and Mahar, *Improving Leadership Effectiveness: The Leader Match Concept.*

11. Schriesheim and Kerr, Theories and measures of leadership: A critical appraisal of current and future directions.

12. Bass, B. M. (1990). *Bass & Stogdill's Handbook of Leadership.* (3rd ed.) New York: The Free Press.

13. Yukl, G. (1998). *Leadership in Organizations* (4th ed.). Upper Saddle River, NJ: Prentice Hall.

14. Schriesheim, C. A., Tepper, B. J. and Terault, L. A. (1994). Least Preferred Coworker score, situational control, and leadership effectiveness: A meta-analysis of contingency theory model performance predictions. *Journal of Applied Psychology,* 79(4) 561–573.

15. Hersey, P., Blanchard, K. H. and Johnson, D. E. (1996). *Management of Organizational Behavior: Utilizing Human Resources* (7th ed.). Upper Saddle River, NJ: Prentice Hall. Graeff, C. L. (1997). Evolution of situational leadership theory: A critical review. *Leadership Quarterly,* 8 (2) 153–170.

16. Vecchio, R. P. (1987). Situational leadership theory: An examination of a prescriptive theory. *Journal of Applied Psychology,* 72, 444–451.

17. Norris, W. R. and Vecchio, R. P. (1992). Situational Leadership theory: A replication. *Group and Organizational Management,* 17(3), 331–342. Fernandez, C. F. and Vecchio, R. P. (1997). Situational leadership theory revisited: A test of an across-job perspective. *Leadership Quarterly,* 8 (1) 67–84.

18. Goodson, J. R., McGee, G. W. and Cashman, J. F. (1989). Situational leadership theory. *Personnel Psychology,* 43, 579–597.

19. House, R. J. and Mitchell, T. R. (1974). Path-Goal theory of leadership. *Journal of Contemporary Business,* 5, 81–97.

20. Ibid.

21. Indvik, J. (1986). Path-goal theory of leadership: A meta-analysis. In *Proceedings of the Academy of Management Meetings,* 189–192.

22. Wofford and Liska, Path-goal theories of leadership: A meta-analysis.

23. Indvik, Path-goal theory of leadership: A meta-analysis.

24. House, R. J. (1996). Path-Goal Theory of leadership: Lessons, legacy, and a reformulated theory. *Leadership Quarterly,* 7, 323–352.

25. Ibid.

26. Yukl, G. (1998). *Leadership in Organizations* (4th ed.). Upper Saddle River, NJ: Prentice Hall.

27. Ibid.

28. Yukl, *Leadership in Organizations* (4th ed.); Dorfman, P. W., Howell, J. P., Hibino, S., Lee, J. K., Tate, U. and Bautista, A. (1997). Leadership in western and Asian countries: Commonalties and differences in effective leadership practices. *Leadership Quarterly,* 8 (3), 233–274.

29. Howell, J. P. and Dorfman, P. W. (1986). Leadership and substitutes for leadership among professional and nonprofessional workers. *Journal of Applied Behavioral Science,* 22(1), 29–46.

Core
Leadership
Behaviors

PART
II

CHAPTER 4

Supportive Leadership Behavior

Learning Objectives
After reading this chapter, you should be able to do the following:

1. Describe supportive leadership as an effective leadership behavior pattern and give examples of supportive leadership behaviors.

2. Explain why supportive leadership is important for individual followers and groups.

3. Describe some of the skills a leader needs to develop into an effective supportive leader.

4. Describe some of the sources of power leaders develop to be supportive of followers.

5. Identify organizational factors which can encourage or discourage supportiveness in leaders.

6. Discuss some of the skills needed for effective listening, which are part of supportive leadership.

7. Explain whether a leader should be equally supportive of all followers or if some followers need more supportiveness than others.

8. Describe several impacts leader supportiveness has on follower psychological reactions and behaviors.

◆ EXAMPLES OF EFFECTIVE SUPPORTIVE LEADERSHIP

- A subordinate approached her supervisor and said she would not be able to make a scheduled committee meeting on Friday because she had a doctor's appointment. She asked if she could reschedule the meeting. The supervisor replied she would check with the other committee members and, if possible, set up the meeting for the first thing Monday morning.
- In describing his performance evaluation, an employee praised his supervisor for not talking down to him; he also said that by encouraging input, observations, and feedback on his own behavior, the supervisor showed respect for the subordinate as a valuable member of the department.
- A military officer showed ongoing concern and respect for subordinate differences in cultural or racial values, life styles, and mores.
- A supervisor was alert to personal problems of subordinates and, once aware of the problems, made a concerted effort to help the subordinate solve them.

- A leader made a conscious effort to encourage and provide "air time" for everyone during staff meetings and to distribute privileges or choice task assignments equitably (1,2).

◆ DEFINITION, BACKGROUND AND IMPORTANCE OF SUPPORTIVE LEADER BEHAVIORS

These are examples of effective supportive leadership behaviors. Supportive leadership involves showing concern for the status, well-being, and needs of followers; demonstrating a kind, considerate, and understanding attitude regarding followers' problems; and fostering followers' professional development. Supportive leaders are friendly and informative, and they encourage open, two-way communication. They also show trust and respect for followers in a way that enhances followers' feelings of personal worth and importance. Keeping followers informed and helping them develop professionally are other marks of supportive leaders (3,4).

Supportiveness is common in effective leaders. Its importance has been well established in industrial, military, educational, human service, and governmental organizations. Its popularity with leaders results from its importance in establishing and maintaining the well-being of followers and groups.

Supportive behaviors are effective because they satisfy people's needs to be liked and appreciated by others, to be respected as capable and valuable, and to be continually improving (5). Supportiveness also helps keep a group together by promoting cohesion among members and keeping individuals from becoming alienated. Some organizations have the same characteristics as dysfunctional families; that is, certain members do not interact effectively, resulting in strife and unhappiness. In organizations, supportive behaviors can help promote the emotional health of individuals and groups (6,7) and improve the leader's interactions with followers. These behaviors are summarized in Figure 4–1.

Many names have been used to describe supportive leader behaviors. Perhaps the earliest term for leader behaviors of this type was consideration, used by researchers at

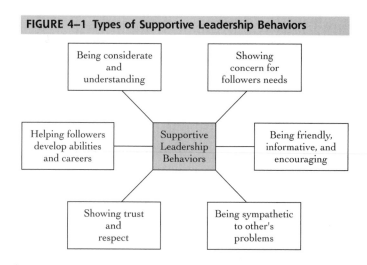

FIGURE 4–1 Types of Supportive Leadership Behaviors

- Being considerate and understanding
- Showing concern for followers needs
- Helping followers develop abilities and careers
- Supportive Leadership Behaviors
- Being friendly, informative, and encouraging
- Showing trust and respect
- Being sympathetic to other's problems

LEADERSHIP IN ACTION: PAT CARRIGAN

Pat Carrigan was the first woman to manage a GM auto assembly plant. She obtained a doctorate in clinical psychology and worked as a teacher in the public schools before becoming a human resource specialist in industry. She started with GM as a human resource consultant and became interested in becoming a line manager. With the help of several other executives in GM, she worked out a five-year plan to prepare herself to become a plant manager. She worked in various aspects of plant operations and served two years as a general plant superintendent. During this time she impressed those who worked with her as a knowledgeable and trustworthy colleague and friend.

Her performance as a plant manager at the Lakewood plant near Atlanta, Georgia was stellar. Grievances were reduced to near zero from a very high level, and discipline incidents were reduced by 82 percent. During her tenure at the Bay City plant in Michigan, productivity increased 40 percent, major budget savings were made, and voluntary self-managed work teams were begun.

Her supportive leadership style is founded on the principle that people are more important than things. Managers at the Bay City plant had the habit of keeping their doors closed. She made a point of keeping her door open, and the other managers learned to do likewise. She believes strongly in personal contact with all employees, and she frequently walked the plant floor talking with workers. Other writers have noted that it is her physical presence, closeness, and concern for employees that earned her their respect and trust. One UAW local president described Carrigan as not having a "phony bone in her body."

Although she is no longer a plant manager at GM, this personal, supportive approach won her the cooperation of employees. She spent time on the factory floor meeting each of the 2,000 workers in the plant, shaking their hand, showing she wanted to listen, and entering into a dialog with them. She showed employees that she wanted to know them as human beings, and they responded with cooperation, respect, and excellent performance.

the Ohio State University during the 1950s and 1960s. At the University of Michigan, the term relationship-oriented behavior was used to refer to supportive leader behaviors, and this term is still popular with consultants and used in the Situational Leadership theory described in chapter 3 (8). Concern for people refers to a similar type of leader behavior and is part of the Managerial Grid Model used for many years in leadership training (9). Researchers have used different methods to measure supportive leadership; and, although each measurement approach is unique, they generally assess most of the behaviors described above. The Leadership in Action box on Pat Carrigan shows how one leader used supportive leadership effectively.

◆ INEFFECTIVE SUPPORTIVE LEADERSHIP

Although the impacts of supportive leadership are usually positive, the following incidents demonstrate how a leader can provide supportiveness that is ineffective because of the follower reactions it produces.

• Community mental health centers are staffed by highly trained mental health professionals—primarily psychologists and social workers. These individuals provide counseling and therapy for center clients. In their roles as caregivers, they are highly attuned to interpersonal processes, particularly those that involve manipulation of others. They deal on a daily basis with clients who feel manipulated and who manipulate others, and their job is to subtly reshape (manipulate) their clients' behavior. This process can make them very sensitive to any manipulation of their own behavior by their manager. In one such center, some managers chose to be supportive by discussing client-related problems openly in meetings and encouraging their staff to do the same. Caregivers saw this behavior as an attempt to manipulate the type of care they gave their clients. As trained professionals, they resented and resisted what they saw as interference in their caregiving activities, and they reacted very negatively to this type of supportive leadership. Managers in other centers, who were more subtle in their supportive behaviors, being friendly, informative, and approachable, for example, had more positive results.

• A new manager was placed in charge of the accounting and billing department of a construction company. The manager was part of a new management group brought in by the board of directors. The company was a rapidly growing family-owned corporation, and the owners were convinced that a professional management team was needed to operate the rapidly growing enterprise. Because the new accounting manager was an "unknown quantity" to the accounting staff, they viewed her as having a mission to "shake up the place" by changing the procedures and possibly some of the accounting staff. When she encouraged them to discuss their problems with her, they felt she was trying to gather data she could use to replace them. They did not trust the motives of the new management group, and a norm developed in the department to "stonewall" the manager whenever she urged them to discuss their problems. All efforts by the new manager to elicit questions, show concern, and demonstrate kindness and understanding were greeted with a matter-of-fact "no problems" by the staff members. A different supportive approach in which the manager provided information about changes or brought in upper management to discuss their plans with the departmental staff would have been more effective.

These examples show that some leaders may use supportive leadership ineffectively with counterproductive results. The leader must be careful how supportiveness is used and tailor the approach to the needs and concerns of the followers. The next section describes how leaders can effectively use supportive leader behaviors to work with followers.

◆ HOW TO BE SUPPORTIVE

Supportive leaders often develop specific skills, traits, and sources of power to help them effectively support their followers. They usually develop good communication skills, effectively conveying their ideas and feelings, listening actively and carefully, and eliciting ideas and feelings from followers. The ability to listen to followers and understand what they are saying is a key element in showing acceptance and consideration. The supportive leader uses communication skills to be responsive to followers' task-related problems, complaints, and personal problems. The leader uses verbal and nonverbal communication to indicate how much followers are valued. Supportive leaders can suspend biases and prejudices while interacting with followers. The Leadership Skills box titled "Supportive Communication" describes the difference between supportive and nonsupportive communication. The self-assessment that follows it is intended to identify important listening skills for supportive leadership.

LEADERSHIP IN PERSPECTIVE: SUPPORTIVE AND NONSUPPORTIVE COMMUNICATION

Supportive communication delivers the message accurately and supports or enhances the relationship between the parties.

Supportive and Nonsupportive Communication

Supportive	*Nonsupportive*
• Problem-oriented	• Person-oriented (naming)
• Descriptive	• Evaluative
• Words and actions consistent	• Incongruent words and actions
• Encouraging	• Puts people down
• Specific	• General or vague
• Interactive (listening)	• One-way (telling)

LEADERSHIP SELF-ASSESSMENT: EFFECTIVE LISTENING

Objective: To help the reader understand and distinguish effective and ineffective listening skills for supportive leadership.

Instructions: Rank the following statements (from 1 to 9) in order of importance for effective listening behavior by a leader.

1. _____ Empathize when someone is speaking by trying to understand the speaker's point of view.

2. _____ Ask questions to show interest and further your understanding.

3. _____ Develop arguments with a speaker's main points while s/he is speaking to be ready to respond.

4. _____ Eliminate physical and psychological distractions when listening.

5. _____ Listen for areas of common interest and agreement.

6. _____ Decide quickly if a message is going to be dull or unimportant and terminate the conversation in order to save time.

7. _____ Actively focus your attention on concepts, ideas, attitudes, and feelings related to the speaker's message.

8. _____ Carefully evaluate the speaker's physical characteristics before comprehending the message.

9. _____ Take into account the speaker's attitudes and beliefs to help understand how the speaker feels about the message.

Interpretation: If you ranked items 1, 2, 4, 5, 7, and 9 as high, then you have a good understanding of effective listening behavior. If you ranked items 3, 6, and 8 as high, you may not be an effective listener and could have difficulty with this aspect of supportive leadership.

Interpersonal skills are closely related to communication skills and are also basic to effective supportive leadership (10). It is through positive, friendly interpersonal relations that the leader supports followers, cooperates with them, develops trust with them, and assists them. Leaders use their interpersonal skills to provide social support when followers are upset or under pressure. Thus, it is within the context of interpersonal relations that the leader shows appreciation and takes an interest in followers' lives. Supportive leaders use interpersonal skills to increase followers' self-confidence, and they accept and understand the diverse beliefs of followers.

Leaders who make an effort to be sociable often develop effective interpersonal and communication skills. A person high in sociability tends to be outgoing and expressive and is often seen as warm, considerate, and giving (11). Sociable leaders enjoy spending time on a regular basis with each follower. They get to know followers and find out about their interests. They are often described as agreeable or easy to get along with, friendly, and cooperative. They tend to maintain a pleasant and cheerful disposition and show consideration and trust toward followers. Leaders who are low in sociability and/or agreeableness are somewhat withdrawn or reserved, cautious in interpersonal relations, and are often insensitive to the needs and feelings of followers. They are also moody, aloof, intolerant, and suspicious in interpersonal relations. These individuals often have difficulty showing effective supportiveness with followers. Sociable and agreeable leaders find it easier to be supportive by showing positive regard and acceptance and are less likely to show rejection, harsh criticism, or personal insults.

Effective supportive leaders also usually develop high levels of competence and expertise at followers' tasks (12). Leaders must have technical and professional competence to provide followers with training and development. In addition, to be a supportive resource in solving problems, the leader must have task-related expertise. Moreover, providing useful feedback on performance requires job-related competence. Effective support of decision making also draws on the leader's technical expertise. High levels of technical competence can also increase the leader's confidence and willingness to support followers.

Being sociable and agreeable probably come naturally to many supportive leaders. But these tendencies can be developed by conscious effort. The same is true for communication, interpersonal, and task skills. Leaders can obtain additional training and coaching in these areas to improve their capabilities to provide supportive leadership effectively.

Regardless of any other skills or traits, a leader's philosophy of leadership will affect the degree of supportiveness shown with followers (13). For example, if a leader believes in a strongly autocratic and heavily directive approach in dealing with subordinates, supportive, caring, concerned, and encouraging behavior will probably not be used with followers. On the other hand, if a leader believes that people are the most important asset and enjoys helping followers develop, then highly supportive behaviors will likely be used with followers. We believe this desire to help followers develop is the most constructive approach for long-term performance and positive follower attitudes.

In addition to developing key skills, supportive leaders also work at developing three types of power sources to help them influence their followers. As leaders build their competence at followers' tasks (described earlier), they increase their expert power and can support followers by providing knowledge, skill, and ability in performing important tasks and solving problems. The more important the follower's problem, the greater the likelihood the leader will use expert power. The follower must recognize the leader's expertise and perceive the leader as a trustworthy source of advice. Effective leaders use expert power to support followers by providing needed knowledge, being available as a source of technical advice, helping individuals solve job problems, providing explanations of processes, and referring followers to needed sources of assistance or information.

As explained in chapter 1, leaders whose personality, accomplishments, and integrity cause followers to admire or identify with them have referent power. Furthermore, when leaders have referent power, followers attribute favorable motives to the leaders, they want their leaders' approval, and they interpret small, apparently insignificant behaviors by leaders as supportive (such as a smile or other friendly gesture). At the same time, supportive behaviors increase the leader's referent power. Examples of supportive behaviors that are both facilitated by referent power and increase it include displaying respect and acceptance, providing help in problem solving, showing interest in followers, and backing them up.

Supportive leaders also develop reward power to satisfy followers needs and wants. Leaders with high reward power are often watched closely by followers, and they see the leader's supportiveness as very significant. Reward power can be used to provide needed resources, a better work schedule, a larger expense account, or advice for followers. Figure 4–2 summarizes skills, traits and sources of power for effective supportive leadership.

Leaders may be encouraged or discouraged from providing supportive leadership by organizational factors that are largely beyond their control. The style preferences of the leader's superior can encourage or discourage a leaders' supportiveness (14). The superior's behavior often conveys the leadership preference of the organization. If the superior is highly supportive with the leader, then the leader will likely be supportive with followers. If the superior is not supportive with the leader, then the leader will likely behave in a similar fashion with followers or will not remain in the organization.

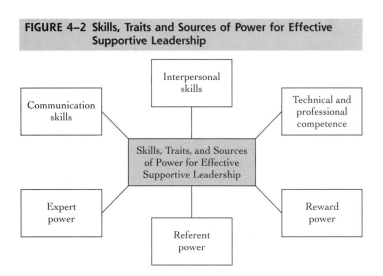

FIGURE 4–2 Skills, Traits and Sources of Power for Effective Supportive Leadership

Because the superior often evaluates the leader's performance, the leader will most likely be sensitive to the superior's style preferences and often reflect them in leadership behaviors. The organizational mission or culture may also encourage or discourage a leader's supportiveness (15). Organizations that provide human services to clients (such as universities or hospitals) or that work with volunteers seem to encourage a supportive leadership style (16). Organizations that encourage high involvement and commitment by their staff also encourage supportiveness (17). Other organizations may not encourage supportive leadership to the same extent, and the leaders may respond with less supportiveness. Thus, organizational characteristics can clearly facilitate or limit the use of supportive leadership behaviors.

As one might expect, leaders from different countries and cultures may express their supportiveness differently. Supportive leaders in Britain are seen as people who share information and welcome followers' suggestions, while those seen as supportive leaders in Japan and Hong Kong appear to focus on interactions with the group in and out of work hours. Japanese leaders are known for spending much time with followers after work hours, eating and drinking while listening to follower concerns and building group solidarity. In the United States, leaders often provide most support for followers

LEADERSHIP IN PERSPECTIVE: SUPPORTIVENESS AND LEADER GENDER

Many popular writers refer to a stereotypical female leadership style that features a high amount of supportiveness of their followers. Female leaders are said to demonstrate more caring for their followers, to be more concerned for their welfare and careers, to provide more helpful advice, and to be more considerate than most male leaders. A comprehensive summary of high quality research on leadership style and gender was conducted by two female researchers. Although these researchers did find differences between male and female leaders, their findings for supportive leadership provides only limited support for the stereotypical leadership styles described by popular writers.

The researchers divided the studies comparing male and female leaders into three groups: experimental studies conducted primarily with college students, assessment center studies conducted on individuals who aspired to leadership positions (this group also contained many students), and practicing leaders. In the first two groups, females playing the role of leaders were significantly more supportive than males. In the third group of studies that focused on actual leaders, there were no differences in supportiveness between male and female leaders.

Several possible explanations have been offered for these findings for actual female leaders. Female leaders may be compelled to adapt more stereotypical male styles as they advance in organizations, or they may find that other leader behaviors that partially replace supportiveness are strongly needed. It does appear, however, that most female leaders are not more supportive than most male leaders.

Source: A. H. Eagly and B. T. Johnson, "Gender and leadership style: A meta-analysis," in R. M. Steers, L. W. Porter and G. A. Bigley, *Motivation and Leadership at Work.* (New York: McGraw-Hill, 1996), 315–345.

during work hours, with "open door" policies and "management by walking around." The focus of all these behaviors, though, is on caring and kindness, which is the hallmark of supportive leadership.

◆ SUPPORTIVENESS AND FOLLOWERS' BEHAVIOR

One important issue for leaders is whether they should provide more interpersonal support to some subordinates than others. Most leaders would answer "yes" to this question. The leader is rare who behaves the same toward each subordinate. To be effective, a leader needs to adapt to different subordinates. How can the leader decide who should receive more support and who should get less? This question addresses the leader's basic influence strategy.

One approach advocates that a leader should use interpersonal support as a reward (18). This approach is closely aligned with behavioral psychology and is based on the operant conditioning model of learning associated with B.F. Skinner. The rationale is that the leader should show most concern, be most considerate, and provide greatest encouragement for the best performers. The intended effect is to positively reinforce good performance. In turn, the thinking goes, the positive reinforcement increases the frequency of the good performance. Research supports the favorable impact of positive reinforcement on performance. It also indicates that leaders tend to show more support for high-performing followers (19).

Still, using supportiveness as positive reinforcement does not address the needs of followers whose performance is less than desired. These employees may need a concerned and encouraging leader to provide them with the confidence necessary to improve their performance. New or young employees who are striving to improve are often not the best performers. Given a nurturing and encouraging supportive leader, who also provides them with the needed task guidance, they may become very good or outstanding performers in the future. Tommy LaSorda, past manager of the Los Angeles Dodgers, attributes his unusual success as a minor and major league manager to providing this type of supportive behavior to young baseball players.

LaSorda represents the approach which says that leaders should provide supportiveness as needed by individual followers rather than as a reward for high performance. Thus, his supportiveness can be a "facilitating condition" stimulating improved follower performance. In addition, of course, subordinates' needs vary over time, so that a normally secure, autonomous, and competent individual may experience personal problems that cause performance to decline, necessitating a temporary increase in supportiveness from the leader. When the problems are solved, the leader can reduce the interpersonal support. The subordinate will return to a normal level of performance and will likely remember that the leader cared enough to respond with kindness when it was needed. Other workers see and hear about leaders who respond positively to followers in this manner. This helps explain why followers who have supportive leaders generally show a high level of job satisfaction. In summary, then, leader supportiveness should be provided for followers who need it. Leaders stimulate and reward followers' performances in whatever ways they can. The use of interpersonal support may be the most immediately available stimulus or reward in a given situation, and most effective when leaders use it both ways. The Leadership in Action box on Stan Smith describes how he provided supportive leadership for followers with very positive results.

LEADERSHIP IN ACTION: STAN SMITH

Until his recent retirement, Stan Smith managed a panty hose manufacturing facility in the southwestern U.S. for Sara Lee Corporation. Under Stan's management, the plant was the most efficient of the five panty hose manufacturers in the Sara Lee organization, and it employed about 800 employees working in three shifts. Stan displayed his supportive leadership by almost never being in his office. He was on the factory floor with his people. He knew the names of every employee on all three shifts.

Stan arrived at the plant early in the morning before the night shift left. He showed his concern for employees by immediately visiting every department, greeting workers, asking how things were going, answering questions, and inquiring about personal or work-related issues. He was present in the plant during the day shift, making the same rounds to each department, and did the same thing one more time after the evening shift came in but before he went home for the night. He thus saw and either talked with or was available to every employee on all three shifts every single work day. He also expected this type of friendly and open behavior from his managerial staff.

Stan also conducted informational meetings during working hours with a different cross section of employees each week. He fostered employee development by instituting a tuition reimbursement program for all employees who wished to take classes at the local colleges. They conducted classes in the plant (free of charge) on English as a second language, as well as other classes to help employees pass their high school equivalency examination. Stan was understandably popular with his employees, and they responded by throwing parties on his birthday, by being productive, and by exhibiting a very low turnover rate.

◆ EFFECTS OF SUPPORTIVE LEADERSHIP

When leaders are supportive, they help satisfy followers' needs for security, acceptance, esteem, and achievement, which makes the workplace more attractive for all concerned (20). Followers typically respond to a leader's concern and kindness by themselves being considerate of others and of the organization. Since the Roman legions, military leaders who see to the needs of their men before they see to their own needs typically derive intense loyalty from the men in times of battle (21). When leaders provide supportive leadership effectively, their followers often become committed to the organization (22), are cooperative, and tend to imitate the leader (23). These results of leader supportiveness are examples of followers' psychological reactions shown earlier in Figure 2–2. A leader who is supportive has other favorable effects—followers are usually more satisfied with their work and their supervision (24), they report less job stress and burnout, their work groups show higher degrees of harmony and cohesiveness (25), and they are less likely to be absent from work, tardy, file a grievance, or quit (26). Supportive leadership also increases followers' self-confidence, lowers anxiety, and minimizes unpleasant and distracting aspects of the work situation (27). Several recent summaries of research have also shown that when leaders are supportive, their followers often perform well on their jobs (28,29).

Although not yet well researched, another follower reaction that may be influenced by supportive leadership is follower empowerment. In a leadership context, the term empowerment is related to motivation. Thus, empowerment is the process by which a leader enhances a follower's feelings of competence or ability to perform, or self-determination, and of the meaningfulness and significance of one's actions (30). By trusting, respecting, and encouraging two-way communications with followers, a supportive leader can create a climate in which followers feel significant and meaningful and believe they will receive the leader's time, help, and assistance when needed. This can increase followers' beliefs in their own capabilities. It can also increase the individuals' confidence that they can govern their own behavior to achieve what is expected of them. Such beliefs affect peoples' willingness to initiate new activities and persevere with tasks. Thus, leader support may be a key factor affecting employee empowerment.

Research in real and simulated organizations shows that supportive leadership has the strongest favorable effects on followers' job satisfaction, including increased satisfaction with supervision, intrinsic task satisfaction, and overall job satisfaction. Next to job satisfaction, leader supportiveness has its strongest effects on increased organizational commitment of followers' and improved job performance (31). However, the effects of a leader's supportiveness on followers are influenced by situational factors. In other words, the positive impacts of supportiveness are generally strongest in certain organizational situations or with certain types of followers. Most studies indicate that a wide range of situational factors should be considered to assess the degree of potential positive impact of a leader's support. Table 4–1 summarizes the impacts of supportive leadership.

Ongoing research outside the United States shows the same positive effects of leader supportiveness in almost every country studied. In Japan, Mexico, Taiwan, Turkey, and India, supportiveness has positive effects on followers' satisfaction and commitment (32,33,34,35). Follower performance was also improved by leader supportiveness in Japan (36). Positive effects of support were especially strong in Japan, Israel, and Germany when the leader was also directive (37). Directive leadership is described in Chapter 6. The combination of leaders' supportive and directive behaviors may be particularly effective in highly industrialized countries. Although some writers have indicated that supportive leadership is less popular in a few countries, such as the Philippines and People's Republic of China, supportiveness seems to be an important aspect of leadership in formal organizations in most countries. It appears that most followers around the world value a leader who shows concern for them, is considerate, listens, and tries to help them with their aspirations and problems.

TABLE 4–1 Impacts of Supportive Leadership

Follower Benefits	*Organizational Benefits*
• satisfaction with work, job, and supervisor	• increased cohesiveness and harmony
• increased commitment to the organization	• lower turnover, absenteeism, lateness, and grievance rates
• reduced stress	• increased cooperation
• increased self-confidence	• increased productivity
• increased performance	

Summary ▪▪

Supportive leadership is a pattern of behaviors involving concern, acceptance, consideration, respect, and a developmental approach toward followers. These behaviors can help preserve the integrity of work groups by building harmony and cohesiveness among members. In general, supportive leadership can be used effectively with beneficial results or ineffectively with poor results.

Supportive leaders rely most heavily on their excellent communication skills, solid interpersonal relations, and technical competence at followers' tasks. These important skills are complemented when leaders make an effort to be sociable and agreeable because by doing so, they show respect and acceptance of followers. The three sources of power that are most important to supportive leadership are expert power, referent power, and reward power.

Organizational factors may encourage or discourage leaders from being supportive with their followers. Leaders usually vary the amount of supportiveness they provide for different followers, depending on followers' needs or performance.

Supportive leadership tends to strongly increase followers' satisfaction with their supervisor, work, and overall job situation. It also helps increase followers' commitment to their organization, lowers followers' stress, and increases group harmony and cohesiveness. These follower and group psychological reactions usually result in increases in follower's performance as well as reduced turnover, grievance rates, tardiness, and absenteeism. Most of the effects of supportive leadership are likely influenced by numerous follower and situational factors to be discussed in chapter 5.

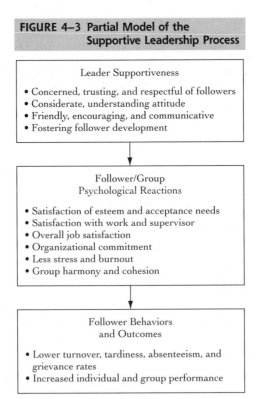

FIGURE 4–3 Partial Model of the Supportive Leadership Process

Leader Supportiveness

- Concerned, trusting, and respectful of followers
- Considerate, understanding attitude
- Friendly, encouraging, and communicative
- Fostering follower development

Follower/Group Psychological Reactions

- Satisfaction of esteem and acceptance needs
- Satisfaction with work and supervisor
- Overall job satisfaction
- Organizational commitment
- Less stress and burnout
- Group harmony and cohesion

Follower Behaviors and Outcomes

- Lower turnover, tardiness, absenteeism, and grievance rates
- Increased individual and group performance

Figure 4–3 summarizes much of this chapter and provides a partial model of the supportive leadership process. The topmost box in Figure 4–3 summarizes the supportive leader behaviors described early in this chapter. The figure shows these behaviors affecting follower and group psychological reactions, which in turn affect follower behaviors and outcomes. In chapter 5 the model depicted in Figure 4–3 will be further explained by adding a discussion of how situations and followers influence the process of supportive leadership.

Key Terms and Concepts in this Chapter

- communication skills
- empowerment
- expert power
- followers' satisfaction

- interpersonal skills
- referent power
- relationship-oriented behaviors

- reward power
- supportive communication
- supportive leader behaviors

Review and Discussion Questions

1. Describe specific supportive leader behaviors that have influenced your behavior in an organization. Identify why each had an impact on your behavior.
2. What situations have you been in where you benefited from or wanted supportiveness from a leader?
3. How might a leader develop the skills and abilities necessary to provide effective supportive behaviors?
4. Describe how a leader could use one or more of the types of power discussed in this chapter to be supportive of followers?
5. Describe how organizational factors could constrain a leader's effective use of supportive leadership.
6. Do you believe that leaders should be more supportive of the best performers, the average performers, or the poor performers? What are the reasons for your position?
7. Why might employees who have supportive managers show high levels of job satisfaction? Could the reasons be different for different individuals?
8. Discuss how supportive leadership could influence followers' feelings of empowerment.
9. What advice would you give a leader on how to use supportive leader behaviors effectively?

Exercise: Impact of Supportive Leadership Behaviors

Instruction: Rank the following supportive leader behaviors in terms of the amount of positive impact you feel they would have on your behavior as a member of a group. The behavior ranked 1 should have the greatest positive impact and the behavior ranked 8 should have the least positive impact.

1. _____ The leader supports you in a dispute with another employee.
2. _____ The leader asks you about your family and your personal interests.
3. _____ The leader keeps you informed about possible changes in your department.

4. _____ The leader helps you do the work when your workload is unusually high.

5. _____ The leader provides training and developmental experiences to help you prepare for a possible future promotion.

6. _____ The leader helps you deal with personal family problems when you ask for help.

7. _____ The leader gives you complete attention when you discuss how to solve a problem confronting the group.

8. _____ When you need to discuss something, the leader is available.

Why would some supportive leadership behaviors have more impact on your behavior than others?

(You might find it interesting to compare your rankings with other individuals.)

◆◆◆ **Case Incident**

A Lack of Self-Confidence?

Ms. Jane Hunt manages the design department of a construction company. Ed Green is her most competent design engineer and he can always be counted on to give a maximum effort on any assignment. Ed has an excellent educational background, having received a bachelors degree in mechanical engineering and a masters degree in civil engineering from a highly respected university.

Ed is very shy and Ms. Hunt feels that he is overly concerned about other people's feelings. Ed cannot complete his projects without the contributions of technical writers, drafters, and typists. However, if he feels someone has a heavy workload, he does not delegate work to them. In fact, he sometimes fails to meet deadlines because he did not give the work to others for completion. If Ed's failure to meet deadlines continues, Ms. Hunt will not be able to assign him important projects. This could mean that Ms. Hunt would not be using Ed's ability effectively.

Everyone in the design department recognizes Ed's competence but they also realize they can avoid doing his work because he is never demanding. They know that Ed will not insist that department standards be met, and he never complains about the quality of work done for him. When technical writing or drafting are not up to standards, he usually tells those doing the work, "Don't bother doing it over; it will be all right." Ms . Hunt knows that it is not all right when standards are not met, so she must have the work redone. Other employees have told Ms. Hunt they think Ed lacks self-confidence and does not realize his own high level of competence.

QUESTIONS

1. Could Ms. Hunt use supportive leadership to positively influence Ed's job performance?

2. What specific supportive leadership behaviors would you recommend to Ms. Hunt to improve Ed's performance?

Endnotes

1. Bartol, K. M. and Butterfield, D. A. (1976). Sex effects in evaluating leaders. *Journal of Applied Psychology,* 61 (4), 446–454.

2. Hendrick, H. W. (1979). Leaders' behavior, subordinate reactions, and perceptions of organizational climate and effectiveness.

Perception and Motor Skills, 49 (3), 803–816.

3. Bass, B. M. (1990). *Bass and Stogdill's Handbook of Leadership* (3rd ed.). Upper Saddle River, NJ: Prentice Hall; Likert, R. (1967). *The Human Organization.* New York: McGraw Hill; Fleishman, E. A. (1953). The description of supervisory behavior. *Journal of Applied Psychology,* 37, 1–6; Bowers, D. G. and Seashore, S. E. (1966). Predicting organizational effectiveness with a four-factor theory of leadership. *Administrative Science Quarterly,* 11, 238–263; House, R. J. and Dessler, G. (1974). The path-goal theory of leadership: Some post hoc and a priori tests. In J. G. Hunt and L. L. Larson (Eds.), *Contingency Approaches to Leadership.* Carbondale: Southern Illinois University Press.

4. DuBrin, A. J. (1998). *Leadership: Research Findings, Practices and Skills.* Boston: Houghton Mifflin Company.

5. Maslow, A. H. (1954). *Motivation and Personality.* New York: Harper & Row.

6. Mitroff, I. I., Mason, R. O. and Pearson, C. (1994). Radical surgery: What will tomorrow's organization's look like? *Academy of Management Executive,* 8 (2), 11–21.

7. Van Maurik, J. (1994). Facilitating excellence: Styles and processes of facilitation. *Leadership and Organizational Development Journal,* 15 (8), 30–35.

8. Hersey, P. and Blanchard, K. H. (1986). *Management of Organizational Behavior: Utilizing Human Resources* (6th ed.). Upper Saddle River, NJ: Prentice Hall.

9. Blake, R. E. and Mouton, J. S. (1984). *The Managerial Grid III,* Houston: Gulf Publishing.

10. Mann, F. C. (1965). Toward understanding the leadership role in formal organizations. In R. Dubin (Ed.), *Leadership and Productivity.* San Francisco: Chandler.

11. Bass, B. M. and Dunteman, G. (1963). Behavior in groups as a function of self, interaction, and task orientation. *Journal of Abnormal and Social Psychology,* 66, 419–428; Fleishman, E. A. and Salter, J. A. (1963). Relation between the leader's behavior and his empathy toward subordinates. *Journal of Industrial Psychology,* 1, 79–84; Fleishman, E. A. (1957). A leader behavior description for industry. In R. M. Stogdill and A. E. Coons (Eds.), *Leader Behavior: Its Description and Measurement.* Columbus: Ohio State University, Bureau of Business Research.

12. Konovsky, M. A. (1986). Antecedents and consequences of informal leader helping behavior: A structured equation modeling approach. Doctoral dissertation, Indiana University, Bloomington; Lindemuth, M. H. (1969). An analysis of the leader behavior of academic deans as related to the campus climate in selected colleges. Doctoral dissertation, University of Michigan, Ann Arbor.

13. Hunt, J. G. and Osborn, R. N. (1980). A multiple influence approach to leadership for managers. In P. Hersey and J. Stinson (Eds.), *Perspectives in Leader Effectiveness.* Ohio University, 47–62.

14. Wagner, L. W. (1965). Leadership style, hierarchical influence, and supervisory role obligations. *Administrative Science Quarterly,* 9, 391–420.

15. Halpin, A. W. (1955). The leader behavior and leadership ideology of educational administrators and aircraft commanders. *Harvard Educational Review,* 25, 18–32.

16. Rawls, J., Ulrich, R. and Nelson, O. (1973). A comparison of managers entering or re-entering the profit and nonprofit sectors. *Academy of Management Journal,* 3, 616–623; Dragon, A. C. (1979). Leader behavior in changing libraries. *Library Research,* 1 (1), 53–66.

17. Ansari, M. D. (1988). Leadership styles and influence strategies: Moderating effect of organizational climate. Paper, International Congress of Psychology, Sydney, Australia; Lombordo, M. M. (1983). I felt it as soon as I walked in. *Issues & Observations,* 3 (4), 7–8.

18. Podsakoff, P. M., Todor, W. D. and Schuler, R. S. (1983). Leader expertise as a moderator of the effects of instrumental and supportive leader behaviors. *Journal of Management,* 9 (2), 173–185.

19. Barrow, J. C. (1976). Worker performance and task complexity as causal determinants of leader behavior, style and flexibility. *Journal of Applied Psychology,* 61, 433–440.

20. Henisath, D. (1998). Finding the word in leadership. *The Journal for Quality and Participation,* 21 (1), 50–51.

21. Sayles, L. (1979). *Leadership: What Effective Managers Really Do . . . and How They Do It.* New York: McGraw-Hill.

22. Dorfman, P. W. and Howell, J. P. (1988). Dimensions of national culture and effective leadership patterns: Hofstede Revisited. In E. G. McGoun (Ed.), *Advances in International Comparative Management,* 3, 127–149; Howell, J. P. and Dorfman, P. W. (1986). Leadership and substitutes for leadership among professional and nonprofessional workers. *Journal of Applied Behavioral Science,* 22, 29–46.

23. Kerr, S. and Slocum, J. W. Jr. (1981). Controlling the performances of people in organizations. In P. C. Nystrom and W. H. Starbuck (Eds.), *Handbook of Organizational Design,* Volume 2. New York: Oxford University Press.

24. Fisher, B. S. and Edwards, J. E. (1988). Consideration and initiating structure and their relationships with leader effectiveness: A meta-analysis. *Best Papers Proceedings,* Academy of Management, Anaheim, CA. 201–215.

25. Kerr, S. and Slocum, J. W. Jr., Controlling the performances of people in organizations; Fisher, B. M. and Edwards, J. E. (1988). Consideration and initiating structure and their relationships with leader effectiveness: A meta-analysis. *Best Papers Proceedings,* Academy of Management Meeting, Anaheim, CA, 201–215; Seltzer, J. and Numeroff, R. (1988). Supervisory leadership and subordinate burnout. *Academy of Management Journal,* 31 (2), 439–446.

26. Yukl, G. (1998). *Leadership in Organizations* (4th ed.). Upper Saddle River, NJ: Prentice Hall.

27. Ibid.

28. Wofford, J. C. and Liska, L. Z. (1993). Path-goal theories of leadership: A meta-analysis. *Journal of Management,* 19 (4), 857–876.

29. Dorfman, P. W., Howell, J. P., Hibino, S., Lee, J. K., Tate, U. and Bautista, J. (1997). Leadership in western and Asian countries: Commonalities and differences in effective leadership processes across cultures. *Leadership Quarterly,* 8 (3), 233–274; Dorfman, P. W., Howell, J. P., Cotton, B. C. G. and Tate. U. (1992). Leadership within the discontinuous hierarchy structure of the military: Are effective leadership behaviors similar within and across command structures? In K. E. Clark, M. B. Clark and D. P. Campbell (Eds.). *Impact of Leadership.* Greensboro, NC: Center for Creative Leadership, 399–416.

30. Spreitzer, G. M. (1992). When organizations dare: The dynamics of individual empowerment in the workplace. Ph.D. dissertation, University of Michigan.

31. Podsakoff, P. M., MacKenzie, S. B. and Bommer, W. H. (1996). Meta-analysis of the relationships between Kerr and Jermier's substitutes for leadership and employee job attitudes, role perceptions, and performance. *Journal of Applied Psychology,* 81 (4), 380–399.

32. Peterson, M. F., Smith, P. B. and Peng, T. K. (1993). Japanese and American supervisors of a U.S. workforce: An intercultural analysis of behavior meanings and leadership style correlates. Working paper: Texas Tech University.

33. Misumi, J. (1985). *The Behavioral Science of Leadership: An interdisciplinary Japanese Research Program.* Ann Arbor: University of Michigan Press.

34. Howell, J. P. and Dorfman, P. W. A comparative study of leadership and its substitutes in a mixed cultural work setting. Presented at the Western Academy of Management Meeting, Big Sky, MT, March; Ayman, R. and Chemers, M. M. (1982). The relationships of managerial behavior to effectiveness and satisfaction in Mexico. Paper, International Conference of Applied Psychology, Edinburgh.

35. Yeh, Q. J. (1995). Leadership, personal traits and job characteristics in R & D organizations: A Taiwanese case. *Leadership and Organizational Development Journal,* 16 (6), 16–27.

36. Kenis, I. (1977). A cross-cultural study of personality and leadership. *Group and Organizational Studies,* 2, 49–60.

37. Ibid.

CHAPTER 5

Situational Dynamics of Supportive Leadership

Learning Objectives
After reading this chapter, you should be able to do the following:

1. Identify organizational situations where supportive leadership is especially effective.
2. Identify situations where supportive leadership is probably not effective.
3. Discuss how leaders can modify situations to increase the effectiveness of their supportive behaviors.
4. Discuss how leaders can modify followers' tasks to replace the need for some supportiveness and still maintain positive follower attitudes and performance.
5. Explain how followers, situations, and supportive leaders affect each other in a dynamic process.

Chapter 4 defined and described how leaders can be supportive and how leader supportiveness affects followers. Even though supportiveness is an important element in most leaders' behavioral repertoire, certain situational factors (including follower characteristics) can make it more or less effective (1,2). This chapter addresses the situational dynamics of supportive leadership—what leaders should look for in a situation to know when supportiveness is most appropriate, how leaders can influence situations to make them more supportive, and how followers, situations, and supportive leaders influence one another.

◆ SITUATIONS WHERE SUPPORTIVENESS MAY OR MAY NOT BE EFFECTIVE

The following are descriptions of situations where supportive leadership may or may not be effective with followers. Place an X next to those situations where you believe supportiveness will be most effective.

1. _____ Followers are under high stress while trying to complete a dangerous task.
2. _____ Followers are new on the job and are unsure of their abilities and insecure about keeping their positions.
3. _____ Followers are a small group of counselors in a student services department of a state university.
4. _____ Followers are very opinionated and stubborn in their point of view.
5. _____ Followers are a large group of people (over 30) who work at widely varying tasks at different locations.
6. _____ Followers' work tasks require creativity and new learning with much competition and possible conflict with other groups.
7. _____ Followers' work involves designing and testing computer programs. They are highly trained and competent and obtain great personal satisfaction from their work.

The situations described in items 1, 2, 3, and 6 would probably result in favorable consequences when a leader uses supportive leadership. These situations reflect a need for supportiveness that can enhance or increase the effectiveness of this leader behavior. Situational characteristics described in items 4 and 5 would likely decrease or neutralize the impact of a leader's supportiveness. These situations indicate followers who may resist or are immune to the positive effects of supportiveness. When these charac-

LEADERSHIP IN ACTION: HERBERT KELLEHER

Herbert Kelleher, chairman of Southwest Airlines, occasionally likes to poke fun at himself for the sake of his employees. Under his leadership, Southwest has had record earnings as well as the top operating margin among the airline industry's large carriers.

Each year Kelleher throws a party for employees to introduce them to the airline's newest television advertising campaign. One recent ad showed Kelleher bumbling a ticket purchase with an expired credit card and missing his plane. Aside from appearing in ads, he shows concern for employees by boarding Southwest planes and joking with the flight crew. He also remembers employee names and sends them birthday cards. He regularly sends letters to all employees describing events in the airline industry and how they will affect Southwest. He listens to employee concerns and takes action—like when he interceded in labor negotiations over a petition by flight attendants against certain types of uniforms. Kelleher's office is tiny, in a barracks-style building located at Dallas's Love Field. He shares this headquarters with other employees, and he makes a clear effort to spread cost cutting equally throughout the company.

In addition to his bottom line results, his concern for employees has resulted in very high marks from employees and union officials. The profit-sharing plan offers both cash and stock ownership to employees. Southwest has not paid less than the maximum allowable cash bonus in 10 years and has placed a substantial portion of the company's ownership in employee hands. The supportiveness and caring attitude he shows for employees, backed up by his actions for their benefit, result in a surprising sense of family at Southwest. One union boss admitted that "Southwest employees are more interested in the health of the company than most groups."

teristics are present, a leader's supportive behaviors will likely produce little or no improvement in follower reactions. Followers in these situations may be subject to other types of influence, and their leaders must often adjust how they influence followers. Item 7 is an example of a situational characteristic that replaces followers' needs for supportiveness from their leader. When followers find their work tasks especially satisfying and the basis for high follower commitment and performance, little supportiveness by their leader is needed. Leaders can sometimes foster the development of these situational characteristics and thereby improve follower attitudes and performance in an indirect manner. These three types of situational characteristics are described in detail in this chapter as they relate to supportive leadership.

The Leadership in Action box with Herb Kelleher describes his supportiveness of employees who must maintain a friendly service orientation while working under stressful conditions. This type of situation calls for supportive behavior by the leader, and Kelleher seems to be effective in this role.

◆ SITUATIONAL FACTORS THAT INCREASE EFFECTIVENESS OF SUPPORTIVE LEADERSHIP

Several characteristics of work tasks and followers have been found to increase the impact of supportive leadership. These characteristics make leader supportiveness especially useful to followers.

TASK, ORGANIZATIONAL, AND FOLLOWER CHARACTERISTICS

First, individuals working at job tasks that are dissatisfying or stressful are particularly responsive to the kind, considerate, and understanding overtures of a supportive leader. Job conditions may be considered dissatisfying or stressful if (1) the task is dangerous or frustrating, (2) the task does not match the subordinate's needs, (3) subordinates are required to deal with hostile customers, and/or (4) subordinates face difficult job deadlines (3). Admiral Richard E. Byrd, American naval officer and polar explorer in the early 1900s, demonstrated supportiveness in a stressful and dangerous situation when he jumped into the icy Antarctic Ocean to rescue one of his crew members who had fallen overboard. Under conditions like these, subordinates appreciate a leader who shows compassion and concern, and they respond with markedly improved psychological reactions.

Second, work tasks that are highly structured also tend to increase the effects of supportive leadership. Highly structured tasks involve execution of rules and procedures that are simple, repetitive, and unambiguous. Once tasks of this nature have been learned, workers may view them as tedious and boring. Thus, workers appreciate a supportive leader who shows a kind and understanding attitude toward them, who humanizes the working conditions. They respond to the supportive leader with significantly improved attitudes and sometimes with improved task performance (4). Structured work tasks are an important situational factor for several leader behaviors described in this book.

Third, work tasks which require creativity or new learning may also increase the impact of supportive leadership. Groups charged with a complex decision-making task often perform best under a supportive leader. And workers faced with new and unfamiliar work tasks perform higher quality work with a supportive leader. It appears that by encouraging and showing confidence in subordinates, a supportive leader helps them overcome the anxiety often caused by a new complex task and allows them to more efficiently apply their collective energies toward effective performance (5).

Several characteristics of the subordinate's work environment have also been found to increase the impact of supportive leadership. First, certain properties of the subordinate's work group can be particularly helpful, probably because an employee typically interacts with coworkers frequently during the workday. Discussions about the work itself, the leader, and the organization are common, and the evidence is clear that employees are influenced by their peers at work. A group that faces much conflict with other groups inside or outside the organization is typically very responsive to a supportive leader (6). The group apparently appreciates the leader's reassurance and concern for their difficult situation. A group that is newly formed is also highly influenced by a supportive leader. In new groups, problems of goal and role definitions are just being worked through, and group members need more support and attention from their leader than in other groups. When this supportiveness is present, they respond favorably with group cooperation and increased energy (7). A dynamic feedback process also occurs with newly formed groups. This means that when group members respond to a supportive leader with increased cohesion and energy, this can cause the leader to respond again with further increases in supportiveness. It thus appears that a newly formed work group offers unusually fertile ground for a supportive leader.

Studies have found that a group that is highly cohesive can increase the effects of supportive leadership. A cohesive group has a high degree of solidarity, unity, and "felt closeness" among the members, and supportive leadership often pays off well in increased productivity as well as improved worker attitudes (8). As with certain other leader behaviors, however, this effect is likely dependent on the norms of the cohesive group. Group norms are shared beliefs among members about how they should or should not behave. A cohesive group is able to enforce its norms for member behavior very effectively because members are attracted to the group and wish to remain in it. If the group norms favor the leader, then the enhancing effect of group cohesion on supportive leadership will result. If group norms oppose the leader, however, the group may combine its efforts to resist the leader's influence, and cohesion can actually decrease the positive effects of a leader's supportive behaviors.

Overall organizational characteristics can also affect the impact of a leader's supportiveness. For example, a high degree of organizational formalization (that is, explicit plans and goals as well as standardized procedures and routines often associated with bureaucratic organizations) seems to make employees more responsive to a leader's supportive behaviors. The supportive leader is apparently seen as a rare source of concern and caring in an otherwise cold, "machine-like" organization and is thus capable of instilling appreciation and especially improved attitudes in subordinates (9).

The organizational or departmental mission can also increase the impacts of a supportive leader. A recent analysis showed that the impact of supportive leadership on follower performance was greatest in educational organizations (10). Although there were significant positive performance and attitudinal results in business, government, and military organizations as well, the impacts were stronger in schools between teachers and administrators. Similarly, several researchers have found that supportive leadership improves group effectiveness in service organizations and departments. These findings occurred in health and human service organizations as well as service departments within manufacturing organizations (11). Thus, the concerned and caring behavior of a supportive leader may be a particularly effective role model for subordinates whose jobs are to interact with and serve others.

A final environmental factor that can increase the effect of a leader's supportiveness occurs when the leader's superior is authoritarian (that is, the superior believes strongly in the need for rules and formal authority and tends to dominate subordinates). In this situation, the leader's supportiveness may have an increased impact on group performance (12). Here, subordinates apparently appreciate the buffering influence their immediate leader provides because it alleviates the tension created by the higher-level authoritarian manager.

Follower characteristics that increase the impacts of supportive leadership include low self-confidence, insecurity, or low self-esteem (13). Followers with these characteristics see the considerate and understanding leader as a source of comfort and encouragement and therefore show positive reactions to this behavior. Followers who expect their leader to be supportive (perhaps because the predecessor was) or who have high needs for achievement, autonomy, and esteem also tend to be positively influenced by supportive leaders. First, a leader who meets their expectations will naturally improve followers' responses (14). And second, since subordinates with these needs likely view the supportive leader as potentially helpful in achieving their goals, they also show higher satisfaction under this type of leadership (15).

INFLUENCING SITUATIONS TO MAKE SUPPORTIVENESS MORE IMPACTFUL

Most leaders are interested in doing whatever they can to make followers more responsive to their leadership. As you probably noticed, many of the factors that increase the impacts of supportive leadership reflect difficult or stressful situations for followers—stressful or dangerous job tasks, many formalized procedures to follow, external group conflict, authoritarian upper-level management, complex tasks, and/or low follower self-confidence, self-esteem, or security. We certainly do not advocate making jobs more stressful or difficult for followers just to increase the impacts of a leader's supportiveness, but leaders must be aware that stressful and difficult situations are common in organizations, and they may be difficult to change in the short run. In these situations, supportive leadership is the behavior of choice for the leader, and it should pay off with significant improvements in followers' reactions and behavioral outcomes. Creating smaller work groups or defining the group mission in terms of human service may also increase the impact of a leaders' supportiveness. Organizational training and socialization programs that build followers' expectations of supportiveness and encourage strong needs for achievement, autonomy, and esteem in followers may also increase the impact of supportiveness. Figure 5–1 summarizes major situational factors that increase the impacts of leader supportiveness. These situational factors help supportive leaders to have strong effects on followers' motivation, attitudes, and performance.

The Leadership in Action box on supportive leadership at Saturn describes how supervisors successfully use this leader behavior in a new automotive assembly plant. The situational factors in this plant make supportiveness an important aspect of the leadership.

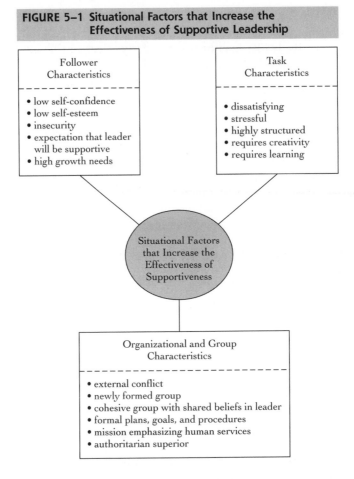

FIGURE 5–1 Situational Factors that Increase the Effectiveness of Supportive Leadership

◆ SITUATIONAL FACTORS THAT DECREASE EFFECTIVENESS OF SUPPORTIVE LEADERSHIP

Some characteristics of situations or followers make supportive leader behavior less important and less impactful on followers. This usually means that supportiveness is not an effective behavior pattern for leaders to use in that situation and a different leadership approach is needed.

TASK, ORGANIZATIONAL, AND FOLLOWER CHARACTERISTICS

A large work group can decrease the impact of supportive leadership on subordinates (16). Leaders are apparently more visible to members of smaller groups (6 to 15 members), and the supportive relationships with members of small groups are more intimate and impactful. In large groups (16 to 34 members), the leader has less opportunity to interact personally with members because the leader is often "spread too thin," reducing the overall impact of supportiveness on group performance and attitudes. Some leaders overcome this factor, like Stan Smith described in chapter 4, but it takes tremendous time and effort to interact with all the members of a very large group.

LEADERSHIP IN ACTION: SUPPORTIVE LEADERSHIP AT SATURN

The Saturn plant in Spring Hill, Tennessee was created for a high level of worker involvement and an emphasis on supporting workers to produce quality automobiles. One form of support used in Spring Hill is encouraging worker development through cross-training. Employees work in teams where members are trained to do all the functions performed by the team. This requires considerable new learning, and teams are given 350 to 700 hours of initial training that covers both technical and team-building aspects of the job. One goal is to develop cohesive teams that can respond to job problems cooperatively. In addition, management provides 92 hours of continuous training a year for each employee, which involves specific technical areas, interpersonal skills, and problem solving.

Saturn workers often operate under considerable stress to meet production goals. This situational factor makes supervisor supportiveness especially important. Supervisors demonstrate trust and respect for workers in these situations through flexible jobs, few firm guidelines, and a minimum of work rules. Worker involvement is encouraged by allowing people to take on added responsibilities as they desire. The basic assumption is that workers can be the most effective managers of complex manufacturing operations, since their familiarity with the work produces better and faster decisions than office-bound managers can make.

For example, to avoid time-consuming purchasing procedures and to speed up repairs, maintenance teams can order many of the tools and parts they need directly from suppliers. The teams can also decide whether to have work done in-house or to contract it to outside companies. In this vein, one maintenance team decided to use an outside supplier to sharpen cutting tools for transmission components because it was cheaper than doing it in-house.

Supportive leadership seems to be paying off for Saturn. The quality is high with low defect rates that rival those of Honda and Nissan. The car has sold well and has received high praise from the automotive press. Saturn workers have demonstrated a high commitment to the company. When a malfunction in the plant's powerhouse stopped the flow of cooling water to the paint shop, the maintenance team worked 36 hours straight to fix the problem.

Followers who are very dogmatic (highly opinionated and unable to incorporate new information effectively) do not respond well to supportive leadership, effectively negating the favorable effects of this type of leadership (17). These individuals are usually quite respectful of formal authority and prefer a strong directive type of leader. A supportive, concerned, and caring leader may be seen as weak or "touchy-feely" and will have little effect on their performance.

Limited evidence indicates that two other situational factors may at least partially decrease the favorable impacts of supportive leadership—a follower whose job is broad in scope (requires a large variety of activities that are important to the organization) and a follower whose job is at a high level in the organization. These two factors are related, in that as one moves to higher levels in an organization, the job often becomes more varied and meaningful for the operation as a whole. An employee in this position apparently becomes more engrossed in the work and relies on the leader to a lesser extent for encouragement and satisfaction of needs. Thus, supportive leadership may have less effect on the attitudes of followers carrying out high level jobs that are broad in scope (18).

Three other situational factors have been proposed that possibly decrease the effects of supportive leadership, although research has yet to validate these suggestions. These include a large spatial or geographic distance between leaders and subordinates, and the existence of little control by the leader over organizational rewards (19). It is argued that a large spatial distance prevents adequate interaction with subordinates, and leaders who do not control organizational rewards will be largely ignored. Researchers also have proposed that followers who are highly trained professionals may resist supportive leadership, though the evidence is unclear at this time. As described with the mental health workers in chapter 4, professional employees tend to value autonomy and self-control and may resist certain supportive influence attempts by their hierarchical leader.

OVERCOMING FACTORS THAT DECREASE EFFECTIVENESS OF SUPPORTIVE LEADERSHIP

Leaders should be aware of situational factors that decrease the impact of supportive leadership so they can work around them. Large groups of followers or dogmatic individuals can be especially problematic. Leaders can break up such groups or perhaps isolate or transfer dogmatic followers. However, high task scope and high job level can motivate many workers, and few leaders would want to decrease this motivation just to make followers more susceptible to supportive leadership. The leader should rely instead on other leader behaviors to influence these individuals.

Overall, few situational characteristics appear to decrease the effectiveness of supportive leadership. This is not the case for other leader behaviors described in later chapters, but it does show that supportive leadership is clearly a very important part of a leader's behavioral repertoire. Figure 5–2 summarizes the major situational factors that can decrease the positive effects of supportive leadership. These factors cause followers to resist or ignore a leader's support but do not improve followers' motivation, attitudes, or performance.

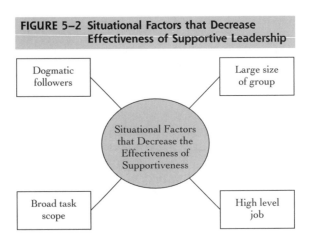

FIGURE 5–2 Situational Factors that Decrease Effectiveness of Supportive Leadership

Dogmatic followers

Large size of group

Situational Factors that Decrease the Effectiveness of Supportiveness

Broad task scope

High level job

LEADERSHIP SELF ASSESSMENT: SUPPORTIVE LEADERSHIP COMMUNICATION

For each of the following leader communications, indicate whether you feel it is supportive or not supportive.

Place an X in front of each supportive leader communication.

1. _____ "I will explain the right way to solve the problem."
2. _____ "I would like to hear your feelings about that incident."
3. _____ "You did a great job on this project."
4. _____ "See me about the methods you will use to complete the project."
5. _____ "Your coworkers and I will cover for you during your absence."
6. _____ "I trust your judgment in this situation."
7. _____ "You must achieve the following goals by the end of the month."
8. _____ "How can I help you with your heavy workload?"
9. _____ "To prevent errors you will need to carefully follow my instructions."
10. _____ "You had a good idea for improving quality."
11. _____ "You can take Friday afternoon off to attend the professional development seminar."

What differentiates the supportive statements from the nonsupportive ones?
Would the supportive leader communications have a different impact on your behavior than the nonsupportive communications? Why?

Key: Supportive communication items are 2, 5, 6, 8, and 11.
Items 1, 4, 7, and 9 address directive communication.
Items 3 and 10 address reward communication.

____

Source: Items adapted from research reported by D. A. Whetten and K. S. Cameron, *Developing Management Skills* (4th ed.) (Reading, MA: Addison-Wesley, 1998).

◆ SITUATIONAL FACTORS THAT REPLACE THE NEED FOR SUPPORTIVE LEADERSHIP

Some situational or follower characteristics can directly improve follower and group attitudes and performance. At times these characteristics can make supportive leadership unnecessary (20,21).

TASK, ORGANIZATIONAL, AND FOLLOWER CHARACTERISTICS

The strongest situational characteristic that replaces the need for supportive leadership is the existence of a work task that is intrinsically satisfying to a worker (22). When people find their work interesting and gratifying, they often derive all the encouragement and psychological support they need from their work and require little, if any, interpersonal support from their supervisor to maintain positive job attitudes. When an occasional setback occurs, a small amount of leader's supportiveness may help. But individuals who "love their work" are often challenged by temporary job setbacks and need little encouragement by the leader to attack and overcome problems on their own.

Another situational characteristic that replaces the need for supportive leadership is a work task that provides its own feedback concerning accomplishment. An example is repairing the brakes on a car and immediately testing them to be sure they work correctly. Research shows that most employees respond with very positive attitudes and motivation when they receive clear and direct feedback on their performance. When this feedback comes directly from their work, it is usually rapid, accurate, satisfying, and motivating (23). Consequently the need for a supportive, encouraging leader is reduced. This is especially true if the employee seeks autonomy and achievement on the job and also finds the work to be inherently satisfying.

When followers place an unusually high degree of importance on tangible organizational rewards, this can replace the need for supportive leadership (24). Specifically, when people are motivated primarily by substantive rewards offered by the organization such as pay raises, promotions, and benefits, they often place little value on a supervisor who concentrates on interpersonal support, encouragement, development, and a caring attitude. To these individuals "the proof is in the pudding," and a good leader is one who comes through with the tangible rewards they value. If these tangible rewards are made available, they will respond with favorable attitudes and performance. A leader who emphasizes a concerned, supportive approach without tangible rewards will have little influence on these followers.

CREATING FACTORS THAT REPLACE THE NEED FOR SUPPORTIVE LEADERSHIP

Creating jobs that are inherently satisfying may make supportive leadership less important while increasing followers' satisfaction and freeing up the leader for other activities. But, intrinsically satisfying jobs must fit the job incumbent. For example, followers who want a challenging job will welcome a task that stretches their capabilities. But if a follower prefers a job that is highly repetitive and predictable, then a challenging job may not be appropriate. Also, building performance feedback into the challenging job will likely result in a more effective performer. If job redesign is not an option, the leader might increase the follower's interest and task satisfaction by switching the employee to a different job. Most employees come to an organization with preexisting values and beliefs about the importance of tangible organizational rewards. If most of a leader's followers are primarily concerned with pay and promotion, then a reward system based on followers' performance may create favorable follower attitudes and performance with little or no supportiveness by the leader. Figure 5–3 summarizes the situational characteristics that have been found to replace the need for supportive leadership. These factors directly improve followers' motivation, attitudes and performance and make supportive leadership at least partially unnecessary.

The Leadership in Action box with youth sports teams provides an example of how a leader's group can develop inherent satisfaction, motivation, and skills at tasks that provide their own feedback and eventually require less interpersonal supportiveness from the leader. Table 5–1 summarizes the three types of situational factors and how they affect the impact of supportive leadership. Figure 5–4 provides an example of how the three types of situational factors can affect supportive leadership by a public school principal.

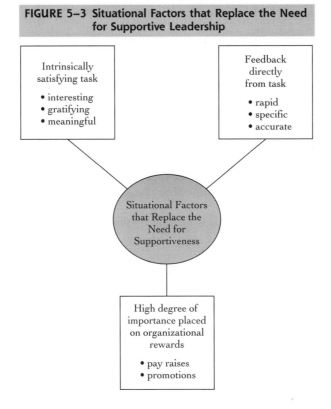

FIGURE 5–3 Situational Factors that Replace the Need for Supportive Leadership

Intrinsically satisfying task

- interesting
- gratifying
- meaningful

Feedback directly from task

- rapid
- specific
- accurate

Situational Factors that Replace the Need for Supportiveness

High degree of importance placed on organizational rewards

- pay raises
- promotions

LEADERSHIP IN ACTION: REPLACING THE NEED FOR SUPPORTIVE LEADERSHIP WITH YOUNG ATHLETES

One of the authors has spent several years coaching youth sports teams. In this situation, supportive leadership is especially effective. Many young participants on these teams have low self-confidence and are insecure about their abilities. They greatly want to improve their skills, their frequently vocal parents expect the coach to be highly supportive, and newly formed sports teams frequently have external conflicts with their opponents. The successful coach usually takes a developmental approach with players at this stage by carefully teaching them fundamental elements of the sport, showing concern for their safety and welfare, answering questions, and being sympathetic and encouraging when their performance is less than they hoped for. Under this type of leadership, the young athletes generally improve, develop a cohesive team spirit, enjoy their experience, and have a successful season.

As these young athletes mature and develop their skills and confidence, the coach can often decrease the degree of interpersonal supportiveness. Competent players develop more interest in the sport and derive satisfaction from their own and the teams' performance. As the players and the team develop, their attitude and motivation are thus maintained at a high level with less interpersonal supportive behavior from the coach. Other leader behaviors become important at this stage such as providing guidance, direction, and recognition for good team performance.

TABLE 5–1 Three Types of Situational and Follower Characteristics that Affect the Impact of Supportive Leadership

Factors that Increase the Effectiveness of Supportiveness	*Factors that Decrease the Effectiveness of Supportiveness*	*Factors that Replace the Need for Supportiveness*
• Followers who are insecure or low in self-confidence and self-esteem • Followers who have high growth needs and expect supportiveness • Dissatisfying or stressful tasks • Highly structured task • Task requires creativity or new learning • Conflict with other groups or organizations • Newly formed or cohesive groups • Extensive formal plans, goals, and procedures • Organizational mission of human service • Authoritarian supervisor	• Dogmatic followers • Large size group • Broad task scope • High-level job	• Intrinsically satisfying task • Feedback directly from task • High importance placed by followers on organizational rewards

FIGURE 5–4 Situational Factors and Supportive Leadership by Public School Principals

Situational factors that could increase effectiveness of a principal's supportiveness

• The teachers feel insecure because of budget cuts that will require reduction in the number of teachers.
• The teachers are experiencing high stress because of student violence in the school.
• The teachers' job requires new learning because of the introduction of computers in the classroom.
• The teachers' job has become more highly structured because the school board has required the coverage of specific content material and development of specific skills.

How Situational Factors can Affect the Impact of Supportive Leadership by a Public School Principal

Situational factors that could decrease the effectiveness of a principal's supportiveness

• Individual teachers have little interaction with the principal because the school is very large.
• The teachers perceive their job to require broad understanding and ability that the principal does not have.

Situational factors that could replace the need for a principal's supportiveness

• The job is intrinsically satisfying: teachers can see the positive impact they are having on students.
• The teachers get direct feedback in the form of improved student performance.

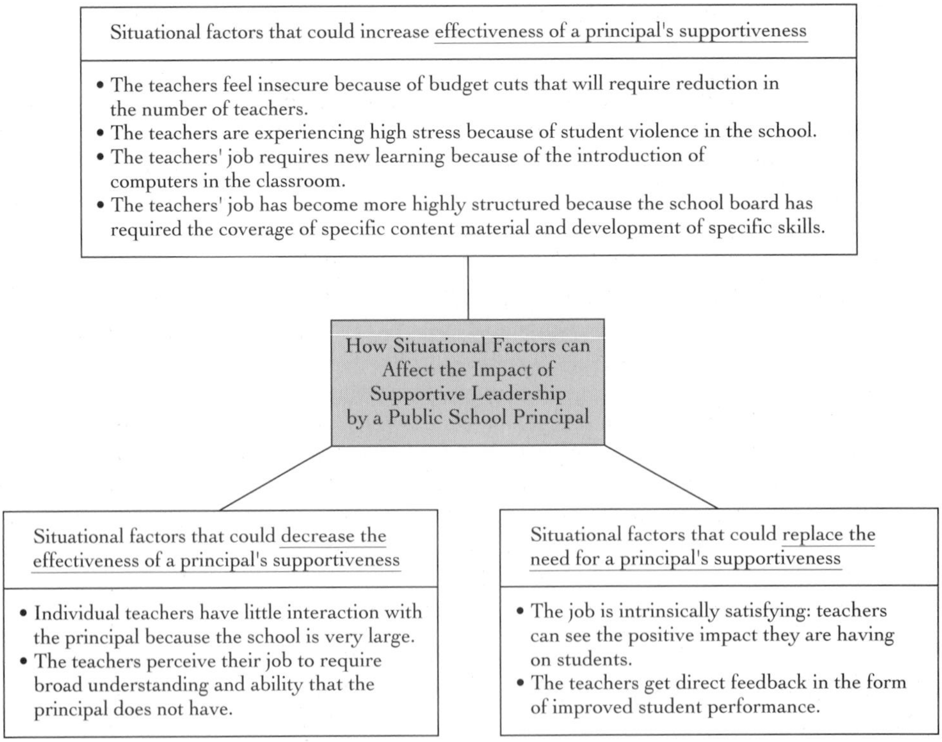

Hopefully the reader now realizes that there is a dynamic interaction among leaders, followers, and situational factors. The three key leadership tasks described in chapter 1 (diagnosing situations–behaving appropriately–modifying situations) reflect this dynamic interaction. Leaders diagnose situations and follower characteristics to determine if they will increase or decrease the effectiveness of supportive leadership (or other leader behaviors). If situational conditions warrant supportiveness, they provide this leader behavior. If factors exist that will decrease the impacts of supportiveness, then the leader considers another leadership approach (described in the following chapters). Situational and follower characteristics thereby influence the type of behavior a leader uses to influence followers. Leaders also determine if followers and situations should be modified to eliminate factors that decrease the effectiveness of supportive leadership or to create factors that replace followers' needs for supportiveness. As described in this chapter, leaders can decrease stressful job situations, provide for followers' training, develop teams, or implement other actions to improve the work situation.

Thus, the leader can take a direct approach and provide a supportive, concerned, and encouraging climate for followers using supportive leader behaviors described in chapter 4. Or the leader can take an indirect approach by modifying and developing followers, groups, and other factors in the job situation to promote and maintain a

LEADERSHIP IN ACTION: CLEASTER MIMS

Cleaster Mims believed that her students were being placed on a "conveyer belt from the school house to the jail house." The same was true of the "boat people" and other immigrants she taught English as a second language. Not enough was expected of the students because they were pigeonholed as low achievers. The teachers were failing the kids and she knew this was wrong for the kids and wrong for society.

Cleaster heard Marva Collins speak about her West Side Preparatory School in Chicago that emphasized academic excellence. She envisioned a similar program in Cincinnati and started to work. She enlisted community volunteers, found space in a church basement, and utilized cast-off furniture and supplies. She started the school without any books, but eventually obtained literature books from a Goodwill store. After five years the school had expanded from 41 to over 200. They purchased their own facility, and were considering boarding students.

Cleaster is president, CEO, principal, and founder of the school. She cares about doing the right things for her students. She developed a program to provide them with a supportive atmosphere that demonstrates a belief in their capabilities and their future. She believes that high expectations can create "a metamorphosis of the mind" if only someone will show they care. She also reflects a spiritual aspect of her leadership when she says: "I feel that I am chosen. When God chooses you, you cannot not do it and find any happiness in life." Her firm moral beliefs have helped her empower the school's teachers to carry out the school's mission.

Source: Adapted from A. Shriberg, C. Lloyd, D. L. Shriberg, and M. L. Williamson, *Practicing Leadership: Principles and Applications.* (New York: John Wiley & Sons, Inc., 1997)

supportive climate. The indirect approach increases followers' independence and self-confidence and alleviates the need for the leader to provide interpersonal encouragement and consideration on a regular basis (25). Some leaders may choose a combination of the direct and indirect approaches, depending on their time constraints, other duties, and the followers involved.

When a leader's direct and/or indirect actions improve followers' satisfaction, commitment and/or performance, this reinforces the leader's approach and s/he will likely continue with the same influence strategy. If the results are not favorable, then the leader must rediagnose the situation to determine if a different strategy is needed to provide for followers' supportiveness needs. Followers' behaviors are therefore an important factor in a leader's decisions about providing direct and/or indirect forms of supportiveness. Providing support through direct interaction with followers probably produces results more quickly than the indirect approach. So, if followers are in an extremely stressful situation, direct supportiveness by the leader is best. But the indirect approach of follower development and situational modification can produce very favorable long-lasting effects for followers and allow the leader more time to pursue other leadership activities.

Summary ■

Effective leaders diagnose situations and followers and attempt to match their behavior to the needs of the situation. Supportiveness is especially warranted when situational and follower characteristics are present to increase its effectiveness. In these situations, leader supportiveness is likely to have the greatest direct impact on followers' psychological reactions and behavioral outcomes. But regardless of conditions, supportive leadership usually has some positive effect on followers.

In other situations, supportive leadership may have smaller direct impacts on followers and therefore be less effective than other leader behaviors. There may be conditions where specific job factors promote high follower satisfaction, commitment, and possibly performance without the need for leader supportive behaviors.

Leaders can sometimes manipulate situational characteristics to make them more favorable. By modifying followers' jobs, work groups, or the organizational mission, leaders can increase the favorable direct effects of supportive behaviors on followers. Leaders can also influence followers indirectly by modifying their work tasks or selection procedures to decrease followers' needs for supportiveness by their leader. This strategy leaves time for the leader to address other follower needs.

Figure 5–5 presents a model of supportive leadership that summarizes the material presented in chapters 4 and 5. Starting at the top of Figure 5–5, supportive behaviors by a leader are shown to influence follower/group psychological reactions, which in turn affect followers' behavioral outcomes. This portion of Figure 5–5 was shown in chapter 4. Situational factors that increase or decrease the effectiveness of leaders' support are now shown on each side of the figure with arrows intersecting the relationship between supportiveness and follower/group psychological reactions. These intersecting arrows indicate that situational and follower characteristics can increase or decrease a leader's effects on followers and groups. The arrows from the leader supportiveness box to the situational factor boxes indicate that leaders can sometimes manipulate situations to improve followers' reactions indi-

FIGURE 5–5 Leadership Process Model for Supportive Leadership

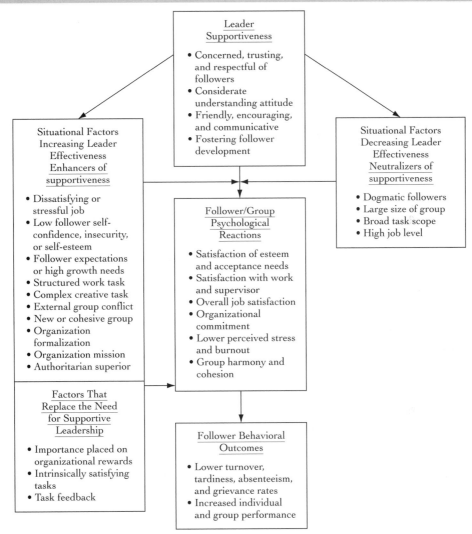

rectly and thereby replace the need to provide supportive behaviors. Other dynamic effects occur among the boxes in Figure 5–5, but these are not shown, in order to prevent the figure from becoming overly complex.

Figure 5–6 is designed to show a leader how to use the model of supportive leadership presented in Figure 5–5. It describes the three key tasks for effective leadership (introduced in chapter 1) as they apply to supportive leadership. Leaders first diagnose the situation by answering a series of questions regarding followers and their task situation (box 1). These questions identify factors that can increase the impacts of supportive leadership. If the answer is "yes" to one or more of these questions, then supportiveness is probably needed and the leader should provide this type of leadership. Once the leader carries out the appropriate supportive behaviors (box 2), follower and situational characteristics should be examined

FIGURE 5–6 Applying the Model of Supportive Leadership

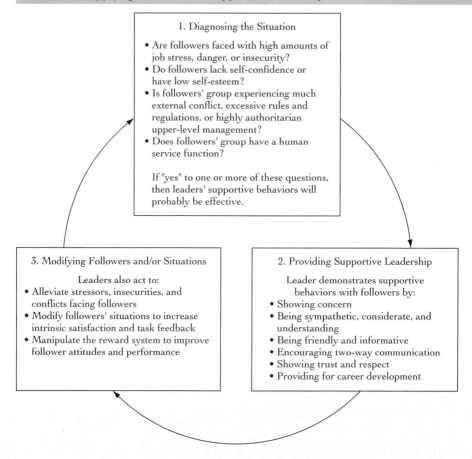

1. Diagnosing the Situation

- Are followers faced with high amounts of job stress, danger, or insecurity?
- Do followers lack self-confidence or have low self-esteem?
- Is followers' group experiencing much external conflict, excessive rules and regulations, or highly authoritarian upper-level management?
- Does followers' group have a human service function?

If "yes" to one or more of these questions, then leaders' supportive behaviors will probably be effective.

3. Modifying Followers and/or Situations

Leaders also act to:
- Alleviate stressors, insecurities, and conflicts facing followers
- Modify followers' situations to increase intrinsic satisfaction and task feedback
- Manipulate the reward system to improve follower attitudes and performance

2. Providing Supportive Leadership

Leader demonstrates supportive behaviors with followers by:
- Showing concern
- Being sympathetic, considerate, and understanding
- Being friendly and informative
- Encouraging two-way communication
- Showing trust and respect
- Providing for career development

to see if any exist that may be decreasing the effectiveness of leader supportiveness. Eliminating these situational factors, if possible, should improve the leader's influence on followers (box 3). The leader should also consider the creation of factors that replace the need for supportiveness to provide for followers' needs without being present (box 3). The process outlined in Figure 5–6 emphasizes the leader's use of supportive behavior to directly satisfy followers' needs as well as situational and follower development strategies that can indirectly satisfy followers' needs and make them less dependent on the leader.

Key Terms and Concepts in this Chapter ▪▪▪▪▪▪▪▪▪▪▪▪▪▪▪▪▪▪▪▪

- authoritarian leader
- cohesive groups
- dissatisfying tasks
- dogmatic followers
- external group conflict
- feedback from task

- group norms
- group size
- insecure followers
- intrinsically satisfying task
- job scope

- job level
- organizational formalization
- organizational rewards
- stressful task
- task structure

Review and Discussion Questions ■

1. Describe a situation you have experienced, observed, or heard about where supportive leadership was effective. Why was supportive leadership appropriate in this situation?

2. Describe a situation you have experienced, observed, or heard about where supportive leadership was not effective. Why was supportiveness not effective in this situation?

3. As a follower, which situational characteristics described in this chapter have had the most impact on your reaction to supportive leadership? How have these characteristics affected you?

4. As a leader, how might you create situational factors to build your influence as a supportive leader?

5. When would it be beneficial to create situational characteristics that decrease the need for supportive leadership?

6. Do you think supportive leadership would be effective by a supervisor in a coal mine? Why or why not?

7. Do you think supportive leadership would be effective by a supervisor of truck drivers for a package delivery company who are paid according to how many packages they deliver?

Leadership Self-Assessment: When Are Supportive Behaviors Needed? ■

Objective: To help the reader apply chapter material by diagnosing situations for supportive leadership.

Instructions: Rate the following situations on whether they require supportive behaviors from the leader. Use the following scale for rating each situation: 5 = highly needed, 4 = needed, 3 = may or may not be needed, 2 = probably not needed, 1 = not needed.

1. Followers are soldering electrical parts onto circuit boards that will be installed in television sets by other workers. 1 2 3 4 5

2. Followers are assigned to handle customer complaints in a large department store. 1 2 3 4 5

3. Followers are sports writers who view and write about professional baseball and football games and players. 1 2 3 4 5

4. Followers work as tellers in a bank. 1 2 3 4 5

5. Followers are police officers who patrol urban areas with high crime rates. 1 2 3 4 5

6. Followers are trained volunteers who provide free family counseling and health advice to low-income families. 1 2 3 4 5

7. Followers are members of a closely knit and successful athletic team. 1 2 3 4 5

8. Followers are traveling sales persons who are paid exclusively based on commissions for their sales. 1 2 3 4 5

9. Followers are members of a newly formed team to develop a mission statement for the organization.	1	2	3	4	5
10. Followers are members of a competent team of computer engineers who are engrossed in designing a new computer and are very well paid.	1	2	3	4	5

Interpretation: If you rated items 1, 2, 4, 5, 6, 7, and 9 highly (a rating of 4 or 5), you correctly diagnosed that these situations normally require supportive leadership. The situations described in items 3, 8, and 10 normally do not require a high degree of supportiveness because other situational and/or follower characteristics often replace the need for supportiveness. Other leader behaviors are probably needed in these situations.

◆◆◆ **Case Incident**

The Friendly Supervisor

Mr. Mike Reeves manages the public relations department of a hospital. The department is responsible for responding to requests from the public and patients for information. There are seven clerks in the department who handle the requests.

Mr. Reeves recently promoted Paula Kemp to office supervisor. Paula had been a clerk in the department for ten years. She was accurate and fast in the preparation of correspondence. Paula was a dependable employee and well liked by the other employees.

As a supervisor Paula does a good job of handing out work assignments, but she does little else to supervise the clerks. She does not like to criticize the clerks and does not enforce office rules. No matter what a clerk does, Paula will not take any disciplinary action. She makes no attempt to check the work of the clerks for compliance with quality standards or to see that work is completed on time. Paula spends most of her time helping out with the work to reduce the load on the clerks in her department. She also invites them to her home each month to socialize and play bridge.

Mr. Reeves has received an increasing number of complaints from other department staff about the poor quality of work by the clerks and the slow turnaround time for clerical work. He has also received complaints about the clerks taking excessively long coffee breaks and spending time on personal phone calls.

The clerks like Paula as a friend, but they are concerned about the effectiveness of her supervision. When Mr. Reeves told Paula that she should focus her effort on supervising to improve the work of the clerks, she said, "These women are my friends, and I don't feel right about cracking down on them."

QUESTIONS

1. Is Paula effective in her supportive leadership behaviors?
2. How would you analyze the effects on employees of Paula's friendship and her efforts to reduce their workload?

3. How could Mr. Reeves use supportive leadership to improve Paula's effectiveness as a supervisor?

Endnotes ▪

1. Hughes, R. L., Ginnett, R. C. and Curphy, G. J. (1996). *Leadership: Enhancing the Lessons of Experience* (2nd ed.) Boston: Irwin.

2. Hellriegel, D., Slocum, J. W. Jr. and Woodman, R. W. (1998). *Organizational Behavior* (8th ed.) Cincinnati, OH: Southwestern College Publishing.

3. Yukl, G. (1998). *Leadership in Organizations* (4th ed.). Upper Saddle River, NJ: Prentice Hall; Griffin, R. W. (1980). Relationships among individual, task design, and leader behavior variables. *Academy of Management Journal,* 23 (4), 665–683; Fiedler, F. E. and House, R. J. (1988). Leadership: a report in progress. In C. Cooper (Ed.), *International Review of Industrial and Organizational Psychology.* Greenwich, CT: JAI Press.

4. Greene, C. (1979). Questions of causation in the path-goal theory of leadership. *Academy of Management Journal,* 22 (1), 22–41; Indvik, J. (1986). Path-goal theory of leadership: A meta-analysis. *Proceedings of the Academy of Management Meeting,* Chicago, 1986; House, R. J. and Dessler, G. (1974). The path-goal theory of leadership: Some post hoc and a priori tests. In J. G. Hunt and L. L. Larson (Eds.), *Contingency Approaches to Leadership.* Carbondale: Southern Illinois University Press; Downey, H. K., Sheridan, J. E., Slocum, J. W. Jr. (1976). The path-goal theory of leadership: A longitudinal analysis. *Organizational Behavior and Human Performance,* 16, 156–176.

5. Burke, W. W. (1965). Leadership behavior as a function of the leader, the follower, and the situation. *Journal of Personality,* 33, 60–81; Schachter, S., Willerman, B., Festinger, L. and Hyman, R. (1961). Emotional disruption and industrial productivity. *Journal of Applied Psychology,* 45, 201–213.

6. Katz, R. (1977). The influence of group conflict on leadership effectiveness. *Organizational Behavior and Human Performance,* 20, 265–286.

7. Greene, C. N. and Schriesheim, C. A. (1980). Leader-group interactions: A longitudinal field investigation. *Journal of Applied Psychology,* 65 (1), 50–59.

8. Schriesheim, J. F. (1980). The social context of leader-subordinate relations: An investigation of the effects of group cohesiveness. *Journal of Applied Psychology,* 65, 183–193; Seashore, S. E. (1954). *Group Cohesiveness in the Industrial Work Group.* Ann Arbor: University of Michigan, Institute for Social Research.

9. Indvik, J. (1986). Path-goal theory of leadership: A meta-analysis. *Proceedings of the Academy of Management Meeting,* Chicago; Miles, R. H. and Petty, M. M. (1977). Leader effectiveness in small bureaucracies. *Academy of Management Journal,* 20, 238–250.

10. Fisher, B. M. and Edwards, J. E. (1988). Consideration and initiating structure and their relationships with leader effectiveness: A meta-analysis. *Proceedings of the Academy of Management Meeting,* Anaheim, CA, 201–215.

11. Woodward, J. (1965). *Industrial Organization: Theory and Practice.* Oxford: Oxford University Press; Schneider, B. (1973). The perception of organizational climate: The customer's view. *Journal of Applied Psychology,* 57, 248–256; Fleishman, E. A., Harris, E. F. and Burtt, H. E. (1955). *Leadership and Supervision in Industry.* Columbus: Ohio State University, Bureau of Educational Research.

12. Hunt, J. G., Osborn, R. N. and Larson, L. L. (1975). Upper level technical orientation and first level leadership within a noncontingency and contingency framework. *Academy of Management Journal,* 18, 476–488.

13. Yukl, G. *Leadership in Organizations* (4th ed.).

14. Manheim, B. F., Rim, Y. and Grinberg, B. (1967). Instrumental status of supervisors as related to workers' perceptions and expectations. *Human Relations,* 20, 387–396.

15. Griffin, R. W. (1980). Relations among individual, task design, and leader behavior variables. *Academy of Management Journal,* 23(4), 665–683.

16. Greene and Schriesheim, Leader-group interactions: A longitudinal field investigation.

17. Weed, S. E., Mitchell, T. R. and Moffitt, W. (1976). Leadership style, subordinate personality, and task type as predictors of performance and satisfaction with supervision. *Journal of Applied Psychology,* 61, 58–66.

18. Griffin, Relations among individual, task design, and leader behavior variables; Indvik, Path-goal theory of leadership: A meta-analysis.

19. Kerr, S. and Jermier, J. M. (1978). Substitutes for leadership: Their meaning and measurement. *Organizational Behavior and Human Performance,* 22, 375–403.

20. DeVries, R. E. (1997). *Need for Leadership: A Solution to Empirical Problems in Situational Leadership Theory,* Ph.D. dissertation, Tilburg University, Netherlands.

21. Dorfman, P. W., Howell, J. P., Tate, U. and Cotton, B. C. G. (1992). Leadership within the "discontinuous hierarchy" structure of the military: Are effective leadership behaviors similar within and across command structures? In R. E. Clark, M. B. Clark and D. P. Campbell (Eds.), *Impact of Leadership,* Greensboro, NC, The Center for Creative Leadership.

22. Howell, J. P. and Dorfman, P. W. (1986). Leadership and substitutes for leadership among professional and nonprofessional workers. *Journal of Applied Behavioral Science,* 22 (1), 29–46.

23. Kerr and Jennier, Substitutes for leadership: Their meaning and measurement.

24. Howell and Dorfman, Leadership and substitutes for leadership among professional and nonprofessional workers.

25. Ingens, O. M. (1995). Situational leadership: A modification of Hersey and Blanchard. *Leadership and Organizational Development Journal,* 16 (2), 36–40.

CHAPTER 6 Directive Leadership Behavior

Learning Objectives
After reading this chapter, you should be able to do the following:

1. Describe directive leadership and give examples of directive leadership behaviors.

2. Explain why directive leadership is important for individual followers and groups.

3. Explain why directive leaders do not need to be authoritarian, autocratic, or punitive to be effective.

4. Describe some of the personal traits and skills that leaders need to develop in order to be effective directive leaders.

5. Describe the sources of power most frequently used by directive leaders.

6. Discuss some of the ways directive leaders can provide effective performance feedback to their followers.

7. Identify organizational factors which can encourage or discourage leaders from being directive.

8. Describe the major impacts directive leadership has on followers' psychological reactions and behaviors.

◆ EXAMPLES OF EFFECTIVE DIRECTIVE LEADERSHIP

- An employee described his supervisor as someone who let him know what work needed to be done, informed him about the quality of his work and how he could improve, and discussed how to handle work-related problems with other employees.
- The supervisor walked along the production line checking the indicators on the machines and asking the operators if they had any problems.
- The production manager told a follower about a rush project that needed top priority and gave the follower suggestions about how to do the project.
- A manager met with an employee for two hours to establish performance goals for the coming year and to discuss the employee's action plans for attaining the goals.

- When Robert C. Hazard, Jr. left his position as CEO of Best Western to become CEO of Quality Inns, he left an organization of confident and capable personnel able to operate with little day-to-day direction. He moved to an organization that had declined and barely avoided bankruptcy. Its personnel needed a directive "hands on" leader like Hazard, who became involved in operations, telling individuals and groups what needed to be done and how to do it, and following up on results. This directive type of leadership behavior was needed to accomplish a turnaround for Quality Inns (1–5).

◆ DEFINITION, BACKGROUND, AND IMPORTANCE OF DIRECTIVE LEADER BEHAVIORS

These examples of leadership in organizations demonstrate effective directive leadership. Directive leadership involves leader activities that guide and structure the actions of group members. In these examples, the leader identified the followers' needs for guidance and information in performing their tasks and provided the necessary inputs to meet those needs.

Leader directiveness has been studied for almost 50 years, and numerous behaviors have been attributed to this leadership pattern. Directive leadership involves defining roles in the group and telling followers what they are expected to do to achieve specific performance goals (6). Directive leaders also plan and schedule work to be done, including assigning responsibilities and tasks to group members (7). They establish and maintain patterns of communication for explaining assignments, rules, and regulations and use their expertise to improve followers' work methods and overcome obstacles. And they monitor and follow up on assignments and work methods to assure the intended results are obtained (8). Two other activities have recently been included as aspects of directive leadership. These include motivating followers to change or improve performance and tracking followers' task skills, as well as training and coaching on new techniques and procedures (9). An effective leader would probably not utilize all these behaviors in a situation where directiveness is needed, but would likely select those directive behaviors that seem appropriate in the situation. Directive leadership behaviors are summarized in Figure 6–1.

Nondirective leaders are hesitant about specifying who, what, and how followers are to accomplish specific task assignments. Nondirective leaders make suggestions only when asked by followers, and they often let followers do the work any way they think best. While this approach can be effective with highly trained and motivated followers, many situations require some type of direction from the leader.

Charles DeGaulle, French general and president, once stated that "men can no longer survive without direction than they can without eating, drinking, or sleeping." Most followers need some direction on the path toward successful effort. Directive leadership alters followers' information, understanding, and ability to accomplish tasks. Directiveness can improve followers' performance capabilities by eliminating wasted effort and focusing attention on effective work methods and key aspects of task performance. Goal setting is a proven technique used by directive leaders for motivating follower performance. Goals provide concrete targets that focus attention and provide

FIGURE 6–1 Types of Directive Leadership Behavior

gauges for performance. Through directive leadership, a leader's intelligence and expertise can be effectively applied to resolving work-related problems (10). Followers may recognize the need for directive leadership, especially when a crisis occurs, when ambiguity regarding management expectations exists, or when the methods for task performance are unclear. But too much directiveness by a leader can create follower resentment and eventually cause grievances, absenteeism, and turnover (11).

Some leaders believe their directiveness is more effective if they maintain a distinct psychological distance from followers (12). If these leaders have little trust in followers, they may become closely controlling as well as autocratic and authoritarian in their interpersonal relations. Authoritarian and autocratic leaders emphasize their formal authority, are cold and hostile, have little concern for followers' needs, and do not allow followers to participate in (provide input to) decision making that affects them on the job. Leadership experts have noted, however, that a leader can be directive without being a threatening autocrat (13).

Effective leaders sometimes use one behavior pattern for making decisions and another pattern for executing decisions after they are made. Leadership in high-technology industries often requires highly trained technical professionals to participate in decision making by providing necessary technical input. High leader directiveness may be needed, however, in carrying out decisions with the same followers when they have little organizational experience in planning or allocating task assignments. Similar situations occur in small business organizations, where a lack of established procedures, control, or information systems fail to provide needed guidance to support independent follower action. Here directive leadership is often needed. It seems clear that leaders can be directive without "lording it over" followers with their formal authority, being hostile and uncaring, or making important job-related decisions without follower input. In a study of managers' communication styles, researchers found effective directive leaders to be dynamic, informative, careful transmitters of information, as well as being frank and open and encouraging two-way communication (14).

Many of the leader behaviors, described here as directive leadership, have a long history. Several were described in the early 1900s as aspects of Taylor's scientific management

LEADERSHIP IN PERSPECTIVE: FREDERICK WINSLOW TAYLOR

One of the best known management writers in the United States in the twentieth century was Frederick Winslow Taylor. He was one of the first individuals to study the activities of people at work. Taylor studied the supervision of men working in the steel industry around 1900, when steel making was very labor intensive. Large work gangs of foreign-born individuals with little education did strenuous physical labor. A firm hand, tempered with kindness, was needed in supervising these workers to assure they knew exactly what was expected of them and how to work according to Taylor's "scientifically" correct methods (15). In Taylor's famous book, *Principles of Scientific Management,* published in 1910, he described how supervisors needed to be very directive with these workers.

The writings of Frederick Taylor were probably responsible for a strong emphasis by U.S. researchers on studying leadership at low levels in organizations. This emphasis on supervisory leadership lasted until the 1970s, and the study of what is now called directive leadership was a major part of this research. This directive leadership pattern is especially important for effective "shop level" supervision of workers. It can also be important for leaders at other organizational levels, depending on the presence of other situational and follower characteristics.

(16) and later as initiating structure in the Ohio State leadership research program. The terms production oriented and concern for production were used in the 1950s, and work facilitation, goal emphasis, and task oriented leadership were popular during the 1960s (17, 18, 19, 20). The term directive leadership became popular in the 1970s with the development of the Path-Goal Theory of leadership (21).

Some of the early measures of this leadership pattern included behaviors which are currently viewed as separate and distinct from a leader's directiveness. Two of these are continually pressuring followers to produce more and threatening and/or taking punitive actions against followers for low performance. Some leaders use these behaviors, but they may not be productive. Threats and pressure often produce negative reactions and are generally viewed as unnecessary to the clarification, guidance, and facilitative functions of directive leadership. Punitive leadership behavior will be discussed in chapter 10. Constantly pressuring followers to produce more is not recommended with today's workforce, especially in developed countries, where the level of worker education has increased to the point that few workers will tolerate this type of leadership approach. Although there are exceptions in some countries with unique cultural beliefs, punitive and pressuring behavior by leaders are typically omitted from current discussions and research on directive leadership.

◆ INEFFECTIVE DIRECTIVE LEADERSHIP

Even though a leader may provide needed directive guidance in a clear manner, if not done in the appropriate context and with other needed information, the results can be inefficiency and ineffectiveness. Researchers (22) provided the following example of ineffective directive leadership:

A new manager clearly defined roles for followers on a project, specified goals to be met and methods to be used, and assured that members knew what was expected by the organization. The followers were experienced, well-meaning employees, however, who had not been receiving adequate performance feedback from their previous manager. These individuals consequently interpreted the leader's highly directive approach as a cue that their previous performance had been inadequate, and they began to change their behavior, which in reality was very effective, in an effort to please the leader. This had the effect of undercutting the reward system and eliminated previously effective behavior patterns.

In chapter 7 we will describe the various situational contexts that make directive leadership most effective. In the above example, the timing and lack of prior feedback resulted in misinterpretation of the leader's directiveness. The timing and appropriateness of directive leadership behaviors for a particular task are critically important. Some tasks require structure and guidance during the goal-setting stage; others require clarification and performance feedback during execution. Some followers need guidance to relate their work to that of other employees; others need technical direction from the leader (23). Effective leaders must carefully diagnose the type of direction needed by a follower and provide it in a timely fashion.

◆ **HOW TO BE DIRECTIVE**

Leaders can develop several skills, personal characteristics, and sources of power to help them effectively direct followers. Two skills are especially important for directive leaders. Communication skills are essential in specifying how followers are to accomplish tasks. Giving followers feedback on their performance also requires effective communication. Communication skills are essential in defining roles of followers and in defining communication patterns. The communication skill of obtaining understanding is necessary in clarifying performance expectations and describing work methods. To motivate followers, the leader must effectively communicate both desired behaviors and incentives for performance. The directive leader must also establish and maintain communication to explain assignments, rules, and procedures.

Leaders' competence at followers' tasks may determine their effectiveness in monitoring work methods to assure that results are obtained. Knowledge about processes, methods, and products is necessary in planning, scheduling, and assigning responsibilities. The directive leader may also need competence in the operation of equipment used by followers to help them accomplish tasks. In order to solve task problems, the leader may also need technical competence related to processes, materials, procedures, or equipment.

Although a number of personal traits are compatible with directive leadership, three traits seem most helpful. Self-confidence includes having high self-esteem, being decisive, and believing in one's ability. The leader with high self-confidence is more likely to attempt to influence followers, attempt difficult tasks, and set high goals. The leader with high self-confidence is not likely to express doubts or act indecisively, both of which can undermine directive leadership. The directive leader's self-confidence can help instill confidence in followers to carry out directions. To be effective, the directive leader needs to be self-confident without being overbearing. Too much self-confidence by a leader may be seen as arrogance, which can produce resentment. For most organizational situations, a moderately high level of self-confidence is probably best.

The term assertiveness refers to being direct in communication and expressing one's position on issues. Assertiveness helps the leader be directive in solving task problems and responding to difficult situations. Guiding followers and structuring the activities of followers often requires the directive leader to show assertiveness. The directive leader's assertiveness can help in informing followers of mistakes, setting high performance expectations, and making legitimate demands for quality performance.

To effectively direct the activities of followers, leaders can benefit from relevant experience. As with competence, experience can provide the leader with the knowledge necessary for guiding and structuring followers' activities. Experience can also be valuable to the leader in training followers in processes and procedures necessary to accomplish tasks. The leader's experience can be of great value in solving task problems, removing barriers to productivity, and achieving quality results. Finally, the more aware followers are of the leaders' extensive experience, the easier it is for the leader to convey expertise. Relevant experience includes previous jobs, education, workshops, and coaching from higher-ups that increase leader's task competence, communication skills, self-confidence, and assertiveness. These traits and skills are evident in effective coaches of college athletic teams. Successful coaches use their experience and expertise as well as assertiveness and self-confidence to communicate their knowledge and understanding to the players in a directive manner. With effort, leaders can build these skills and personal characteristics to increase the effectiveness of their directive leadership.

Effective directive leaders often develop three sources of power to make their directions especially impactful. These are legitimate power, expert power, and resource/connection power. Two other sources of power that can make a leader's directions impactful are reward and coercive power, but they will be discussed in chapter 10.

Legitimate power supports directive leadership because followers' compliance is based on the belief that the leader has the right to provide the direction, and followers are obligated to comply. Followers normally perceive their leaders as having the right to influence because of the position they occupy. Managers usually have the legitimate right to assign specific tasks, schedule work, define work methods, and monitor performance.

Expert power helps directive leadership because followers believe that the leader has a high level of knowledge, skill, and ability for performing tasks. Expert power is especially useful in directive leadership because it enables the leader to make effective plans and strategies, solve problems, and achieve task objectives. When followers depend on the leader for advice and problem solving, the leader's ability to direct followers' behavior is enhanced. If expert power is to help the leader be more effective in providing direction, the follower must recognize the leader's expertise and believe the leader is trustworthy as a source of knowledge.

Resource/connection power in the form of access to important information also helps directive leaders because it enables them to provide followers with data and supporting information to justify their directions. When followers see that a leader's directions are justified by clear evidence of past performance, they are more likely to view the directions as helpful. Leaders may provide information on past performance, market demands, company operations, new technology, or other areas that can influence employees' task efforts and achievement. Figure 6–2 summarizes the skills, traits, and sources of power for effective directive leadership.

LEADERSHIP SELF-ASSESSMENT: PROVIDING EFFECTIVE PERFORMANCE FEEDBACK

Instructions: Indicate the extent to which you would engage in the following behaviors when providing feedback to others on their performance, using a scale of (5) almost always; (4) usually; (3) occasionally; (2) seldom; (1) almost never. I would:

1. provide specific examples of effective and ineffective behaviors.   5   4   3   2   1

2. focus my feedback on the person's intent and motives.   5   4   3   2   1

3. provide feedback that focuses on obtaining understanding and solving problems.   5   4   3   2   1

4. provide feedback on situations, regardless of whether the person receiving the feedback has control over them.   5   4   3   2   1

5. fix blame on individuals who are responsible for problems.   5   4   3   2   1

6. avoid overloading individuals with too much feedback at one time.   5   4   3   2   1

7. focus on the other person's needs and what will be helpful to him or her.   5   4   3   2   1

8. criticize individuals when they deserve it.   5   4   3   2   1

9. focus on the future in providing feedback and how future performance can be more effective.   5   4   3   2   1

10. take into account the other person's attitudes, beliefs, and values to assure understanding of my feedback.   5   4   3   2   1

Interpretation: If you rated items numbered 1, 3, 6, 7, 9, and 10 as 4 or 5, then you are probably effective at giving feedback. These items focus on the receiver's behavior, understanding, needs, and values and are oriented toward improving future performance. If you rated items numbered 2, 4, 5, and 8 as 4 or 5, you may be ineffective at providing feedback. These items do not focus on the receiver's behavior and/or are not oriented toward improving future performance.

Source: Items based on K. Karp, "The lost art of feedback," in J. W. Pfeiffer (Ed.), *The 1987 Annual: Developing Human Resources.* (San Diego: University Associates, 1987), 237–245 and Waldroop, J. and Butler, T., "The executive as coach," *Harvard Business Review,* November–December 1996, 111–130.

Several writers have pointed out that leaders are often not completely free to choose their behavioral strategies because organizational requirements influence the amount of directive behavior required of the leader (24,25,26). For example, leaders may be required to specify and enforce company standards, objectives, and work deadlines or to coordinate followers' activities with other departments, all requiring directive leadership (27). Leaders usually respond to a high degree of threat or stress by being directive (28).

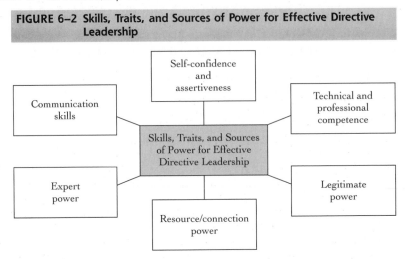

FIGURE 6–2 Skills, Traits, and Sources of Power for Effective Directive Leadership

The stress may come from pressure of the leader's superior for immediate results, from managers higher up in the organization, from low follower performance, or from a decline in organizational profits (29,30,31,32,33,34). A highly bureaucratic climate with authoritarian policies and centralized decision making can also cause supervisors to be directive in their behavior (35). These organizational conditions create expectations by superiors and sometimes followers that leaders should be directive.

This Leadership in Action box for the women's America's Cup team shows the importance of directive leadership in this highly stressful situation.

◆ EFFECTS OF DIRECTIVE LEADERSHIP

As described earlier, the purpose of directive leadership is to help individuals and groups of followers perform work tasks efficiently and effectively. Because leaders usually possess greater authority, experience, and expertise than followers, they often provide information on management expectations for followers and on performance plans, rules, and regulations. They also provide guidance on correct and updated work methods, and they schedule or assign tasks. They monitor and follow up on assignments, thereby motivating followers to avoid loafing. This section summarizes the overall impacts of directive leadership. In reading and thinking about these impacts, two factors should be kept in mind.

First, much of the research on directive leadership has addressed its combined effects with supportive leadership. Consequently, in many studies it is difficult to distinguish separate effects for these two patterns of behavior. Where it is possible to separate the effects, we have done so. When the combined effects could not be clearly separated, we have reported them as combined impacts.

Second, the research on directive leadership indicates that its effects on followers are often strongly influenced by situational and follower characteristics. Usually, however, situational factors do not change the direction of directive leadership's effect. Instead, they change the amount of positive (or negative) effect. For example, if a follower is working on a highly structured task, the follower will likely see little need for directive leadership. Therefore, directiveness usually has a smaller impact (although it is usually still positive) on this follower's satisfaction than on one with a less structured task.

LEADERSHIP IN ACTION: WOMEN AND LEADERSHIP IN THE AMERICA'S CUP RACE

In 1995, a group of dedicated individuals set out to be the first women's team ever to enter the America's Cup sailing race. They had many difficulties, but eventually managed to race neck and neck with seven other teams composed exclusively of men. The lessons they learned about leadership made a vivid impression on all the crew members.

The team planners decided at an early stage to sail without a skipper. "We wanted teamwork to be the driving force behind the team. We thought that if we set things up so the leadership duties were shared, instead of having one person in charge, it would encourage working together as a team." They believed that the women would be more consensus oriented than men and would avoid the power struggles that had occurred on previous men's teams.

This decision to have no skipper prevented the team from developing and performing to its potential. The members did not resolve conflicts and differences. They strove to keep the appearance of harmony and a "smooth façade" rather than confronting difficult problems. The unresolved conflicts festered and continued to interfere with the team effort. For example, during the early races the helms person and tactician could not agree on a course of action. Because neither was the leader, neither could pull rank, so the team made and repeated mistakes in several races. A lack of clear directive leadership from a single skipper was clearly hurting the team's performance.

Ann Jardim is cofounder of the Simmons Graduate School of Management in Boston, the only all-female business school in the U.S. Jardim was not surprised that the team had problems with a lack of leadership. She stated, "Women tend to generate teams of equals. We're not hierarchical—we operate by consensus. As a result, we don't generate leaders. Men are born followers; women aren't. Men need to establish hierarchies, find leaders; women don't. . . . The very idea that groups need leadership has to be taught to women, and it should have been hammered into your group."

The team planners decided to replace the tactician with a highly experienced skipper (team leader). This new skipper had the proven expertise to direct the team. By insisting that disagreements be faced and worked out, the skipper gained the respect and cooperation of all the crew members when quick decisions were needed. Eventually a "calm confidence settled over the boat."

The group came together, addressed the problems confronting them, and performed admirably. Although they did not win, they learned the importance of having a strong directive leader to address safety issues, tactics, and countless other quick decisions that arise during a race. These decisions require "one voice that can rise above the din of the water, the sails, the ropes, and the other crew members." Once the leadership and other conflicts were resolved, the group coalesced into the type of team that can compete in the America's Cup race.

_____

Source: Anna Seaton Huntington, "A ship with no captain," *HR Magazine,* November, 1997, 94–99.

Lack of task structure usually means a follower welcomes a leader's directive guidance and tends to respond with considerably higher satisfaction. In both cases (high and low task structure) skillful directive leadership will often increase follower satisfaction, if only because it shows the leader is interested in the follower's performance. But the impact is usually largest in low task structure situations.

EFFECTS ON FOLLOWER/GROUP PSYCHOLOGICAL REACTIONS

Directive leadership has one of its most important psychological effects on followers' role clarity (36,37,38). Followers' clear understanding of their correct role in accomplishing work tasks as well as their relationships with their leader and peers is usually essential to effective task performance. When a leader provides information about expectations, guides a follower in the use of work methods, or assigns a task that utilizes the follower's ability, the leader is providing a clear picture for the follower of what needs to be done. This clear picture often relieves followers' uncertainty and tension; followers know exactly how they are supposed to behave. The leader is, in a sense, providing structure for the follower. Most people welcome some structure and predictability in their lives. An example is when a college professor hands out a course syllabus early in the semester to clarify requirements and due dates for class assignments. This structure helps people concentrate on important issues, and the directive leader provides this by clarifying followers' roles. Thus, role clarity also often leads to positive employee attitudes and improved performance (39).

Another follower psychological reaction to directive leadership, sometimes as the result of improved role clarity, is follower satisfaction. Satisfaction with the work one does, satisfaction with supervision, and overall satisfaction with one's job and organization have all shown improvements from a leader's directiveness (39,40,41,42,43,44). Increases in follower satisfaction have been found with volunteers, nursing supervisors, school principal, departments in state governments, and numerous business settings. Some early measures of directive leadership, which included punitive, autocratic, and authoritarian dimensions, found decreases in follower satisfaction to result from leader directiveness. However, current measures of directive leadership that delete these other dimensions generally find positive impacts on follower satisfaction.

Another psychological reaction affected by directive leadership, often when combined with supportive leadership, is followers' level of stress and a related outcome of stress—job burnout. Researchers have noticed that a leader's behavior can be a source of job stress or it can help followers avoid and cope with job stress. In early research that used punitive and autocratic definitions of directive leadership, a high degree of directiveness seemed to increase followers' stress. This is certainly understandable to anyone who has worked for a punitive autocratic leader. However, when assessed with current measures, which focus instead on information, expertise, and guidance, leader directiveness appears to lower followers' stress levels and increase their ability to deal with job stress (45). This is supported by findings that directive leadership (as well as supportive leadership) results in lower job burnout among followers (46).

The psychological reactions of the leader's group are also often affected by directive leadership. Group cohesion has been the most frequently studied group-level psychological reaction. Group cohesion refers to the "felt closeness" or perceived solidarity among group members. A cohesive group has a strong "we feeling," and members have a sense of unity and togetherness with other group members. Cohesive groups are usually effective in controlling members' behavior, and thus, the members usually act together in important task-related situations. Directive leaders who are not also arbitrarily punitive, autocratic, or authoritarian tend to have highly cohesive groups of followers (47, 48). Similar increases in group cohesion result when directive leadership is combined with supportive leadership (49,50). Two other group psychological reactions that may be improved by directive leadership are the quality of relations among group members (51,52) and the level of group motivation that is "focused on achieving organizational goals" (53). These results have been found consistently in business organizations, schools, and health care settings.

EFFECTS ON FOLLOWERS' PERFORMANCE AND BEHAVIOR

Many researchers have studied the effects of directive leadership on followers' performance and behavior in different organizations. One finding was that in large organizations with several levels of management, directive leaders tend to receive higher merit ratings than nondirective leaders (54,55,56,57). This is especially true in business organizations where followers are working under time constraints—such as in manufacturing departments. It is less true in service departments, where time constraints are often not critical. In schools, a high degree of directiveness combined with high supportiveness tends to result in high merit ratings for administrators (58,59). This may indicate that in organizations that emphasize quality of human service, directive leadership is most effective when combined with supportiveness.

Studies of followers' performance and productivity as outcomes of directive leadership are generally also quite positive. Directive leaders usually have higher performing or more productive followers than nondirective leaders (60,61,62,63,64). In addition, several researchers in education and health care settings have reported that increased leader directiveness resulted in improved department or organizational effectiveness and/or efficiency (65,66). In educational and training settings, several studies show trainee or student scores on achievement tests to be higher when administrators and/or teachers are highly directive, sometimes when combined with supportive leadership (67,68). Overall, it appears that the guidance, expertise, and attention to followers' task performance by directive leaders usually pays off.

Other outcomes of directive leadership have been studied to a lesser extent than those reported above, and the results are less consistent. Early measures of directiveness indicated that increased absenteeism, grievances, and turnover sometimes resulted, especially when the leader failed to also be supportive. One interesting early study showed that high levels of directiveness (which at that time still included authoritarian and autocratic behaviors) were tolerated by followers with no increases in grievances or turnover only when the leader was also highly supportive (69). More recent studies with updated measures of leader directiveness show reductions in intentions to quit and no increases in actual turnover from directive leadership (70), regardless of the level of a leader's supportiveness (71).

Numerous researchers have found the directive leadership pattern impactful in many countries (72,73,74). In Japan, for example, directive leadership is highly acceptable to followers, because they view it as directly connected to accepting their organizations' mission and goals. Numerous studies in Japan have shown directive behaviors to result in high performance in many organizational settings (75). Other researchers have reported positive impacts of directiveness (often along with supportive leadership) among Israeli foremen and nurses (76). Recent studies of managers and supervisors in Mexico, Taiwan, and Korea also found positive impacts of leader directiveness on follower psychological reactions and perceptions (77). One researcher also found directiveness to have important impacts on follower satisfaction and performance in Saudi Arabia (78). Directive leadership is clearly an important part of a leader's behavioral repertoire in many countries.

LEADERSHIP IN ACTION: DIRECTIVE LEADERSHIP IN MEXICO

Mexico has a culture which combines the histories of the Spanish Conquistadors who invaded Mexico in the 16th century and the Indians who occupied that country for thousands of years. The predominant leadership model of the Spaniards was militaristic and authoritarian. After arriving in the new world, their leaders burned their ships before proceeding overland. The Indian culture emphasized religious leaders who were considered omnipotent and their direction's were never questioned. This dual history has resulted in a predominant leadership pattern in Mexico of the autocratic patron who makes decisions and gives clear directions to compliant followers.

Status differences are still predominant in Mexico where high-status paternalistic leaders are expected to take care of and direct followers' activities. These cultural expectations reinforce the importance of strong directive leadership in Mexico. This is supported by recent research showing directive leadership improves followers' commitment, job clarity, and performance in business organizations in Mexico.

Source: P. W. Dorfman, J. P. Howell, S. Hibino, J. K. Lee, U. Tate, and A. Bautista, "Leadership in Western and Asian Countries: Commonalities and differences in effective leadership processes across cultures," *Leadership Quarterly,* (1997) 8(3), 133–274.

TABLE 6–1 Major Effects of Directive Leadership

Follower Benefits	Organizational Benefits
• role clarity	• increased cohesiveness and harmony
• clear expectations	• high quality relations among group members
• satisfaction with work and supervisor	• reductions of intentions to quit
• satisfaction with organization	• group arousal focused on achieving organizational goals
• lower stress	• improved efficiency and/or effectiveness
• increased performance	

Recently, researchers using updated statistical techniques have summarized the most extensive and consistent effects of directive leadership (79,80). Specifically, modern directive leadership had strong positive effects on improved role clarity, satisfaction with supervision, and overall job satisfaction. It also appeared to elicit a moderate to strong improvement in followers' satisfaction with work and their performance. Clearly, leader directiveness has important positive impacts on followers' role clarity, satisfaction, and performance. In addition, increased group cohesiveness and reduced stress may result from nonpunitive directive leadership. Though other psychological reactions of followers have been studied, the small number of studies and/or less consistent results makes generalizations difficult at this time.

The effects described here are often influenced by situational or follower characteristics that can increase, decrease, or replace the effects of directive leadership. Thus, the impacts are general tendencies to be expected in light of certain situational and follower characteristics that exist in a specific leadership context. Table 6–1 summarizes the major effects of directive leadership. The important situational and follower characteristics that affect directive leadership will be discussed in chapter 7.

Summary ▪▪▪

Directive leadership is a pattern of behaviors that involves providing guidance and structure for followers to help them carry out their tasks and effectively contribute to successful group performance. It involves defining roles of group members, clarifying expectations, planning and scheduling, explaining work methods, monitoring and following up on assignments, and motivating or coaching. Leaders can be directive without overemphasizing their formal authority and still allow followers to have input to decision making. Effective directive leadership improves followers' information, understanding, and ability to deal with work tasks.

Self-confidence and assertiveness are the two personal traits of directive leaders that seem to be most helpful. Effective directive leaders also develop good communication skills, competence, and experience, and they work to develop their own legitimate power, expert power, and resource/connection power (especially access to key information needed by followers).

When carried out in a timely and effective manner, directive leadership increases followers' role clarity, satisfaction, and performance. It also probably increases group cohesion and reduces stress for followers. Many of these effects of directive leadership are influenced by situational and follower characteristics to be described in chapter 7. Figure 6–3 provides a partial model of the directive leadership process and summarizes many of the findings reported in chapter 6. In chapter 7 we will add relevant situational and follower characteristics to complete the leadership process model for directive leadership.

FIGURE 6–3 Partial Model of the Directive Leadership Process

Leader Directiveness

- Guiding and structuring follower activities
- Defining roles and communication patterns
- Clarifying expectations and work methods
- Planning, scheduling, and assigning responsibilities
- Monitoring and following up on assignments
- Motivating and conveying expertise

Follower/Group Psychological Reactions

- Role clarity
- Satisfaction with supervision and job
- Intrinsic satisfaction with work
- Lower job stress and burnout
- Group cohesion

Follower Behaviors and Outcomes

- Department and organization effectiveness
- Increased individual and group performance
- High merit ratings for leaders
- Reduced intentions to quit

Key Terms and Concepts in this Chapter ■ ■ ■ ■ ■ ■ ■ ■ ■ ■ ■ ■ ■ ■ ■ ■ ■

- assertiveness
- bureaucratic climate
- communication skills
- directive leadership
- expert power

- initiating structure
- legitimate power
- performance feedback
- production oriented
- resource/connection power

- role clarity
- self-confidence
- satisfaction with supervisor and job
- task oriented

Review and Discussion Questions ▦ ▦ ▦ ■

1. Describe specific directive leader behaviors that have influenced your behavior. For these leader behaviors, identify why they had an impact on your behavior. If you have little or no work experience, think of one of your past teachers for this question.

2. How might a leader develop the skills and abilities necessary to provide directive leadership behaviors effectively?

3. Which types of power do you think would be most helpful for directive leaders in the organization where you work or plan to work?

4. Describe how a leader's values or beliefs could constrain the leader's effective use of directive leadership.

5. Should leaders be more directive of the best performers, the average performers, or the poor performers? What are the reasons for your position?

6. Why might employees who have directive managers show low levels of job satisfaction? Could the reasons be different for different individuals?

7. Describe how directive leadership might influence followers' feelings of empowerment.

8. What advice would you give a leader on how to use directive leader behaviors effectively?

Exercise: Self-Assessment of Directive Leader Behaviors ■ ■ ■ ■ ■ ■ ■ ■ ■ ■ ■ ■

Directions: Rate the following directive leadership behaviors by circling the number on the 1-to-5 scale that best indicates your evaluation of their importance in supervising employees in a fast-food restaurant.

	Low Importance			High Importance	
The supervisor:					
1. communicates her authority as a leader.	1	2	3	4	5
2. clearly spells out performance expectations.	1	2	3	4	5
3. plans and schedules work for employees.	1	2	3	4	5
4. assigns responsibilities and tasks to individuals.	1	2	3	4	5
5. conveys to employees the methods to solve problems.	1	2	3	4	5
6. explains rules and procedures to employees.	1	2	3	4	5
7. monitors work methods to assure good results.	1	2	3	4	5
8. defines work roles for individuals.	1	2	3	4	5

9. identifies problems and acts decisively to solve them. 1 2 3 4 5
10. sets goals and priorities for employees. 1 2 3 4 5

Compare your evaluations with a colleague's evaluations and discuss the results.

Source: The items for this self-assessment are derived from research by Jon P. Howell and Peter W. Dorfman, "Leadership and Substitutes for Leadership Among Professional and Nonprofessional Workers," *Journal of Applied Behavioral Science,* 22 (1), 1986, 29–46.

◆◆◆ **Case Incident**

Implementing the New System

Mr. Burns, production manager, began his weekly meeting with supervisors by stating, "The new production control system will eliminate our current problem of excessive costs due to rejects that do not meet quality control standards. Every supervisor is to make this system work effectively."

"But Mr. Burns," said Brian Woods, a senior supervisor who had been with the company for ten years, "I have met with the other supervisors and we have identified eleven changes that must be made to the new system before it will operate effectively."

"Now Brian," replied Mr. Burns, "This system has worked well at other plants. The industrial engineers have made all the necessary adjustments and assured me that this system will be effective. I'm not going to argue about redesigning the system. You just have to make it work like the other plants."

"But Mr. Burns," replied Woods, "we should work out the problems before we try to implement the system."

Mr. Burns looked directly at Brian and in a loud voice said, "Woods, it sounds like you are trying to prevent the new system from being effective, and I'm beginning to wonder if you are against my attempts to eliminate the excessive costs."

Mr. Burns then looked at the group of supervisors and asked: "Are there any questions?"

There were no questions and the meeting was adjourned.

QUESTIONS

1. What problems in directive leadership, if any, are illustrated by Mr. Burns's behavior?
2. Do you think Mr. Burns's directive leadership will result in the effective implementation of the new system? If not, how could Mr. Burns have been more effective?

3. Should Mr. Burns have combined his directive behaviors with other leader behaviors to influence the supervisors' behavior? If so, how?

Endnotes

1. Klauss, R. and Bass, B. M. (1982). *Interpersonal Communication in Organizations.* New York: Academic Press.
2. Penley, L. E. and Hawkins, B. (1985). Studying interpersonal communication in organizations: A leadership application. *Academy of Management Journal,* 28(2), 309–326.
3. Yukl, G. (1998). *Leadership in Organizations* (4th ed.). Upper Saddle River, NJ: Prentice Hall.

4. Graen, G., Dansereau, F. Jr. and Minami, T. (1972). Dysfunctional leadership styles. *Organizational Behavioral Human Performance,* 7, 216–236.

5. Muczyk, J. P. and Reimann, B. C. (1987). The case for directive leadership. *Academy of Management Executive,* 1(3), 301–311.

6. Hellriegel, D., Slocum, J. W. Jr. and Woodman, R. W. (1998). *Organizational Behavior* (8th ed.). Cincinnati, Ohio: Southwestern.

7. Peterson, R. S. (1997). A directive leadership style in group decision making can be both virtue and vice: Evidence from elite and experimental groups. *Journal of Personality and Social Psychology,* 72(5), 1107–1121.

8. Muczyk and Reimann, The case for directive leadership.

9. Fiedler, F. (1987). When to lead, when to stand back. *Psychology Today,* 26–27.

10. Fiedler, F. E. and Garcia, J. E. (1987). *New Approaches to Effective Leadership: Cognitive Resources and Organizational Performance.* New York: Wiley.

11. Fleishman, E. A. and Harris, E. F. (1962). Patterns of leadership behavior related to employee grievances and turnover. *Personnel Psychology,* 15, 43–56.

12. Korman, A. K. (1966). "Consideration," "initiating structure" and organizational criteria—a review. *Personnel Psychology,* 18, 349–360.

13. Bass, B. M. (1990). *Bass and Stogdill's Handbook of Leadership* (3rd ed.), New York: The Free Press.

14. Penley, L. E. and Hawkins, B. (1985). Studying interpersonal communication in organizations: A leadership application. *Academy of Management Journal,* 28(2), 309–326.

15. Taylor, Frederick W. (1910). *Principles of Scientific Management.* NY: Harper & Brothers.

16. Ibid.

17. Katz, D., Maccoby, N. and Morse, N. C. (1950). Productivity, supervision and morale in an office situation. Ann Arbor: University of Michigan, Institute for Social Research.

18. Blake, R. R. and Mouton, J. S. (1964). *The Managerial Grid.* Houston, TX: Gulf.

19. Bowers, D. G. and Seashore, S. E. (1966). Predicting organizational effectiveness with a four-factor theory of leadership. *Administrative Science Quarterly,* 11, 238–263.

20. Fulk, J. and Wendler, E. R. (1982). Dimensionality of leader-subordinate interactions: A path-goal investigation. *Organizational Behavior and Human Performance,* 30, 241–264.

21. Indvik, J. (1986). Path-goal theory of leadership: A meta-analysis. *Proceedings of the Academy of Management,* Chicago, 189–192.

22. Graen, G., Dansereau, F. Jr. and Minami, T. (1972). Dysfunctional leadership styles. *Organizational Behavior and Human Performance,* 7, 216–236.

23. Bass, B. M. (1965). *Organizational Psychology.* Boston: Allyn & Bacon.

24. Stewart, R. (1967). *Managers and their Jobs: A Study of Similarities and Differences in the Way Managers Spent their Time.* London: Macmillan.

25. Stewart, R. (1976). *Contrasts in Management.* Maidenhead, Berkshire, England: McGraw-Hill: UK.

26. Stewart, R. (1982). Choices for the Manager: A Guide to Understanding Managerial Work. Upper Saddle River, NJ: Prentice Hall.

27. Katzell, R. A., Miller, C. E., Rotler, N. G. and Venet, T. G. (1970). Effects of leadership and other inputs on group processes and outputs. *Journal of Social Psychology,* 80, 157–169.

28. Bass, *Bass and Stogdill's Handbook of Leadership.*

29. Greene, C. N. (1975). The reciprocal nature of influence between leader and subordinate. *Journal of Applied Psychology,* 60, 187–193.

30. Greene, C. N. (1979). Questions of causation in the path-goal theory of leadership. *Academy of Management Journal,* 22, 22–41.

31. Lowin, A. and Craig, J. R. (1968). Participative decision making: A model, literature, critique, and prescription for research. *Organizational Behavior and Human Performance,* 3, 68–106.

32. Fleishman, E. A., Harris, E. F. and Burtt, H. E. (1955). Leadership and Supervision in Industry. Columbus: Ohio State University, Bureau of Educational Research.

33. Hall, D. T. and Mansfield, R. (1971). Organizational and individual response to external stress. *Administrative Science Quarterly,* 16, 533–547.

34. Bass, B. M., Brader, M. S. and Breed, W. (1967). Profitability and good relations: Which is cause and which is effect? (Brief No. 4) Pittsburgh: University of Pittsburgh, Management Research Center.

35. Roberts, N. C. (1986). Organizational power styles: Collective and competitive power under various organizational conditions. *Journal of Applied Behavioral Science,* 22, 443–458.

36. Fulk and Wendler, Dimensionality of leader-subordinate interactions: A path-goal investigation.

37. Indvik, Path-goal theory of leadership: A meta-analysis.

38. Podsakoff, P. M., Toder, W. D. and Schuler, R. S. (1983). Leader expertise as a moderator of the effects of instrumental and supportive leader behaviors. *Journal of Management,* 9, 173–185.

39. Smith, E. E. (1957). The effects of clear and unclear role expectations on group productivity and defensiveness. *Journal of Abnormal and Social Psychology,* 55, 213–217.

40. Fulk, J. and Wendler, E. R. (1982). Dimensionality of leader-subordinate interactions: A path-goal investigation. *Organizational Behavior and Human Performance,* 30, 241–264.

41. Indvik, Path-goal theory of leadership: A meta-analysis.

42. Kellogg, C. E. and White, D. D. (1987). Leader behaviors and volunteer satisfaction with work: The effect of volunteer maturation level. Paper, Academy of Management, New Orleans.

43. Schriesheim, C. A. and Murphy, C. J. (1976). Relationship between leader behavior and subordinate satisfaction and performance: A test of some situational moderators. *Journal of Applied Psychology,* 61, 634–641.

44. House, R. J., Filley, A. C. and Kerr, S. (1971). Relation of leader consideration and initiating structure to R and D subordinates' satisfaction. *Administrative Science Quarterly,* 16, 19–30.

45. Graham, F. C. (1982). Job stress in Mississippi cooperative extension service county personnel as related to age, gender, district, tenure, position and perceived leadership behavior of immediate supervisors. *Dissertation Abstracts International,* 43(7A), 2180.

46. Seltzer, J. and Numeroff, R. E. (1988). Supervisory leadership and subordinate burnout. *Academy of Management Journal,* 31, 439–446.

47. Berkowitz, L. (1953). An exploratory study of the roles of aircraft commanders. USAF Human Resources Research Center and Research Bulletin, No. 53–65, 1–27.

48. Katzell, R. A., Miller, C. E., Rotler, N. G. and Venet, T. G. (1970). Effects of leadership and other inputs on group processes and outputs. *Journal of Social Psychology,* 80, 157–169.

49. Christner, C. A. and Hemphill, J. K. (1955). Leader behavior of B–29 commanders and changes in crew members' attitudes toward the crew. *Sociometry,* 18, 82–87.

50. Greene, C. N. and Schriesheim, C. A. (1980). Leader-group interactions: A longitudinal field investigation. *Journal of Applied Psychology,* 65, 50–59.

51. Nealy, S. M. and Blood, M. R. (1968). Leadership performance of nursing supervisors at two organizational levels. *Journal of Applied Psychology,* 52, 414–422.

52. Sheridan, J. E. and Vredenburgh, D. J. (1979). Structural model of leadership influence in a hospital organization. *Academy of Management Journal,* 22, 6–21.

53. Greene, C. N. and Schriesheim, C. A. (1980). Leader-group interactions: A longitudinal field investigation.

54. Rubenowitz, S. (1962). Job oriented and person oriented leadership. *Personnel Psychology,* 15, 387–396.

55. Dunteman, G. H. and Bass, B. M. (1963). Supervisory and engineering success associated with self, interaction, and task orientation scores. *Personnel Psychology,* 16, 13–22.

56. Fleishman, E. A. and Harris, E. F. (1962). Patterns of leadership behavior related to employee grievances and turnover. *Personnel Psychology,* 15, 43–56.

57. Fleishman, E. A. and Simmons, J. (1970). Relationship between leadership patterns and effectiveness ratings among Israeli foremen. *Personnel Psychology, 23,* 169–172.

58. Halpin, A. W. (1956). The leader behavior of school superintendents. Columbus: Ohio State University, College of Education.

59. Seeman, M. (1957). A comparison of general and specific leader behavior descriptions. In R. M. Stogdill and E. A. Coons (Eds.), *Leader behavior: Its description and measurement.* Columbus: Ohio State University, Bureau of Business Research.

60. Indvik, Path-goal theory of leadership: A meta-analysis.

61. Mann, F. C., Indik, B. P. and Vroom, V. H. (1963). The productivity of work groups. Ann Arbor: University of Michigan, Survey Research Center.

62. Gekoski, N. (1952). Predicting group productivity. *Personnel Psychology, 5,* 281–291.

63. Likert, R. (1955). *Developing Patterns of Management.* American Management Association, General Management Series, No. 178, New York.

64. Dagirmanjian, S. (1981). The work experience of service staff in mental health service organizations and its relationship to leadership style and organizational structure. Dissertation Abstracts International, 43(58), 1609.

65. Blaihed, S. A. (1982). The relationship between leadership behavior of the chief executive officer in the hospital and overall hospital performance. Dissertation Abstracts International, 43(7A), 2169.

66. Hemphill, J. K. (1955). Leadership behavior associated with the administrative regulations of college departments. *Journal of Educational Psychology, 46,* 385–401.

67. Hood, P. D. (1963). Leadership climate for trainee leaders: The army AIT platoon. Washington, D.C.: George Washington University, Human Resources Research Office.

68. Keeler, B. T. and Andrews, J. H. M. (1963). Leader behavior of principals, staff morale, and productivity. *Alberta Journal of Educational Research, 9,* 179–191.

69. Fleishman and Harris (1962). Patterns of leadership behavior related to employee grievances and turnover.

70. Hunt, J. G., Osborne, R. N. and Martin, H. J. (1979). A multiple influence model of leadership. Unpublished manuscript. Carbondale: Southern Illinois University Press.

71. Dorfman, P. W., Howell, J. P., Hibino, S., Lee, J. K., Tate, U. and Bautista, A. (1997). Leadership in western and Asian countries: Commonalities and differences in effective leadership practices. *Leadership Quarterly,* 8(3), 233–274.

72. Ibid.

73. Matsai, T., Ohtsuke, Y. and Kikuchi, A. (1978). Consideration and structure behavior as reflections of supervisory interpersonal values. *Journal of Applied Psychology, 63,* 259–262.

74. Misumi, J. (1985). *The Behavioral Science of Leadership: An Interdisciplinary Japanese Research Program.* Ann Arbor: University of Michigan Press.

75. Misumi, J. and Peterson, M. F. (1985). The Performance-Maintenance (PM) theory of leadership: Review of a Japanese research program. *Administrative Science Quarterly,* 30, 198–223.

76. Fleishman, E. A. and Simmons, J. (1970). Relationship between leadership patterns and effectiveness ratings among Israeli foremen. *Personnel Psychology, 23,* 169–172.

77. Dorfman, Howell, Hibino, Lee, Tate and Bautista. Leadership in western and Asian countries: Commonalities and differences in effective leadership practices.

78. Al Gattan, A. R. A. (1985). Test of the path-goal theory of leadership in the multinational domain. Paper, Academy of Management Meeting, San Diego, CA.

79. Indvik, Path-goal theory of leadership: A meta-analysis.

80. Fisher, B. M. and Edwards, J. E. (1988). Consideration and initiating structure and their relationships with leader effectiveness: A meta-analysis. Best Papers Proceedings, Academy of Management. Anaheim, CA, 201–205.

CHAPTER 7

Situational Dynamics of Directive Leadership

Learning Objectives
After reading this chapter, you should be able to do the following:

1. Identify organizational situations where directive leadership is especially effective.

2. Identify situations where directive leadership is probably not effective.

3. Explain how leaders can modify situations to make their directive leadership more effective.

4. Explain how leaders can modify followers' work situation to make followers less dependent on directive leadership.

5. Discuss how followers, situations, and directive leaders interact and affect each other in a dynamic process.

Chapter 6 described the pattern of directive leadership and gave examples of directive behaviors used by leaders. We also described important effects of leader directiveness and pointed out that certain situational factors make directive leadership more or less effective. Chapter 7 addresses the situational dynamics of directive leadership (1). These dynamics include what leaders should look for in a situation to know when directive leadership is needed and how they can help followers obtain directive guidance from other sources. We also discuss how directive leaders, followers, and situational factors affect one another.

◆ SITUATIONS WHERE DIRECTIVE LEADERSHIP MAY OR MAY NOT BE EFFECTIVE

The following are descriptions of situations where directive leadership may or may not be effective with followers. Place an X next to those situations where you believe leader directiveness will be most effective.

1. _____ Followers view themselves as capable and experienced individuals who desire to work independently without supervision by their leader.

2. _____ Followers are members of a large work group and must coordinate their activities with one another to successfully complete their work tasks.

3. _____ The leader has a high degree of expertise at followers' work tasks and is very supportive of followers.

4. _____ Followers work in an organization where clear written plans, procedures, and goals exist for their work, and feedback on their performance comes directly from a computer display of individual productivity.

5. _____ Followers work in a cohesive group whose members have little or no desire to meet their leaders' performance goals.

6. _____ Followers' work on tasks that require them to follow specific procedures.

7. _____ Followers are new at their jobs and need guidance from their leader about effective work methods and what the leader expects of them.

8. _____ Followers work in autonomous groups whose members are highly trained and experienced and help one another with task and work related problems.

Some of the situations described above reflect a need for directive leadership. The situations numbered 2, 3, 6, and 7 are examples where followers typically need and re-

---

LEADERSHIP IN ACTION: JOHN F. WELCH— CHAIRMAN OF GE

John F. Welch is directing a new quality program for General Electric's worldwide operations. He describes how he pours his energy into clarifying expectations and structuring activities for his people regarding the program. "You have to tell your people that quality is critical to survival, you have to demand that everyone gets trained . . . you have to say 'We must do this!' " An aspect of the quality control program Welch is directing involves training "black belts" in statistical and other quality measures. He makes his expectations clear to younger managers by informing them that they have no future at GE unless they become black belts. After their training, he assigns them to roam GE plants and holds them responsible for setting up quality improvement projects.

Shifting GE's emphasis from manufactured products to supplying services is another strategy Welch is directing. He provides planning and guidance for managers to help them emphasize services, such as medical diagnostics, and expand spare parts and engine overhauls while de-emphasizing equipment sales with declining profit margins. He constantly clarifies his expectations that managers must obtain and keep a dominant position in whatever business GE enters. This is the overall goal he stresses as GE acquires companies with profitable market niches in the United States and abroad. He also assigns "stretch goals" to his managers, expecting them to attain huge gains in market power.

Laurence Bossidy left GE in the early 1990s to take over Allied Signal. He said that Welch directs his managers with specific objectives of staying ahead of the competition. "I think Jack's done it for 15 years . . . and they are going to be able to keep it going."

Source: William M. Carley, "Charging Ahead: To Keep GE's Profits Rising, Welch Pushes Quality Control Plan," *The Wall Street Journal.* January 13, 1997.

spond favorably to directive behaviors by their leader. These situations therefore enhance the positive effects of directive leadership. Two of the above situations have the opposite effect on leader effectiveness. Items 1 and 5 describe situations where followers simply do not desire any direction by their leader. When the leader directs these followers regarding how their work should be done, they may become uncooperative. These situational characteristics can therefore decrease or neutralize the effects of directiveness on the followers described. Two other situations described above actually replace followers' needs for directiveness from their leader. Items 4 and 8 are examples of these situations, where followers obtain guidance and direction from members of their work group or other sources and require little or no direction by their leader. These situations often yield very favorable results for followers and leaders. This chapter describes these three types of situations and offers leadership strategies for influencing the situations to improve follower, group, and organizational results.

The Leadership in Action box on John Welch, chief executive of General Electric, shows how directive leadership can be used at the top of a very large corporation to drive company strategies. Welch is a highly effective directive leader.

SITUATIONAL FACTORS THAT INCREASE EFFECTIVENESS OF DIRECTIVE LEADERSHIP

Several task and environmental characteristics have been found to enhance the effects of directive leadership. These factors increase the effectiveness of directive leadership in influencing followers.

TASK, ORGANIZATIONAL, AND FOLLOWER CHARACTERISTICS

When followers' work tasks are highly structured, requiring a specific set of procedures for successful completion, leader directiveness usually results in high levels of follower and group performance (2, 3, 4, 5, 6, 7). A work task with high structure has predefined steps that enable a competent worker to perform effectively. Though followers may dislike directive leadership with structured unambiguous tasks, their performance improves consistently when leaders are directive. This is probably because the existence of task structure gives the leader a clearly correct set of steps to use in guiding followers. By monitoring followers' performance, directive leaders also keep followers focused on their work. Two other task characteristics that increase the effects of leader directiveness are a high degree of task interdependence among followers and direct communications between customers and followers (8, 9). Task interdependence occurs when a follower must closely coordinate his/her work with others in order to achieve a high level of performance. An example is a group of medical workers in a hospital emergency room. An emergency room also often involves direct communications between various staff members and patients. Both of these situational conditions (combined of course with the life-and-death nature of the business) likely increase the importance of performing tasks correctly, which can increase followers' responsiveness to the leader's directive guidance.

The existence of a high degree of stress also often allows directive leadership to have a strong favorable impact on followers. This finding first occurred in early studies of military combat (10) and has since been supported by studies in health care and numerous other organizations (11, 12). The emergency room example described in the previous paragraph is also a high stress environment, necessitating directive leadership. Workers under high stress appreciate the guidance provided by a directive leader and typically respond with high job satisfaction, low levels of job burnout, and high performance. The sources of stress studied have included stress with one's leader, the existence of internal group conflict, role conflict, and combat conditions. Two researchers recently reported findings supporting job stress as an enhancer of directive leadership, and they suggested that directive leaders who were highly experienced were particularly effective under stress, more so than directive leaders who were highly intelligent (13). They cited earlier studies to justify this prediction, but research is only beginning to appear that tests their prediction in organizations.

When followers work in a relatively large group (more than four or five persons), directive leadership usually has a favorable effect on followers' psychological reactions, including improved job satisfaction, group arousal, and group cohesion (14, 15). Some writers have suggested that this result occurs because larger groups are less cohesive. It seems likely, however, that a directive approach is necessary and effective in large groups primarily to guide and coordinate the large number of people so they don't act at cross purposes with one another. Coordination is difficult with large groups, and leaders must give more attention to directing members to assure it is achieved. A positive group performance norm may also enhance the impact of directiveness on follower performance (16). A performance norm is a shared expectation among group members about the amount and/or quality of performance they should achieve. When a group of followers has a positive performance norm, it shares a desire to help the leader reach performance goals and responds positively to her guidance. This positive attitude is often found on successful athletic teams.

When working in a mechanistic organization structure (a bureaucracy with many hierarchical levels and decisions communicated downward from higher levels) and/or when the leader's position is at a fairly low level within the structure, the impact of the leader's directiveness on followers' satisfaction is enhanced (17, 18). In an organization where many decisions are made at higher levels and communicated downward, followers generally expect supervisory leaders to be directive to assure the decisions are carried out. Their positive reaction in the form of higher satisfaction may occur because the leader meets their expectations.

Certain leader characteristics or behaviors also increase the impact of directiveness on followers' performance and/or perceptions. A directive leader who possesses a high need for achievement (the desire to excel) (19), a high degree of expertise at the follower's task (20), and/or a high degree of supportiveness (21, 22) typically has favorable impacts on individual follower performance, group performance, and subordinate role clarity (23, 24, 25). The enhancing effect of supportiveness should not be interpreted to mean that all leaders should be highly directive and highly supportive of their followers. In fact, one researcher has pointed out that a moderately high amount of directiveness and supportiveness (rather than extremely high on both) may be the optimal combination of these two leader behaviors for many situations (26). It is easy to imagine how leaders who are highly competent at followers' tasks, show concern for followers, and display a strong desire for excellent performance can be effective in directing their followers.

A small number of studies show follower characteristics can increase the effectiveness of leader directiveness. When ROTC cadets possessed a high need for achievement, their leaders' directiveness resulted in high levels of follower satisfaction (27).

LEADERSHIP IN PERSPECTIVE: FOLLOWERS' GENDER AND RACE

Two follower characteristics have often been assumed to influence the impact of directive leadership—gender and race. Reviews of empirical findings from laboratory studies (28) and field studies in real organizations (29) conclusively show that follower gender does not consistently increase or decrease the impact of directive leadership on followers' psychological reactions or behaviors (30, 31). Though studies have found significant differences related to follower gender, the findings are not consistent, and other situational factors have most likely affected the results and confused the interpretations. The same conclusion is appropriate for followers' race, although less good research is available on directive leadership and follower race than on gender. At this time, no clear consistent evidence indicates that followers' race increases or decreases the impact of a leader's directiveness. Leaders may behave somewhat differently when followers are a different race, but the evidence does not show the impact of directive leadership to be consistently different. More research is needed in the area of race and leader effectiveness, especially with the increasing global integration of the U.S. economy.

A similar result occurred for professional research and development workers who preferred their job requirements to be specific and clear (32, 33). Followers who have high need for achievement may welcome the leader's helpful direction in successfully completing their tasks. High desire for clarity by followers means they want and appreciate a leader's explanations and guidance for completing their job tasks.

Recent international studies have focused on how situational and follower characteristics enhance the impacts of directive leadership in various countries. One study of Mexican managers and professionals showed that followers who believed in the need for "masculine" (strongly assertive) leaders were more satisfied with directive supervision. This study also found that beliefs in paternalism (leaders should take care of followers) enhanced the impact of directiveness on followers' performance (34). Another study found that a leader's task expertise was a consistent enhancer of directiveness in Japan, Taiwan, Korea, and Mexico (35). More research is underway to better understand how situational and follower characteristics affect directive leadership in different cultures. The Leadership in Perspective box on followers' gender and race describes research on these two follower characteristics and directive leadership.

INFLUENCING SITUATIONS TO MAKE DIRECTIVENESS MORE IMPACTFUL

Because high task structure increases the impact of leader directiveness on follower performance, leaders may be interested in building this task characteristic into followers' jobs. This can be done through job design programs that create clear stepwise methods and procedures for followers' job tasks. Certain types of jobs are obviously more suited to this approach than others, and more will be said about task structure later in this chapter. As noted, however, high task structure may also decrease the positive effect of directiveness on follower satisfaction, so leaders are best advised to also be supportive of followers. Training leaders to become experts in methods and procedures and to communicate this expertise via directive leadership should also significantly increase leaders' directive impacts on follower performance. Leader training that focuses on developing task expertise and providing supportive leader behavior can enhance the favorable effects of directive leadership.

Stress on followers and a bureaucratic organization structure can also increase the effects of leader directiveness. Most leaders will not wish to increase follower stress levels or to increase bureaucracy, but they should remember that directive leader behavior is an effective strategy when followers face these job conditions. Increasing the size of followers' work groups, influencing the groups' production norm (through a group reward system), and recruiting followers who have a high need for clarity will increase the need for a leader's directiveness and probably its impact. However, creating small groups and recruiting followers with low need for clarity can sometimes replace the need for directive leadership (to be discussed below), which can also improve followers' psychological reactions and performance and give the leader added time for other tasks. Figure 7–1 summarizes the major situational factors that make directive leadership especially effective.

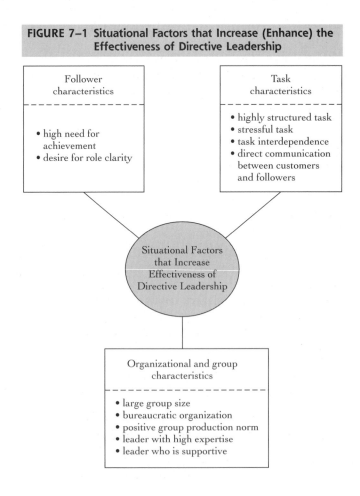

FIGURE 7–1 Situational Factors that Increase (Enhance) the Effectiveness of Directive Leadership

Follower characteristics

- high need for achievement
- desire for role clarity

Task characteristics

- highly structured task
- stressful task
- task interdependence
- direct communication between customers and followers

Situational Factors that Increase Effectiveness of Directive Leadership

Organizational and group characteristics

- large group size
- bureaucratic organization
- positive group production norm
- leader with high expertise
- leader who is supportive

LEADERSHIP IN ACTION: DIRECTIVE LEADERSHIP WAS NEEDED, BUT NOT PROVIDED

Jon P. Muczyk and Bernard C. Reimann provided a good example of what can happen when a leader fails to provide directive leadership when it is sorely needed—the "Iran-gate" affair of the early 1980s. President Ronald Reagan's espoused management style was, "Surround yourself with the best people you can find, delegate authority, and don't interfere as long as the overall policy you've set is being carried out." (p. 307). This nondirective style apparently worked well "until two of his former key aids, Chief of Staff James Baker III and Treasury Secretary Donald Regan, decided to swap jobs." Don Regan decided to streamline the White House operation, and in the process he isolated the President from key sources of information. President Reagan's nondirective style kept him from following up on specific assignments of staff members, and he, in effect, lost control over the actions of his subordinates. Since he had lost information and control systems with his new chief of staff, he discovered too late about actions of certain subordinates that may eventually have led to the Iran-Contra affair.

Source: J. P. Muczyk and B. C. Reimann. "The case for directive leadership," *Academy of Management Executive,* 1(3) (1987): 301–311.

The Leadership in Action box shows how a personnel change created a situation where directive leadership was needed. When the needed leader direction was not provided, this resulted in followers' actions that were out of control and eventually damaged the leader's reputation.

◆ SITUATIONAL FACTORS THAT MAKE DIRECTIVE LEADERSHIP LESS EFFECTIVE

Some situational characteristics can reduce or eliminate (neutralize) the impact of directiveness on followers. Most leaders would like to eliminate these situational factors if they could identify them. There are occasions, however, when these factors may be advantageous to an organizational unit or to followers. This can occur in government or universities where incompetent administrators become entrenched in their position and cannot be removed. In these situations, creating neutralizers is sometimes the only means to minimize damage to a group or organization.

TASK, ORGANIZATIONAL, AND FOLLOWER CHARACTERISTICS

Although a high degree of task structure was described earlier as increasing the impact of directive leadership on follower performance, the influence of task structure on the directive leadership-follower satisfaction relationship is quite different. When followers' work tasks are highly structured, the impact of leader directiveness on followers' intrinsic job satisfaction and general job satisfaction is actually reduced (36, 37, 38, 39, 40). A recent summary of research on directive leadership confirmed this neutralizing effect for follower satisfaction (41). It appears that when followers face job tasks with predefined procedures and steps, they dislike a leader reiterating these procedures to them through directive leadership, even though this reiteration can help their performance.

Characteristics of the follower's work group may also decrease the impact of directive leadership, although this is a complex situational factor. Studies of group cohesion (the "felt solidarity" or closeness among group members) indicate both neutralizing and enhancing effects. Cohesion among group members causes them to act together, cooperating with or resisting the leader. The key factor appears to be the type of performance norm that develops within the cohesive group. If a low performance norm exists, indicating little desire or effort by members to meet the leader's performance goals, then the impact of directive leadership on follower performance is decreased—a neutralizing effect (42, 43). This neutralizing effect is especially strong when the group is highly cohesive (44). This neutralizing effect was observed in a county hospital where an outside management team had been brought in by the board of directors to implement several new administrative systems. The existing middle management group disliked the "outsiders" and provided little cooperation in meeting the goals they were given. After a long and difficult implementation period, the systems were installed and the "outside team" left. Local managers replaced the outsiders and cooperation of the middle managers was restored.

High performance norms may increase (enhance) the impact of directive leadership. Clearly a follower's work group affects how the follower reacts to a leader's directiveness. People respond to pressures by their fellow workers, and these pressures may enhance or overwhelm a leader's influence. It seems evident that task and group characteristics can be important situational factors that decrease the impacts of directive leadership.

Two studies reported follower characteristics that decreased the impacts of a leader's directiveness. Leader directiveness had little impact when followers were highly experienced (45). Also, the impact of directive leadership on followers' role ambiguity was reduced when followers were highly competent at their task and desired independence in their work (46). These findings are consistent with other research indicating that experienced, capable followers who desire autonomy may resist directive leadership (47).

OVERCOMING FACTORS THAT DECREASE EFFECTS OF DIRECTIVE LEADERSHIP

Leaders should become aware of situational factors that decrease the impacts of their directive behavior so they can either modify the situation or choose alternate behavioral strategies. Rather than creating a high degree of task structure for followers (which could improve performance but lower satisfaction), the leader might be better served by working to create high performance norms among followers. Leaders can influence group performance norms through group-based reward systems and good-natured competition with other groups. Increasing ones own legitimacy through expertise and effectively representing the group's interests are also effective strategies. Training programs that focus on creating these conditions will help the leader overcome possible neutralizers such as task structure and low group performance norms. It may also be advisable to hire capable followers who like to work independently without close supervision, even though

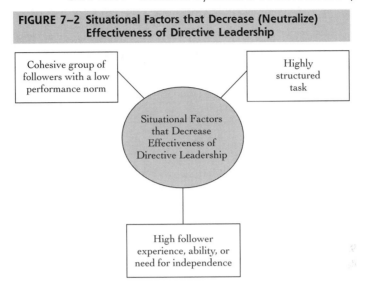

FIGURE 7–2 Situational Factors that Decrease (Neutralize) Effectiveness of Directive Leadership

directive leadership is probably not the most effective leader behavior to emphasize with these followers. Other leader behaviors such as providing rewards, to be discussed later in this book, are effective in this situation. Figure 7–2 summarizes the situational characteristics that decrease the effectiveness of directive leadership. When these characteristics exist, followers often ignore or resist a leader's directiveness, and leaders must use another type of influence to guide and motivate followers.

◆ SITUATIONAL FACTORS THAT REPLACE THE NEED FOR DIRECTIVE LEADERSHIP

Effective leaders can often identify or create situational and follower characteristics that provide needed guidance and structure for followers. These factors can increase followers' ability to perform without continuous direction from the leader. Leaders can then perform other important functions such as designing participation and reward systems or obtaining key resources. These activities can require considerable time and effort, and identifying factors that replace the need for directive leadership is an important step toward making time available for these activities.

TASK, ORGANIZATIONAL, AND FOLLOWER CHARACTERISTICS

The strongest situational characteristic that replaces the need for directive leadership is autonomous work groups or team operations where followers interact frequently with one another and obtain guidance and input for their work tasks from coworkers (48, 49, 50). When competent coworkers are available and followers are members of a work team with collective responsibilities for task accomplishment, direction from leaders can become unnecessary. Team structures of this type have become increasingly common in large organizations during the late 1990s. Another important situational characteristic

LEADERSHIP SELF-ASSESSMENT: DIRECTIVE ATTITUDES AND BEHAVIORS

Indicate whether you mostly agree or mostly disagree with the following statements. Relate the statements to any work situation, including sports, community activities, and school activities, in which you have been responsible for the work of others. If a work situation does not come to mind, imagine how you would act or think.

	Mostly Agree	Mostly Disagree
1. I keep close tabs on productivity figures, and interpret them to the group.	_____	_____
2. I send frequent e-mail messages to group members, giving them information and guidance about work procedures.	_____	_____
3. I clearly specify the quality goals our group needs to achieve.	_____	_____
4. I maintain clear-cut standards of performance.	_____	_____
5. When I conduct a meeting, the participants can count on a clear agenda.	_____	_____
6. Specifying productivity goals at the beginning of each week is essential for good performance.	_____	_____
7. I schedule the work for our group members to assure tasks are completed on time.	_____	_____
8. I monitor and follow up on work that does not meet standards.	_____	_____
9. I spend at least 20 percent of my work week either planning myself or helping team members with their planning.	_____	_____
10. I spend a good deal of time instructing group members in how to solve technical or business problems.	_____	_____

If you responded "mostly agree" to eight, nine, or ten of the above statements, you have a strong orientation toward directive leadership. If you responded "mostly disagree" to five or more of the statements, you may have a preference to use other leader behaviors to influence followers.

———
Source: Adapted from A. J Dubrin, *Leadership: Research Findings, Practice, and Skill.* (Boston: Houghton Mifflin Company, 1998) pp. 92–93.

that replaces the need for directive leadership is a high degree of organizational formalization, for example, explicit plans, procedures, goals, and responsibilities assigned by the organization to specific followers. When tasks, work strategies, and/or methods are clearly specified in writing, there may be little need for directive leadership (51, 52). The replacement effects of clearly specified plans, procedures, and work methods are often found in organizational units with repetitive tasks and low levels of stress, such as a maintenance battalion in the peacetime military.

A third situational factor that can replace leader directiveness is built-in feedback from the follower's task (53). This type of performance feedback is often provided by computer displays of individual or group productivity (54), which gives followers frequent up-to-date information on the effectiveness of their work methods and progress toward assigned goals. This feedback can alleviate the need for monitoring and direction by the leader. Competent followers can take timely action based on feedback received directly from the task. Fourth, a predictable flow of work that is often routine and repetitive has also been shown to replace directive leadership (55, 56). Once the routine and predictable tasks are mastered, workers have little need for direction by a leader. Finally, one recent research study found a large number of years working for a given leader resulted in high performance by the follower and completely negated (neutralized) the influence of the leader's directive behaviors (57). Years with a supervisor may be a useful way of measuring a follower's experience, confidence, job ability, or simply job "savvy." Followers with these characteristics can provide their own job guidance with little or no direction needed from their leader (58).

CREATING FACTORS THAT REPLACE THE NEED FOR DIRECTIVE LEADERSHIP

Creating situational factors that replace leader directiveness may be best achieved by establishing autonomous work teams of followers. If the teams are provided with direct task feedback and authority to make and implement work-related decisions, this strategy can improve followers' psychological reactions and performance and give leaders more time. Of course, followers must be experienced, competent, and committed to performing well in order for autonomous work teams to have a desirable effect.

This strategy of granting independence to teams can be effectively complemented by (1) designing production systems that provide a predictable flow of work and (2) developing specific procedures to be used in performing tasks. Retaining highly experienced and capable followers who have worked with the leader for many years can provide another source of guidance and structure for group members who are less experienced and can alleviate the need for the leader's directiveness. Figure 7–3 summarizes the situational characteristics that can replace the need for directive leadership. These factors provide guidance and motivation for followers and make directive leadership at least partially unnecessary.

In this Leadership in Action box, Gerry Gladstone failed to recognize that the situational and follower characteristics he faced in Allied Machinery were very different from his previous position. The new situational factors required more directive leadership behavior, which Gerry failed to provide. This led to his unsuccessful performance as president of Allied.

Table 7–1 summarizes the three types of situational and follower characteristics and how they influence the effectiveness of directive leadership. Figure 7–4 provides an example of how the three types of situational factors can affect directive leadership by a public school principal.

FIGURE 7–3 Situational Factors that Replace the Need for Directive Leadership

Feedback directly from task

Organizational formalization

Large number of years with leader

Situational Factors that Replace the Need for Directive Leadership

Autonomous work groups
or
team operations

Predictable flow of work
or
routine and repetitive work

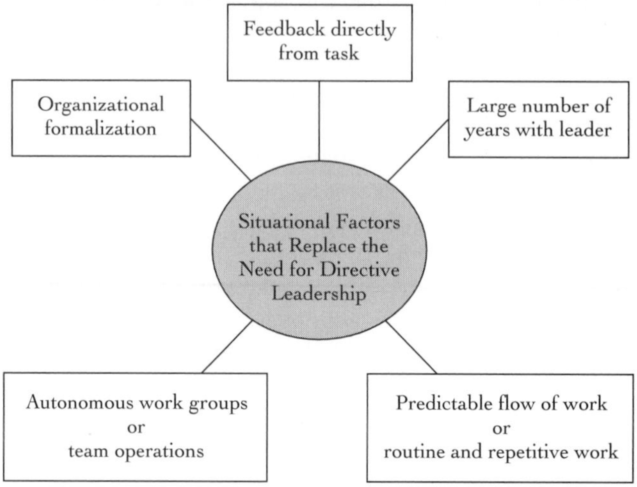

LEADERSHIP IN ACTION: A NEED FOR DIRECTIVE LEADERSHIP

Gerry Gladstone has had a lesson in leadership. He worked his way up to general manager of the machinery division of a large conglomerate. His division was one of the most profitable in the company when he accepted the presidency of Allied Machinery, a smaller competitor that was in need of new leadership to reverse its declining performance. A year later Allied's performance is still declining, even though the industry is rapidly expanding. Gerry is beginning to realize he was "spoiled" in his earlier position. In his job as general manager in the conglomerate, Gerry had learned to rely on high-quality subordinates and organizational support systems. Well-developed procedures for processing orders and for inventory control as well as sophisticated computer information systems had allowed him to use extensive participative leadership and delegation with followers. His democratic style included little directiveness, and he came to believe his style was the only way to lead.

The organization at Allied was quite different. The managers reporting to him had considerably lower capabilities and initiative than his former subordinates. They were accustomed to clear direction and close monitoring from their president. Allied did not have the well-developed procedures or the information system Gerry was accustomed to using. Without clear direction and follow-up from Gerry, his managers often made errors or failed to meet deadlines. Without adequate standardized procedures or reliable control systems, Gerry did not learn of the failures until it was too late. Allied's performance went from bad to worse in several key areas, and the board asked Gerry to resign as president a year after he took the job.

Source: Adapted from J. P. Muczyk and B. C. Reimann, "The case for directive leadership," *Academy of Management Executive,* 1(3) (1987): 301–311.

TABLE 7–1 Situational and Follower Characteristics that Affect the Impact of Directive Leadership

Factors that Increase the Effectiveness of Directive Leadership	*Factors that Decrease the Effectiveness of Directive Leadership*	*Factors that Replace the Need for Directive Leadership*
• Followers' tasks are highly structured (here directive leadership improves follower performance) • Followers' tasks require cooperation with others and/or direct communication with customers • Followers are under high stress • Followers are members of a large work group • Followers' work group has a positive productivity norm • Organization is highly bureaucratic • Leader is a supervisor at a fairly low level in the organization • Leader has a high level of need for achievement, is supportive, or an expert at followers' tasks • Followers have "masculine" or "paternalistic" values • Followers prefer clear and specific job requirements	• Followers work in a cohesive group with a low performance norm • Followers are highly competent and experienced at their work tasks • Follower's tasks are highly structured (here directive leadership does not improve followers' satisfaction) • Followers have a strong need for independence	• Followers work in autonomous work teams • Organization has extensive goals, plans, and procedures for guiding followers behavior • Followers' tasks provide regular feedback on performance • Followers' work is routine and predictable • Followers have many years of experience working with the leader

◆ ASSESSING THE DYNAMICS OF DIRECTIVE LEADERSHIP

Leaders carry out the three key leadership tasks of diagnosing situations, behaving appropriately, and modifying situations (see chapter 1) when providing effective directive leadership. When leaders diagnose situations and find one or more characteristics that increase the effectiveness of directive leadership (see table 7–1), they should be directive with followers. Followers in these situations respond positively to a directive leader. If the leader's situational diagnosis identifies factors that would decrease the effects of directiveness (see table 7–1), then other types of leader behaviors will most likely be preferable.

A leader should also attempt to determine if situational characteristics can be modified to eliminate factors that decrease leader effectiveness or to create factors

FIGURE 7–4 Influence of Situational Factors on the Directive Leadership of Public School Principals

Situational factors that could <u>increase the effectiveness of a principal's directiveness</u>

- Due to increased enrollments, the principal supervises a large number of teachers.
- The principal has extensive experience in teaching, and the teachers perceive the principal as having high teaching ability.
- The teachers are experiencing high stress because of student violence in the school.
- The teachers work closely together and reinforce high group norms for excellence in education.
- The teachers' job has become more highly structured because the school board has required the coverage of specific content material and development of specific skills.

How Situational Factors can Affect the Impact of Directive Leadership by Public School Principals

Situational factors that could <u>decrease the effectiveness</u> of a principal's directiveness

- The classes are team taught by highly cohesive groups of teachers.
- The teachers have a level of experience and ability that exceeds that of the principal.
- The teachers have a high need for independence that is satisfied by teaching with their own unique methods.

Situational factors that could <u>replace the need</u> for a principal's directiveness

- The teachers have worked for a large number of years for the same principal.
- The school system has a detailed set of work rules that the teachers must follow.
- The teachers get direct feedback in the form of improved student performance.

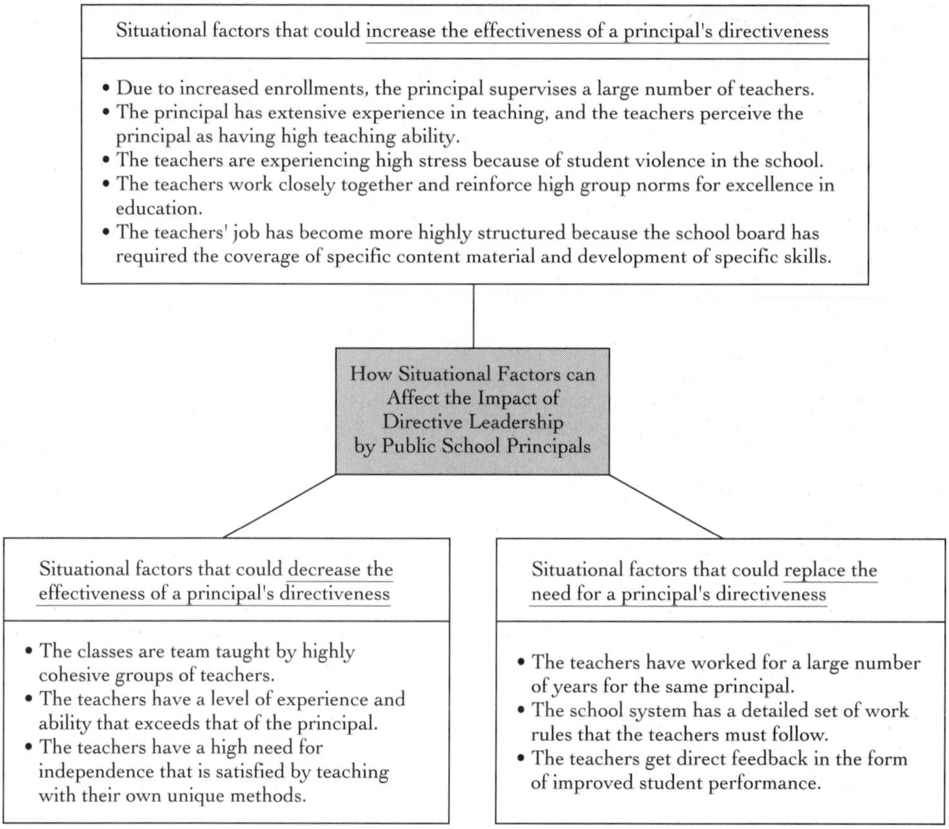

that replace directive leadership (see table 7–1). Leaders can improve the work situation and replace the need for directive guidance from the leader by creating autonomous work teams; designing tasks that provide followers with direct performance feedback and/or are routine and predictable; designing and communicating goals, plans, and procedures for the work; or developing a cohesive group of followers with many years of experience.

When leaders act to modify situations in this manner, they force followers to take increased responsibility for managing their own work. They also empower followers by providing nonleader sources of guidance on the job such as capable coworkers, standardized plans, goals and procedures, and relevant work experience. Followers can turn to these sources to control and guide their own work efforts without requiring regular direction from the leader. This allows the leader to focus on other responsibilities.

When a leader provides direction resulting in favorable psychological reactions and behaviors from followers, this encourages the leader to continue the strategy. If the results are disappointing, the leader can shift her attention to the follower's work situation. When the leader identifies follower or situational characteristics she can modify to increase her influence on followers or to replace her directiveness with other sources of guidance, she can benefit followers by working to change the situation. Followers' reactions and behaviors as well as situational characteristics thus affect the directive strategy of the leader. Directive leader behaviors are often needed with some follower tasks, but they may not be necessary for all tasks. As followers gain experience and skill and identify coworkers who are knowledgeable and helpful, the leader can often decrease the directive behaviors. This allows followers to develop into capable self-managing performers who take pride in their work and are willing to help others on the job.

Summary

Research shows that leaders adapt their directive behavior to the organizational situations they face. When important situational factors that increase the impacts of directive leader behavior are present, this behavior will be highly effective in influencing followers' psychological reactions and behavioral outcomes. Although differences exist among countries and cultures regarding the type of directive leader behavior most appropriate for followers, some type of directiveness seems especially effective in cultures where followers have highly masculine or paternalistic values.

When important situational and follower characteristics that decrease the impact of directive leader behavior on followers are present, the leader had best try to modify the situation or use another behavioral strategy to influence followers. When situational factors that replace the need for directiveness by a leader exist, this leader behavior will be partially or completely unnecessary because the situation provides needed guidance and structure for followers on their work tasks. In these situations, the leader can decrease the amount of active guidance provided for followers and concentrate on other needed leader behaviors that are often underattended.

Figure 7–5 describes a process model of directive leadership that summarizes many of the major findings regarding directive leader behavior described in chapters 6 and 7. Directive behaviors shown at the top of Figure 7–5 influence follower and group psychological reactions, which in turn affect followers' behavioral outcomes. Situational factors (including follower characteristics) that increase, decrease, or replace the need for leader directiveness are shown on each side of Figure 7–5, with arrows intersecting the relationship between directiveness and follower/group psychological reactions. These arrows indicate that the situational factors can increase or decrease the leader's effects on followers and groups. Arrows from the leader directiveness box to the situational factor boxes show that leaders can sometimes modify situations to create more favorable leader-follower interactions. The arrow from the situational factor box on the left shows certain factors can affect follower/group reactions to replace the effects of directive leadership. To keep Figure 7–5 from becoming too complicated, other possible dynamic effects among the boxes are not shown.

Figure 7–6 is designed to show a leader how to use the model of directive leadership presented in Figure 7–5. It describes the three key tasks for effective leadership as they apply to leader directiveness. Leaders first diagnose the situation by answering a series of questions regarding followers and their task situation (box 1). These questions basically identify the existence of situational factors that increase (enhance) the impacts of directive leadership. If

FIGURE 7–5 Process Model of the Directive Leadership Process

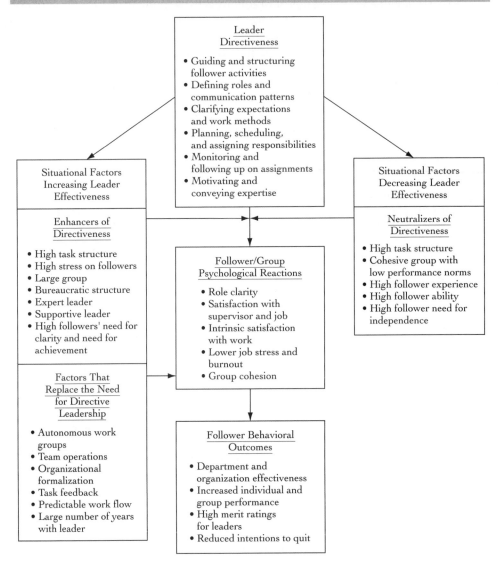

the answer is "yes" to one or more of these questions, then directiveness is probably needed and the leader should provide this type of leadership (box 2). At the same time, the leader should examine the follower and situational characteristics to see if important factors exist that can decrease (neutralize) the effects of directiveness. The existence of one or more strong enhancers will likely overwhelm most neutralizers, but the leader would do well to eliminate neutralizers whenever possible. The creation of situational factors that replace directiveness should also be considered to help provide for followers' needs without active direction from the leader (box 3).

FIGURE 7–6 Applying the Model of Directive Leadership

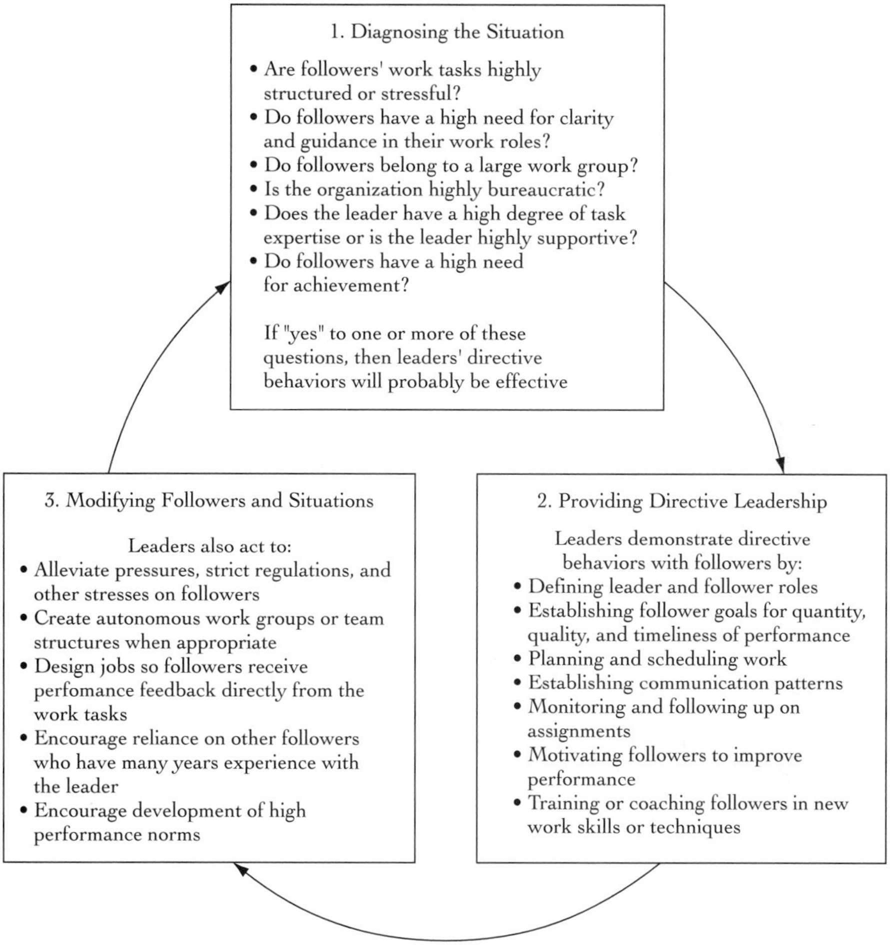

1. Diagnosing the Situation

- Are followers' work tasks highly structured or stressful?
- Do followers have a high need for clarity and guidance in their work roles?
- Do followers belong to a large work group?
- Is the organization highly bureaucratic?
- Does the leader have a high degree of task expertise or is the leader highly supportive?
- Do followers have a high need for achievement?

If "yes" to one or more of these questions, then leaders' directive behaviors will probably be effective

3. Modifying Followers and Situations

Leaders also act to:
- Alleviate pressures, strict regulations, and other stresses on followers
- Create autonomous work groups or team structures when appropriate
- Design jobs so followers receive perfomance feedback directly from the work tasks
- Encourage reliance on other followers who have many years experience with the leader
- Encourage development of high performance norms

2. Providing Directive Leadership

Leaders demonstrate directive behaviors with followers by:
- Defining leader and follower roles
- Establishing follower goals for quantity, quality, and timeliness of performance
- Planning and scheduling work
- Establishing communication patterns
- Monitoring and following up on assignments
- Motivating followers to improve performance
- Training or coaching followers in new work skills or techniques

Key Terms and Concepts in this Chapter ▪

- autonomous work groups
- group cohesion
- group performance norms
- intrinsic satisfaction
- mechanistic organization structure

- need for achievement
- need for independence
- organizational formalization
- stress

- supportiveness
- task structure
- task interdependence

Review and Discussion Questions ▪▪▪▪▪▪▪▪▪▪▪▪▪▪▪▪▪▪▪▪▪▪▪▪▪▪▪▪

1. What are the common situational characteristics that cause directive leadership to be highly effective?

2. Describe a situation you have experienced or observed where directive leadership was not effective. Explain why directiveness did not have a favorable impact on followers.

3. In your current job (or a job you hope to obtain), which follower or situational characteristics would make directive leadership highly effective? Which characteristics would make it ineffective?

4. As a leader, how might you create situational factors to build your influence as a directive leader?

5. Do you think directive leadership would be an effective strategy for a supervisor of fire fighters? Why or why not?

6. Do you think directive leadership would be an effective strategy for a supervisor of highly trained, experienced, and capable assemblers of desktop computers? Why or why not?

Exercise: Analysis of Directive Leadership ▪▪▪▪▪▪▪▪▪▪▪▪▪▪▪▪▪▪▪▪▪▪▪▪

1. Describe a situation you have experienced, observed, or heard about that requires some type of directive leadership.

2. What is it about this situation that makes directive leadership necessary and appropriate?

3. What specific directive leadership behaviors would be *most effective* in this situation?

4. What specific directive leadership behaviors would be *ineffective* in this situation?

◆◆◆ **Case Incident**

A Type of Direction

Scott Davis is the manager of a plant that manufactures camping equipment. The employees are highly trained and experienced in their jobs, and their performance has been excellent. Mr. Davis recently promoted Will Taylor to be supervisor of the department that manufactures sleeping bags. Will has worked in the plant for the past twelve years and has the best production record in the department.

After a month of Will's supervision, his employees in the sleeping bag department requested a meeting with Mr. Davis. They stated that Will was making it impossible for them to achieve their production goals. They characterized Will as a dictator and perfectionist.

Comments by the employees included: "Will is rejecting finished sleeping bags that meet quality specifications because they do not meet his criteria for perfection." "The only way to do the job is his way." "The job of supervisor has made him a dictator." "He demands that every work station be cleaned up twenty times a day." "He stands over us like we didn't know how to do our jobs." "He tells you that the job must be done exactly the way he would have done it." "If he keeps up his loud orders, we will need to get earplugs."

QUESTIONS

1. What are possible problems in Will Taylor's directive style?

2. Would Will be more effective if he modified his methods of directiveness? If so, how?

3. What should Mr. Davis do to help Will improve his supervision?

Endnotes

1. Trevelyan, R. (1998). The boundary of leadership: Getting it right and having it all. *Business Strategy Review,* 9(1), 37–44.

2. Griffin, R. W. (1980). Relationships among individual, task design, and leader behavior variables. *Academy of Management Journal,* 23, 665–683.

3. Wofford, C. Jr. (1971). Managerial behavior, situational factors, productivity and morale. *Administrative Science Quarterly,* 16, 10–12.

4. Downey, A. K., Sheridan, J. E. and Slocum, J. W. Jr. (1976). The path-goal theory of leadership: A longitudinal analysis. *Organizational Behavior and Human Performance,* 16, 156–176.

5. Indvik, J. (1986). Path-goal theory of leadership: A meta-analysis. Proceedings, Academy of Management, Chicago, 189–192.

6. Wolcott, C. (1984). The relationship between the leadership behavior of library supervisors and the performance of their professional subordinates. Dissertation Abstracts International, 45(5A), 1507.

7. Kahai, S. S., Sosik, J. J. and Avolio, B. J. (1997). Effects of leadership style and problem structure on work group process and outcomes in an electronic meeting system environment. *Personnel Psychology,* 50(1), 121–146.

8. Fry, L. W., Kerr, S. and Lee, C. (1986). Effects of different leader behaviors under different levels of task interdependence. *Human Relations,* 39, 1067–1082.

9. Childers, T. L., Dubinsky, A. J. and Skinner, S. J. (1990). Leadership substitutes as moderators of sales supervisory behavior. *Journal of Business Research,* 21, 363–382.

10. Halpin, A. W. (1954). The leadership behavior and combat performance of airplane commanders. *Journal of Abnormal and Social Psychology,* 49, 19–22.

11. Numeroff, R. E. and Seltzer, J. (1986). The relationship between leadership factors, burnout, and stress symptoms among middle managers. Paper, Academy of Management, Chicago.

12. Misumi, J. and Sako, H. (1982). An experimental study of the effect of leadership behavior on followers' behavior of following after the leader in a simulated emergency situation. *Japanese Journal of Experimental Psychology,* 21(1), 49–59. Cited in J. Misumi, The Behavioral Science of Leadership: An Interdisciplinary Japanese Research Program. Ann Arbor: University of Michigan Press.

13. Fiedler, F. E. and Garcia, J. E. (1987). *New Approaches to Effective Leadership: Cognitive Resources and Organizational Performance.* New York: Wiley.

14. Greene, C. N. and Schriesheim, C. A. (1980). Leader-group interactions: a longitudinal field investigation. *Journal of Applied Psychology,* 65(1), 50–59.

15. Schriesheim, C. A. and Murphy, C. J. (1976). Relationship between leader behavior and subordinate satisfaction and performance: A test of some situational moderators. *Journal of Applied Psychology,* 61, 634–641.

16. Howell, J. and Frost, P. (1988). A laboratory study of charismatic leadership. *Organizational Behavior and Human Decision Processes,* 43, 243–269.

17. Nealy, S. M. and Blood, M. R. (1968). Leadership performance of nursing supervisors at two organizational levels. *Journal of Applied Psychology,* 52, 414–422.

18. Cooper, R. and Payne, R. (1967). Personality orientations and performance in football

teams: Leaders' and subordinates' orientations related to team success. Birmingham, England: University of Aston, Organizational Group Psychology.

19. Mayes, B. T. (1979). Leader needs as moderators of the subordinate job performance-leader behavior relationship. Paper, Academy of Management Meeting, Atlanta, GA.

20. Podsakoff, P. M., Todor, W. D. and Schuler, R. S. (1983). Leadership expertise as a moderator of the effects of instrumental and supportive leader behaviors. *Journal of Management, 9,* 173–185.

21. Calloway, D. W. (1985). The promise and paradoxes of leadership. *Directors and Boards,* 9(2), 12–16.

22. Cleveland, H. (1980). Learning the art of leadership: The worldwide crisis in governance demands new approaches. Unpublished manuscript. Cited in B. M. Bass (1990) *Bass & Stogdill's Handbook of Leadership,* (3rd ed.) New York: The Free Press.

23. Podsakoff, Toder, and Schuler, Leader expertise as a moderator of the effects of instrumental and supportive leader behaviors.

24. Smith, E. E. (1957). The effects of clear and unclear role expectations on group productivity and defensiveness. *Journal of Abnormal and Social Psychology,* 55, 213–217.

25. Kellogg, C. E. and White, D. D. (1987). Leader behaviors and volunteer satisfaction with work: The effect of volunteer maturation level. Paper, Academy of Management, New Orleans.

26. House, R. (1987). The 'All things in Moderation' leader. *Academy of Management Review,* 12, 164–169.

27. Mathieu, J. E. (1990). A test of subordinates' achievement and affiliation needs as moderators of leader path-goal relationships. *Basic and Applied Social Psychology,* 11(12), 179–189.

28. Bartol, K. (1978). The sex structuring of organizations: A search for possible causes. *Academy of Management Review,* 3, 805–815.

29. Larwood, L., Wood, M. M. and Inderlied, S. D. (1978). Training women for management: New problems, new solutions. *Academy of Management Review,* 3, 584–593.

30. Marsh, M. K. and Atherton, R. M. Jr. (1981). Leadership, organizational type, and subordinate satisfaction in the U. S. Army: The hi-hi paradigm sustained. *Journal of Social Relations,* 9, 121–143.

31. Graham, F. C. (1982). Job stress in Mississippi cooperative extension service county personnel as related to age, gender, district, tenure, position and perceived leadership behavior of immediate supervisors. *Dissertation Abstracts International,* 43(7A), 2180.

32. Keller, R. T. (1989). A test of the path-goal theory of leadership with need for clarity as a moderator in research and development organizations. *Journal of Applied Psychology,* 74, 208–212.

33. Kroll, M. J. and Pringle, C. D. (1985). Individual differences and path-goal theory: The role of leader directiveness. *Southwest Journal of Business and Economics,* 2(3), 11–20.

34. Dorfman, P. W. and Howell, J. P. (1988). Dimensions of National Culture and Effective Leadership Patterns: Hofstede Revisited. *Advances in International Comparative Management,* 3, 127–150.

35. Dorfman, P. W., Howell, J. P., Hibino, S., Lee, J. K., Tate, U. and Bautista, A. (1997). Leadership in western and Asian countries: Commonalties and differences in effective leadership practices. *Leadership Quarterly,* 8(3), 233–274.

36. Jurma, W. E. (1978). Leadership structuring style, task ambiguity, and group member satisfaction. *Small Group Behavior,* 9, 124–134.

37. Badin, I. J. (1974). Some moderator influences on relationships between consideration, initiating structure, and organizational criteria. *Journal of Applied Psychology.* 59, 380–382.

38. Johns, G. (1978). Task moderators of the relationship between leadership style and subordinate responses. *Academy of Management Journal,* 21, 319–325.

39. Dessler, G. (1973). An investigation of the path-goal theory of leadership. Doctoral

Dissertation, Baruch College, City University of New York.

40. Kinicki, A. J. and Schriesheim, C. A. (1978). Teachers as leaders: A moderator variable approach. *Journal of Educational Research,* 70, 928–935.

41. Indvik, Path-goal theory of leadership: A meta-analysis.

42. Howell, J. and Frost, P. (1988). A laboratory study of charismatic leadership. *Organizational Behavior and Human Decision Processes,* 43, 243–269.

43. Hernandez, S. R. and Kaluzny, A. D. (1982). Selected determinants of performance within a set of health service organizations. Proceedings, Academy of Management, New York, 52–56.

44. Howell, J. P. and Dorfman, P. W. (1981). Substitutes for Leadership: Test of a construct. *Academy of Management Journal,* 24, 714–728.

45. Vecchio, R. P. (1987). Situational leadership theory: An examination of a prescriptive theory. *Journal of Applied Psychology,* 72, 444–451.

46. Howell, J. P. and Dorfman, P. W. (1986). Leadership and substitutes for leadership among professional and nonprofessional workers. *The Journal of Applied Behavioral Science,* 22(1), 29–46.

47. Kerr, S. and Jermier, J. (1978). Substitutes for leadership: Their meaning and measurement. *Organizational Behavior and Human Performance,* 22, 374–403.

48. Manz, C. C. and Sims, H. P. Jr. (1987). Leading workers to lead themselves: The external leadership of self-managing work teams. *Administrative Science Quarterly,* 32, 106–129.

49. Wall, T. D., Kemp, N. J., Jackson, P. R. and Clegg, C. W. (1986). Outcomes of autonomous workgroups: A long-term field experiment. *Academy of Management Journal,* 29, 280–304.

50. Cherns, A. (1976). The principles of sociotechnical design. *Human Relations,* 29, 783–792.

51. Howell and Dorfman, Substitutes for leadership: Test of a construct.

52. Kerr and Jermier, Substitutes for leadership: Their meaning and measurement.

53. Schriesheim, C. A. and Denisi, A. S. (1981). Task dimensions as moderators of the effects of instrumental leadership: A two sample replicated test of path-goal leadership theory. *Journal of Applied Psychology,* 66, 589–597.

54. Cherns, A. (1976). The principles of sociotechnical design. *Human Relations,* 29, 783–792.

55. Wall, J. (1986). *Bosses.* Lexington, MA: D. C. Heath.

56. Comstock, D. S. and Scott, W. R. (1977). Technology and structure of subunits: Distinguishing individual work efforts. *Administrative Science Quarterly,* 22, 177–202.

57. Mossholder, K. W., Niebuhr, R. E. and Norris, D. R. (1980). Effects of dyadic duration on the relationship between leader behavior perceptions and follower outcomes. *Journal of Organizational Behavior,* II, 379–388.

58. Cox, C. and Makin, P. J. (1994). Overcoming dependency with contingency contracting. *Leadership and Organizational Development Journal,* 15(1), 21–27.

CHAPTER 8 Participative Leadership Behavior

Learning Objectives
After reading this chapter you should be able to do the following:

1. Describe participative leadership behaviors and provide examples of specific leader behaviors.

2. Explain why participative leadership can have positive influences on follower behaviors.

3. Explain why participative leadership can have negative effects on follower behaviors.

4. Describe skills and abilities that are needed to be an effective participative leader.

5. Identify how participative leaders can effectively use sources of power.

6. Describe the individual and organizational benefits that can result from effective participative leadership.

◆ EXAMPLES OF EFFECTIVE PARTICIPATIVE LEADERSHIP

1. When a leader asked for followers' input on a decision, he treated himself on par with them and did not emphasize any status differences between himself and followers. He did not coerce them to accept a solution he favored nor did he impose his opinions. In this manner, followers sensed a situation of trust, inspiration, and responsibility for making a good decision.

2. A department manager asked her immediate and highly experienced subordinates for help in designing a new office layout. She reviewed with them the needs of the department and then asked them to come up with a plan they both could agree on that would meet those needs. The new layout was approved with very few modifications, and everyone was pleased with the results.

3. The dean of a business school in the western United States asked the accounting department faculty to help in recruiting and replacing their department head who was retiring. A group of faculty was selected by the department. The group advertised the position, reviewed and interviewed applicants, invited the most qualified for a visit, and then polled the department members to select the three individuals they found most acceptable. The group then met with all other department heads and administrators in the college and solicited their input on the three finalists. The three were then ranked by the

group in terms of their suitability for the department head position. The individual ranked first was offered the position with the dean's approval but declined to accept. The second ranked candidate was then offered the job and accepted. Nearly all the department faculty and administrators were happy with the decision as well as the process used.

4. Project managers often lack the technical knowledge needed to make important decisions on high-tech jobs. They supervise highly trained professional employees who are closer to the technical problems and have better information, but the manager may have broader knowledge than the technical professional on matters involving other parts of the system or on external pressures. By sharing their ideas through participative one-on-one or group discussions, the manager and the specialist can often arrive at better decisions than either deciding alone (1,2,3).

These are examples of effective participative leadership behaviors by leaders.

◆ DEFINITION, BACKGROUND, AND IMPORTANCE OF PARTICIPATIVE LEADERSHIP BEHAVIORS

Leaders make decisions on many issues—assigning people to jobs, obtaining supplies and equipment, modifying strategies or procedures, or nurturing new group members. For each decision, leaders weigh alternatives and select strategies they believe to be optimal. Many employees, volunteers, and other participants in today's organizations believe they have a right to be involved in and/or influence the decisions that affect them. Their reaction to a decision can be affected by the extent to which the leader consults them and allows them to provide input to the decision process. Frequently employees have extensive experience, information, training, and knowledge that can improve the quality of decisions. For these reasons, leaders often provide opportunities for followers to give input, especially when the decisions will affect followers in some way. When leaders involve followers in the decision processes they are practicing participative leadership.

Managers and researchers have used two meanings for participative leadership. Historically, the most common meaning has been to involve followers in some way in decisions that leaders would otherwise make on their own—through consulting with individuals or holding meetings with groups of followers to discuss decision issues (4). The leader often retains the final authority to make the decision, but followers provide information and ideas that the leader carefully considers in arriving at the final decision. The other meaning of participative leadership goes a bit further. Leaders involve followers in the decision process (such as discussing decision situations or evaluating alternatives) but also share decision-making power with followers by allowing them to directly affect the decision outcomes. Some writers believe that participation exists only when followers share decision-making power equally with the leader (5,6).

In this book, participative leadership refers to numerous behaviors by leaders that involve and include followers in various aspects of the decision process. These behaviors include group discussion sessions or individualized one-on-one meetings in which leaders share decision-making power with followers. This definition thus includes the aspect of sharing the leader's power. It also includes leader actions such as obtaining information from followers, asking their opinions about decision alternatives, or obtaining their ideas about how particular strategies might be implemented. The latter activities may allow the leader to make the final decision, but followers have been involved in and indirectly influence the decision process by providing inputs and assessments that the leader then incorporates into deliberations and the final decision. Our definition of participative leadership includes elements of both the earlier meanings used by managers and researchers.

Participative leadership includes describing a decision problem to a group of followers and asking for their input on the implications of various alternative solutions already developed by the leader. It also involves holding informal conversations with individual followers to draw their ideas out and listening carefully to understand and incorporate their information into a decision solution. Participative leaders hold group meetings with followers to describe the decision situation and ask for followers' suggested solutions. They make sure that all group members who wish to express an opinion about a decision issue are given plenty of opportunity to do so and assure that all follower ideas and contributions are given serious consideration. When recommendations of followers are not implemented as part of the decision solution, participative leaders explain to followers why their suggestions were not included. When a leader and follower disagree, the participative leader may hold a discussion session to air both sides of the disagreement and help resolve the issue. Participative leaders sometimes even assign a decision problem to followers for their resolution (7,8,9,10).

Clearly many variations on these behaviors exist. The increasing level of education and increased feelings of equality in the workforce of the United States and other western countries have produced a widespread desire for upward mobility and interesting work. These factors have resulted in increased pressures from many workers for more participation opportunities. When followers in these countries describe their concept of an ideal leader, they usually include participative leadership behavior as one of the top three qualities (11). Many individuals believe that participative leadership is a major part of effective leadership. Figure 8–1 summarizes major types of participative leadership behaviors.

Participation may also include individuals outside the leader's immediate group of followers, such as peers, upper level leaders, or individuals outside the organization (12). Even though decisions can sometimes benefit from this type of consultation, especially in highly technical environments, the traditional meaning of participative leadership fo-

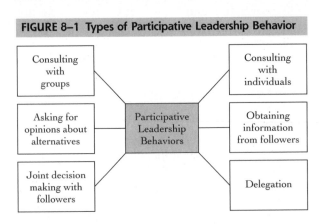

FIGURE 8–1 Types of Participative Leadership Behavior

Consulting with groups

Consulting with individuals

Asking for opinions about alternatives

Participative Leadership Behaviors

Obtaining information from followers

Joint decision making with followers

Delegation

cuses on inclusion of the leader's followers in decisions. This is the meaning used by most experts on participation, and their work will be summarized in this chapter.

In thinking about participative leadership in relation to the other leader behaviors, the reader should keep in mind that participation deals with making decisions, whereas directive leadership (described in chapters 6 and 7) often deals with executing a decision once it has been made. Leadership writers have noted that "a leader can be participative . . . by consulting employees during the decision-making phase, yet still be directive by following up closely on progress toward the ends that have been mutually decided on (13)." This approach might be appropriate for new followers who have up-to-date technical knowledge useful in making decisions but little experience in how to implement that knowledge in a specific organization. Participative and directive leadership can often be used together in a complementary fashion to achieve effective results.

In the United States and many other developed countries, individuals are taught and encouraged to participate in school, at home, at work, and in their communities. They therefore develop an expectation to participate, and the chance to participate leads to positive attitudes (14). As noted, the rising education of the workforce in these same countries reflects a widespread desire for increased independence, achievement, influence, and personal growth. Participative leadership appeals directly to these needs of organizational members by providing opportunities for satisfaction, and this further increases follower morale and satisfaction. Thus rewarded, followers are often motivated to participate actively with their leader to assure continued satisfaction. In many developing countries (such as Mexico or Peoples Republic of China), values other than participation are often emphasized, such as obedience, submission, and respect for authority. In these countries, participative leadership may not be effective (15).

From a group or organizational standpoint, participative leadership improves the availability and flow of information for decision making. For example, followers often have more current information regarding work tasks than do leaders, and their involvement produces better decisions, made with more timely information. Participation also allows followers to learn more about implementing new programs or procedures after decisions are made (16). Some writers have suggested that leaders use participative leadership because they believe it is politically correct and therefore necessary to increase the acceptance of the leader's ideas (17). Clearly, participative leadership has many possible benefits. Bear in mind, however, that no single leadership behavior pattern is perfect for every situation. The situational factors that affect participative leadership are discussed in the next chapter.

One form of participative leadership has been common in Europe for several decades. Specifically, legislation in Sweden, Norway, and the former Yugoslavia and West Germany establishes workers' counsels to advise high-level decision makers or requires union representation on boards of directors. These programs have been used extensively. In the United States and Japan, the approach is more informal and flexible than in Europe. In this case the participative behaviors by a leader are based on a personal relationship between the leader and followers, not on national legislation. Leaders may have casual conversations with a single follower or a prescheduled meeting with an entire work group. This approach to participation allows the leader to adapt behavior to the needs of the situation. It may also permit followers to focus input on decisions that affect them most (18). Experts on participative leadership believe that the informal approach is more impactful on individuals and on group productivity than is

LEADERSHIP IN ACTION: WILMA MANKILLER

Wilma Mankiller, former chief of the Cherokee Nation, is the only woman to have ever held this prestigious office. She was leader of the second largest tribe in the United States, with over 140,000 followers and a budget that exceeded $75 million.

As a participative leader, she found that developing teams is an ideal way to solve problems. According to Mankiller, consulting and collaborating with followers are the key ingredients of a good leader. These skills have also helped to revitalize the tribe. As an example of the faith that she placed in her followers, Mankiller says "after every major upheaval, we have been able to gather together as a people and rebuild a community and a government."

Because she is a woman, Mankiller met with opposition in the beginning of her term of office. But Mankiller feels that being a woman was eventually the key to her success. Studies in the 1980s and 1990s found that women often choose a participative approach to leadership. Wilma agrees. As a woman, she was "more of a team builder, my unscientific observations are that men make unilateral decisions and charge ahead . . . There are exceptions to that, but women tend to . . . do things in a more consultative and collaborative way."

Source: "Wilma Mankiller former Principle Chief of the Cherokee Nation"
http://www.powersource.com/powersource/gallery/people/wilma.html

the legislative approach (19). Although many organizations have implemented quality circles, quality improvement groups, semiautonomous or self-managed work teams, and other programs, it is the informal approach that is described in this and the following chapter.

One expert (20) points out that in formal organizations, some participative leadership may be politically necessary to get a leader's decisions approved and implemented. For example, upper management may want assurance that followers are committed to carrying out a decision. Follower involvement in making the decision may be important in obtaining this assurance. The Leadership in Action box on Wilma Mankiller describes participative behaviors by a leader.

Some writers have described a continuum that shows how a leader can use degrees of participation to include followers in various types of decision situations (21,22). Figure 8–2 shows these different degrees of participation. First, little or no participation is used under the autocratic decision approach—the leader makes the decision with or without input from followers. Next, some participation takes place with the consultation approach—the leader obtains ideas and evaluations from followers, individually or as a group, and uses them to make the decision. With the consultation approach, the leader often obtains follower reactions to the decision option chosen. Increased levels of participation occur with consensus/group decision making, where the leader and followers discuss the decision problem and make the decision together. With this approach followers often have as much influence on the outcome as the leader. Finally, delegation represents the maximum amount of participation, where the leader assigns a decision problem to one or more followers

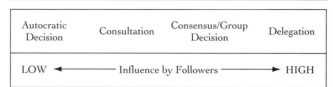

FIGURE 8–2 Degrees of Participation

Autocratic Decision	Consultation	Consensus/Group Decision	Delegation

LOW ◄──────── Influence by Followers ────────► HIGH

Source: Adapted from Gary Yukl (1998) *Leadership in Organizations.* Prentice Hall, Upper Saddle River, New Jersey.

TABLE 8–1 Effective Delegation

TO DELEGATE EFFECTIVELY	
Do	***Avoid***
• understand your authority and responsibility	• lack of agreement on authority and responsibility
• clearly communicate performance expectations	• lack of understanding of group's objectives
• make followers responsible for results	• involvement of followers not trained to effectively perform
• delegate challenging responsibilities	• showing a lack of confidence in followers
• show confidence in followers' ability to perform	• requiring "nothing less than perfection"
• reward accomplishment	• making followers feel insecure

to decide. The leader may provide overall guidance or maintain veto power over the follower's decision.

Real leaders vary their use of these different forms of participation. Some leaders, for example, use consensus decision making only with one or two trusted followers; others prefer large group meetings where all points of view are heard. Some leaders use delegation only after carefully specifying guidelines and limits to the decision option chosen and may require that the final decision be subjected to the leader's approval before implementation (23). Other leaders give followers complete freedom in arriving at and implementing a solution. Most leaders use different combinations of participation at different times, adapting them to each situation and group of followers.

Some writers have argued that delegation is a different form of decision making than participation and is more oriented to follower development (24,25). However, research shows that followers see delegation as only one type of participation used along with other approaches to obtain their involvement (26,27). Consultation and consensus decision making are also excellent learning opportunities for followers. Delegation is an end point in the continuum of participation, in which followers evaluate and make decisions on their own, with a minimum of guidance and oversight by their leader, but it is certainly not the only participative procedure conducive to follower development.

Table 8–1 indicates some leader actions that tend to improve the effectiveness of delegation.

◆ INEFFECTIVE PARTICIPATIVE LEADERSHIP

Like other leader behaviors, participative leadership can be used ineffectively. The following incidents describe leaders' use of participative leadership behaviors in an inappropriate manner:

1. A leader called a meeting, supposedly to obtain follower input on a decision problem. During the discussion it became apparent to followers that the leader had already made the decision, and the meeting's purpose was merely to give followers the perception of participation. When followers realized the leader's real objective, some "tuned out" the discussion entirely and said nothing, whereas others told the leader they favored the option he had already selected.

2. The department's morale was very low due to low wages and a poor benefits package. The manager decided to implement a participation program in which groups of workers in a given job category would discuss how their work could be done more efficiently. Workers saw the participation program as a gimmick to manipulate them and to divert their attention from real issues.

While participative leadership behavior can be used very effectively at times, these two incidents make it clear that in certain situations, and with certain leader motives, participative behaviors and techniques can be rendered not only ineffective but potentially disastrous. The Leadership in Perspective box describes the history of participative leadership and how it may not be effective in all cultures.

◆ HOW TO BE PARTICIPATIVE

Effective leaders typically have or develop specific traits, skills, and sources of power to help them carry out participative leadership with their followers. One very important leader trait with regard to participation is integrity. When the leader is honest with followers, they learn to trust the information and other input the leader provides. When the leader is known to be ethical in dealings both inside and outside the followers' group, they trust the leader to behave consistently with the group's values and to be fair to all group members. When the leader keeps her word, accurately represents the group's position in important issues, and gives credit to members for valuable contributions, follower loyalty and commitment to the group are generated (28). When they feel trust, loyalty, and commitment, followers actively participate with the leader and other members in problem solving and decision making for the group's benefit.

Leaders socialized need for power is another trait that helps them use participative behaviors effectively. Leaders whose personalities include a strong need for power like to influence and control their environment. The socialized form of need for power causes leaders to enjoy coaching and developing followers to build their influence over their environment. They are typically not aggressive or dominant with followers, and they are seldom defensive. They willingly take advice from others who have relevant knowledge and are careful about abusing their position of power. These factors enable a leader to garner followers' ideas and cooperation in a participative manner and effectively address group problems and decisions (29).

LEADERSHIP IN PERSPECTIVE: HISTORY OF PARTICIPATIVE LEADERSHIP

In the year 529, St. Benedict described consultation with followers as an important part of leaders' decision making in the administration of monasteries (30). In 1513, Machiavelli described a similar, though somewhat limited, approach in the administration of governmental affairs. In the 1850s, John Stuart Mill advocated participation in the administration of public affairs.

In U.S. industry in the late 1800s, independent craftsmen were prevalent, and so were strengthening labor unions. Both of these institutions tried to keep control of actual work methods in the hands of employees (31). In the early 1900s, Frederick Taylor's "scientific management" sought to give control of work methods to management (32). Taylor's success assured that management-centered control of workers' activities was prevalent, until research in the 1930s and 1940s addressed the shortcomings of management-centered decision making. During the 1950s and 1960s, writers developed management approaches that increased worker involvement in decision making. These approaches did not return control of work activities to workers, however; instead they simply included workers in discussions of important issues to improve collective effort and motivation and to overcome resistance to the tremendous changes that were beginning to affect U.S. industry (33).

Participative leadership has been written about and researched under several names including consultative decision making, joint decision making, power sharing, decentralization, democratic management, and delegation. Famous early studies on democratic management included discussions of participative leadership as well as other leader behaviors (34,35). A classic study addressed participation as a method for overcoming resistance to change in an industrial organization (36). Research programs at the University of Michigan clearly identified participative leadership as a key aspect of a leader's effectiveness (37). The leadership research program at Ohio State University included participation in early measures of consideration—a type of supportive leadership (38). After leader directiveness and supportiveness, the largest amount of research on leaders' behavior has dealt with participation (39).

Nearly all the new management programs developed in the past 30 years in the United States have included some attention to participative leadership. Many distinguished writers advocate participative approaches as the key to increasing the quality and competitiveness of U. S. industry (40). However, not all countries and cultures value the individualism and independence that characterize the American culture and make participation so appealing there. While participation is undoubtedly an important element in a leader's behavioral repertoire in the United States and other western countries, this is not necessarily the case elsewhere.

Leaders who are effective at self-monitoring can diagnose situations well and adapt their behavior based on social cues from their environment. These individuals learn from the feedback they receive from others and develop an understanding of how their behavior affects others. They also are effective at resolving conflicts with others (41). All these behavioral traits can help a leader obtain and keep group support that is needed for participative decision making.

Participative leaders also develop effective listening skills. These were described in chapter 4 on supportive leadership. In order to promote the trust and cooperation needed for effective follower participation, leaders must demonstrate active listening behaviors such as concentration, careful attention, and providing verbal and nonverbal feedback to followers. This shows that the leader values followers' ideas and input and encourages their further participation.

Effective participative leaders often have a high level of assertiveness skills, but they are not aggressive. They stand up for their own and their group's rights while making it easy for others to do the same. They are not hostile, domineering, or pushy. They do not polarize issues but phrase their statements in order to open an honest dialogue with followers. They make honest statements about their own ideas and feelings and show their willingness to address followers' ideas through mutual discussion and problem solving. These assertiveness skills model and encourage similar behaviors from followers, and they create a constructive environment for participative problem solving and decision making (42).

Participative leaders also demonstrate empathy and social insight. They learn to understand their followers' attitudes, motives, and needs regarding key issues. They recognize the interests, goals, and values that followers have in common and how they are aligned with their own. This empathy and insight usually come from a leader's experience in participative problem-solving situations. They use this understanding to facilitate cooperation and discussion, to build harmony among followers, and to influence followers to pursue collective goals through participative discussions.

A final skill of participative leaders is managing conflict among followers. When two or more group members have interests or goals that seem incompatible, conflict and disagreement can disrupt the productive discussion needed for effective participation. It is important for leaders to determine the source of conflicts when they do occur and to address them proactively. Though conflict resolution strategies will vary with the situation, leaders must recognize that the followers' environment can be a critical factor in the amount of conflict followers perceive and experience. A leader's careful assessment of the organization's expectations of followers, the adequacy of resources, the degree of interdependence with others, and communication problems may be important to resolving conflicts among followers. Conflicts between followers regarding values, beliefs, and goals are often addressed effectively by strategies which encourage collaboration and sharing of desired outcomes. Once conflicts are addressed, followers can get back to the business of joint problem solving and decision making.

Effective leaders usually attempt to develop and utilize at least three types of power to assist them in carrying out participative leadership. When leaders emphasize these sources of power, followers tend to respond well to participation opportunities.

A leader's legitimate power is important for gaining followers' confidence in the participative process. Followers need to know the leader has the authority to invite their involvement in making decisions. The leader must also be in a position to implement decisions that result from follower participation. If followers are uncertain about the leader's authority to use their input to implement group decisions, they will likely have little motivation to respond to participative behaviors by their leader. A leader's legitimate power thus gives followers confidence that their participation can have a meaningful and useful result.

A leader who has substantial connection/resource power can often minimize conflict and facilitate interactions among followers. Competition among members for scarce resources is a very common source of conflict in groups. Leaders who can provide ample resources remove this problem and allow members to concentrate their efforts on problem solving and decision making. When members' work-related needs are met, they are unlikely to be anxious about their jobs and are more accommodating with coworkers. The leader who has connections and networks that include influential others outside the group will likely be highly respected by followers. This respect typically results in willing cooperation and active participation when leaders solicit follower input for decisions.

A leader's expert power is also an asset to participative leadership, just as it is to supportive and directive leadership. The leader who has expert power can facilitate followers' participation by providing knowledge, skill, and ability that support their involvement in the decision-making process. The more important the decision, the greater the likelihood that the leader's expert power will be a factor in supporting follower participation. The leader can provide followers with needed knowledge, be available as a source of technical advice, provide explanations of processes, and refer followers to needed sources of assistance or information. Figure 8–3 summarizes the skills, traits, and sources of power for effective participative leadership.

Leaders do not all use the same amount of participation, and a given leader will usually vary the type or amount of participation used with followers in different situations (43). Personal characteristics of leaders can influence their use of participative leadership. For example, although the leader's gender is not conclusively related to leader directiveness or supportiveness, current research shows that female leaders tend to use participative approaches to decision making more frequently than male leaders (44). It may be that the social skills of women who have achieved leadership positions allow them to incorporate others more easily into the decision process, or perhaps, female leaders are more frequently censured than male leaders when they are autocratic (45). The Leadership in Action box on Wilma Mankiller is a good example of a female leader's participative approach.

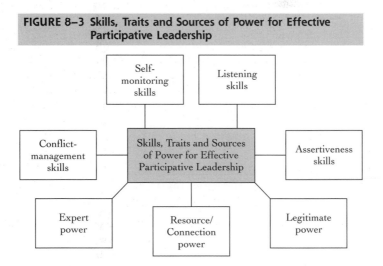

FIGURE 8–3 Skills, Traits and Sources of Power for Effective Participative Leadership

LEADERSHIP SELF-ASSESSMENT: OBTAINING EFFECTIVE PARTICIPATION

Instructions: Indicate the extent to which you engage in the following behaviors when obtaining the participation of others in decision making, using a scale of
(5) almost always; (4) usually; (3) occasionally; (2) seldom; (1) almost never.

1. I take time to understand followers' preferences
   before trying to obtain their participation in decisions.   1   2   3   4   5

2. I involve everyone in making decisions, regardless
   of their needs and wants.   1   2   3   4   5

3. I provide others with clear information on the
   objectives and desired results of their participation.   1   2   3   4   5

4. I have people participate in decisions regardless of
   their knowledge or ability to make effective
   contributions.   1   2   3   4   5

5. I get input from others to clarify their reasons for
   suggesting alternative decisions or actions.   1   2   3   4   5

6. I make evaluative comments on the decision input
   from others before I fully understand their position.   1   2   3   4   5

7. After making comments about an individual's
   suggestions, I allow the individual to further
   explain his/her ideas.   1   2   3   4   5

8. I immediately let people know when they make
   suggestions that I disagree with.   1   2   3   4   5

9. I reward individuals who contribute ideas and
   suggestions by comments showing appreciation.   1   2   3   4   5

10. I take into account the other person's attitudes,
    beliefs, and values in order to obtain effective
    participation.   1   2   3   4   5

Interpretation: If you rated items 1, 3, 5, 7, 9, and 10 as 4 or 5, you are probably using participative leadership effectively. If you rated items 2, 4, 6, and 8 as 4 or 5, you may not use participative leadership effectively.

Source: Items adapted from research by P. W. Dorfman, J. P. Howell, B. C. G. Cotton and U. Tate, "Leadership within the 'discontinuous hierarchy' structure of the military: Are effective leadership behaviors similar within and across command structures?" In K.E. Clark, M.B. Clark and D.P. Campbell (Eds.), *Impacts of Leadership.* Greensboro, North Carolina: Center for Creative Leadership.

Some studies have shown that leaders who have much work experience or are highly educated are more participative (46,47,48,49). These factors may allow the leader to be comfortable and secure with the leadership position and less threatened by potentially conflicting ideas. Followers often desire to be involved in decisions that affect them, and experienced or educated leaders may recognize and respond to their desires.

LEADERSHIP IN PERSPECTIVE: WHAT ARE GROUPS GOOD AT DOING?

Many years ago a famous learning psychologist named Robert Thorndike (50) conducted an experiment that showed how the type of problem was a critical factor in determining if an individual or a group was more effective at finding a solution. His results showed that groups were much better at solving crossword puzzles, but individuals were better at constructing them. Both of these tasks are complex but there are important differences.

Vroom and Jago (51) pointed out that solving crossword puzzles involves solving a large number of small, loosely connected problems, each having one correct answer. One can begin anywhere, jump around randomly, and still solve the puzzle efficiently. Members of a group can work independently and effectively to solve the puzzle. In constructing crossword puzzles, however, there is no single correct solution, and any word added must be coordinated with previous words and those added later. Instead of being loosely coupled, the words must be tightly coupled in order and sequence, making coordination very important. Groups are less effective at completing this type of project, as they also are at writing a novel or composing a symphony. Groups can address themselves to large projects with numerous independent subtasks, but they are much less effective at combining complex patterns of highly interconnected tasks into a single integrated whole.

Leaders' perceptions of their followers also influence their use of participative leadership. For example, participative leadership is likely to be used in the following circumstances: when the leader perceives followers as having competence, expertise, or essential information to make a quality decision; when follower acceptance of the decision outcome is essential; when followers need to develop their decision skills; or when followers share organizational goals with the leader (52,53,54,55). It is understandable that leaders carefully consider their followers when making a commitment to use participative leadership.

Some organizational factors constrain or prevent a leader from using participative leadership. For example, participation is difficult to use effectively when the leader works in a highly bureaucratic organization or has very little time to make a decision (56,57). If the leader is highly authoritarian or there is a large social or occupational status difference between leader and followers, the leader may have less confidence in followers and therefore be less likely to involve them in decisions (58,59). These constraints make sense, although they are based on limited research in organizations.

The appropriateness of participative leadership in different cultures and countries is difficult to determine because leadership practices must be consistent with the cultural norms in each society. These norms determine the amount and type of worker participation that is expected in that culture (60). If there is a tradition or "cultural imperative" of participation (as in the United States), then participation is often expected; if there is a tradition of authoritarian decision making, then participation is not expected, and followers may dislike it.

In a classic study of international management, three well-known researchers surveyed leaders in fourteen countries. They found that leaders in all countries professed a belief in the importance of participation, but most of the leaders outside the United States did not trust the average follower's capability to show initiative and share leadership responsibilities (61). Later studies showed this tendency was less pronounced but still present when leaders outside the United States described only followers of their own nationality. These findings probably result from cultural mandates that make leaders feel they should approve of participation even though they may not believe it is the most effective approach.

It is likely that the meaning of participative leadership is also different in different cultures. One writer noted that in Japan participation means that followers are given the honor of presenting their views to organizational superiors (62). In the United States, participation often means not only that followers can present their ideas, but that those ideas are reflected in the decisions made. If there is no evidence that the followers' input is included in the decisions, then American workers are more likely to feel that genuine participation has not taken place. This distinction is another example of how cultural norms affect the meanings, expectations, and effectiveness of participation as well as other types of leader behavior. Clearly leaders must consider the cultural norms and expectations of followers and peers when they use participative leadership.

The Leadership in Perspective box shows that group problem solving is highly effective at certain types of tasks, but not all tasks.

◆ EFFECTS OF PARTICIPATIVE LEADERSHIP

Numerous books, chapters, and research articles published in the United States during the past thirty years have focused on the effects of participative leadership. A large portion of these publications are qualitative descriptions of specific management programs or other examples of participation in real organizations (63,64,65). Another large group of studies is quantitative in nature, meaning that researchers actually measured the extent of participative leadership and its effect on followers' satisfaction, performance, commitment to decisions, and other important outcomes. These studies allow a good assessment of the real effects of participation, because the researchers are careful to rule out other possible causes of positive or negative results. Although researchers do not uniformly agree about what to conclude from this research, several recent summaries have helped to discern some general patterns (66,67,68,69).

EFFECTS ON FOLLOWER/GROUP PSYCHOLOGICAL REACTIONS

Participative leadership has a very consistent favorable effect on the satisfaction of followers, including satisfaction with their leader, with their work, and general satisfaction with their organization and job situation (70,71,72,73). Laboratory studies and studies of real organizations generally find that followers like participative leadership better than autocratic leadership, especially in the United States (74). Several reasons are usually given for this finding. First, when asked to participate, followers can reflect their own interests and concerns in the outcomes of decisions that affect them. Second, participation gives followers an opportunity to utilize their own untapped talents, and this helps satisfy their needs for competence, self-fulfillment and personal growth. Third, it allows followers to make a significant contribution to a valued group, thereby satisfying needs for esteem and accomplishment.

Participative leadership also improves followers' motivation and commitment to decisions. This commitment is often shown by less resistance to change produced by the decision, by smoother implementation of the decision option chosen, and/or by increased acceptance and motivation to make the decision work (75,76). One writer described the reason for this result of participation by emphasizing that people support what they build (77). By participating in the decision, followers often have their self-esteem tied to its outcome. They may also see it as beneficial to them, and they likely understand the reasoning behind the decision better than if they had not participated.

EFFECTS ON FOLLOWERS' PERFORMANCE AND BEHAVIOR

A large number of studies have reported that participative leadership results in high levels of performance or productivity with followers or groups of followers. These studies were conducted with many different types of followers and organizations, such as U.S. Army officers and NCOs (78), library directors (79), U.S. Army clerks (80), aerospace firms (81), light manufacturing firms (82), and other types of formal organizations (83,84). Although some researchers still disagree about whether improved performance results from participation, there are sound reasons for expecting improved performance. First, increased amounts of information are likely available from followers to help identify and evaluate alternative courses of action. Second, increased motivation to participate and to successfully implement decisions results, because participation helps satisfy followers' esteem and social needs.

Numerous studies have indicated that the quality of decisions is improved with participative leadership (85,86,87,88). A quality decision is highly likely to help attain organizational goals because it is well reasoned and consistent with available information and organizational goals and objectives (89). High-quality decisions result from participation because more complete information is available to participants, and a more comprehensive discussion of the decision situation and possible alternatives often occurs.

Much recent research on decision quality deals with the model of participative leadership originally developed by Vroom and Yetton (90) and further developed by Vroom and Jago (91). Their model emphasizes follower and situational characteristics of each decision problem and provides advice on how to use participative techniques to involve followers in decision making. These researchers report that the impact of participation on decision quality is highly affected by factors such as the existence of shared goals among followers, the amount of knowledge and information possessed by followers, group size, disagreement among participants, and the nature of the problem. These situational factors will be discussed in detail in the next chapter on situational factors and participative leadership. At this point, it seems safe to say that participative leadership affects decision quality, but the type and degree of impact depends on the decision situation.

Researchers also point to the development of followers as an outcome of participation. Including followers in discussions to generate and evaluate decision options develops their decision making skills and may improve relations among followers. Participative discussions may also help integrate individual and organizational goals and improve followers' "self-management" skills.

Participative leadership can also have several possible undesirable results. First, participative decision making usually takes more time than autocratic decisions, and this may be a critical factor in decision success (such as in a medical team facing an emergency). Participative discussions also take followers away from other tasks. Although they can benefit from the participative discussions, the urgency of their other tasks and decreased productivity during discussion sessions must be evaluated to determine which is more important. One writer also described the training costs for both leaders and followers to prepare them for effective consultation, group decision making, or delegation. Other support costs include meeting rooms and staff support to assure that necessary information is available to those who are participating in decisions (92). Finally, some managers are not comfortable with participation and will resist if encouraged to use it. In turn, resistance can cause resentment and lost productivity for those working with this manager, so the final decision to use participation should probably be left to the individual manager.

The impact of participative leadership in other countries depends on the norms and expectations that exist there. Studies in western Europe generally find that participative leadership has positive effects, particularly on follower satisfaction (93). One study compared the participative practices of German and British managers and found they were quite similar in the degree of participation used for different types of decisions. As in the United States, the more formal education the managers had, the more they used participative leadership. These findings likely reflect the cultural similarities between the United States and western Europe.

In the Middle East, the predominant cultures differ dramatically from that of the United States and western Europe, and the impacts of participative leadership are more varied. One researcher found that Turkish supervisors were significantly less participative than Americans and that the followers of Turkish supervisors were significantly less satisfied with participative leadership than were followers of American supervisors. The same researcher also found that Turkish supervisors were more authoritarian than Americans, which explained their low level of participativeness (94). However, researchers in India found that Indian college students responded to participative leadership in a laboratory study by showing increased productivity (95). In Nigeria, participative leadership was not effective in improving follower performance or satisfaction for construction workers and teachers (96). Similar results occurred in Latin America and Asia. In a recent study of five countries, researchers showed that participative leadership had positive impacts in the United States only, and not in Mexico, Korea, Taiwan, or Japan (97). It appears that participative leadership behaviors, as described here, may not be effective in certain countries or groups of countries where the culture does not include egalitarianism and popular participation by all persons.

Summary

Participative leadership consists of involving followers in making decisions that the leader would otherwise make alone. Participative behaviors include consulting with followers to obtain their input, meeting with groups of followers to jointly generate and explore alternatives, or delegating decisions to individuals or groups to make on their own with or without the final approval of the leader.

Participative leadership gives followers opportunities to satisfy needs for competence, self-control, independence, esteem, and personal growth. Participation has a long history as a leadership technique and has been particularly popular in the United States and parts of western Europe for several decades. Female leaders and/or leaders who are highly experienced and educated tend to be participative with followers. Leaders also tend to use participative behaviors when followers are competent, when they share the organization's goals with the leader, when followers must implement the decision, or when they need to develop their decision skills.

Overall, the evidence shows that participative leadership improves followers' satisfaction and performance, although the effects are not strong and are most likely heavily influenced by characteristics of followers and the decision situation. Some evidence indicates that participation increases follower commitment to decisions and decision quality, but this also is likely affected by the situation. Participative leadership also has drawbacks: it takes time, removes followers from other tasks, requires training and other support, and may be resisted by some managers. Figure 8–4 summarizes much of this chapter in terms of the Leadership Process Model described in chapter 2. Participative leader behaviors are shown as influencing follower and group psychological reactions, which affect important follower behaviors and outcomes. Chapter 9 will describe the effects of various follower and situational characteristics on participative leadership.

FIGURE 8–4 Partial Model of the Participative Leadership Process

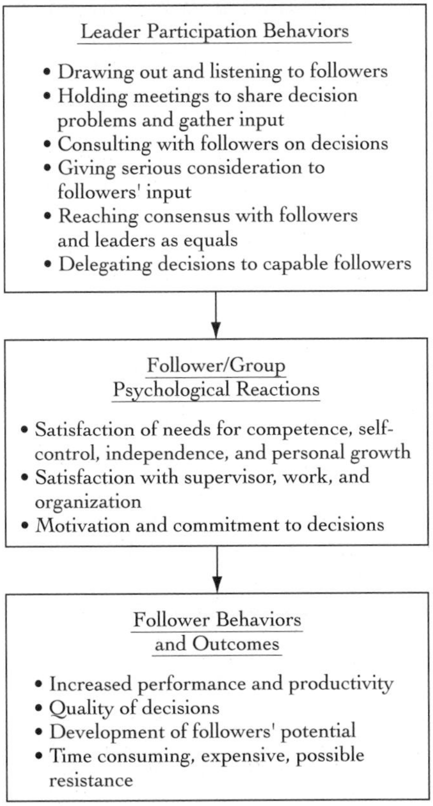

Leader Participation Behaviors

- Drawing out and listening to followers
- Holding meetings to share decision problems and gather input
- Consulting with followers on decisions
- Giving serious consideration to followers' input
- Reaching consensus with followers and leaders as equals
- Delegating decisions to capable followers

↓

Follower/Group Psychological Reactions

- Satisfaction of needs for competence, self-control, independence, and personal growth
- Satisfaction with supervisor, work, and organization
- Motivation and commitment to decisions

↓

Follower Behaviors and Outcomes

- Increased performance and productivity
- Quality of decisions
- Development of followers' potential
- Time consuming, expensive, possible resistance

Key Terms and Concepts in This Chapter ▪

- assertiveness skill
- connection/resource power
- consensus group decisions
- consultation
- delegation
- development of followers

- empathy
- expert power
- joint decision making
- legitimate power
- listening skills

- managing conflict
- participative leadership
- quality of decisions
- self-monitoring
- socialized need for power

Review and Discussion Questions ▪

1. Describe participative leader behaviors that had a positive effect on your behavior. Why did these leader behaviors have a positive effect on you?
2. Describe participative leader behaviors that were ineffective and had a negative effect on you. Why did these leader behaviors have a negative effect on you?
3. What could a leader do to develop some of the skills and traits needed to provide effective participative leadership?
4. What advice would you give to a leader on how to use and not use power to be effective in participative leadership?
5. Should most leaders be more participative with their followers? What are the reasons for your position?
6. Do some employees dislike and avoid managers' attempts to get them to participate in decision making? If so, how would you explain their avoidance behavior?
7. Describe a situation where someone delegated responsibility to you. Did the delegation result in effective or ineffective performance? Can you explain why?
8. What specific behaviors should a leader engage in to be effective as a participative leader?

Exercise: Actions to Obtain Participation ▪

You supervise a group of copy editors in a medium-sized publishing firm. While talking with employees at the company recognition dinner your manager became convinced that the employees in your department were not participating in departmental decisions. Employees told your manager that they had suggestions and ideas to improve the productivity in your department. They mentioned methods for cutting costs and increasing quality that impressed your manager. They also told him of grievances that he felt had the potential for producing major problems in employee relations. As a supervisor, you have been told to take courses of action to obtain employee participation on possible improvements in your department.

Evaluate the following list of actions to obtain participation from your employees. Which actions would you take? Why? Which actions would you avoid taking? Why?

1. Take a confidential survey of employees to obtain suggestions for improving the department.
2. Offer a monthly award for the best suggestion to cut costs or improve quality.

3. Provide employees with additional information on customers, quality control standards, costs, and how individual jobs contribute to department productivity.
4. Have the human resources department meet with employees to determine problems and complaints.
5. Become better friends with employees by participating with them in activities outside of work.
6. Have employees elect a representative group to evaluate ideas for improving productivity and make recommendations to you.
7. Establish a suggestion program so employees can make suggestions by using a suggestion box.
8. Listen in on employees' conversations whenever possible.
9. Have an open door policy and encourage employees to provide input on pending decisions.
10. Hold weekly meetings with employees to share important issues with them and obtain their input.

◆◆◆ **Case Incident**

Let's All Be Participative Managers

John Peterson is president of JP Chemical Corporation. He is committed to continually improving the company's management through the use of modern management practices. To get new ideas, he attended a management development seminar at a local university. The seminar focused on using participation to improve productivity and to increase employee commitment to their jobs. Mr. Peterson became convinced that all his managers needed to immediately implement participative management practices.

To ensure implementation of participative management, Mr. Peterson sent an e-mail to all the company managers that stated: "I am convinced that we must immediately begin to practice participative management. The attachments to this e-mail are the handouts from the university management development seminar that explain how to practice participative management. I expect each of you to implement the practices in the attachments starting next week. As a company, we are now committed to practicing participation. Any managers who do not implement participative practices will find it impossible to remain with this company."

QUESTIONS

1. Do you think President Peterson's e-mail will result in effective participative practices by the managers? Why?
2. How do you think managers will react to the message in the e-mail? How would you feel if you were one of the managers who received Mr. Peterson's e-mail?
3. Do you think Mr. Peterson should have approached implementing participative practices in a different way? If so, how?

Endnotes ■

1. Sinha, T. N. and Sinha, B. P. (1977). Styles of leadership and their effects on group productivity. *Indian Journal of Industrial Relations*, 13(2), 209–223.
2. Vroom, V. H. and Jago, A .G. (1988). *The New Leadership: Managing Participation in Organizations*. Upper Saddle River, NJ: Prentice Hall.
3. Sayles, L. R. (1989). *Leadership: Managing in real organizations*. (2nd ed.) New York: McGraw-Hill.
4. Bass, B. M. (1990). *Bass & Stogdill's Handbook of Leadership*. New York: The Free Press.
5. Ibid.
6. Vroom, V. H. and Jago, A. G. (1988). *The New Leadership: Managing Participation in Organizations*.
7. Ibid.
8. Bass, B. M. *Bass & Stogdill's Handbook of Leadership*.
9. Muczyk, J. P. and Reimann, B. C. (1987). The case for directive leadership. *Academy of Management Executive*, 1(3), 301–311.
10. Wexley, K. N. and Snell, S. A. (1987). Managerial power: A neglected aspect of the performance appraisal interview. *Journal of Business Research*, 15, 45–54.
11. Graves, L. M. (1983). Implicit leadership theory: A comparison to two-dimensional leadership theory. *Proceedings: Eastern Academy of Management*, Pittsburgh, PA, 93–95.
12. Yukl, G. (1998). *Leadership in Organizations*. (4th ed.) Upper Saddle River, NJ: Prentice Hall.
13. Muczyk, J. P. and Reimann, B. C. The case for directive leadership.
14. Kenis, I. (1977). A cross-cultural study of personality and leadership. *Group and Organizational Studies*, 2(1), 49–60.
15. Lawler, E. E. III. (1986). *High Involvement Management*. San Francisco: Jossey-Bass.
16. Miller, K. I. and Monge, P. R. (1986). Participation, satisfaction and productivity: A meta-analytic review. *Academy of Management Review*, 29, 727–753.
17. Clark, A. W. and Witherspoon, J. A. (1973). Manager's conflict: Democratic management versus distrust of people's capacity. *Psychological Reports*, 32(3), 815–819.
18. Lawler, E. E., Renwick, P. A. and Bullock, R. J. (1981). Employee influence on decisions: An analysis. *Journal of Occupational Behavior*, 2, 115–123.
19. Vroom, V. H. and Jago, A. G. *The New Leadership: Managing Participation in Organizations*.
20. Yukl, G. *Leadership in Organizations*.
21. Vroom, V. H. and Jago, A. G. *The New Leadership: Managing Participation in Organizations*.
22. Tannenbaum, R. and Schmidt, W. H. (1958). How to choose a leadership pattern. *Harvard Business Review*, 36, March-April, 95–101.
23. Yukl, G. *Leadership in Organizations*.
24. Leana, C. R. (1987). Power relinquishment versus power sharing: Theoretical clarification and empirical comparison of delegation and participation. *Journal of Applied Psychology*, 72 (2), 228–233.
25. Locke, E. A. and Schweiger, D. M. (1979). Participation in decision making: One more look, in B. M. Staw (Ed.), *Research in Organizational Behavior*, Vol. 1: 265–339. Greenwich, CT: JAI Press.
26. Bass, B. M. *Bass & Stogdill's Handbook of Leadership*.
27. Bass, B. M., Valenzi, E. R., Farrow, D. L. and Soloman, R. J. (1975). Management styles associated with organizational, task, personal and interpersonal contingencies. *Journal of Applied Psychology*, 60, 720–729.
28. Yukl, G. *Leadership in Organizations* (4th ed.).
29. Bass, B. M. *Bass & Stogdill's Handbook of Leadership*.
30. Vroom, V. H. and Jago, A. G. *The New Leadership: Managing Participation in Organizations*.
31. Ibid.
32. Taylor, F. W. (1911). *Principles of Scientific Management*. New York: Harpers.
33. Vroom, V. H. and Jago, A. G. *The New Leadership: Managing Participation in Organizations*.

34. Lewin, K. and Lippitt, R. (1938). An experimental approach to the study of autocracy and democracy: A preliminary note. *Sociometry,* 1, 292–300.

35. Lippitt, R. (1940). An experimental study of the effect of democratic and authoritarian group atmospheres. *University of Iowa Studies in Child Welfare,* 16, 43–95.

36. Coch, L. and French, J. R. P. (1948). Overcoming resistance to change. *Human Relations,* 1, 512–532.

37. Likert, R. (1967). *The Human Organization: It's Management and Value.* New York: McGraw-Hill.

38. Bass, B. M. *Bass & Stogdill's Handbook of Leadership.*

39. Yukl, G. *Leadership in Organizations* (4th ed.).

40. Lawler, E. E. III. *High Involvement Management.*

41. Dobbins, G. H., Long, W. S., Dedrick, E. J. and Clemons, T. C. (1990). The role of self-monitoring and gender on leadership emergence: A laboratory and field study. *Journal of Management,* 16, 609–618.

42. Hughes, R. L., Ginnett, R. C. and Curphy, G. J. (1996). *Leadership: Enhancing the Lessons of Experience.* Chicago: Irwin.

43. Hill, W. A. (1973). Leadership style: Rigid or flexible? *Organizational Behavior and Human Performance,* 9, 35–47.

44. Eagly, A. H. and Johnson, B. T. (1990). Gender and leadership style: A meta-analysis. *Psychological Bulletin,* 108(2), 233–256.

45. Jago, A. G. and Vroom, V. H. (1982). Sex differences in the incidence and evaluation of participative leader behavior. *Journal of Applied Psychology,* 67, 776–783.

46. Seversky, P. M. (1982). Trust, need to control, and the tendency to delegate: A study of the delegation behavior of superintendents. *Dissertation Abstracts International,* 43(9A), 2851.

47. Heller, F. A. and Yukl, G. (1969). Participation, managerial decision-making, and situational variables. *Organizational Behavior and Human Performance,* 4, 227–241.

48. Bass, B. M. *Bass & Stogdill's Handbook of Leadership.*

49. Jago, A. G. and Vroom, V. H. Sex differences in the incidence and evaluation of participative leader behavior.

50. Thorndike, R. L. (1938). On what type of task will a group do well? *Journal of Abnormal and Social Psychology,* 33, 409–413.

51. Vroom, V. H. and Jago, A. G. *The New Leadership: Managing Participation in Organizations.*

52. Field, R. H. G., Read, P. C., and Louviere, J. J. (1990). The effects of situation attributes on decision making choice in the Vroom-Jago model of participation in decision making. *Leadership Quarterly,* 1, 165–176.

53. Vroom, V. H. and Jago, A. G. *The New Leadership: Managing Participation in Organizations.*

54. Leana, C. R. Power relinquishment versus power sharing: Theoretical clarification and empirical comparison of delegation and participation.

55. Jago, A. G. (1978). A test of spuriousness in descriptive models of participative leader behavior. *Journal of Applied Psychology,* 63, 383–387.

56. Leana, C. R. Power relinquishment versus power sharing: Theoretical clarification and empirical comparison of delegation and participation.

57. Mohr, L. B. (1977). Authority and democracy in organizations. *Human Relations,* 30, 919–947.

58. Vroom, V. H. (1960). *Some Personality Determinants of the Effects of Participation.* Upper Saddle River, NJ: Prentice Hall.

59. Mohr, L. B. (1977). Authority and democracy in organizations. *Human Relations,* 30, 919–947.

60. Grunwald, W. and Bernthal, W. F. (1983). Controversy in German management: The Harzburg model experience. *Academy of Management Review,* 8(2), 233–241.

61. Haire, M., Ghiselli, E. E. and Porter, L. W. (1966). *Managerial Thinking: An International Study.* New York: Wiley.

62. Kerr, S. (1984). Leadership and participation. *Working paper,* University of Southern California.

63. Peters, T. J. and Waterman, R. H., Jr. (1982). *In Search of Excellence: Lessons from*

America's Best-Run Companies. New York: Harper and Row.

64. Lawler, E. E. III. *High Involvement Management.*

65. Kouzes, J. M. and Posner, B. Z. (1987). *Credibility: How Leaders Gain and Lose it, Why People Demand it.* San Francisco: Jossey-Bass.

66. Cotton, J. L., Vollrath, D. A., Froggett, K. L., Lengnick-Hall, M. L. and Jennings, K. R. (1988). Employee participation: Diverse forms and different outcomes. *Academy of Management Review, 13, 8–22.*

67. Leana, C. R., Locke, E. A. and Schweiger, D. M. (1990). Fact and fiction in analyzing research on participative decision making: A critique of Cotton, Vollrath, Froggett, Lengnick-Hall and Jennings, *Academy of Management Review, 15, 137–146.*

68. Wagner, J. A. III, and Gooding, R. Z. (1987). Shared influence and organizational behavior: A meta-analysis of situational variables expected to moderate participation-outcome relationships. *Academy of Management Journal, 30, 524–541.*

69. Wagner, J. A. III, (1994). Participation effects on performance and satisfaction: A reconsideration of research evidence. *Academy of Management Review, 19 (2), 312–330.*

70. Dorfman, P. W., Howell, J. P., Cotton, B. C. G. and Tate, U. (1992). Leadership within the "discontinuous hierarchy" structure of the military: Are effective leadership behaviors similar within and across command structures? In K. E. Clark, M. B. Clark and D. P. Campbell (Eds.), *Impacts of Leadership.* Greensboro, North Carolina: Center for Creative Leadership.

71. Pace, L. A., Hartley, D. E. and Davenport, L. A. (1992). Beyond situationalism: Subordinate preferences and perceived leader impact. In K. E. Clark, M. B. Clark and D. P. Campbell (Eds.), *Impacts of Leadership.* Greensboro, North Carolina: Center for Creative Leadership.

72. York, R. O. and Denton, R. T. (1990). Leadership behavior and supervisor performance: The view from the bottom. *The Clinical Supervisor.* 8(1), 93–108.

73. Indvik, J. (1986). Path-goal theory of leadership: A meta-analysis. *Proceedings of the Academy of Management.* 189–192, Chicago.

74. Bass, B. M. *Bass & Stogdill's Handbook of Leadership.*

75. Delva, W. L., Wacker, J. and Teas, K. (1985). Motivational antecedents: A test of predictor models. *Psychological Reports, 56, 447–461.*

76. Tichy, N. and Devanna, M. (1986). *Transformational Leadership.* New York: Wiley.

77. Bass, B. M. *Bass & Stogdill's Handbook of Leadership.*

78. Dorfman, P. W., Howell, J. P., Cotton, B. C. G. and Tate, U. Leadership within the "discontinuous hierarchy" structure of the military: Are effective leadership behaviors similar within and across command structures?

79. Solomon, R. J. (1976). An examination of the relationship between a survey feedback O.D. Technique and the work environment. *Personnel Psychology, 29, 583–594.*

80. Reeder, R. R. (1981). The importance of the superior's technical competence in the subordinates' work. *Dissertation Abstracts International, 42(6A), 2830.*

81. Hinrichs, J. R. (1978). An eight-year follow-up of a management assessment center. *Journal of Applied Psychology, 63, 596–601.*

82. Bowers, D. G. and Seashore, S. E. (1966). Predicting organizational effectiveness with a four-factor theory of leadership. *Administrative Science Quarterly, 11, 238–263.*

83. Miller, K. I. and Monge, P. R. Participation, satisfaction and productivity: A meta-analytic review.

84. Lawler, E. E. III. *High Involvement Management.*

85. Leana, C. R. (1985). A partial test of Janis' group think model: Effects of group cohesiveness and leader behavior on defective decision making. *Journal of Management, 11, 5–17.*

86. Mitroff, I. I. and Mason, R. O. (1981). The metaphysics of policy and planning: A reply to Cosier. *Academy of Management Review, 6, 649–651.*

87. Mitroff, I. I. (1982). Dialectic squared: A fundamental difference in perception of the meanings of some key concepts in social science. *Decision Science,* 13, 222–224.

88. Lorge, I., Fox, D., Davitz, J. and Brenner, M. (1958). A survey of studies contrasting the quality of group performance and individual performance, 1920–1957. *Psychological Bulletin,* 55, 337–370.

89. Vroom, V. H. and Jago, A. G. *The New Leadership: Managing Participation in Organizations.*

90. Vroom, V. H. and Yetton, P. W. (1973). *Leadership and Decision Making.* Pittsburgh: University of Pittsburgh Press.

91. Vroom, V. H. and Jago, A. G. *The New Leadership: Managing Participation in Organizations.*

92. Hammer, M. and Champy, J. (1993). *Reengineering the Corporation.* New York: Harper Business.

93. Drenth, P. J. D and Koopman, P. L. (1984). A contingency approach to participative leadership: How good? In J. G. Hunt, D. Hosking, C. A. Schriesheim, and R. Stewart, (Eds.) *Leadership and Managers: International perspectives on managerial behavior and leadership.* New York: Pergamon.

94. Kenis, I. A cross-cultural study of personality and leadership.

95. Sinha, T. N. and Sinha, B. P. Styles of leadership and their effects on group productivity.

96. Ejiogu, A. M. (1983). Participative management in a developing economy: Poison or placebo. *Journal of Applied Behavioral Science,* 19(3), 239–247.

97. Dorfman, P. W., Howell, J. P., Hibino, S., Lee, J., Tate, U. and Bautista, A. (1994). Leadership in western and Asian countries: Commonalties and differences in effective leadership processes and substitutes across cultures. *Leadership Quarterly,* 8(3), 233–274.

CHAPTER 9

Situational Dynamics of Participative Leadership

Learning Objectives
After reading this chapter you should be able to do the following:

1. Identify characteristics of followers that make participative leadership highly effective and characteristics that make it ineffective.

2. Identify organizational and task characteristics that make participative leadership highly effective and characteristics that make it ineffective.

3. Describe how leaders can modify situations to increase the effectiveness of their participative leadership.

4. Explain how leaders can modify followers' work situations to make followers less dependent on the leader's participative leadership.

5. Describe how followers, situations, and participative leaders interact and affect each other in a dynamic process.

◆ SITUATIONS WHERE PARTICIPATION MAY OR MAY NOT BE EFFECTIVE

In the previous chapter participative leadership was described in detail, as were leaders' traits, skills, and sources of power that help leaders effectively use participation with their followers. The effects or impacts of participative leadership were also described, and it was noted that often the results may depend on the type of followers involved or the situation in which the leaders' participative behavior takes place. With certain types of followers or in specific situations, participation can be very effective. With other followers or other situations, participation may not be effective. This chapter describes the situational and follower characteristics that may determine how much influence a participative leader has on followers. It also addresses how leaders can influence situations to allow for effective participation.

The following are situations in which participative leadership may or may not be effective. Place an X next to those situations where you believe participation will be most effective.

1. _____ Followers are working on tasks that are very important for the organization's success.

2. _____ Followers' acceptance and commitment are needed to successfully implement a decision.

3. _____ Followers' work tasks are highly predictable and repetitive with no variation in the methods for completion.

4. _____ The leader must make several emergency decisions immediately with very little time to gather input and information.

5. _____ The leader and followers work in an environment that is extremely uncertain and rapidly changing.

6. _____ Followers are highly competent and possess knowledge and information needed to make an effective decision.

7. _____ An extensive set of written rules, regulations, and procedures exist to direct followers in their work and decision making.

8. _____ Followers have high needs for independence and seek opportunities for achievement and self-fulfillment on the job.

Several of the situations described above reflect a need for participative leadership. Items 1, 2, 5, 6, and 8 include follower and situational factors that can make participative leadership especially useful and effective with followers. Other situations can do the opposite. That is, they can make participation ineffective as an influence strategy. Items 3 and 4 are examples of such situations—that is, participative leadership will not be expected and will have little value to followers, or there is inadequate time to use participation effectively. Followers may reject a leader who attempts to use participative behaviors in these situations. Item 7 describes a situation where an organizational factor replaces the need for participative leadership by the leader. In this situation, written rules, procedures, and regulations provide clear guidance for leaders and followers in how decisions are to be made, making participation unnecessary. In this situation, the leader had best choose another strategy to influence followers. The situational and follower characteristics that make participative leadership highly effective, ineffective, or unnecessary are described in detail in this chapter.

The Leadership in Action box with Bob Gore describes his extremely participative leadership style, which helps produce responsibility and creativity throughout his company. Employees seem to respond very favorably to this participative leadership pattern at W. L. Gore & Associates.

◆ SITUATIONAL FACTORS THAT INCREASE EFFECTIVENESS OF PARTICIPATIVE LEADERSHIP

When certain characteristics of the situation or of followers are present, a leader's participative behaviors have very positive effects on followers' psychological reactions or behaviors. These situational and follower characteristics are enhancers of participative leadership.

LEADERSHIP IN ACTION: BOB GORE—PRESIDENT OF W. L. GORE & ASSOCIATES

Bob Gore is such a strong advocate of participative management that he refers to employees at every level as his associates. W. L. Gore & Associates, makers of Gore-Tex, employs approximately 10,000 people worldwide without a hierarchy. The "lattice" structure at Gore-Tex is intentionally decentralized to allow individuals to work across disciplines. Gore's associates participate in business issues ranging from forecasting and planning to developing strategies for distribution and market positioning. Associates at Gore are also asked to participate in developing new product concepts, building teams, reorganizing, and troubleshooting—all issues that are important to the organization's success.

Bob Gore's style of participative leadership borrows heavily from the Socratic method of interactive questioning. Gore's associates marvel at his ability to listen to them and interact with them by only asking questions. One associate noted that "Gore made almost no statements during the whole 90-minute meeting, but instead asked hundreds of questions—from market forecasts to technical requirements to the associate's 'dream' for the business." Through this style of participation, associates at Gore are made to feel that not only their ideas for the functional operations are considered but their vision for the organization as a whole matters.

Within Gore's philosophy of leadership lies a healthy respect for the contributions that individuals can make. For Gore, the contributions reside not only in the finished product or idea, but in the process by which the product or idea was conceived. For example, one associate was surprised to learn, after her project was accepted, that Gore wanted to "access her thinking process" because he was so impressed with its value. So at W. L. Gore & Associates, participative leadership allows employees to feel as though both their ideas and the processes by which ideas are conceived are valuable to the overall success of the organization.

Source: S.W. Angrist, Classless capitalists. In Wright, P.L. and Robbins, S.P. (Eds.), *Organizational Theory,* (Upper Saddle River, NJ: Prentice Hall, 1978), 126–128 and Pacanowsky, M. (1995). Team tools for wicked problems. *Organizational Dynamics,* 23 (3), 36–51.

TASK, ORGANIZATIONAL, AND FOLLOWER CHARACTERISTICS

When followers' tasks are especially important for the leader's group or organization, the impact of participative leadership on follower performance is usually strong and positive (1,2,3,4). Followers carrying out important tasks are probably competent and take seriously their leader's invitations to influence decisions, with favorable results. Another important enhancer of participative leadership occurs when follower acceptance and/or commitment to a decision are essential to carry out the decision (5,6). Inviting followers to participate in the decision process helps them understand and shape the decision process, thus increasing their "ownership" of the decision outcome and their acceptance and commitment to carry it out.

Environmental uncertainty is another situational characteristic that enhances the impact of participation on followers and/or organizational performance (7,8,9,10). Here the input of followers is important in responding to a high degree of uncertainty faced by the group or organization. Participative leadership is an effective way of obtaining as much relevant information and as many ideas as possible in order to effectively address the uncertainty.

The conditions within the leader's group are also important to participative leadership. If the group is harmonious and trusts the leader, these conditions tend to enhance a participative leader's impact on group performance (11). On the other hand, if conflict exists among followers, good conflict management skills enhance the leader's impact on group effectiveness (12). Here the leader is restoring the trust and camaraderie needed to encourage followers to participate wholeheartedly with the leader in decision making.

Certain characteristics of followers make them especially responsive to participative leader behaviors. The characteristic that most frequently enhances participative leadership is followers' job competence, expertise, knowledge, and information relevant to the decision task. These follower characteristics increase the impact of leader participation behaviors on follower and group performance (13,14,15,16,17,18,19,20,21,22). Furthermore, highly competent and knowledgeable followers often expect to have an impact on leadership decisions that affect them. As we will see, this expectation is not always present in other countries, but the enhancing effect of follower competence and knowledge has been found in many types of organizations in the United States.

Two other characteristics that can enhance the effects of leader participation on follower satisfaction and performance are followers' needs for independence (23,24,25) and growth (26). In other words, followers who prefer to work independently and/or who seek self-fulfillment and achievement opportunities at work respond very positively to leaders' efforts to involve them in decision making. They probably see the leaders' invitation as a compliment to their capabilities, they value the chance to further develop and demonstrate their competence, their self-esteem is increased, and their positive attitudes and efforts are consequently heightened. A related follower characteristic that also enhances leader participativeness is internal locus of control, which is the tendency of certain people to see themselves as having personal control of their lives and environment (27,28). These individuals do not believe in fate. They believe they control their own destiny through their own decisions and actions. When leaders solicit their input on decisions, they naturally respond positively with heightened satisfaction.

The amount of participation followers expect also enhances the impact of participation on their satisfaction and sometimes on group performance. Followers expect participation when it is used by other leaders in the organization (29), when it has been used for other decisions (30), or when their prior leader used it in decision making. When a leader meets their expectations and involves them in decisions, they respond with improved satisfaction and perhaps with improved performance. Figure 9–1 summarizes the situational factors that increase the effectiveness of participative leadership.

INFLUENCING SITUATIONS TO MAKE PARTICIPATIVE LEADERSHIP MORE EFFECTIVE

The single most potent enhancer of participative leadership is follower competence, knowledge, and information. Organizations can cultivate this factor with training and development programs as well as selection and coaching for followers. Assigning competent followers to perform important tasks further enhances the impact of the leader's

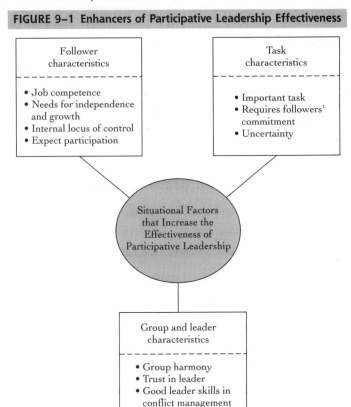

FIGURE 9–1 Enhancers of Participative Leadership Effectiveness

participation. Programs that increase the responsibility, autonomy, and importance of followers' work tasks can also enhance the impact of a leader's participativeness.

An uncertain environment also enhances participation's impact, although we do not advocate withholding information from followers simply to enhance a participative leader's impact. If a leader takes on a new project (such as developing a new product), having followers participate in decision making will likely be very effective because the activity is uncertain.

Several other follower characteristics also enhance participation by a leader. For one, followers who expect to participate in decision making respond well to the opportunity. Here precedence is important. When leaders use participation successfully in specific situations, they create the expectation among followers that they will use it in the future. Every manager knows the importance of precedent in the eyes of followers. Since followers who have a great need for independence, achievement, and self-fulfillment or who believe they control their own destiny respond well to participation, careful recruitment programs that bring these individuals into the organization should enhance the value of participative behaviors.

Organizational development and team-building programs can be used to build harmony and trust in the leader's group of followers. These conditions encourage collective

LEADERSHIP IN PERSPECTIVE: RESEARCH ON PARTICIPATIVE LEADERSHIP

Victor Vroom and Arthur Jago have been studying participative leadership among managers in the United States for many years. They have noticed that the level of participation used by many managers has steadily increased since the 1970s. They note that the society and workforce, as well as the products produced and the business environment, have all changed significantly since the days of Frederick Taylor and World War II. Vroom and Jago view the major reasons for the increase as an adaptation to current conditions. They also identified two critical aspects of these conditions that characterize today's organizations and encourage participation.

First, managers today face greater complexity in the decisions they make than did managers decades ago. Technological innovations, foreign competition, and the changing role of government toward business mean that managers often do not have all the knowledge they need to make good decisions on their own. More and more they must integrate the knowledge and capabilities of different specialists to arrive at informed and effective decisions. This requires participative leadership.

A second major reason for increased participation by leaders is the nature of the labor force in organizations today. Followers are more educated than workers earlier in this century. They often possess more ability to contribute toward effective decisions and expect to be involved. Leaders who use an autocratic decision style will likely face greater resistance today than previously. Both of these situational factors—environmental complexity and an increasingly educated workforce—probably contribute to the increase in participative approaches taken by many of today's leaders.

Source: Adapted from Victor H. Vroom and Arthur G. Jago, *The New Leadership* (Upper Saddle River, NJ: Prentice Hall, 1988).

team effort and enhance participative leadership. Such programs can be conducted by staff personnel, outside consultants, or managers who are experienced in team building.

The Leadership in Perspective box on participative leadership describes how economic and workforce trends in the United States have created a situation in many organizations where participative leadership is especially popular.

◆ SITUATIONAL FACTORS THAT DECREASE EFFECTIVENESS OF PARTICIPATIVE LEADERSHIP

Situational factors exist that make participative leadership less important and therefore less effective with followers. When these factors exist, leaders should consider using other behavior patterns to influence followers.

TASK, ORGANIZATIONAL, AND FOLLOWER CHARACTERISTICS

A high degree of task structure in followers' work decreases the amount of satisfaction and performance that results from participative leadership (31,32,33,34,35). Task structure refers to the existence of predictable and reliable methods for successful task performance. Repetitive tasks are often high in task structure, and research indicates that repetitive tasks do decrease the impact of participative leadership (36). Experienced leaders know that some workers appreciate predictable work methods and expect to have little influence on the leader's decisions. These workers often respond to nonparticipative leaders with satisfaction and good performance. For this type of worker, then, a high degree of task structure can decrease the effects of participative leadership.

A recent summary of research on participative leadership identified task complexity as a factor that decreases the impact of leader participativeness on follower satisfaction and acceptance of decisions (37). This was the single most significant finding from this summary, and it may appear to contradict the neutralizing effects described previously regarding task structure. In fact there has been a controversy among leadership researchers about how task characteristics affect the impact of participative leadership. However, task complexity in this summary seemed to involve problem-solving situations that required processing unusual information and dealing with considerable uncertainty. Individuals who perform such tasks are likely to be highly trained and experienced professionals, and they may require little input and discussion with their leader. Consequently, these individuals are not highly influenced by participative leader behaviors. Professional workers are also usually satisfied and committed to their organizations, which is consistent with our expectations that the effects of task complexity are to replace the need for participative leadership.

The existence of a large group can also decrease the effects of a leader's participative behaviors on followers' satisfaction. This is probably due to the difficulty of all members effectively sharing information and feeling they can influence a decision. Other researchers have reported that short time deadlines, emergencies, or a desire for quick results decrease the impact of participation on decision effectiveness (38,39,40). The time requirements of many participative processes make them prohibitive or ineffective in these situations.

One set of follower characteristics has shown consistent, decreasing effects on leaders' participation behaviors. When followers are passive, apathetic, and/or willing to accept autocratic decisions, leader participation behaviors do not improve follower satisfaction or commitment to decisions (41,42,43). These followers apparently do not want to involve themselves with the leader in decision making, and when the leader tries to involve them, they react with low satisfaction and little commitment to decisions. Another follower characteristic that has decreased the effects of leader participation in some situations is follower authoritarianism. Authoritarian followers prefer to have their behavior controlled by others. We would therefore expect them to prefer not to be consulted or involved in leadership decisions. This neutralizing effect was found in initial studies of parcel delivery workers and first line supervisors (44,45) but was not found in a later follow-up study (46). Another researcher explored the possibility that the type of task may affect how authoritarian followers reacted to participation and found the neutralizing effect occurred only when followers worked on highly repetitive tasks (47). Recall that repetitive and/or structured tasks were also neutralizers of participation. When such tasks are performed by authoritarian followers, the neutralizing effect may be particularly strong. Figure 9–2 summarizes the situational and follower characteristics that decrease effectiveness of participative leadership.

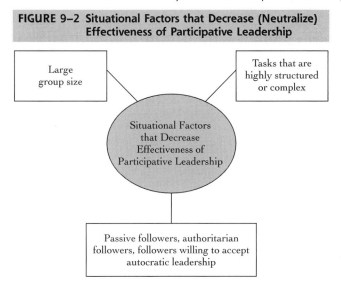

FIGURE 9–2 Situational Factors that Decrease (Neutralize) Effectiveness of Participative Leadership

OVERCOMING FACTORS THAT DECREASE EFFECTIVENESS OF PARTICIPATIVE LEADERSHIP

Recall that leaders must know which situations are not compatible with participative leader behaviors. If they can recognize these situations, leaders can modify or work around them when necessary.

The followers' task structure and complexity are both possible neutralizers, especially when combined with certain types of followers. Task redesign can be used to manipulate the structure and complexity of followers' tasks, and selection procedures can help determine if specific personality types are well matched with certain jobs. A participative leader may wish to avoid placing authoritarian followers on jobs with high task structure, due to the neutralizing effect. Since highly trained professionals may be the only persons qualified to do complex problem-solving tasks, the leader may simply need to use behaviors other than participative ones to influence these individuals.

When leaders face emergency decisions or those with short time deadlines, participation is not effective. In some cases, the leader may be able to extend deadlines or learn of needed decisions sooner and thus provide more time for participative leadership. Emergencies and decisions with short time horizons do occur occasionally, and leaders are wise to avoid participative approaches when faced with these situations.

A large-sized group of followers can also neutralize the impact of participative leadership. In these situations the leader may be able to create subgroups. These subgroups can operate with some autonomy but will allow the leader to involve members in useful discussions of decision issues. This approach may help prevent the isolation some individuals experience in large groups.

Followers who are passive and apathetic or are authoritarian and willing to accept a leader's autocratic decisions also decrease the effectiveness of participative leadership behaviors. In the short run a leader can probably not do much to change these factors, and she should use other leader behaviors to influence followers. Charismatic

LEADERSHIP IN ACTION: PARTICIPATIVE LEADERSHIP AT GENERAL MOTORS

General Motors has been described as the world's largest corporate bureaucracy with a long history of autocratic decision making by powerful top-level executives. In the late 1980s, GM had been through difficult times with tremendous foreign competition and inefficient production facilities. It had tried numerous programs to overcome the inefficiencies with limited success. Its chief executive officer, Roger Smith, agreed to try a more participative approach to involve employees in the decision process.

This change was difficult for the GM management. It required persuading managers to encourage and accept ideas and challenges from their subordinates, something they were unaccustomed to doing. It also involved convincing subordinates that the management really meant it when they asked for input. Given the long history of top-down decision making, this was probably the biggest hurdle.

After struggling with these difficulties, GM began to see some results. At the Lake Orion factory, managers began to involve plant workers in discussions with engineers on the full-sized models. Historically, workers found out about the new models only when production began. But after introducing the participative approach, they were able to reduce product planning time by six months.

In the Buick City complex, managers got together with union leaders. They indicated that they needed to increase productivity and showed figures that demonstrated how the plant was using more man-hours per car than all other GM plants. This participative approach resulted in faster production line speed, a productivity level above the corporate average, and zero grievances. Participative leadership seems to be having real bottom-line benefits at General Motors.

_____

Source: Adapted from *The Wall Street Journal,* January 12, 1988.

leadership behaviors may be effective in overcoming apathetic and passive behavior. Over time, attrition and selection processes can bring in more involved and committed followers who appreciate and respond to participative leadership. The Leadership in Action box shows how General Motors has implemented participative leadership approaches to help solve productivity problems. Although GM met with difficulties, the participative approach seems to yield favorable results.

◆ SITUATIONAL FACTORS THAT REPLACE THE NEED FOR PARTICIPATIVE LEADERSHIP

One situational characteristic that replaced the need for participative leadership behavior among commissioned and noncommissioned U.S. Army officers was organizational formalization—the degree of formal rules, regulations, and procedures specified for followers to direct their activities (48). When extensive rules and regulations were present, as is often the case in the military, the impact of leader participativeness on follower satisfaction with their work was significantly reduced. However, the presence of organizational formalization also had a positive impact of its own on followers' satisfaction with work—replacing a normal impact of participative leadership. We should not assume from this single study that organizational formalization is always a replacement for a leader's participation. However, this study does show that formalization can replace the need for this leader behavior.

CREATING FACTORS THAT REPLACE THE NEED FOR PARTICIPATIVE LEADERSHIP

As noted earlier, the creation of factors that replace the need for leadership helps "free up" a leader for other needed activities, adds to the stability of the leader's unit when the leader is absent, and helps followers take on added responsibility and become more independent. Since few researchers have attempted to identify factors that replace the need for participative leadership, the only situational characteristic that has been confirmed to have replacement effects occurred in the sample of U.S. Army officers described earlier. The U.S. military probably operates with more formal rules and procedures than many nonmilitary leaders find comfortable. Although this potential leadership replacement is often under the control of the organization's management (more rules and procedures can always be created), it may require a very high degree of organizational formalization to effectively replace participative leadership.

Although not yet tested by researchers, we believe that two other task characteristics may combine with individual follower traits to create replacements for participation. Highly structured tasks, when performed by followers who are authoritarian or have a low need for independence, may replace the need for participative leadership. Thus, the leaders might create the right combination of situational and follower traits with their recruitment and selection strategy. Highly complex tasks, when performed by highly trained and/or professional workers, may also replace the need for participative leadership. Here again, recruiting and selecting well-trained and professional individuals for jobs of this type may create replacements for participation. These possible replacements are speculative at this time and are therefore excluded from the summary figures later in this chapter. Table 9–1 summarizes the three major types of situational and follower characteristics that affect the impact of participative leadership. Figure 9–3 provides an example of how situational factors can affect the impact of participative leadership by a public school principal.

◆ ASSESSING THE DYNAMICS OF PARTICIPATIVE LEADERSHIP

A dynamic interaction occurs between a participative leader, followers' needs and expectations, and important situational factors. When leaders determine that situational and follower characteristics are present that will increase (enhance) the effects of participative leadership (see table 9–1), they should use participation to involve followers in decision making and problem solving. If the leader's diagnosis identifies factors that decrease (neutralize) the effects of participation (see table 9–1), the leader should probably use other leader behaviors to influence followers. If situational factors exist that replace the need for participative leadership (see table 9–1), then this leadership pattern is probably unnecessary, and the leader should look to other possible needs of their followers.

TABLE 9–1 Situational and Follower Characteristics that Affect the Impact of Participative Leadership

Factors that Increase the Effectiveness of Participativeness	Factors that Decrease the Effectiveness of Participativeness	Factors that Replace the Need for Participativeness
• Task importance • Task requires followers' commitment • Environmental uncertainty • Leader's conflict-management skills • Group harmony and trust • Followers' job competence and knowledge • Followers' need for independence and growth • Followers' internal locus of control • Followers expect participation	• Task structure • Task complexity • Large group size • Short time deadlines • Passive followers • Authoritarian followers • Followers willing to accept autocratic leadership	• Many formal rules and procedures

FIGURE 9–3 Example of the Influence of Situational Factors on the Participative Leadership of Public School Principals

Situational factors that could <u>increase</u> effectiveness of a principal's participativeness

- The teachers feel their job of teaching is very important and that they have a high degree of competence in teaching.
- The teachers are experiencing high uncertainty because of disagreements on the board of education about curriculum and financing of the school system.
- The principal is recognized as having outstanding conflict-management skills.
- The teachers cooperate with each other and there is a high degree of harmony in their relations.

How Situational Factors can Affect the Impact of Participative Leadership by a Public School Principal

Situational factors that could <u>decrease</u> the effectiveness of a principal's participativeness

- The teachers' job is highly complex because of the diverse cultural backgrounds of the students and their levels of preparation.
- The teachers have become very passive and discouraged because they lack resources to do their jobs.

Situational factors that could <u>replace</u> the need for a principal's participativeness

- The teachers' job is regulated by extensive formal rules and procedures laid down in employee handbooks and curriculum mandates.
- The teachers are teaching highly complex subject matter which makes use of their extensive specialized training.

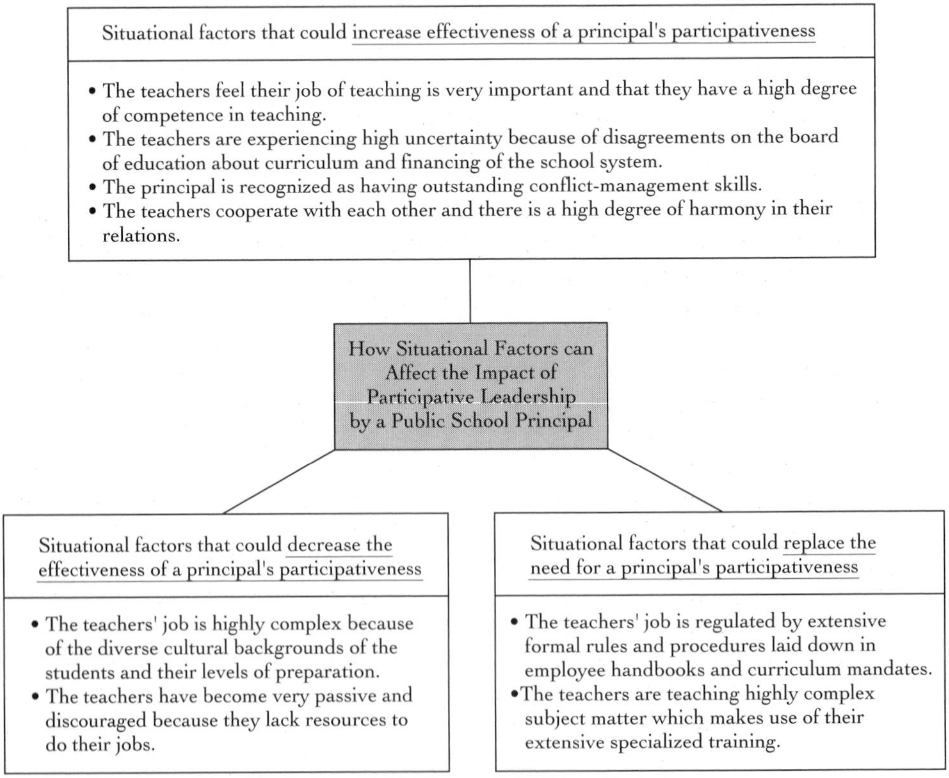

Effective participative leaders also assess situations and followers to determine if they can be modified. If leaders can eliminate factors that decrease the positive effects of participation or create factors that increase the effectiveness of participation, they can make the situation more favorable to participative leadership. As indicated earlier, leaders can provide training and development to increase followers' competence and job knowledge; redesign followers' jobs to increase their responsibility and importance; use selection and job placement to create a group of followers who are independent, achievement oriented, nonauthoritarian, and expect participation; and use team building to create group harmony with small groups of followers. Moreover, leaders can sometimes get deadlines extended to allow time for effective participation. All these actions can create a situation in which participative leadership is highly effective. Leaders may also create formal written guidelines to inform decision makers how to make decisions without using participation, although this approach may be most useful in organizations that have historically relied heavily on written guidelines, rules, and procedures. Since only one situational factor has been found to clearly replace the need for participative leadership, leaders had best concentrate their efforts on modifying situations to create enhancers and eliminate neutralizers of participative leadership.

Followers' reactions to the leader's efforts to modify their situation will affect the leader's future participation behaviors as well as future efforts at situational modification. Followers thus influence the participation-related behaviors of their

---

LEADERSHIP IN ACTION: JOHN W. GARDNER ON MORAL LEADERSHIP

John W. Gardner, who has served six presidents of the United States in various leadership capacities, noted that the characteristics followers expect of an ethical leader are at least partly determined by the culture. But in the United States today he believes that morally acceptable leaders are often identified by their objectives for their followers.

A continuing commitment to the development of human possibilities is a basic social objective and major goal of ethical leaders. He quoted Thomas Jefferson who said, "We hope to avail the nation of those talents which nature has sown as liberally among the poor as the rich, but which perish without use, if not sought for and cultivated." In pursuing this objective, Gardner believes leaders have an obligation to encourage the active involvement of followers in decision making and the pursuit of group goals.

Gardner also quoted Al Sloan, who ran General Motors Corporation for 35 years, on this issue. Sloan said he worried about how to keep managers around the country awake and thinking about what they could contribute to the future of General Motors. "And the only way to do that is to push some decisions in their direction."

Gardner believes that ethical leaders constantly strive to enliven individuals all down the line to share in the leadership task of making decisions and carrying them out. This requires leaders who delegate, consult and listen to followers, respect human possibilities, and remove obstacles to followers' participation. He ends by quoting Lyman Bryson who stated, "A democratic way of doing anything is a way that best keeps and develops the intrinsic power of men and women."

Source: John W. Gardner, *On Leadership,* (New York: The Free Press, 1990).

leader. Overall, however, with increasing levels of formal education and training of the working population in western countries, participative leadership seems to be a frequently effective leadership response to followers' needs. The Leadership in Action box on John W. Gardner describes ethical issues of participative leadership in the United States.

Summary ▪▪

Leaders will be most effective with participative behaviors if they display them when enhancers of participation are present. In these situations, leaders will likely have strong positive effects on followers' psychological states and behavioral outcomes. Participative leadership will have less impact on followers when important replacements or neutralizers are present. When these situational and follower conditions exist, leaders will likely be most effective if they avoid using participative leadership behavior and choose a different behavior pattern (such as directive or supportive leadership) to influence followers' psychological reactions and behaviors.

Figure 9–4 shows the Process Model of Participative Leadership, which summarizes material from chapters 8 and 9 on how situational factors influence the effects of participative leadership on follower psychological reactions and behavioral outcomes. Participative leader behaviors are shown at the top of Figure 9–4, affecting follower and group psychological reactions that, in turn, affect followers' behaviors and outcomes. Situational factors are shown on each side of Figure 9–4. The arrows from situational factor boxes intersect the arrow connecting participative leader behaviors with follower and group psychological reactions. This intersection shows that situational factors can increase or decrease the effects of participative leadership on followers' reactions. Participative leader behaviors are also connected with arrows to situational factors, showing that leaders can modify the situations to make them more favorable for the leader's influence attempts. The factors that may replace the need for participative leadership are shown at the left of Figure 9–4 with an arrow directly affecting follower reactions.

Figure 9–5 is designed to help the leader use the information summarized in Figure 9–4. It shows the three key leadership tasks of diagnosing situations, providing leadership, and modifying followers and situations. Leaders first diagnose the situation by answering the questions regarding followers and their work situation shown in box 1. These questions assess the existence of factors that can increase or decrease the effects of participative leadership on followers' reactions. If the answer is "yes" to one or more of these questions, then followers will probably expect and value a participative approach by their leader. The leader then provides the appropriate participative behaviors shown in box 2. The leader also examines the followers' situation to determine if it can be modified to eliminate possible neutralizers and/or create enhancers of participative leadership. The leader might also determine if factors can be created that replace the need for participation. If situations can be modified to improve the effectiveness of leaders and followers, then the leader uses the information in box 3. The leader then rediagnoses the situation and reconsiders the amount of participative leader behaviors that are needed. Figure 9–5 is thus a dynamic model of continually diagnosing situations, providing participative leadership, modifying situations, rediagnosing situations, and so on. It thus represents the dynamic nature of the leadership process model described in this book.

FIGURE 9–4 Leadership Process Model of Participative Leadership

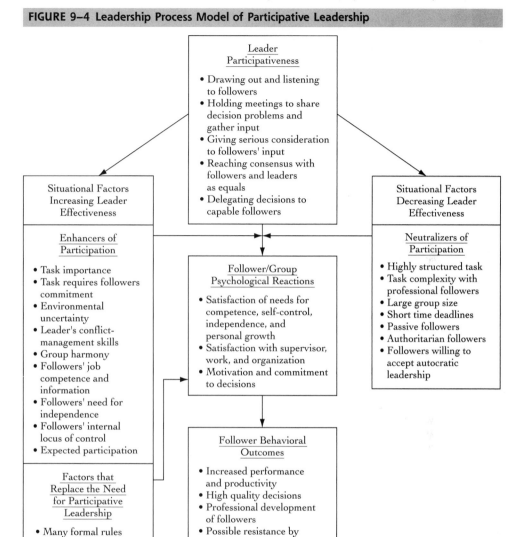

Key Terms and Concepts in this Chapter

- acceptance of decisions
- commitment to decisions
- environmental uncertainty
- group harmony

- growth needs
- independence needs
- locus of control
- organizational formalization

- participative leadership
- passive followers
- task complexity
- task structure

FIGURE 9–5 Applying the Model of Participative Leadership

1. Diagnosing the Situation

- Are followers highly competent and knowledgeable; do they work on important tasks; is their commitment essential to carry out the leader's decisions?
- Do followers value achievement, independence, and self-fulfillment; view themselves as controlling their own lives; feel harmony and trust with the leader; and expect to participate in decisions?
- Is the leader effective in obtaining follower input and skilled at conflict management?
- Is there much environmental uncertainty?

If "yes" to one or more of these questions, followers will expect and value participative leadership.

3. Modifying Followers and/or Situations

Leaders also act to:
- Increase formal rules and procedures that prescribe how to deal with emergencies and short time deadlines
- Redesign tasks to increase their importance and followers' independence
- Build group harmony
- Develop followers' job competence and knowledge
- Eliminate highly structured tasks and large groups
- Reassign followers who are passive, authoritarian, or desire autocratic leadership

2. Providing Participative Leadership

Leaders demonstrate participative behaviors with followers by:
- Holding informal conversations with individual followers to obtain information related to decisions
- Sharing decision problems with groups of followers to solicit their ideas or suggested solutions
- Assigning a decision problem to followers who are competent and desire to handle it
- Allowing "air time" for all followers who desire it when discussing decision problems
- Inviting input and discussion on points of disagreement regarding decision problems
- Explaining to followers why ideas or solutions are not implemented

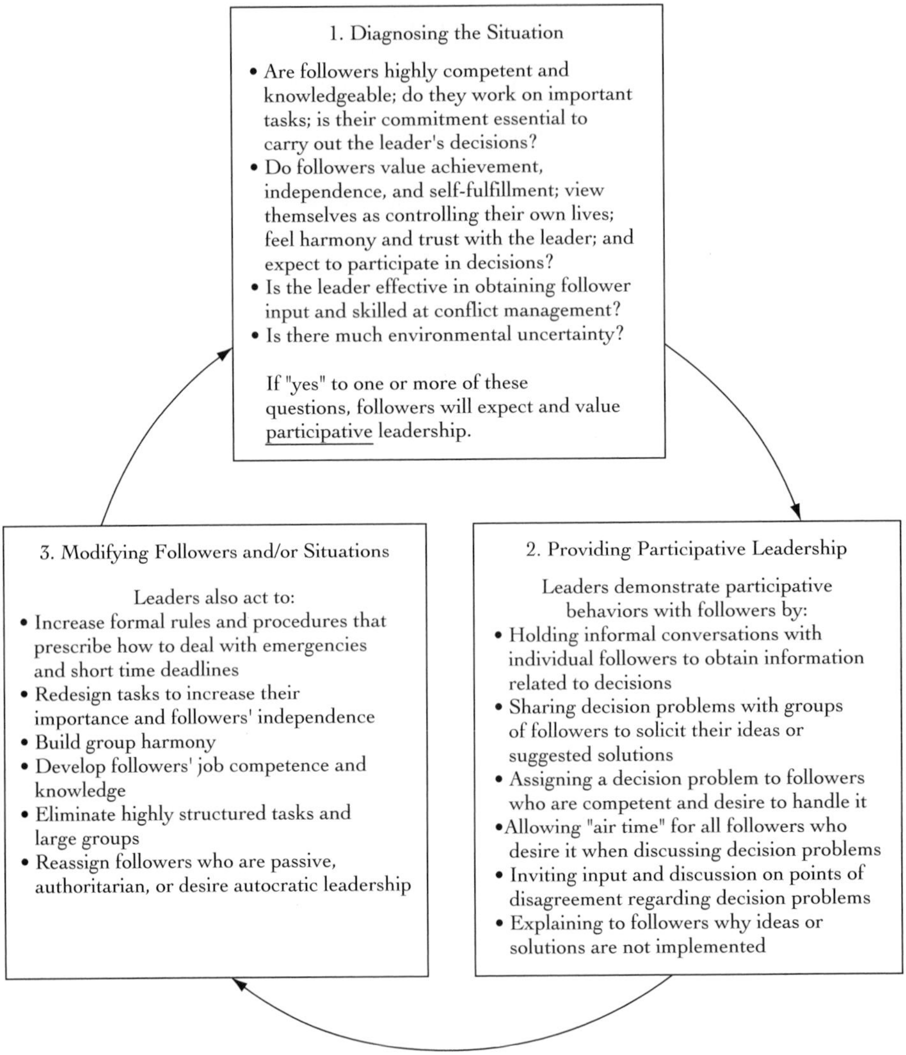

Review and Discussion Questions ▪▪▪▪▪▪▪▪▪▪▪▪▪▪▪▪▪▪▪▪▪▪▪▪▪▪▪▪▪▪

1. Give several specific examples of situational factors that could cause participative leadership to be highly effective. For each, explain why they would increase the leader's impact on followers.

2. Give several specific examples of situational factors that could cause participative leadership to be less effective. For each, explain why they decrease the leader's impact on followers.

3. Which of the situational characteristics described in this chapter do you feel have had the most impact on your reaction to participative leadership?

4. Which of your personal characteristics or skills would increase (or decrease) your impact as a participative leader?

5. As a leader, how might you create situational factors to build your influence as a participative leader?

6. Discuss the values or benefits to leaders of creating factors that replace the need for participative leadership.

Exercise: Choosing an Appropriate Leadership Behavior ■■■■■■■■■■

TASK 1: (5 Minutes)

Read the following scenario carefully and then respond to the statements that follow about how you would behave if you were a leader in this situation.

You supervise one of several small final-assembly departments for a medium-sized producer of top-of-the-line camping equipment. You are not sure why, but the quality of camping lanterns produced in your department has been declining. There have been some small changes recently in the lanterns' design, but employees in your department are experienced and knowledgeable about the lanterns and their quality has been very good in the past. Morale in the department is good and employees usually take pride in the company's products. The lanterns are an important part of the company's product line and customer complaints are increasing about the decreased quality.

TASK 2: (15 Minutes)

Based on the material presented thus far in this book (chapters 1–9), rate each of the following triads of statements according to how much you agree with them as an appropriate leader behavior by the supervisor in this situation. For each triad, rate the statement you believe is most appropriate and impactful as a 1, rate the statement you think is least appropriate as a 3, and rate the other statement as a 2. You must rate all the statements in each triad as a 1, 2, or 3. Mark your answers in the *Your Answer* column and complete all five triads of statements. For a given triad of statements, your answers might look like the following:

Your Answer
1. __3__
2. __1__
3. __2__

	Your Answer	Triad Answer

Triad I
1. Show concern for the status and well-being of the followers. 1. _____ _____
2. Describe the problem to a few key employees in the department and ask for their ideas on possible solutions. 2. _____ _____
3. Tell followers that the lanterns have fallen below quality standards and they must improve their quality. 3. _____ _____

Triad II
4. Emphasize the appropriate work methods and task assignments to all employees in the department. 4. _____ _____

	Your *Answer*	*Triad* *Answer*

5. Be friendly and encourage two-way communication with followers.

5._____ _____

6. Hold a group meeting with all employees in the department and ask for their input on alternative solutions which have already been developed.

6._____ _____

Triad III

7. Assure that all employees' ideas and contributions are given serious consideration.

7._____ _____

8. Demonstrate a kind and understanding attitude toward your employees during this difficult time period.

8._____ _____

9. Keep close track of followers' task skills and coach them on work methods as needed.

9._____ _____

Triad IV

10. Assign the quality problem to your employees and ask them to develop a solution.

10._____ _____

11. Show trust and respect toward your employees for their good performance in the past.

11._____ _____

12. Carefully review work assignments and assure correct procedures are followed.

12._____ _____

Triad V

13. Reassign your employees to different tasks to decrease their boredom.

13._____ _____

14. Hold informal conversations with each employee in the department to draw out their ideas on how to solve the quality problem.

14._____ _____

15. Be approachable and sympathetic regarding followers' problems.

15._____ _____

Task 3 (20–30 Minutes)

Now form groups of three people with others in your class. Complete a *Triad Solution* to the 15 statements by coming to agreement within your group on how each statement should be rated. Discuss each statement with others in your group in order to reach agreement.

Task 4 (20–30 Minutes)

The instructor will now discuss this scenario and the statements about leadership behavior by relating them to the Leadership Process Model and leader behaviors described thus far in the book.

Endnotes ■

1. Drenth, P. J. D. and Koopman, P. L. (1984). A contingency approach to participative leadership: How good? In J. G. Hunt, D. Hosking, C. A. Schriesheim and R. Stewart, (Eds.) *Leadership and Managers: International Perspectives on Managerial Behavior and Leadership*. New York: Pergamon.

2. Bass, B. M. and Shackleton, V. J. (1979). Industrial democracy and participative management: A case for synthesis. *Academy of Management Review,* 4, 393–404.

3. Murnighan, J. K. and Leung, T. K. (1976). The effects of leadership involvement and the importance of the task on subordinates performance. *Organizational Behavior and Human Performance,* 17, 299–310.

4. Lawrence, L. C. and Smith, P. C. (1955). Group decision and employee participation. *Journal of Applied Psychology,* 39, 334–337.

5. Bass, B. M. (1990). *Bass & Stogdill's Handbook of Leadership.* New York: The Free Press.

6. Vroom, V. H. and Jago, A. G. (1988). *The New Leadership: Managing Participation in Organizations.* Upper Saddle River, NJ: Prentice Hall.

7. Heller, F. A. and Wilpert, B. (1981). *Competence and Power in Managerial Decision-Making: A Study of Senior Levels of Management in Eight Countries.* London: Wiley.

8. Lawrence, L. C. and Lorsch, J. W. (1967). *Organization and Environment.* MA: Harvard University Press.

9. Burns, T. and Stalker, G. M. (1969). *The Management of Innovation.* Chicago: Quadrangle Books.

10. Roby, T. B., Nicol, E. H. and Farrell, F. M. (1963). Group problem solving under two types of executive structure. *Journal of Abnormal and Social Psychology,* 67, 550–556.

11. Bass, B. M., Valenzi, E. R. and Farrow, D. L. (1977). External environment related to managerial style. *Proceedings, International Conference on Social Change and Organizational Development,* Dubrovnik, Yugoslavia.

12. Crouch, A. G. and Yetton, P. (1987). Manager behavior, leadership style, and subordinate performance: An empirical extension of the Vroom-Yetton conflict rule. *Organizational Behavior and Human Decision Processes,* 39, 65–82.

13. Dorfman, P. W., Howell, J. P., Hibino, S., Lee, J., Tate, U. and Bautista, A. (1997). Leadership in western and Asian countries: Commonalties and differences in effective leadership processes and substitutes across cultures. *Leadership Quarterly,* 8 (3), 233–274.

14. Leana, C. R. (1986). Predictors and consequences of delegation. *Academy of Management Journal,* 29, 754–774.

15. Bass, B. M. *Bass & Stogdill's Handbook of Leadership.*

16. Bass, B. M. and Ryterband, E. C. (1979). *Organizational Psychology* (2nd ed.). Boston: Allyn & Bacon.

17. Filley, A. C., House, R. J. and Kerr, S. (1976). *Managerial Process and Organizational Behavior* (2nd ed.) Glenview, IL: Scott Foresman.

18. Locke, E. A. and Schweiger, D. M. (1979). Participation in decision making: One more look. In B.M. Staw (Ed.), *Research in Organizational Behavior,* Vol. 1: 265–339. Greenwich, CT: JAI Press.

19. Fiedler, F. and Garcia, J. E. (1987). *New approaches to effective leadership: Cognitive resources and organizational performance.* New York: Wiley.

20. Heller, F. A. and Wilpert, B. *Competence and Power in Managerial Decision-Making: A Study of Senior Levels of Management in Eight Countries.*

21. Hersey, P. and Blanchard, K. H. (1982). *Management of Organizational Behavior: Utilizing Human Resources* (4th ed.) Upper Saddle River, NJ: Prentice Hall.

22. Vroom, V. H. and Jago, A. G. *The New Leadership: Managing Participation in Organizations.*

23. Kenis, I. (1977). A cross-cultural study of personality and leadership. *Group and Organizational Studies,* 2(1), 49–60.

24. House, R. J. and Dessler, G. (1974). The path-goal theory of leadership: Some posthoc and a priori tests. In J. G. Hunt and L. L. Larson (Eds.), *Contingency Approaches to Leadership.* Carbondale: Southwestern Illinois University Press.

25. Vroom, V. H. (1959). Some personality determinants of the effects of participation. *Journal of Abnormal and Social Psychology,* 59, 322–327.

26. Griffin, R. W. (1980). Relationships among individual, task design, and leader behavior variables. *Academy of Management Journal,* 23(4), 665–683.

27. Mitchell, T. R., Smyser, C. M. and Weed, S. E. (1975). Locus of control, supervision and work satisfaction. *Academy of Management Journal, 18,* 623–630.

28. House, R. J. and Dessler, G. (1974). The path-goal theory of leadership: Some posthoc and a priori tests. In J. G. Hunt and L. L. Larson (Eds.), *Contingency Approaches to Leadership.* Carbondale: Southwestern Illinois University Press.

29. Lowin, A. (1968). Participative decision making: A model, literature, critique, and prescription for research. *Organization Behavior and Human Performance, 3,* 68–106.

30. Miller, K. I. and Monge, P. R. (1986). Participation, satisfaction and productivity: A meta-analytic review. *Academy of Management Review, 29,* 727–753.

31. Indvik, J. (1986). Path-goal theory of leadership: a meta-analysis. *Proceedings of the Academy of Management.* 189–192, Chicago.

32. Vroom, V., Grant, L. D. and Cotton, T. S. (1969). The consequences of social interaction in group problem solving. *Organizational Behavior and Human Performance, 44,* 77–95.

33. Shaw, M. E. and Blum, J. M. (1964). Effects of leadership style upon group performance as a function of task structure. *Journal of Personality and Social Psychology, 3,* 238–242.

34. Dunnette, M. D., Campbell, J. P. and Jaastad, K. (1963). The effect of group participation on brainstorming effectiveness for two industrial samples. *Journal of Applied Psychology, 47,* 30–37.

35. Field, R. H. G. (1982). A test of the Vroom-Yetton normative model of leadership. *Journal of Applied Psychology, 67,* 523–532.

36. Schuler, R. (1976). Participation with supervisor and subordinate authoritarianism: A path-goal theory reconciliation, *Administrative Science Quarterly, 21*(2), 320–325.

37. Wagner, J. A. III, and Gooding, R. Z. (1987). Shared influence and organizational behavior: A meta-analysis of situational variables expected to moderate participation-outcome relationships.

38. Bass, B. M. and Barrett, G. V. (1981). *People, Work and Organizations: An Introduction to Industrial and Organizational Psychology.* Boston: Allyn & Bacon.

39. Vroom, V. H. and Jago, A. G. *The New Leadership: Managing Participation in Organizations.*

40. Hahn, C. P. and Trittipoe, T. G. (1961). Situational Problems for Leadership Training: III. Review for Petty Officers of Leadership Research. Washington, D.C.:Naval Contract Report, Institute for Research.

41. Vroom, V. H. and Jago, A. G. *The New Leadership: Managing Participation in Organizations.*

42. Bass, B. M. and Barrett, G. V. *People, Work and Organizations: An Introduction to Industrial and Organizational Psychology.*

43. Hahn, C. P. and Trittipoe, T. G. (1961). *Situational Problems for Leadership Training: III. Review for Petty Officers of Leadership Research.* Washington, D.C.:Naval Contract Report, Institute for Research.

44. Vroom, V. H. Some personality determinants of the effects of participation.

45. Kenis, I. (1978). Leadership behavior, subordinate personality, and satisfaction with supervision. *Journal of Psychology, 48*(1), 99–107.

46. Tosi, H. (1970). A reexamination of personality as a determinant of the effects of participation. *Personnel Psychology, 23,* 91–99.

47. Schuler, R. (1976). Participation with supervisor and subordinate authoritarianism: A path-goal theory reconciliation.

48. Dorfman, P. W., Howell, J. P., Cotton, B. C. G. and Tate, U. (1992). Leadership within the 'discontinuous hierarchy' structure of the military: Are effective leadership behaviors similar within and across command structures? In K. E. Clark, M. B. Clark and D. P. Campbell (Eds.), *Impacts of Leadership.* Greensboro, North Carolina: Center for Creative Leadership.

Academy of Management Journal, 30, 524–541.

CHAPTER 10

Leader Reward and Punishment Behaviors

Learning Objectives
After reading this chapter you should be able to do the following:

1. Explain how leaders can use rewards and punishments to have positive influences on followers.
2. Explain why leaders' use of rewards and punishments can sometimes have negative effects on followers.
3. Describe the skills and abilities that a leader needs to effectively use rewards and punishments.
4. Give specific examples of effective and ineffective reward and punishment behaviors by leaders.
5. Describe the benefits to individuals and organizations that can result from a leader's effective reward and punishment behaviors.

◆ EXAMPLES OF EFFECTIVE LEADER REWARD AND PUNISHMENT BEHAVIORS

1. A supervisor established a new policy that any member of the department who brought in a new client would earn 10 percent of the contracted fees.
2. In the McDonald's organization, the cook who makes the fastest high-quality hamburgers in the United States is awarded the title "All American Hamburger Maker." This title implies great status in the company.
3. Many schools and school districts select an outstanding teacher for "teacher of the year" awards. Besides significant status, these awards are sometimes accompanied by cash bonuses.
4. Because a head coach praised and rewarded players when they performed well, they were willing to accept his extreme reprimands and extra grueling practice time when they performed poorly.
5. A supervisor expressed genuine disappointment to group members when their performance was well below standard.
6. A leader reduced a follower's rate of pay for repeated periods of low performance. This not only caused the punished follower to increase his

efforts, but other followers also increased their performance to avoid similar punishment (1,2,3).

The incidents described here are examples of effective leader reward and punishment behaviors.

◆ DEFINITION, BACKGROUND, AND IMPORTANCE OF LEADER REWARD AND PUNISHMENT BEHAVIORS

The use of rewards and punishments to influence followers' behavior is probably as old as the concept of "leadership" itself. Homer told of King Agamemnon promising rewards to Achilles, the great military leader, if he defeated the Trojans (4). Military history is also filled with examples of followers being punished by their leaders for not being successful. Twentieth-century psychologists studied the impacts of rewards and punishment on experimental subjects and clarified how these influence strategies affected them (5).

Early psychological research resulted in a principle of behavior known as the Law of Effect, which essentially states that a specific behavior will increase in frequency if it is followed by a reward. A corollary is that a behavior which is not followed by a reward (or is followed by a punishment) will decrease in frequency. The rationale for these principles is that people have innate tendencies to seek pleasure and avoid pain. Rewards bring pleasure, and people consequently seek to attain them; punishments are painful and will therefore be avoided. Subsequent research findings from many areas of social behavior support these principles by showing that rewards and punishments can have strong effects on the behavior of animals and humans (6,7,8,9,10,11).

In recent years, organizational researchers have focused on how leaders can effectively administer rewards and punishments in order to influence followers' behavior in specific ways. Leader reward behaviors provide desirable outcomes (positive reinforcers) for followers when they help achieve organizational goals (12). Managers in high-performing organizations make a conscious effort to reward any action of organizational members that are valuable to the organization (13). These managers recognize that tangible and intangible rewards that they control can help satisfy followers' needs for recognition, self-esteem, achievement, security, and physical necessities.

Because people enjoy being recognized and rewarded for a job well done, rewards improve followers' psychological reactions. A simple compliment and pat on the back are powerful rewards because they can be used frequently and "on the spot" with no time delay. In turn, followers' improved psychological reactions keep them committed to the organization. Providing meaningful rewards to followers when they perform well also gives them the information and incentives (motivation) they need to effectively direct their own behavior. The rewards tell followers what behaviors the leader sees as important and they increase the chances followers will repeat those behaviors to obtain future rewards. When leaders reward good performance with material benefits, they are "putting their money where their mouth is," and this increases followers' confidence in the integrity of their leader and the organization.

Leader punishment behaviors provide *aversive* outcomes (punishment) or remove desirable outcomes when followers hinder achievement of organizational goals (14). Many followers realize the importance of these behaviors when they are used carefully. A recent nationwide survey showed that almost 50 percent of workers believe that managers are too lenient with poor performers (15). When leaders punish followers for rule violations, lack of effort, or poor performance, they provide followers with useful information on what behaviors the leader does not want. Followers generally recognize that it is useful to have information on what leaders want and do not want.

Formal leaders in organizations usually command numerous resources that they can use to reward or punish followers. Effective reward behaviors include giving special recognition to a follower whose work is outstanding, recommending a significant pay increase for someone whose performance is high, giving positive feedback when a follower performs well, acknowledging improvement in a follower's work, commending a follower who does better than average work, or informing the leader's boss when a follower does outstanding work (16). Effective punishment behaviors are showing displeasure if a follower's work is below departmental standards, imposing fines for repeated rule violations, reprimanding a follower if his work is consistently below his capabilities, recommending that a follower receive no pay increase if his work is below standard, or giving undesirable job assignments to followers who are late to work (17). Different leaders control different types of rewards and punishments, but all leaders use some types of rewards and punishments to influence their followers' behavior. Figures 10–1 and 10–2 summarize several effective reward and punishment behaviors.

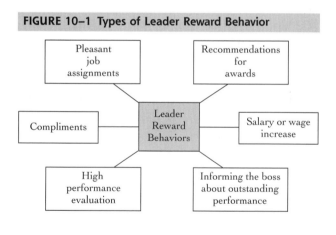

FIGURE 10–1 Types of Leader Reward Behavior

Pleasant job assignments — Recommendations for awards — Compliments — Leader Reward Behaviors — Salary or wage increase — High performance evaluation — Informing the boss about outstanding performance

FIGURE 10–2 Types of Leader Punishment Behavior

Verbal reprimand — Unpleasant job assignment — Fines for rule violation — Leader Punishment Behaviors — Reduced privileges — Low performance evaluation — Extra work

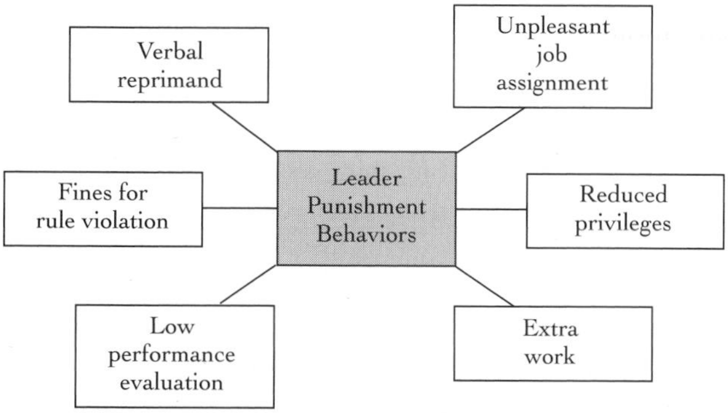

LEADERSHIP IN ACTION: INFORMAL REWARDS IN THE MILITARY

A management consultant was conducting a training session with a group of military officers. One colonel resisted the use of rewards to influence followers' behavior. Shortly thereafter, the colonel's superior officer, a general, decided to praise him for his handling of an important presentation. The general folded a piece of paper in half, wrote "Bravo" on the front, and wrote more specific complimentary remarks on the inside.

The general called the colonel in, praised him, and gave him the card. The colonel read the card, stood up abruptly, and walked out. The general was dumbfounded and thought he had offended the colonel. After a few minutes the general went to check on the colonel and found he had stopped at every office on the way out to show off his "Bravo" card. He was smiling and being congratulated by everyone who saw it. The colonel later printed his own recognition cards with "Wonderful" on the front.

Source: Adapted from B. Nelson, *1001 Ways to Reward Employees.* (New York: Workman Publishing, 1994).

◆ THE PROCESS OF SOCIAL EXCHANGE

The use of rewards and punishments by a leader has been described as a process of social exchange between the leader and followers (18). The leader wants certain behavior from a follower such as attendance, a clean work area, responsiveness, or good performance. The leader also controls certain items that followers either want (rewards) or would like to avoid (punishments). An unwritten contract is established between the leader and followers that each will provide what the other wants. This contract is usually informal and is not specified in detail. As long as both perceive the contract as fair and the benefits to each party outweigh their costs, they will tend to have a mutually satisfying and productive relationship. This social exchange has been found in virtually all leader-follower relationships—soldiers and military leaders, voters and political bosses, street gang leaders and members, as well as managers and employees (19).

Leader rewards and punishments may be tangible (a raise in pay or a demotion) or intangible (a compliment or a sarcastic remark). Both types can have significant impacts on followers. Research shows that organizational leaders use more intangible rewards to influence followers than tangible (20). This is probably due to the ability of leaders to use intangible rewards such as praise, recognition, and appreciation on short notice. When a follower does something that the leader desires, an immediate compliment by the leader is very useful to assure the follower knows the leader is pleased with the behavior. When several of these informal rewards are followed by a tangible reward (such as a pay increase), the follower is effectively encouraged to repeat the desired behavior in the future. The Leadership in Action box describes an informal reward system used by military officers that was very effective.

LEADERSHIP IN PERSPECTIVE: EFFECTIVE USE OF REWARDS

Influencing behavior through the use of rewards is most likely to be effective when the rewards have the following basic characteristics:

1. The rewards offered by the leader are highly valued by the follower. Tailor rewards to individuals.
2. The rewards are large enough for the followers to expend the effort required.
3. The follower will receive the rewards immediately after the desired behavior.
4. The follower believes the leader is sincere and the rewards will actually be received.
5. The rewards should be tied to high performance, and the leader should not reward low performance.
6. The leader should strive to be consistent and fair in rewarding behaviors.

◆ CONTINGENT REWARDS AND PUNISHMENTS

Effective use of rewards and punishments must be a consequence of specific follower behaviors. Another way of stating this is that the rewards and punishments must be contingent on the follower's behavior. That is, a follower must know that a compliment or pay raise is a direct result of specific behaviors or a high level of performance. Making the follower aware of this contingency allows the follower to focus efforts on repeating the behavior or performance to obtain the reward again. A similar process occurs with leader punishment. When the leader expresses dissatisfaction with a follower's poor attendance and states that repeated poor attendance will result in the follower's dismissal, the follower now has the knowledge needed to avoid further punishment. In both cases, making the reward/punishment contingent on specific follower behaviors and informing followers of this contingency provide the incentive and knowledge for followers to direct their behavior to attain rewards and avoid punishment.

In addition to clarifying the type of behavior or performance a leader prefers, tangible and intangible rewards also improve interpersonal relations and increase followers' satisfaction. Popular management writers have pointed out that everyone likes to be complimented and that tangible rewards are valued by followers (21). It is probably best to give intangible rewards such as praise or compliments on an occasional basis. Complimenting a follower every day for coming to work on time will probably embarrass the follower or make the leader seem less than genuine. Some evidence from laboratory research indicates that tangible rewards provided by a leader may reduce the inherent satisfaction and motivation of followers when they complete certain challenging tasks. That is, in some research studies, tangible rewards appeared to cause followers to perform only for the tangible reward, not for the inherent interest of the task. However, this research is not well supported in real organizations where people work for a living (22,23). When people perform well at job tasks that they find interesting and challenging, they are usually happy and motivated to continue their good performance when a leader rewards them. The box on guidelines for effective use of rewards provides leadership advice from research on leader reward behaviors.

◆ REWARDING DESIRED BEHAVIOR

It is important for a leader to let followers know what tangible rewards are available and how they can obtain them. Leaders must be very careful about what is rewarded and how followers see the rewards as being distributed. One expert described numerous examples where leaders say they want one thing and reward something else (24). For example, organizational leaders may say they want followers who are original and think independently, but they reward those who conform. Orphanage directors say they want to place orphans with foster homes, yet their salaries and budgets are based on the number of children living in the orphanage. In both these situations, the rewards are not consistent with the stated goals. However, what is rewarded will be encouraged and probably repeated by those receiving the rewards. Leaders must carefully analyze which behaviors are rewarded and how the reward contingencies are viewed by followers. Table 10–1 provides examples of what leaders hope for and what often gets rewarded.

◆ THE USE OF PUNISHMENT

Leaders' punishment behavior involves telling followers about possible punishments and administering them. The act of punishing involves imposing penalties and removing positive stimuli when followers demonstrate inappropriate or undesired behavior. B.F. Skinner was an influential psychologist and writer who argued that punishment was not effective, had undesirable side effects, and should be avoided. Some researchers and practicing leaders believe that punishment causes anxiety, passivity, withdrawal, or aggression toward the leader. Research reviews show, however, that these side effects are not common and improvement in behavior is much more the rule (25,26). Some have suggested that punishment is unethical or nonhumanitarian and reflects an "eye for an eye" approach to leadership. This argument confuses punishment as a "payback" for past performance with the current view of contingent punishment as "future oriented," to help suppress or eliminate harmful behavior. Contingent punishment has been used effectively to suppress alcoholism and destructive workplace behavior (27,28,29). Lead-

TABLE 10–1 Examples of what is Hoped for Versus what often Gets Rewarded

What is hoped for	What gets rewarded
• quality work	• fast work
• lasting solutions	• quick fixes
• creativity	• conformity
• cooperation	• aggressiveness
• simplification	• complication
• risk taking	• risk avoiding

ers must evaluate the future consequences of undesirable or destructive behaviors if they do nothing to stop them. Some experts suggest it is more humane to punish disruptive behavior and stop its recurrence than to ignore it while hoping it will go away and allowing continued conflicts, hostility, and open insubordination to interrupt the activities of an entire group.

Some writers have suggested that punishment only eliminates undesirable behavior temporarily, until the threat of punishment is gone. This ignores the responsibility of leaders to regularly monitor follower activities and to reward the positive behaviors that replace those punished. Other writers have suggested that cohesion and esprit de corps are heightened if a group is subjected to harsh punishment. Fraternity initiations and basic military training seem to reflect this belief. Careful research shows, however, that harsh noncontingent punishment *lowers* group cohesion, whereas less severe forms of punishment do not have this effect (30).

When followers create conflict, repeatedly break rules, are hostile or insubordinate, or abuse drugs or alcohol on the job, some type of severe punishment is probably the most effective leadership strategy. In contrast, to eliminate lack of effort on the job, mild forms of punishment such as expressing disappointment or giving negative feedback are often adequate, especially when combined with promised rewards for good performance.

Refusing to comply with a leader's request is a common reason for imposing punishments such as a strong verbal reprimand, an unpleasant job assignment, or (if repeated) suspension or termination. A low level of effort resulting in low job performance will often be dealt with by withdrawal of privileges, not being considered for promotion, or a reduction in pay. For many followers, simply having one's poor performance or inappropriate behavior pointed out by the leader (known as negative feedback) is sufficiently unpleasant to change the follower's behavior. Being told why their behavior was not appropriate and how to perform correctly in the future can be especially helpful to inexperienced followers. But followers must also be told what

---

LEADERSHIP IN PERSPECTIVE: CONSTRUCTIVE PUNISHMENT

Influencing behavior by using punishments is most likely to be effective when the leader's punishment behavior has the following characteristics:

1. The leader directs the punishment against the follower's behavior, not the person.

2. The punishment is done in private.

3. The leader handles the punishment in a low key, unemotional manner.

4. The leader takes direct responsibility for the punishment and does not attribute the punishment as coming from someone else.

5. The punishment promptly follows the undesirable behavior or poor performance.

6. The punishment is consistent for similar undesirable behaviors and poor performance.

7. The punishment is accompanied by information on how the follower can perform effectively.

they have done correctly and that the leader recognizes and appreciates this behavior. Contingent reward behavior should be used with contingent punishments whenever possible.

Management by exception is one type of contingent punishment behavior in which the leader monitors performance and does not acknowledge or reward desirable behaviors, but only intervenes with directiveness and punishment when followers do not perform well. This approach has *not* proven effective in industrial organizations, although there is some evidence it can be useful in military organizations (31,32). The box on guidelines for constructive punishment summarizes effective leadership approaches for using contingent punishment.

◆ INEFFECTIVE LEADER REWARD AND PUNISHMENT

Not all reward and punishment behaviors by leaders are effective. Ineffective use of leader reward behaviors are demonstrated by the following actions:

1. A leader was just as likely to praise a follower when he performed poorly as when he performed well. At first followers liked getting the leader's praise, but it had no effect on their behavior. Because they had not earned the praise, after a while they began to view the leader as incompetent.

2. The owner-manager of a small retail business awarded bonuses equally to all employees whenever he felt he could afford it. The manager hoped the bonuses would encourage followers to increase their efforts and raise performance. But because the bonuses were not contingent on individual or group performance, employees had no way of knowing when or why they were awarded. The bonuses therefore had no effect on performance.

Ineffective use of leader punishment behaviors are demonstrated by the following actions:

1. A supervisor expressed extreme displeasure and criticized a follower's work, even though the follower had performed well compared to other group members.

2. A leader repeatedly punished his followers with severe verbal reprimands, unpleasant task assignments, and extra work. Because no followers were spared from the penalties and they were administered for trivial actions, the followers came to view them as "part of the job," and they lost any impact they may have had if administered more selectively.

3. A leader always punished followers in public. The leader believed that embarrassing followers in front of their peers was an effective way to change their behavior. Followers reacted by resenting the leader and resisting her directions whenever they could (33).

As the above examples show, rewards and punishments can be misused so that they have no effect or severely damaging effects. In most of these examples, rewards and punishments were not provided contingent on followers' performance, the punishment was excessive, or was not done in private. When leader rewards and punishments are not administered contingent on follower behaviors or performance, they have little effect or a detrimental effect. The detrimental effect is especially pronounced when a leader administers noncontingent punishment behaviors.

LEADERSHIP SELF-ASSESSMENT: USING REWARD AND PUNISHMENT BEHAVIORS

Instructions: Indicate the extent you would engage in the following reward and punishment behaviors to influence followers. Use a scale of (5) very frequently; (4) frequently; (3) occasionally; (2) seldom; (1) almost never.

1. I would give positive feedback to my followers when they perform well.　　　　　　　1　2　3　4　5

2. I would show my displeasure with followers when their work is below acceptable standards.　1　2　3　4　5

3. I would praise followers frequently regardless of their performance.　　　　　　　　1　2　3　4　5

4. I would be quick to acknowledge an improvement in the quality of a follower's work.　　1　2　3　4　5

5. I would sometimes criticize a follower's work even if it is above acceptable standards.　　1　2　3　4　5

6. When followers' work is not up to par, I would point it out to them.　　　　　　　1　2　3　4　5

7. Even when followers perform poorly on the job, I would still commend them.　　　　1　2　3　4　5

8. I would reprimand followers now and then even if they performed well, just to keep them in line.　1　2　3　4　5

9. I would offer a bonus to all followers who exceed performance for quantity and quality.　　1　2　3　4　5

Interpretation: If you rated items 1, 4, and 9 as four or five, you would probably use leader contingent reward behaviors effectively. If you rated items 2 and 6 as four or five, you probably use leader contingent punishment behaviors effectively. If you rated items 3 and 7 as four or five, you would use noncontingent reward behavior. If you rated items 5 and 8 as four or five, you would use noncontingent punishment behavior. Contingent reward and punishment behaviors are much more effective at influencing followers' behavior than noncontingent reward and punishment.

Source: Adapted from research questionnaires originally developed by P. M. Podsakoff, P. W. Dorfman, J. P. Howell, and W. D. Todor, "Leader reward and punishment behaviors: A preliminary test of a culture-free style of leadership effectiveness," *Advances in International Comparative Management*, 2 (1986): 95–138.

◆ HOW TO REWARD AND PUNISH FOLLOWERS

Leaders can develop behavioral traits, skills, and sources of power to help them use reward and punishment behaviors effectively. Leaders who prefer to make their own decisions and take responsibility for those decisions are often inclined to use rewards to influence followers. These leader traits are often accompanied by a high amount of self-confidence by the leader (34,35). Leaders usually develop these three personal factors through leadership experience, and these qualities allow leaders to act based on their own assessments of situations. They actively monitor followers' behavior and performance and use the information they obtain to effectively reward or punish followers.

Of course, leaders must be skilled at accurately monitoring and measuring followers' performance in order to provide rewards contingently. Performance evaluation is a notoriously difficult process to carry out accurately. Followers doing repetitive tasks are usually more easily evaluated than managerial or professional workers doing complex technical or service-oriented tasks. Thus, the leader must develop performance measures for followers that inspire their confidence. Skills at evaluating followers' performance are also developed through experience as well as formal training.

Effective leaders often develop several sources of power to help them use reward and punishment behaviors. When leaders have reward power (they control important tangible rewards such as bonuses or promotions), they can use those rewards to encourage certain follower behaviors and performance. High-level managers typically control more tangible rewards than low-level managers, although middle- and low-level supervisors usually control some tangible rewards. Leaders at all levels control intangible or social rewards such as compliments and personal recognition. A leader's coercive power (control over important punishments such as demotion or termination) can be used to influence followers through punishment behaviors. Leaders in some organizations have more control over tangible punishments than in other organizations. Nearly all leaders control intangible and social punishments such as negative performance feedback. Today, leaders' abilities to use physical and many tangible punishments are highly restricted. But even the captain of an intramural softball team has the power to cheer for a player who gets an important base hit or to suggest to another player the need to work on base-running skills.

A leader who holds a high-level position in an organization has a high amount of legitimate power that can be used to influence followers. Most followers are very respectful of leaders who work at high levels and respond quickly to their requests. These leaders also usually control major rewards and punishments that are important to followers. One recent study showed that a small amount of leadership behavior by a high-level leader had a much stronger effect on followers than a large amount of the same leader behavior by a low-level leader (36). The leader's legitimate power is clearly one important factor that helps a leader use rewards and punishments effectively.

Leaders' connection/resource power can also be developed to help them use rewards and punishments to influence followers. When leaders cultivate contacts with high-level managers, they can sometimes obtain resources they can use to reward followers. Leaders often develop extensive networks in the organization to provide the political influence they may need to obtain approval for a follower's promotion. When followers are aware that their leader has extensive contacts at higher levels in the organization, they often view potential punishments as more significant because leaders at higher levels may become involved. This increases the potential impact of their leader's punishment behaviors. Figure 10–3 summarizes the traits, skills, and power sources that can be developed to help a leader effectively use rewards and punishments.

Two organizational factors can reduce or constrain a leader's ability to control important rewards: (1) labor contracts and civil service agreements that specify pay levels for employees and (2) organizational reward systems, policies, or procedures that define when employees will receive rewards or that require time-consuming formal ap-

FIGURE 10–3 Traits, Skills, and Sources of Power that Help a Leader Effectively Use Rewards and Punishments

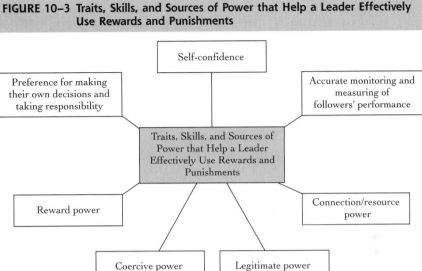

provals by upper management (37). Leaders should probably emphasize intangible rewards and other leader behaviors to influence followers in these situations.

As with leader's reward behavior, legal restrictions may significantly limit the use of certain types of punishment that were common in the past. For example, employment laws, previous court decisions, labor contracts, and civil service agreements severely limit managers' ability to dismiss employees. Legal limitations also exist for other types of disciplinary actions such as demotions or suspension without pay.

Certain leader characteristics may also limit a leader's use of contingent punishment behavior. For example, one military study of multiracial groups showed that when both leaders and followers were the same race (black or white), the leader was less likely to use punishment than when leader and followers were of a different race (38). Some researchers have found that male leaders are more inclined to use contingent reward and punishment behaviors than female leaders, but other studies show no differences between male and female leaders on these behaviors (39,40,41,42). More studies are needed on the effects of leaders' race and gender before definite conclusions are possible. The Leadership in Action box describes how one organizational leader uses rewards to obtain high performance at Motorola.

◆ EFFECTS OF LEADER REWARD AND PUNISHMENT

As described earlier, followers enjoy leaders' reward behaviors because they help satisfy followers' needs for recognition, self-esteem, achievement, security, and physical necessities. When rewards and punishments are provided contingent on followers' performance, followers are aware of what the leader wants and does not want. In order to administer rewards and punishments contingently, leaders must monitor and evaluate followers' behavior and performance. Monitoring and evaluation in themselves can have

LEADERSHIP IN ACTION: ROBERT GALVIN— CHAIRMAN OF MOTOROLA

Robert Galvin's use of rewards at Motorola is partially responsible for the company's rise to the top of the semiconductor industry. Employees in Motorola's self-managed work teams can earn up to 41 percent of their base salaries in bonuses for meeting certain goals. According to Galvin, the only way the reward structure can work is if there is a clear and complementary relationship between employee performance and rewards. Workers receive financial rewards for innovation and for productive manufacturing of state-of-the-art technology that generates high profitability.

Galvin understands that employees will not take participation in decision making seriously unless they can share the rewards. Galvin believes that rewards should go to those who independently find imaginative ways to support the goals and philosophy of the corporation. For example, a production worker discovered that 10 percent of the screws being used broke during production. This worker took the initiative to call the vendor and work through the problem. At the end of the year the company had realized considerable savings, which the worker shared. Another employee discovered that 40 percent of the gold used in their semiconductors was wasted during production. After eliminating over 50 places where gold had been lost, the company reduced the waste to zero and shared the savings with the employees. Motorola has established a reward program for production workers and administrative staff. For example, a group of secretarial workers pooled together all their loose office supplies and harvested a year's worth of supplies. Motorola shared the savings with employees for not having to buy office supplies.

Galvin also believes in rewarding entrepreneurial behavior, long-term thinking, and customer satisfaction. To encourage long-term thinking, Motorola measures and rewards managerial performance over as long as a six year time frame. Galvin rewards entrepreneurial behavior by promoting employees who have shown themselves to successfully challenge inappropriate assumptions made by top management.

Galvin also uses contingent punishments. When an internal audit revealed bookkeeping discrepancies in a Motorola sales department, Galvin directed 20 managers to make retribution by contributing $8,500 to charity. The results of Galvin's reward and punishment structure at Motorola include an increase in product quality and productivity, improvements in safety and cleanliness, need for less staff due to employees' willingness to carry an extra workload and share in the rewards, cooperation between shifts to keep production running smoothly, and decreased turnover as fewer people quit in search of greener pastures.

Source: R. Galvin, "What a message," *Across the Board,* 34(8) (1997): 12–14; J. O'Toole, *Vanguard Management* (New York: Berkley Books, 1985); J. O'Toole, *Leading Change* (San Francisco: Jossey-Bass Publishers, 1995).

positive impacts on followers' psychological reactions and behavioral outcomes. The effects of leader reward and punishment behaviors are further described in this section.

EFFECTS OF LEADER REWARD BEHAVIOR

Numerous studies of leaders' contingent reward behavior show that this behavior results in improvements in follower performance (43, 44,45,46). This favorable impact is also supported by research on behavior modification in organizations (47,48) and studies of leaders over time (49,50,51,52). Other studies show the positive effects of contingent reward behavior on group productivity, enthusiasm, cohesiveness (53,54), and other follower behaviors including compliance with the leader's requests (55,56,57). The popular management literature also indicates that tangible and intangible rewards are used extensively in effective organizations (58,59).

Some writers have suggested that if leaders use reward power extensively, followers will view their relationship with the leader as strictly economic, and they will seldom do more than is required for the reward. They further suggest that extensive use of rewards will erode loyalty and commitment to the leader and the organization. However, many studies show that a leader's contingent reward behavior improves followers' psychological reactions such as satisfaction with supervision, organizational commitment, and job clarity (60,61). These findings and the fact that leader reward behavior also increases followers' ratings of their leader imply that rewards do not erode followers' attitudes toward the leader or the organization (62,63). Followers are generally happier with their leader and with those around them when they are well rewarded.

It is important to remember that these positive effects assume rewards are provided contingent on follower behavior and/or performance. Studies of leader reward behaviors which are not contingent on follower performance generally show no effects or decreases in followers' psychological reactions and performance (64).

There is a popular belief among experts on international leadership and management that a leader's contingent reward behavior is effective only in certain types of cultures. These cultures are usually described as individualist. Individualist cultures are composed of loosely knit social frameworks where people are expected to look out for themselves, and emphasis is placed on individual initiative and independence (the United States is one example). In these cultures leaders are assumed to spend much time monitoring individual followers' behavior and performance and guiding and controlling followers by appealing to their individual self-interests through contingent rewards and punishments. Cultures that are not individualist are often described as collectivist. These cultures have tight-knit social frameworks where various groups (families, clans, or work groups) look after their members (the Peoples' Republic of China is an example). Individuals in collectivist cultures are expected to look out for the group first (not themselves), and individual initiative and independence are not valued as they are in individualist cultures. Here individual guidance and control are maintained by group loyalty, not individual self-interest.

The belief that a leader's contingent rewards are effective only in individualist cultures has been contradicted by recent research findings from organizations in collectivist countries such as Taiwan, Japan, South Korea, and Mexico. These findings concern intangible (social) rewards such as a leader's compliments, praise, and recognition for followers' good performance. Even in collectivist cultures, when leaders provide intangible rewards of this type contingent on followers' performance, they result in improvements in follower psychological reactions and sometimes performance (65,66). These same results have been found in highly individualist business organizations in the United States. This evidence needs further collaboration, but it appears that performance-contingent social rewards by the leader have universally positive impacts on followers in both collectivist and individualist cultures. It may be that a leader's contingent tangible rewards have less impact in collectivist countries than in individualist countries. This possibility must be carefully tested in studies in both types of cultures before final conclusions are reached.

EFFECTS OF LEADER PUNISHMENT BEHAVIOR

Some early studies showed that a leader's emphasis on punishment decreased followers' satisfaction with their leader (67,68) or produced hostility, absenteeism, withdrawal, tension, and passivity in followers (69,70,71,72,73). However, more recent studies show that contingent punishment behavior does *not* decrease follower satisfaction or performance (74,75,76), probably because followers view contingent punishment as fair. In fact, several researchers have found that leaders' contingent punishment behavior can actually improve follower or group performance (primarily by eliminating undesirable behaviors) when used in combination with contingent reward behavior (77,78,79,80,81). It appears that a leader's contingent punishment should be used along with a liberal amount of contingent reward behavior.

A totally different pattern of results has occurred when leader punishment is not contingent on follower performance. This type of punishment often results in decreases in followers' satisfaction with work, with supervision, with coworkers, and sometimes in performance, commitment to the organization, role clarity, and group cohesion (82,83,84,85). Clearly, followers react very negatively when they are punished for reasons unrelated to their behavior or performance.

LEADERSHIP IN PERSPECTIVE: PUNISHMENT AND MORAL LEADERSHIP

Some managers do not believe in punishment. They believe that punishment hurts followers' feelings and makes them resent and resist future leader requests. These managers maintain that rewards and other leader behaviors are all that is necessary to obtain needed behavior from followers. But destructive follower behaviors sometimes require strong and immediate action by the leader. These follower behaviors can be damaging to other followers or the organization, and punishment is usually the quickest way to stop the damage and correct the behavior.

One example is sexual harassment, which causes personal physical and/or psychological harm to employees, damages careers, and creates legal liabilities for managers and organizations. Individuals who commit sexual harassment do not usually stop this behavior on their own. They often derive personal satisfaction from their power over others and do not want to relinquish this power. Leaders must make it clear to followers that sexual harassment will not be tolerated through training programs that define and give examples of inappropriate behavior, clear policies and procedures on reporting it, and the consequences (punishment) to those who sexually harass others. When incidents occur that are substantiated, leaders must follow through with the specified punishment to assure that everyone knows the leader is serious. Leaders who take firm punitive action in these situations develop a reputation for high moral conduct and promote trust and respect from followers.

Research evidence also suggests that contingent punishment behaviors have an impact only in certain cultures. Contingent social punishment (such as reprimands or negative feedback) have had almost no effects on followers' psychological reactions or performance in studies of organizations in collectivist cultures (86). In contrast, comparison studies from the United States found that contingent social punishment behaviors improved followers' organizational commitment and job clarity. It thus appears from this limited evidence that leaders' contingent punishment is primarily useful in individualist cultures. When leaders administer punishments that are not contingent on followers' behavior or performance, followers' reactions are universally negative. The Leadership in Perspective box on punishment and moral leadership shows how this leader behavior can result in followers' respect and trust.

Summary ▪

Leader reward and punishment behavior involves providing desirable outcomes (positive reinforcers) for followers when their behavior helps achieve organizational goals and providing aversive outcomes (punishment) or removing desirable outcomes when their behavior hinders achievement of these goals. Rewards and punishments may be tangible (a raise or a demotion) or intangible (a compliment or expressing disappointment for low performance). Their use represents part of a social exchange between leaders and followers—leaders provide certain services including rewards and punishments, and followers provide specific activities and task performance in return.

Rewards and punishments address our natural desire to seek pleasure and avoid pain. They also appeal to our needs for recognition, self-esteem, achievement, security, and physical necessities. When administered contingent on followers' performance, rewards and punishments provide followers with information and motivational incentives that they need to effectively direct their own behavior. To effectively influence follower behavior, the leader must carefully monitor and measure follower behavior and/or performance and administer rewards and punishments contingently.

Leaders' contingent reward behavior results in improved follower performance, compliance with leader requests, satisfaction, organizational commitment, role clarity, and follower ratings of the leader's effectiveness. Leaders' noncontingent reward behavior, however, has little if any consistent impact on followers' psychological states or performance.

Leaders' contingent punishment behavior may have positive effects on followers' performance when combined with leaders' contingent reward behavior. When used in this manner, contingent punishment does not decrease followers' satisfaction, probably because followers view it as a fair complement to contingent reward behavior. When leader punishment behavior is not contingent on follower performance, however, decreases are likely in followers' satisfaction, performance, commitment, role clarity, and group cohesion. Followers clearly react negatively when they do not know the reason for punishment.

Figure 10–4 summarizes the major findings described in this chapter. Leaders' reward and punishment behaviors are shown influencing follower and group psychological reactions, which affect follower behaviors and outcomes. Situational factors that affect these leadership processes are described in chapter 11.

FIGURE 10–4 Partial Model of Leader Reward and Punishment Behaviors

Leader Reward and Punishment
Behaviors

- Giving pleasant job assignments
- Giving compliments and recognition
- Recommending awards and promotions
- Increasing salary or wages
- Giving reprimands and criticism
- Giving unpleasant job assignments
- Giving low performance evaluations and demotions
- Reducing privileges or giving extra work

↓

Follower/Group
Psychological Reactions

- Satisfaction of needs for recognition, self-esteem, achievement, and security
- Role clarity
- Satisfaction with supervisor and work
- Commitment to organization

↓

Follower Behaviors
and Outcomes

- Performance and productivity
- Compliance with leader requests
- Group cohesiveness
- Follower enthusiasm

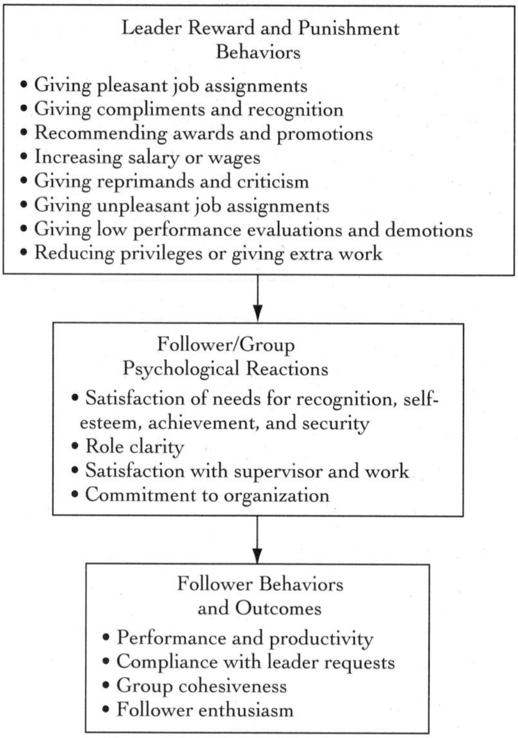

Key Terms and Concepts in this Chapter ▪▪▪▪▪▪▪▪▪▪▪▪▪▪▪▪▪▪▪▪▪▪▪

- coercive power
- connection/resource power
- contingent punishment behavior
- contingent reward behavior
- group cohesiveness

- job clarity
- law of effect
- leader punishment behavior
- leader reward behavior
- legitimate power
- management by exception

- organizational commitment
- organization reward systems
- reward power
- satisfaction with supervision
- social exchange

Review and Discussion Questions ▪▪▪▪▪▪▪▪▪▪▪▪▪▪▪▪▪▪▪▪▪▪▪▪▪▪▪▪

1. Describe specific leader reward behaviors that have influenced your behavior. In what way did they influence you?

2. Describe specific leader punishment behaviors that have influenced your behavior. In what way did they influence you?

3. Describe a situation you experienced in which a leader's reward behavior was needed.

4. Describe a situation you experienced in which a leader's punishment behavior was needed.

5. Describe how a leader can develop the sources of power described in this chapter to help him/her provide leader reward or punishment behaviors effectively.

6. Have you ever experienced a situation in which a leader was constrained from using a reward or punishment when it was really needed? If so, describe this situation.

7. Why do you think contingent reward behavior is more effective in influencing followers than noncontingent reward behavior? What about contingent punishment behavior versus noncontingent punishment?

◆◆◆ **Case Incident**

How Can You Influence Gary's Behavior?

You supervise six tellers in a savings and loan company. The tellers handle opening accounts, deposits, withdrawals, and loan payments. The tellers can have a major effect on customer satisfaction.

There are very few complaints about the behavior of the tellers, with the exception of Gary Thompson. When customers ask Gary a question, he comes to you to check on the answer. If you are busy, Gary keeps the customers waiting until he can check with you or someone else. It seems to you that he checks with you on every minor detail related to his job. Gary's dependence on you

has been increasing, and he wants approval for decisions that the other tellers routinely make on their own. He is consuming a great deal of your time by seeing that everything is done exactly the way you want it done.

Gary appears to have a strong desire to do a good job. He is always at work on time, very polite, dresses exceptionally well, and tries to cooperate with the other employees.

Your "gut" feeling is that you are sick and tired of answering Gary's questions and listening to the customer complaints about having to wait on Gary to complete routine transactions.

QUESTIONS

1. What would be your analysis of Gary's behavior? What do you think is being rewarded and how is it being rewarded by the supervisor?

2. If you were Gary's supervisor, what changes would you want in Gary's behavior?

3. What specific leader behaviors would you use to change Gary's behavior?

Endnotes

1. Yukl, G. A. (1998). *Leadership in Organizations* (4th ed.). Upper Saddle River, NJ: Prentice Hall.

2. Hughes, R. L., Ginnett, R. C. and Curphy, G. J. (1996). *Leadership: Enhancing the Lessons of Experience* (2nd ed.). Chicago, IL: Irwin.

3. Yukl, G. A. and Van Fleet, D. D. (1982). Cross situational, multimethod research on military leader effectiveness. *Organizational Behavior and Human Performance*, 30, 87–108.

4. Bass, B. (1990). *Bass and Stogdill's Handbook of Leadership* (3rd ed.). New York: The Free Press.

5. Skinner, B. F. (1974). *About Behaviorism*. New York: Knopf.

6. Feldman, M. D. and MacCulloch, M. J. (1965). The application of anticipatory

avoidance learning to the treatment of homosexuality: Theory, technique and preliminary results. *Behavior Research and Therapy,* 2, 165–183.

7. Bucher, B. and Lovaas, O. I. (1968). Use of aversive stimulations in behavior modification. In M. R. Jones (Ed.), Miami symposium on the prediction of behavior, 1967: Aversive stimulation. Coral Gables, Florida: University of Miami Press.

8. Balke, B. G. (1965). The application of behavior therapy to the treatment of alcoholism. *Behavior Research and Therapy,* 3, 75–85.

9. Johnston, J. M. (1972). Punishment of human behavior. *American Psychologist,* 27, 1033–1054.

10. Rimm, D. C. and Masters, J. C. (1974). *Behavior therapy: Technique and empirical findings.* New York: Academic Press.

11. Parke, R. D. (1972). Some effects of punishment on children's behavior. In W. W. Hartup (Ed.), *The young child: Reviews of research.* (Vol. 2), Washington D.C. : National Association for the Education of Young Children.

12. Szilagyi, A. D. (1980). Causal inferences between leader reward behavior and subordinate performance, absenteeism, and work satisfaction. *Journal of Occupational Psychology,* 53, 195–204.

13. Peters, T. J. and Waterman, R. H. (1982). *In Search of Excellence.* New York: Harper & Row.

14. Schriesheim, C. A., Hinkin, T. R. and Tetrault, L. A. (1991). The discriminate validity of the leader reward and punishment questionnaire (LRPQ) and satisfaction with supervision: A two sample, factor analytic investigation. *Journal of Occupational Psychology,* 64, 159–166.

15. Viega, J. F. (1988). Face your problem subordinates now! *Academy of Management Executive,* 2, 145–152.

16. Podsakoff, P. M., Todor, W. D., Grover, R. A. and Huber, V. L. (1984). Situational moderators of leader reward and punishment behaviors: Fact or fiction. *Organizational Behavior and Human Performance,* 34, 21–63.

17. Ibid.

18. Hollander, E. P. (1987). College and university leadership from psychological perspective: A transactional view. Paper, Invitational interdisciplinary colloquium on leadership in higher education, National Center for postsecondary governance and finance, Columbia University, New York.

19. Bass, *Bass and Stogdill's Handbook of Leadership.*

20. Ibid.

21. Peters and Waterman, *In Search of Excellence.*

22. Steers, R. M., Porter, L. W. and Bigley, G. A. (1996). *Motivation and Leadership at Work* (6th ed.). New York: McGraw-Hill.

23. Eisenberger, R. and Cameron, J. (1996). Detrimental Effects of Reward: Reality or Myth? *American Psychologist,* 3 (11), 1153–1166.

24. Steers, Porter and Bigley, *Motivation and Leadership at Work.*

25. Powell, J. and Azrin, N. (1968). The effects of shock as a punisher for cigarette smoking. *Journal of Applied Behavior Analysis,* 1, 63–71.

26. Kazdin, A. E. (1975). Behavior modification in applied settings. Homewood, IL: Dorsey.

27. Harris, S. and Ersner-Hershfield, R. (1978). Behavioral suppression of seriously disruptive behavior in psychotic and retarded patients: A review of punishment and altercations. *Psychological Bulletin,* 85, 1352–1375.

28. Balke, The application of behavior therapy to the treatment of alcoholism.

29. Rimm and Masters, *Behavior Therapy: Technique and Empirical Findings.*

30. Blake, R. J. and Potter, E. H. III (1992). Novice leaders, novice behaviors, and strong culture: Promoting leadership change beyond the classroom. In K. E. Clark, M. B. Clark and D. P. Campbell (Eds.), *Impact of Leadership.* Greensboro, NC: The Center for Creative Leadership.

31. Bass, *Bass and Stogdill's Handbook of Leadership.*

32. Colby, A. H. and Zak, R. E. (1988). Transformational leadership: A comparison of Army and Air Force perceptions. (Report 88-0565). Air Command and Staff College, Air University, Maxwell AFB, AL.

33. Hughes, Ginnett and Curphy, *Leadership: Enhancing the Lessons of Experience.*

34. Hinton, B. L. and Barrow, J. C. (1976). Personality correlates of the reinforcement propensities of leaders. *Personnel Psychology,* 29, 61–66.

35. Bass, *Bass and Stogdill's Handbook of Leadership.*

36. Dorfman, P. W., Howell, J. P., Cotton, B. C. G. and Tate, U. (1992). Leadership within the "discontinuous hierarchy" structure of the military: Are effective leadership behaviors similar within and across command structures. In K. E. Clark, M. B. Clark and D. P. Campbell (Eds.), *Impact of Leadership.* Greensboro, NC: Center for Creative Leadership.

37. Yukl, *Leadership in Organizations.*

38. Scontrino, M. P., Larson, J. R. Jr. and Fiedler, F. (1977). Racial similarity as a moderator variable in the perception of leader behavior and control. *International Journal of Intercultural Relations,* 1(2), summer, 111–117.

39. Kappelman, S. K. (1981). Teachers' perceptions of principals' bases of power in relation to principals' style of leadership. Doctoral dissertation, University of New Orleans, New Orleans.

40. Ansari, M. A. (1989). Effects of leader sex, subordinate sex, and subordinate performance on the use of influence strategies, *Sex Roles,* 20(5–6), 283–293.

41. Baker, L. D., Di Marco, N. and Scott, W. E. Jr. (1975). Effects of supervisor's sex and level of authoritarianism on evaluation and reinforcement of blind and sighted workers. *Journal of Applied Psychology,* 60, 28–32.

42. Szilagyi, A. D. (1980). Reward behavior of male and female leaders: A causal inference analysis, *Journal of Vocational Behavior,* 16, 59–72.

43. Williams, M. L., Podsakoff, P. M. and Huber, V. (1992). Effects of group-level and individual-level variation in leader behaviors on subordinate attitudes and performance. *Journal of Occupational and Organizational Psychology,* 65, 115–129.

44. Yammarino, F. J. and Bass, B. M. (1990). Long-term forcasting of transformational leadership and its effects among naval officers. In K. E. Clark and M. B. Clark (Eds.), *Measures of Leadership.* West Orange, NJ: Leadership Library of America, 151–170.

45. Podsakoff, P. M., Todor, W. D. and Skov, R. (1982). Effect of leader contingent and non-contingent reward and punishment behaviors in subordinate performance and satisfaction. *Academy of Management Journal,* 25, 810–821.

46. Szilagyi, A. D. (1980). Causal inferences between leader reward behavior and subordinate performance, absenteeism, and work satisfaction. *Journal of Occupational Psychology,* 53(3), 195–204.

47. Luthans, F. and Kreitner, R. (1975). *Organizational Behavior Modification.* Glenview, IL: Scott, Foresman.

48. Schneier, C. E. (1974). Behavior modification in management: A review and critique. *Academy of Management Journal,* 17, 528–548.

49. Greene, C. N. (1976). A longitudinal investigation of performance-reinforcing behaviors and subordinate satisfaction and performance. *Proceedings,* Midwest Academy of Management, St. Louis, MO., 157–185.

50. Greene, C. N. (1976). Causal connections among cohesion, drive, goal acceptance, and productivity in work groups. Paper, Academy of Management, Kansas City, MO.

51. Sims, H. P. and Szilagyi, A. D. (1978). A causal analysis of leader behavior over three different time lags. Paper, Eastern Academy of Management, New York.

52. Sims, H. P. (1977). The leader as manager of reinforcement contingencies: An empirical example and a model. In J. G. Hunt and L. L. Larson (Eds.), *Leadership: The cutting edge.* Carbondale: Southern Illinois University Press.

53. Podsakoff, P. M. and Todor, W. D. (1985). Relationships between leader reward and punishment behavior and group process and productivity. *Journal of Management,* 11, 55–73.

54. George, J. M. (1995). Assymetrical effects of rewards and punishments: The case of social loafing. *Journal of Occupational and Organizational Psychology,* 68 (4), 327–338.

55. Herold, D. M. (1977). Two-way influence processes in leader-follower dyads. *Academy of Management Journal, 20,* 224–237.

56. Thamhain, H. J. and Gemmill, G. R. (1974). Influence style of project managers: Some project performance correlates. *Academy of Management Journal,* 17, 216–224.

57. Warren, D. I. (1968). Power, visibility, and conformity in formal organizations. *American Sociological Review,* 6, 951–970.

58. Kouzes, J. M. and Posner, B. Z. (1987). *The Leadership Challenge: How to Get Extraordinary Things Done in Organizations.* San Francisco: Jossey-Bass.

59. Peters and Waterman, *In Search of Excellence.*

60. Williams, Podsakoff and Huber, Effects of group level and individual-level variation in leader behaviors on subordinate attitudes and performance.

61. Dorfman, P. W., Howell, J. P., Hibino, S., Lee, J. K., Tate, U. and Bautista, A. (1997). Leadership in western and Asian countries: Commonalities and differences in effective leadership processes across cultures. *Leadership Quarterly,* 8(3), 233–274.

62. Hollander, E. P. (1992). The essential interdependence of leadership and followership. *Current Directions in Psychological Science,* 1(2), 71–75.

63. Korukonda, A. R. and Hunt, J. G. (1989). Pat on the back versus kick in the pants: An application of cognitive inference to the study of leader reward and punishment behaviors. *Group and Organization Studies,* 14(3), 299–324.

64. Podsakoff and Todor, Relationships between leader reward and punishment behavior and group process and productivity.

65. Fahr, J. L., Podsakoff, P. M. and Cheng, B. S. (1987). Culture-free leadership effectiveness versus moderators of leadership behavior: An extension and test of Kerr and Jermier's "substitutes for leadership" model in Taiwan. *Journal of International Business Studies,* 18, 43–60.

66. Dorfman, Howell, Hibino, Lee, Tate and Bautista, Leadership in western and Asian countries: Commonalities and differences in effective leadership processes across cultures.

67. Bachman, J. G., Smith, C. and Slesinger, J. A. (1966). Control, performance and satisfaction: An analysis of structural and individual effects. *Journal of Personality and Social Psychology,* 4, 127–136.

68. Weschler, I. R., Kahane, M. and Tannenbaum, R. (1952). Job satisfaction, productivity and morale: A case study. *Occupational Psychology,* 26, 1–4.

69. Bachman, J. G., Bowers, D. G. and Marcus, P. M. (1968). Bases of supervisory power: A comparative study in five organizational settings. In A. S. Tannenbaum (Ed.), *Control in Organizations.* New York: McGraw-Hill.

70. Ivancevich, J. M. and Donnelly, J. H. (1970). An analysis of control, bases of control, and satisfaction in an organizational setting. *Academy of Management Journal,* 13, 427–436.

71. Riecken, H. W. (1952). Some problems of consensus development. *Rural Sociology,* 17, 245–252.

72. Sheridan, J. E. and Vredenburgh, D. J. (1978). Usefulness of leadership behavior and social power variables in predicting job tension, performance, and turnover of nursing employees. *Journal of Applied Psychology,* 63, 89–95.

73. Martinko, M. J. and Gardner, W. L. (1982). Learned helplessness: An alternative explanation for performance deficits. *Academy of Management Review,* 7, 195–204.

74. Arvey, R. D., Davis, G. A. and Nelson, S. M. (1984). Use of discipline in an organization: A field study. *Journal of Applied Psychology,* 69, 448–460.

75. Podsakoff, Todor, Grover and Huber, Situational moderators of leader reward and punishment behaviors: Fact or fiction?

76. Podsakoff, Todor and Skov, Effect of leader contingent and noncontingent reward and punishment behaviors on subordinate performance and satisfaction.

77. Arvey, R. D. and Ivancevich, J. (1980). Punishment in organizations: A review, propositions, and research suggestion. *Academy of Management Review,* 51, 123–132.

78. Podsakoff, Todor and Skov, Effect of leader contingent and noncontingent reward and punishment behaviors on subordinate performance and satisfaction.

79. Korukonda and Hunt, Pat on the back versus kick in the pants: An application of cognitive inference to the study of leader reward and punishment behaviors.

80. Williams, M. L., Podsakoff, P. M. and Huber, V. (1992). Effects of group-level and individual-level variation in leader behaviors on subordinate attitudes and performance. *Journal of Occupational and Organizational Psychology,* 65(2), 115–129.

81. Podsakoff, P. M. and Todor, W. D. (1985). Relationships between leader reward and punishment behavior and group processes and productivity. *Journal of Management,* 11(1), 55–73.

82. Podsakoff, Todor, Grover and Huber, Situational moderators of leader reward and punishment behaviors: Fact or fiction?

83. Podsakoff, P. M., Dorfman, P. W., Howell, J. P. and Todor, W. D. (1986). Leader reward and punishment behaviors: A preliminary test of a culture-free style of leadership effectiveness. *Advances in International Comparative Management,* 2, 95–138.

84. Williams, Podsakoff and Huber, Effects of group-level and individual-level variation in leader behaviors on subordinate attitudes and performance.

85. Podsakoff and Todor, Relationship between leader reward and punishment behavior and group process and productivity.

86. Dorfman, Howell, Hibino, Lee, Tate and Bautista, Leadership in western and Asian countries: Commonalities and differences in effective leadership processes across cultures.

CHAPTER

11

Situational Dynamics of Leader Reward and Punishment Behaviors

Learning Objectives
After reading this chapter you should be able to do the following:

1. Describe follower characteristics that can make leader reward and punishment behaviors highly effective and characteristics that make them ineffective.

2. Describe organizational and task situations where leader reward and punishment behaviors will likely be highly effective and where they may be ineffective.

3. Discuss how leaders can modify situations to increase the effectiveness of their reward and punishment behaviors.

4. Describe how leaders can modify followers' work situations to make them less dependent on the leader's reward and punishment behaviors.

5. Explain how followers, situations, and leader reward and punishment behaviors interact and affect each other in a dynamic process.

In chapter 10, leader reward and punishment behaviors were described. The overall importance of leaders providing rewards and punishments contingent on followers' behavior or performance was emphasized. The general effects on followers of leaders' reward and punishment behaviors were also reported.

Although contingent reward and punishment behaviors often result in increased levels of performance and better attitudes, specific situational and follower characteristics may cause these leader behaviors to have a greater or lesser impact. Chapter 11 addresses these situational and follower characteristics.

Leaders' reward and/or punishment behaviors may or may not be appropriate in the situations described below. Place an "R" next to those situations where you believe leader *reward* behavior can be effective in influencing followers, place a "P" where you think leader *punishment* behavior can be effective, and place an "N" where you believe *neither* of these leader behaviors will be effective.

1. _____ The leader controls rewards that are important to followers and has a reputation for administering those rewards in a fair and impartial manner.
2. _____ Followers are highly skilled design engineers doing complex work, and good performance measures for their work have not been developed at this time.
3. _____ The leader is held in high esteem by followers and in the past has rewarded them for good performance. Recently, however, they have refused to follow the leader's directions on two consecutive assignments resulting in poor performance.
4. _____ Followers' job performance is a direct result of their effort on the job.
5. _____ Followers work at locations that are physically distant from their leader, making it difficult for the leader to accurately gauge their performance on a regular basis.
6. _____ Followers are highly trained professionals who derive intense satisfaction from their work and place little value on the rewards controlled by the leader.
7. _____ The leader possesses a high degree of expertise at followers' work tasks and has clearly explained to followers the criteria for good performance.
8. _____ A follower has been warned about demonstrating impolite and abusive behavior with other workers and customers, but this behavior has continued. The follower indicated she understands the necessity of treating coworkers and customers in a considerate manner, and she seems to be an emotionally stable individual.

A leader's contingent reward behaviors would probably be very effective in three of these situations. Items 1, 4, and 7 all include situational factors that make reward behaviors a useful influence strategy for leaders. The situations described in items 3 and 8 reflect a need for some type of punishment behavior by the leader. Here the followers' behavior requires correction, and followers are likely to respond to reasonable punishments in a mature manner. Items 2, 5, and 6 describe situations where neither reward nor punishment behaviors by the leader is likely to be effective with followers. Either the leader is unable to do a good job at evaluating followers' performance (making it very difficult to use rewards and punishments effectively), or followers are motivated by other factors that can replace the need for leaders' rewards and punishments. These situational and follower characteristics that make leaders' rewards and punishments effective, ineffective, or unnecessary are described in this chapter.

◆ SITUATIONAL FACTORS THAT INCREASE EFFECTIVENESS OF LEADER REWARD AND PUNISHMENT BEHAVIORS

Certain situational and follower characteristics can increase or enhance the impact of a leader's reward and punishment behaviors on followers' psychological reactions and behaviors. Practicing leaders are often very interested in these factors because they can make followers more responsive.

TASK, ORGANIZATIONAL, AND FOLLOWER CHARACTERISTICS

When leaders have control over substantial tangible rewards, they are a highly effective influence strategy (1,2) because followers believe in the leader's ability to provide valued rewards that have been promised. The leader's rank in the organization is closely related to control over rewards, since higher-ranking leaders often have larger and more varied rewards at their disposal. A compliment or appreciative comment from a high-level leader can be very satisfying and encouraging to an employee who seldom interacts with anyone other than an immediate supervisor or coworkers. In general, control over substantial rewards and high rank can enhance the effects of the leader's reward behavior on followers (3).

Several factors related to the performance-appraisal process increase the effects of leaders' contingent reward behavior on followers' job performance. These factors especially increase the impacts of tangible rewards. When good measures of follower performance are used by leaders to administer contingent rewards, when the rewards and performance criteria are clearly explained before the evaluation, and when rewards are distributed fairly and timely rather than arbitrarily or a long period of time after follower's performance, then leader-provided tangible rewards have an especially strong impact on follower performance (4,5).

When leaders are recognized as experts in followers' tasks, this tends to increase the impact of the leader's contingent reward behavior on followers' psychological reactions, including their commitment to the organization, satisfaction with work, and job clarity (6). Leaders' expertise increases followers' respect for the leader and their responsiveness to the leader's influence. When followers belong to a cohesive work group, the impact of a leader's contingent rewards on followers' performance can be enhanced (7,8). As described in earlier chapters, the effect of a cohesive work group on the leader's influence depends on the groups' performance norms, but when the norms are positive and encourage high performance, the results are usually favorable.

When rewards are valued and expected by followers, the leader's reward behavior is especially impactful (9,10,11). Moreover, when followers' performance is determined by their skill and effort, a leader's contingent reward behavior will have strong effects on followers' performance (12). These situational factors are present at the Lincoln Electric Company in Cleveland, Ohio where highly skilled employees are paid based strictly on the amount of good product they produce. They also receive quarterly bonuses from company profits. The size of bonus for each employee is determined by several indicators of their individual performance. Employees at Lincoln work very hard and are quite productive because they know they will be well compensated for their effort.

Regarding situational factors that increase effectiveness of leaders' contingent punishment behavior, research showed that when individuals viewed a leader as having high status and esteem, they reacted more favorably to punitive behavior than when the leader had low status and esteem (13). Thus, in this situation, the leader's status and esteem enhanced the effectiveness of punishment behavior, although another writer suggested that overuse of punishment by the leader may eventually undermine status and esteem (14).

A large variety of tasks performed by followers also may enhance the impact of a leader's contingent punishment behavior (15). In one line of research, which involved government workers, followers probably found contingent punishment to be helpful in clarifying appropriate and inappropriate behavior on the wide variety of tasks they perform. Task variety has not been studied extensively as a leadership enhancer, but this finding indicates it is worthy of more research. And, as indicated in chapter 10, when leader contingent punishment behavior was used concurrently with contingent reward behavior, the effects of both were increased (16).

Researchers have proposed several other leader activities as potential enhancers of leader punishment behavior (17). The leader activities include assuring the punishment is consistent with organizational rules and policies, administering it in private and making it appropriately severe, allowing followers to express their opinions and to appeal tangible punishments, and assuring that the leader's demeanor is not unpleasant. These behavioral factors are consistent with psychological research on learning, and leaders who keep them in mind are likely to yield positive results from their punishment behaviors.

Follower characteristics that may enhance the impacts of a leader's punishment include the follower's belief in a just world (a belief that people get what they deserve), their positive affectivity (a general positive outlook and self-concept), and their effective emotional coping behaviors (lack of worry or negative thinking, not interpreting negative feedback personally, maintaining an optimistic and effective approach to life). Followers with these characteristics are probably mature individuals who will interpret reasonable punishments as useful feedback they can use to guide their future behavior. Each of these factors is worthy of future research to confirm its enhancing effects. Figure 11–1 summarizes the enhancers of leader reward and punishment behaviors. The Leadership in Perspective box on rewards and punishments in team sports shows how specific follower and situational characteristics enhance a coach's influence.

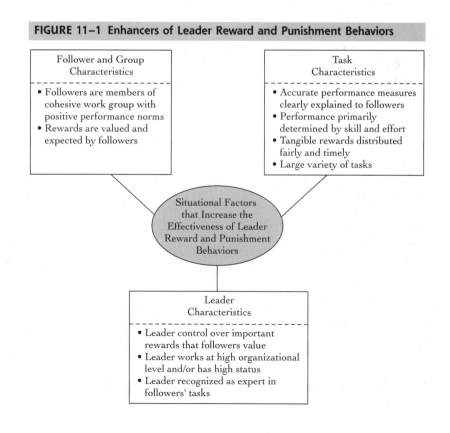

FIGURE 11–1 Enhancers of Leader Reward and Punishment Behaviors

Follower and Group Characteristics
- Followers are members of cohesive work group with positive performance norms
- Rewards are valued and expected by followers

Task Characteristics
- Accurate performance measures clearly explained to followers
- Performance primarily determined by skill and effort
- Tangible rewards distributed fairly and timely
- Large variety of tasks

Situational Factors that Increase the Effectiveness of Leader Reward and Punishment Behaviors

Leader Characteristics
- Leader control over important rewards that followers value
- Leader works at high organizational level and/or has high status
- Leader recognized as expert in followers' tasks

> ## LEADERSHIP IN PERSPECTIVE: REWARDS AND PUNISHMENT IN TEAM SPORTS
>
> Basketball, football, and baseball players love to play their game. The best performing players on a team are normally part of the starting lineup. Therefore, being chosen as a "starter" is one of the most valued rewards a coach can give a player. The next most important reward a coach controls is playing time. The players who contribute the most to a team usually play the most minutes or innings in a game. The high value players place on starting and playing time and the control of these factors by the coach both enhance their effects on the players' behavior and performance. But, because coaches can also withhold these two factors, they can be used to punish players for inappropriate behavior. Players are often pulled from the starting lineup or their playing time is reduced for missing practice, breaking team rules, lack of hustle, or poor performance. Effective coaches use the starting lineup and playing time as rewards for maximum effort and high performance and as punishments for inappropriate behavior by team members.

INFLUENCING SITUATIONS TO MAKE LEADER REWARDS AND PUNISHMENTS MORE EFFECTIVE

One set of factors that enhances the impact of leader reward behavior deals with followers' performance and how it is evaluated by the leader. To assure rewards are contingent on followers' performance, the leader must obtain and use accurate performance measures. These performance measures may be included in the organization's performance-evaluation system, or the leader may create them. Performance measures should be clearly explained and the rewards identified for specific behaviors or performance levels. When followers achieve desired performance levels, rewards should be provided in an equitable and timely fashion.

Leaders who are at low levels in an organization and control few tangible rewards may attempt to negotiate with their superiors to obtain more reward power. They can also assure followers that they control some valued rewards (such as task assignments, work schedules, etc.). If leaders talk frankly with followers and think about their desires, values, and the work situation, they can often identify innovative and valued rewards. If these rewards are used along with intangible social rewards like praise, they can overcome constraints on leaders' power to control other tangible rewards and enhance the leaders' impacts (18).

Leaders can increase their task expertise by continually updating their skills and knowledge and making themselves available to assist followers with task problems. They can encourage development of cohesive work groups by helping groups succeed at work tasks, providing resources for groups, and increasing opportunities and rewards for follower interaction. These strategies will increase the leaders' perceived expertise, and the cohesion among followers and will likely also encourage group norms that are supportive of the leader. These factors should enhance the impact of the leader's contingent reward behavior.

Increasing perceived expertise can also increase the leader's status and esteem in the eyes of followers. Superiors can increase a leader's status by making public state-

LEADERSHIP IN ACTION: HOW LEADERS CAN REWARD FOLLOWERS

The following are examples of rewards used by leaders in several organizations.

A Pat-on-the-Back Award is given by managers to employees at Bush Gardens who do an outstanding job. Receiving the award is recorded in the employee's personnel file.

At Amway Corporation employees who are commended in customers' letters are sent flowers.

When an employee at Pacific Gas & Electric has a noteworthy achievement, the manager rings a ship's bell.

As a reward for outstanding performance at South Carolina Federal financial services, the top managers serve lunch to the high-performance employees.

All employees who worked on the first Apple Macintosh computer had their signatures placed on the inside of all the Macintoshes manufactured.

Founder of IBM, Thomas J. Watson Sr., wrote checks on the spot to employees who were doing an outstanding job.

Managers at Bell Atlantic named cellular telephone sites after highly productive employees.

Mary Kay Cosmetics rewards the top independent sellers with pink Cadillacs and diamond rings.

ments about a leader's competence, capabilities, and accomplishments and championing the leader to those outside the leader's group. These strategies can enhance both reward *and* punishment behaviors. If leaders use liberal doses of contingent reward behavior (tangible and intangible) along with carefully selected punishment behaviors, they can increase the impacts of both these behavioral strategies.

In implementing enhancers of contingent punishment behavior, leaders should assure that followers view punishments as contingent on their actions or performance. Making punishment consistent in all situations and for all followers also helps assure maximum effect from punishment. Consistency tells followers when to expect punishment, and they can use this knowledge to control their own behavior and avoid punishment.

◆ SITUATIONAL FACTORS THAT DECREASE EFFECTIVENESS OF LEADER REWARD AND PUNISHMENT BEHAVIORS

Several situational characteristics can decrease the effectiveness of a leader's contingent reward behavior. These factors neutralize the impact of the leader's behaviors on followers.

TASK, ORGANIZATIONAL, AND FOLLOWER CHARACTERISTICS

A large spatial distance between the leader and followers has been seen to decrease the impact on followers' psychological reactions and job performance. This distance is common in many service organizations, and its neutralizing effect has been found in studies of government workers in the United States and Taiwan and in hospitals, universities, insurance companies, and public utilities in the United States (19,20,21). Individuals who work at locations distant from their leader often have a high degree of job autonomy (independence from their leader). Examples of these types of workers are salespersons, technicians, construction workers, military personnel, other service and professional workers, and increasing numbers of individuals working in their homes. It is often difficult for a leader to regularly gauge performance and to reward followers in these situations. Contingent reward behavior may therefore not be especially effective. Although this limitation may apply especially to nontangible social rewards, leaders in these situations should probably emphasize other leadership behaviors described in this book to influence followers.

The existence of a closely knit cohesive work group with antileader norms can decrease the impact of a leader's reward behavior on followers' satisfaction with work, satisfaction with coworkers, and job clarity (22,23). When individuals work in a group with mutual support and camaraderie, they can derive many of their social rewards from coworkers rather than the leader. If followers do not value their leader's input, they may actually develop a norm of noncooperation with the leader. As noted earlier, however, a cohesive group can also enhance the effect of leader reward behavior when group members share a positive productivity norm.

Studies have also shown that a high degree of organizational formalization can decrease the impact of a leader's contingent reward behavior on followers' performance (24,25). Organizational formalization can also replace certain leader behaviors. Written plans, goals, and guidelines can clarify task requirements for followers and facilitate effective performance, which can sometimes produce follower satisfaction without rewards from leaders. This situational characteristic, then, is an important neutralizer or replacement of reward behavior and must be carefully considered by leaders when attempting to use rewards to influence followers.

One other situational neutralizer of reward behavior has been suggested, although no studies have confirmed its effect. When followers' performance is largely determined by factors outside their control (such as bad luck, poor weather, machine breakdowns, or errors by other people), then the impact of leaders' contingent reward behavior is likely decreased (26). This suggested neutralizer makes sense because a leader's rewards can affect only factors that are under followers' control. However, the effects of these situational factors are likely temporary. We suspect that once performance is under the control of the follower, a leader's contingent reward behavior will again become effective for influencing followers.

Two follower characteristics have also been noted as neutralizers of leaders' contingent reward behavior. First, followers' indifference toward organizational rewards can decrease the effect of leader rewards on follower performance (27,28,29). Logically, if followers do not value the tangible or intangible rewards offered by a leader, those rewards will have little effect on their attitudes and behavior. Second, followers' intrinsic task satisfaction decreased the impact of a leader's contingent rewards on follower satisfaction in one study (30). This finding should be further investigated in future research.

Several writers have proposed other follower characteristics that may decrease the impacts of a leader's contingent reward behavior. First, when followers do not believe they can perform well enough to receive rewards, they may not respond to a leader's promised rewards (31). Second, if followers believe rewards are provided in a capricious and arbitrary manner and are not based on an accurate assessment of their performance, they will probably not respond to them (32,33). These suggested neutralizers are consistent with research on motivation in organizations (34). Future research is needed to verify their neutralizing effect on leaders' contingent reward behavior.

Two situational factors act as neutralizers of leaders' contingent punishment behavior. A large spatial distance between a leader and followers can decrease the impact of contingent punishment on followers' satisfaction (35). Also, when workers have an opportunity to interact with one another in the leader's absence or observe others disobeying the leader, they are less likely to be influenced by a leader's punishment behavior (36). It appears that spatial distance and a highly interactive (cohesive) group of followers with antileader norms may have the same neutralizing effects on a leader's contingent punishment behavior as on contingent reward behavior. Figure 11–2 summarizes situational factors that decrease effectiveness of leader reward and punishment behaviors.

OVERCOMING FACTORS THAT DECREASE EFFECTIVENESS OF LEADER REWARDS AND PUNISHMENTS

When followers work autonomously or at a distance from the leader, it is difficult for the leader to adequately monitor their performance and behavior in order to administer contingent rewards and punishments. It is often best in these situations to seek followers with professionalism, work experience, and intrinsic task satisfaction and to offer

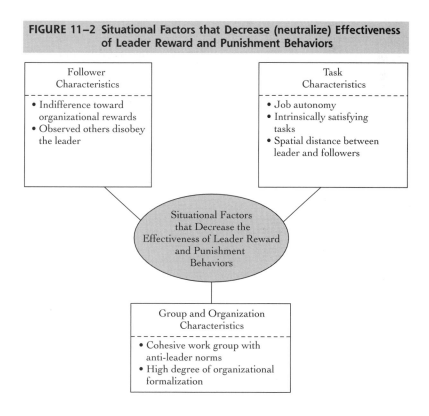

FIGURE 11–2 Situational Factors that Decrease (neutralize) Effectiveness of Leader Reward and Punishment Behaviors

Follower Characteristics
- Indifference toward organizational rewards
- Observed others disobey the leader

Task Characteristics
- Job autonomy
- Intrinsically satisfying tasks
- Spatial distance between leader and followers

Situational Factors that Decrease the Effectiveness of Leader Reward and Punishment Behaviors

Group and Organization Characteristics
- Cohesive work group with anti-leader norms
- High degree of organizational formalization

LEADERSHIP IN ACTION: LEADING SOCIAL WORKERS

Social workers often work in poor urban or rural areas with high crime rates. They provide advice, counseling, and representation for individuals and families who need help in seeking employment, collecting welfare, or obtaining other social services. They usually meet with clients on their own with no manager present to administer organizational rewards or punishments. But the type of individual who becomes a social worker is not motivated primarily by leaders' rewards and punishments. These individuals often feel a "calling" to help the less fortunate in our society. They undergo considerable formal education and practical training to prepare them to work independently. This education and training socializes them to take professional pride in the service they provide. They get considerable intrinsic satisfaction from helping their clients. These factors usually overcome any need for leaders' rewards and punishments to influence social workers to do their best for clients. Leaders in this situation should probably provide continuous training and development opportunities and resources to help the social workers serve their clients most effectively.

them additional training and education. These replacements for leaders' rewards and punishments are discussed in the next section of this chapter. The leader will also likely rely on other leadership behaviors that do not require continuous monitoring, such as supportive and charismatic ones.

When cohesive work groups with antileader norms, intrinsically satisfying tasks, or indifference toward organizational rewards neutralize leader reward behaviors, leaders can try to foster a professional pride in followers so that they will perform at high levels without regular monitoring and contingent rewards. Additional training or group development approaches may transform these follower and group characteristics into useful replacements for leaders' rewards and punishments, providing motivation and guidance independent of the leader. The Leadership in Action box on leading social workers describes how situational factors that neutralize leaders' rewards and punishments can be overcome.

◆ SITUATIONAL FACTORS THAT REPLACE THE NEED FOR LEADER REWARD AND PUNISHMENT BEHAVIORS

Some studies have shown that situational characteristics can act as replacements for leaders' contingent reward and punishment behaviors. Several characteristics of the task, the organization, and followers can replace the need for these leader behaviors.

TASK, ORGANIZATIONAL, AND FOLLOWER CHARACTERISTICS

A high degree of organizational formalization (numerous plans, goals, and/or procedures to guide organizational members) or an organization-wide reward system can replace the impact of a leader's contingent reward behavior on followers' satisfaction or performance (37,38). A formal organizational reward system that operates independently of the leader can be one aspect of overall plans, goals, and procedures designed to guide followers' activities. Examples occur with individuals who sell life insurance or real estate and earn a fixed commission on their sales regardless of their leader's behavior. Under these conditions, the guidance aspects of a leader's informal rewards and punishments can become less important to followers.

A closely knit, cohesive work group with strong performance norms can also replace the effects of a leader's contingent rewards (39,40,41). Cohesive work groups are a good source of guidance and good feelings for followers. Also, the existence of a leader with high expertise at followers' tasks or high rank can replace the need for a leader's reward behavior (42). Here followers react favorably to requests by leaders with status, prestige, or know-how without requiring rewards for their behavior.

Much of the research reported here is quite recent and has been conducted outside the United States. In contrast, several studies in the United States have found *no* situational characteristics that replace leaders' contingent reward and punishment behaviors (43,44,45,46). However, this may be partially due to inconsistent research methods. Also, many researchers have overlooked the distinctions between leadership enhancers, neutralizers, or replacements, making it difficult for the reader to asses the results. The scarcity of findings in the United States may also be due to the individualistic nature of the culture. Individualism may make followers highly responsive to rewards and/or punishments from their leader. In fact, more follower characteristics than situational factors have been found to replace leaders' contingent reward and punishment behaviors in the United States. At this point, the limited evidence suggests that situational characteristics seldom act as replacements for leaders' contingent reward and punishment behaviors in the United States, although situational replacements may be more common in other countries.

Several characteristics of followers may replace effects of leaders' contingent reward behavior. The most frequently occurring replacement effects have occurred with followers who are highly professional, have extensive schooling, or have many years of work experience. These factors all provide followers with relevant knowledge and ability that they can apply to their work tasks, independent of the leader's guidance. In turn, they may at least partially replace the impact of reward behavior on followers' satisfaction, job clarity, and job performance in the United States and other countries (47,48,49). Replacement effects of this type may also occur if a long period of training or experience has created in followers a high degree of pride in doing a good job and the desire to control their own behavior (50,51). These individuals do not rely on leader-provided reinforcement for their motivation and job satisfaction.

Another follower replacement that may be related to the professionalism and experience of followers is indifference toward organizational rewards. This characteristic is found in followers who derive their motivation and satisfaction from sources other than the leader or their employing organization. They are usually committed to their work and derive pleasure from doing it well. These replacement effects have occurred most often in studies of managers (52,53). Intrinsic task satisfaction is a related characteristic that can also replace the effects of reward behavior on followers' satisfaction (54,55). Thus, for followers who enjoy their work and derive their motivation and satisfaction from work activities rather than from their leader's reinforcement, the effects of the leader's contingent reward behavior can be minimal and unnecessary.

The pattern of findings for follower characteristics indicates strong replacement effects for followers who have considerable schooling and professional training or experience, and who derive more satisfaction from doing their jobs well than from the rewards offered by their leader. The same may be true with regard to contingent punishment, but no research was available on that subject. We suspect, however, that many of the follower characteristics that replace leader reward behavior will do the same for intangible leader punishments.

CREATING FACTORS THAT REPLACE THE NEED FOR LEADER REWARD AND PUNISHMENT BEHAVIOR

Follower characteristics are the most important replacements for a leader's contingent reward behavior. Leaders who select highly trained professional followers and/or those with considerable work experience can rely on those followers to carry out many required tasks on their own. The leader who develops followers and delegates important tasks will also increase followers' motivation to work autonomously and without continuous reward behavior by the leader. Designing jobs and task assignments that match individuals with their interests will create high levels of intrinsic task satisfaction in followers, further increasing their desire to perform independently and at high levels. As the leader's group of followers become increasingly professional, experienced, and intrinsically satisfied with their work tasks, they will derive most of their motivation from these tasks and will be less reliant on leader-provided organizational rewards. This will free up the leader for other leadership activities.

Two situational characteristics that show the most promise as replacements for leader reward behavior are cohesive work groups with strong performance norms and

TABLE 11–1 Situational and Follower Characteristics that Affect the Impact of Leader Reward and Punishment Behavior

Factors that Increase the Effectiveness of Reward and Punishment Behavior	*Factors that Decrease the Effectiveness of Reward and Punishment Behavior*	*Factors that Replace the Need for Reward and Punishment Behavior*
• Leader controls important rewards that are valued and/or expected by followers	• Spatial distance between leader and followers	• High degree of professionalism
• Leader works at a high organizational level	• Followers' job autonomy	• Years of schooling and work experience by followers
• Accurate measures of performance used and clearly explained	• Intrinsically satisfying tasks	• Intrinsically satisfying tasks
• Tangible rewards distributed fairly and timely	• Indifference toward organizational rewards	• Indifference toward organizational rewards
• Performance determined by skill and effort	• Existence of cohesive work groups with antileader norms	• Formalized group or organizational reward system
• Leader is recognized as expert in followers' tasks or has high ability	• High degree of organizational formalization	
• Cohesive work group exists with positive performance norms		
• Rewards are valued and expected by followers		

group or organizational reward systems. Cohesive groups with strong performance norms can be developed by helping the group attain a high level of performance, by providing adequate resources for the group, increasing the group's status, and increasing the opportunities for favorable interaction among group members. Recall that the weight of evidence indicates that cohesive groups with strong performance norms generally improve follower and group psychological reactions and performance. They may do this as enhancers or replacements of leaders' reward and punishment behaviors. Group or organizational reward systems (such as gainsharing plans) also improve followers' psychological reactions and behaviors, possibly as replacements for leader reward behaviors. Leaders should therefore encourage and work toward designing reward systems of this type to alleviate some of the need for the leader to regularly provide tangible rewards contingent on followers' behaviors. Since empirical findings on replacements for leader punishment behaviors are almost nonexistent, little can be said at this time regarding the creation of replacements for this leader behavior. Table 11–1 summarizes the three types of situational and follower characteristics that affect the impact of a leader's reward and punishment behavior. Figure 11–3 provides an example of the influence of situational factors on the reward and punishment behaviors of public school principals.

FIGURE 11–3 Influence of Situational Factors on the Reward and Punishment Behaviors of Public School Principals

Situational factors that could increase effectiveness of a principal's reward and punishment behaviors

- The principal has control over raises and performance evaluations that teachers value highly as rewards.
- The principal is recognized by the teachers as having a high degree of expertise in their jobs.
- The teachers' achievements are determined by their own skill and effort.
- The teachers believe that in the past rewards have been distributed in a fair and timely manner.

How Situational Factors can Affect the Impact of Reward and Punishment Behaviors by a Public School Principal

Situational factors that could decrease the effectiveness of a principal's reward and punishment behaviors

- The rewards controlled by the principal are considered trivial by the teachers.
- The teachers have formed highly cohesive work groups that identify with the teachers' union and have antileader norms.

Situational factors that could replace the need for a principal's reward and punishment behaviors

- The teachers are highly professional with extensive education and experience.
- The teachers get intrinsic satisfaction from their jobs because they can observe positive student outcomes.

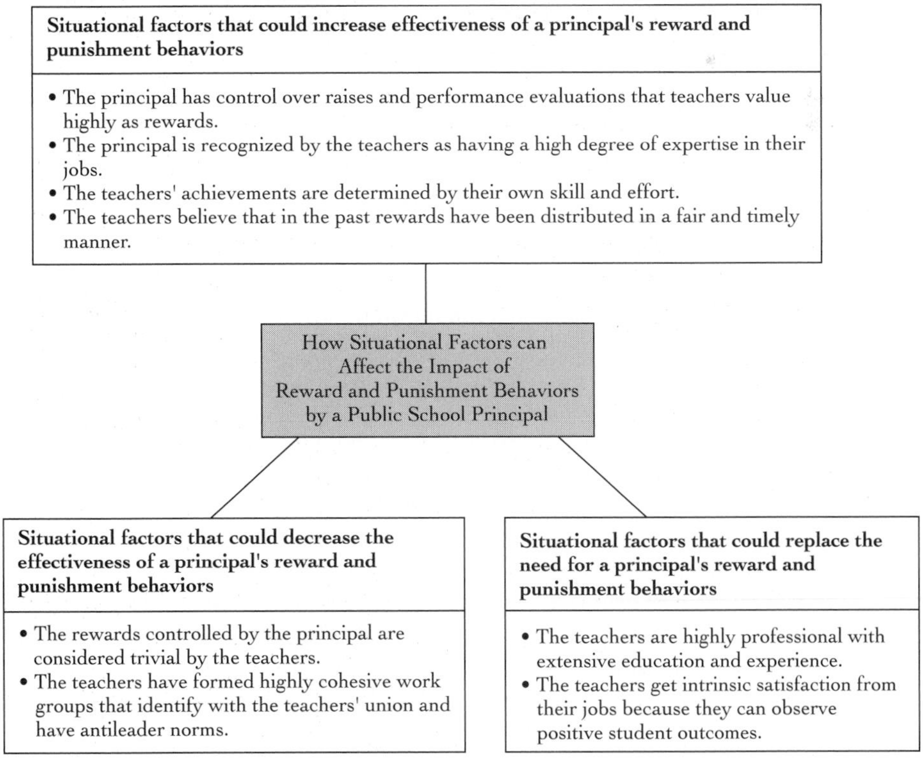

◆ ASSESSING THE DYNAMICS OF LEADER REWARD AND PUNISHMENT BEHAVIORS

Leaders' reward and punishment behaviors, followers' background and personal characteristics, and the organizational situation all interact to affect how leaders influence their followers. If the leader's diagnosis of the situation identifies follower or situational characteristics that increase (enhance) the effectiveness of reward and punishment behaviors (see table 11–1), then the leader can probably use this behavior pattern as an effective influence strategy with followers. If the leader's diagnosis identifies factors that decrease (neutralize) the effects of a leader's rewards and punishments (table 11–1), the leader should consider other leader behaviors to influence followers. If the leader diagnoses followers' characteristics that replace the need for the leader's rewards and punishments (table 11–1), then this leader behavior may be unnecessary with these followers. The leader can then concentrate on other behavior patterns to satisfy follower needs. Leaders must consider situational and follower characteristics before using rewards and punishments to influence followers.

Effective leaders also diagnose situations to determine if they can make them more favorable. Leaders can sometimes create enhancers or eliminate neutralizers to make their reward and punishment behaviors more effective. Leaders can do this by developing accurate measures of followers' performance, negotiating with superiors for more control over valued rewards, administering them in a fair and timely manner, or increasing their own status and expertise through advanced technical training. They can also create cohesive follower groups with high-performance norms by providing adequate resources, helping followers succeed at tasks, advertising followers' achievements, and creating opportunities for favorable followers' interactions. These and other possible strategies can create a situation where a leader's rewards and punishments are particularly effective at influencing followers.

Leaders can also create replacements for their rewards and punishments to enable followers to work independently. They can do this by hiring or developing highly professional and experienced followers who can perform well without the leader's regular guidance. Through individual follower development, careful delegation of challenging job tasks, thoughtful job design, and training experiences, individuals can become autonomous performers who are less reliant on their leaders for regular guidance and rewards. Leaders can also develop formalized group or organizational reward systems (such as gainsharing) that encourage or discourage specific follower behaviors and operate independently of the leader.

If important enhancers exist or can be created for a leader's reward and punishment behaviors, then followers will likely respond favorably to this behavior by their leader. However, if followers do not respond to the leader's rewards and punishments and the leader does not succeed at creating enhancers or eliminating critical neutralizers, then replacements for this leader behavior are needed. The leader should then attempt to create those follower or organizational characteristics that enable followers to perform effectively with little direct help from their leader. The leader thus uses rewards and punishments and/or modifies the followers' situation based on followers' reactions to the leader as well as diagnosis of situational conditions and followers' characteristics.

Summary ■■

Although a leader's contingent reward and punishment behaviors generally improve followers' psychological reactions and behaviors, certain situational and follower characteristics make these leader behaviors more or less effective. Leaders need to be aware of these factors and select influence strategies that will maximize their effectiveness. Providing rewards and punishments and modifying followers' work situations are both useful strategies to influence followers' behaviors.

Figure 11–4 presents a Leadership Process Model of leaders' contingent reward and punishment behavior. This model integrates the discussion in chapter 10 on impacts of contingent reward and punishment with the chapter 11 material on situational factors that can increase, decrease, or replace the effects of these leader behaviors. Reward and punishment behaviors are shown at the top of figure 11–4. Downward arrows show these leader behaviors influencing follower and group psychological reactions which in turn affect follower behavioral outcomes. Important situational factors are shown on each side of the figure. Arrows from the situational factor boxes which intersect the downward pointing arrow from the leader behavior box indicate that situational factors can increase, decrease, or replace the effects of leaders' reward and punishment behaviors. Arrows also connect the leader behavior box with situational factor boxes, indicating that leaders can modify the situation or followers to make the results more favorable. The single arrow connecting the situational factor box on the left side of figure 11–4 with follower and group psychological reactions shows that certain replacements for leaders' rewards and punishments may affect psychological reactions. Another arrow could be shown in figure 11–4 from follower behavioral outcomes to the leader behavior box at the top of the model. This would show that followers' behavior can affect future leader behaviors, which is certainly true and is mentioned in this chapter. This and other possible effects are deleted in order to keep the figure 11–4 from becoming overly complex.

Figure 11–5 is shown to help the leader use the information from figure 11–4 in a real leadership situation. Similar to comparable figures in the earlier chapters, it shows the three key leadership tasks of diagnosing situations, providing leadership, and modifying followers and situations. Leaders first diagnose the situation by answering the questions in box 1. If the answer is "yes" to one or more of these questions, then important enhancers exist in that situation and a leader's rewards and punishments will likely be effective with followers. The leader then provides the appropriate rewards or punishments shown in box 2. The leader assesses his impacts on followers and examines the followers' situation to determine if it can be modified to make it more effective for the leader and followers. Box 3 shows possible modifications that create replacements for leaders' reward and punishment behaviors, enabling followers to work more independently of the leader. The leader might also modify the situation by creating more enhancers or eliminating neutralizers, although these are not shown in order to keep figure 11–5 from becoming too complex. The leader then rediagnoses the situation (box 1) and reconsiders the amount and type of reward and punishment behavior that is needed. If the answer is "no" to all the questions in box 1, then the leader should probably consider other leader behaviors and/or assess the situation and followers for possible modification. Figure 11–5 represents the dynamic nature of leader reward and punishment behaviors.

FIGURE 11–4 Leadership Process Model of Leader Reward and Punishment Behaviors

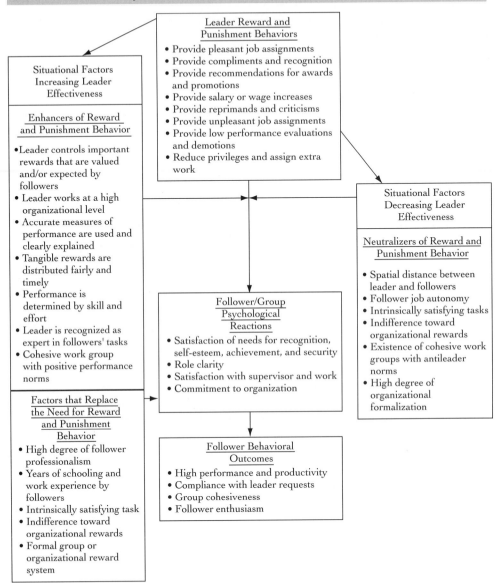

Key Terms and Concepts in this Chapter ▪ ▪ ▪ ▪ ▪ ▪ ▪ ▪ ▪ ▪ ▪ ▪ ▪ ▪ ▪ ▪ ▪

- cohesive work groups
- contingent punishment behaviors
- contingent reward behaviors
- coping behaviors
- individualism
- intrinsic task satisfaction
- job autonomy
- organizational formalization
- organization-wide reward systems
- performance norms
- positive affectivity
- professionalism

FIGURE 11–5 Applying the Model of Leader Reward and Punishment Behaviors

1. Diagnosing the Situation

- Does leader have control over important rewards that are valued by followers?
- Does leader work at a high level in the organization?
- Are accurate measures of performance used and clearly explained?
- Are tangible rewards distributed fairly and timely?
- Is performance determined by skill and effort?
- Is the leader recognized as an expert in the followers' tasks?
- Are there cohesive work groups with positive performance norms?

If "yes" to one or more of these questions, followers will expect and value reward and punishment leader behavior.
If "no," consider other leader behaviors or situational modification.

3. Modifying Followers and/or Situations

Leaders also act to:

- Develop a high degree of follower professionalism
- Provide additional schooling and task training for followers
- Develop intrinsically satisfying tasks by modifying job structure

2. Providing Reward and Punishment Behaviors

Leaders demonstrate reward and punishment behaviors with followers by:

- Pleasant job assignments
- Compliments and recognition
- Recommendations for awards and promotions
- Salary or wage increases
- Reprimands and criticisms
- Unpleasant job assignments
- Low performance evaluations and demotions
- Reduced privileges and extra work

Review and Discussion Questions

1. Describe a situation you have experienced or observed where a leader effectively used rewards or punishments. Why was the leader's use of rewards or punishments effective in this situation?

2. Describe a situation you have experienced or observed where a leader's use of rewards or punishments was not effective. Why was the leader's use of rewards or punishments not effective in this situation?

3. Give several specific examples of situational factors that could cause leader reward and/or punishment behavior to be highly effective. For each example, explain why the situational factors would increase the leader's impact on followers.

4. Give several specific examples of situational factors that could cause leader reward and/or punishment behavior to be less effective. For each example, explain why the situational factors would decrease the leader's impact on followers.

5. As a follower, which of the situational characteristics described in this chapter have had the most impact on your reaction to leaders' use of rewards and punishments? How have these characteristics affected your reaction to leaders' use of rewards and punishments?

6. As a leader, how could you create situational factors that would increase your influence when using rewards and punishments?

7. Do you think reward and punishment leader behaviors would be effective for a military commander? Why or why not?

Exercise: Choosing an Appropriate Leadership Style ▪▪▪▪▪▪▪▪▪▪▪▪▪

TASK 1: (5–10 Minutes)

Read the following scenario carefully and think about how you would behave if you were a leader in this situation.

You manage an automotive accessories and repair department in a large department store. Profit margins of department stores are being squeezed by large discount chains, resulting in numerous department store closings nationwide. Auto accessories such as batteries, shock absorbers, and other items have always been a major profit center in your store, generating a large percentage of the store's total revenue and earnings. Total sales of the automotive department have been at a moderate to low level during the winter and early spring and the rest of the store has been doing even worse.

The salespeople in your department are all fairly young (in their 20s and 30s), about half graduated from high school (none attended college), and all have families with small children. They are paid on an hourly basis, and several of them have other jobs in their off hours to supplement their income. They get along fairly well but each is so busy and involved with his own family that there is little social interaction among them outside work. They are generally experienced, capable, and highly independent.

From your experience, you know that store traffic always increases in the summer, and customers are interested in making sure their cars are comfortable, safe, and reliable for summer vacations. A successful salesperson in this department is one who is up-to-date on all product specifications, is outgoing and polite to customers, helps customers troubleshoot problems with their cars, and follows up on customer inquiries with an attempt to close each sale. All these activities are directly related to the effort and skill of the salesperson. Your store has a reputation for quality products and service, which the store management believes must be maintained. The store manager has emphasized that you must significantly increase the sales of your department or the entire store will be threatened with possible closing. The manager has confidence in you and believes that department managers should have the freedom to lead and motivate their people as they see fit.

TASK 2: (15 Minutes)

Rate each of the following triads of statements according to how much you agree with them as an appropriate leader behavior by the manager in this situation. For each triad, rate the statement you believe is most appropriate and impactful as a 1, rate the statement you think is least appropriate as a 3, and rate the other statement as a 2. You must rate all the statements in each triad as a 1, 2, or 3. No two items in a triad can be given the same rating. Mark your answers in the *Your Answer* column and complete all five triads of statements. For a given triad of statements, your answers might look like the following:

YOUR ANSWER

1. ___3___
2. ___1___
3. ___2___

	Your Answer	Triad Answer

TRIAD I

1. Tell salespeople that they must increase sales during the summer. _____ _____

2. Be friendly and encourage followers to keep up the high-quality service they provide. _____ _____

3. Revise the compensation system so salespeople are paid commissions based on the amount of their sales. _____ _____

TRIAD II

4. Hold a group meeting with all departmental employees to ask for their ideas on how to increase sales while maintaining quality of service. _____ _____

5. Emphasize appropriate sales techniques and the importance of closing all sales. _____ _____

6. Provide coupons for local grocery stores to salespeople who reach a specific sales goal. _____ _____

TRIAD III

7. Keep followers informed and let them know you trust them to do a good job. _____ _____

8. Inform the store manager whenever a salesperson reaches a high level of sales or provides outstanding service to customers. _____ _____

9. Closely monitor salespeople to be sure they use effective sales techniques. _____ _____

TRIAD IV

10. Show concern for the status and well-being of all department employees during this stressful period. _____ _____

11. Recommend a pay increase for an employee whose sales are unusually high. _____ _____

12. Write a letter of commendation for an employee whose sales and service are outstanding. _____ _____

TRIAD V

13. Conduct a review/training session with salespeople about product characteristics and correct sales techniques. _____ _____

14. Be approachable and sympathetic about employees' problems and concerns. _____ _____

15. Provide coupons for gasoline to salespeople who receive repeated compliments from customers about their good service. _____ _____

TASK 3 (20–30 Minutes)

Now form groups of three people with others in your class. Complete a *Triad Solution* to the 15 statements by coming to agreement within your group on the ratings for each statement. Discuss each statement with others in your group in order to reach agreement.

TASK 4 (20–30 Minutes)

The instructor will now discuss this scenario and the statements about leadership behavior by relating them to the Leadership Process Model and leader behaviors described thus far in the book.

◆◆◆ **Case Incident**

Move the Supervisors?

Pam Hill is the site manager for a government contractor doing highly technical and complex design and testing of military systems. The work is being done on a military installation under the control of the military. Ms. Hill is responsible for two development teams that are working on the project. One team works the day shift and the other works the night shift.

The day shift (7:00 a.m. to 4:00 p.m.) is ahead of schedule and under budget. It has an excellent safety record with no lost time for accidents. The day shift has been commended by the military commander for excellent security and has had no security violations. The team is highly cohesive, and members cooperate with each other. The supervisor of the day shift has received very high performance evaluations from both management and team members.

The night shift (4:30 p.m. to 12:30 a.m.) is behind schedule and over budget. It has a poor safety record with three lost-time accidents in the previous month. The night shift has been written up twice for security violations, and a third violation could result in the government suspending the contract. Team members on the night shift have filed numerous grievances related to interpersonal conflicts on the team, and they do not seem to cooperate with each other. The supervisor of the night shift has received very low performance evaluations from both management and team members.

Ms. Hill feels she must do something immediately to correct the problems on the night shift. To achieve a quick improvement in the situation, she has decided to move the supervisor on the day shift to the night shift and to move the supervisor on the night shift to the day shift.

QUESTIONS

1. If you were one of the supervisors involved, how would you interpret Ms. Hill's action in terms of who and what is getting rewarded and punished?
2. Do you think this action by Ms. Hill will improve performance on the night shift? Why?
3. What effect do you think Ms. Hill's action will have on the day shift? Why?
4. If you were advising Ms. Hill, what actions would you advise her to take?

Endnotes ▪▪▪

1. Hughes, R. L., Ginnett, R. C., Curphy, G. J. (1993). *Leadership: Enhancing the Lessons of Experience.* Homewood, IL: Irwin.

2. Arvey, R. D. and Ivancevich, J. M. (1980). Punishment in organizations: A review, propositions and research suggestions. *Academy of Management Review,* 5, 123–132.

3. Howell, J. P., Dorfman, P. W., Hibino, S., Lee, J. K. and Tate U. (1994). Leadership in western and Asian countries: Commonalities and differences in effective leadership processes and substitutes across cultures. Bureau of Business Research, New Mexico State University.

4. Lawler, E. E. III. (1971). *Pay and Organizational Effectiveness.* New York: McGraw-Hill.

5. Luthans, F., Paul, R. and Baker, D. (1981). An experimental analysis of the impact of contingent reinforcement on salespersons' performance behavior. *Journal of Applied Psychology,* 64, 314–323.

6. Howell, Dorfman, Hibino, Lee and Tate, Leadership in western and Asian countries: Commonalities and differences in effective leadership processes and substitutes across cultures.

7. Podsakoff, P. M., Todor, W. D., Grover, R. A. and Huber, V. L. (1984). Situational moderators of leader reward and punishment behavior: Fact or fiction? *Organizational Behavior and Human Performance,* 34, 21–63.

8. Howell, Dorfman, Hibino, Lee and Tate, Leadership in western and Asian countries: Commonalities and differences in effective leadership processes and substitutes across cultures.

9. Ilgen, D. R., Fisher, C. D. and Taylor, M. S. (1979). Consequences of individual feedback on behavior in organizations. *Journal of Applied Psychology,* 64, 349–371.

10. Bennis, W. G, Berkowitz, N., Affinito, M. and Malone, M. (1958). Authority, power, and the ability to influence. *Human Relations,* 11, 143–155.

11. Bass, B. (1990). *Bass and Stogdill's Handbook of Leadership* (3rd ed.). New York: The Free Press.

12. Yukl, G. A. (1998). Leadership in Organizations (4th ed.). Upper Saddle River, NJ: Prentice Hall.

13. Iverson, M. A. (1964). Personality impressions of punitive stimulus persons of differential status. *Journal of Abnormal and Social Psychology,* 68, 617–626.

14. Bass, *Bass and Stogdill's Handbook of Leadership.*

15. Podsakoff, Todor, Grover and Huber, Situational moderators of leader reward and punishment behavior: Fact or fiction?

16. Brass, D. J. and Oldham, G. R. (1976). Validating an in-basket test using an alternative set of leadership scoring dimensions. *Journal of Applied Psychology,* 61, 652–657.

17. Ball, G. A., Trevino, L. K. and Sims, H. P. Jr. (1992). Understanding subordinate reactions to punishment incidents: Perspectives from justice and social effect. *Leadership Quarterly,* 3(4), 307–333.

18. Hughes, Ginnett and Curphy, *Leadership: Enhancing the Lessons of Experience.*

19. Podsakoff, Todor, Grover and Huber, Situational moderators of leader reward and punishment behavior: Fact or fiction?

20. Fahr, J. L., Podsakoff, P. M. and Cheng, B. S. (1987). Culture-free leadership effectiveness versus moderators of leadership behavior: An extension and test of Kerr and Jermier's "substitutes for leadership" model in Taiwan. *Journal of International Business Studies,* 18, 43–60.

21. Podsakoff, P. M., Niehoff, B. P., MacKenzie, S. B. and Williams, M. L. (1993). Do substitutes for leadership really substitute for leadership? An empirical investigation of Kerr and Jermier's situational leadership model. *Organizational Behavior and Human Decision Processes,* 54, 1–44.

22. Podsakoff, Dorfman, Howell and Todor, Leader reward and punishment behaviors: A preliminary test of a culture-free style of leadership effectiveness.

23. Podsakoff, Niehoff, MacKenzie and Williams, Do substitutes for leadership really substitute for leadership? An

empirical investigation of Kerr and Jermier's situational leadership model.

24. Podsakoff, Dorfman, Howell and Todor, Leader reward and punishment behaviors: A preliminary test of a culture-free style of leadership effectiveness.

25. Podsakoff, Todor, Grover and Huber, Situational moderators of leader reward and punishment behavior: Fact or fiction?

26. Yukl, *Leadership in Organizations* (4th ed.).

27. Podsakoff, Todor, Grover and Huber, Situational moderators of leader reward and punishment behavior: Fact or fiction?

28. Ilgen, Fisher and Taylor, Consequences of individual feedback on behavior in organizations.

29. Podsakoff, Dorfman, Howell and Todor, Leader reward and punishment behaviors: A preliminary test of a culture-free style of leadership effectiveness.

30. Ibid.

31. Larson, J. R. (1984). The performance feedback process: A preliminary model. *Organizational Behavior and Human Performance,* 33, 42–76.

32. Ibid.

33. Bass, *Bass and Stogdill's Handbook of Leadership.*

34. Pinder, C. (1998). *Work Motivation in Organizational Behavior,* Upper Saddle River, NJ: Prentice Hall.

35. Fahr, Podsakoff and Cheng, Culture-free leadership effectiveness versus moderators of leadership behavior: An extension and test of Kerr and Jermier's "substitutes for leadership" model in Taiwan.

36. Stotland, E. (1959). Peer groups and reactions to power figures. In D. Cartwright (Ed.), *Studies in Social Power.* Ann Arbor: University of Michigan, Institute for Social Research.

37. Howell, Dorfman, Hibino, Lee and Tate, Leadership in western and Asian countries: Commonalities and differences in effective leadership processes and substitutes across cultures.

38. Markham, S. E. (1988). The pay-for-performance dilemma revisited: An empirical example of the importance of group effects. *Journal of Applied Psychology,* 73, 172–180.

39. Howell, Dorfman, Hibino, Lee and Tate, Leadership in western and Asian countries: Commonalities and differences in effective leadership processes and substitutes across cultures.

40. Bass, *Bass and Stogdill's Handbook of Leadership.*

41. Tsur, E. (1983). The kibbutz way of life — structure and management of the kibbutz. *Kibbutz Studies,* November, 23–31.

42. Howell, Dorfman, Hibino, Lee and Tate, Leadership in western and Asian countries: Commonalities and differences in effective leadership processes and substitutes across cultures.

43. Podsakoff, Niehoff, MacKenzie and Williams, Do substitutes for leadership really substitute for leadership? An empirical investigation of Kerr and Jermier's situational leadership model.

44. Dorfman, P. W., Howell, J. P., Cotton, B. C. G. and Tate, U. (1992). Leadership within the "discontinuous hierarchy" structure of the military: Are effective leadership behaviors similar within and across command structures? In K. E. Clark, M. B. Clark and D. P. Campbell (Eds.), *Impact of Leadership.* Greensboro, NC: Center for Creative Leadership.

45. Podsakoff, Dorfman, Howell and Todor, Leader reward and punishment behaviors: A preliminary test of a culture-free style of leadership effectiveness.

46. Howell, Dorfman, Hibino, Lee and Tate, Leadership in western and Asian countries: Commonalities and differences in effective leadership processes and substitutes across cultures.

47. Podsakoff, Dorfman, Howell and Todor, Leader reward and punishment behaviors: A preliminary test of a culture-free style of leadership effectiveness.

48. Howell, Dorfman, Hibino, Lee and Tate, Leadership in western and Asian countries: Commonalities and differences in effective leadership processes and substitutes across cultures.

49. Jacoby, J., Mazursky, D., Troutman, T. and Kuss, A. (1984). When feedback is ignored: Disutility of outcome feedback. *Journal of Applied Psychology,* 69, 531–545.

50. Parsons, C. K., Herold, D. M. and Turlington, B. (1981). Individual differences in performance feedback preferences. Paper, Academy of Management Meeting, San Diego, CA.

51. Bass, B. M. (1967). Social behavior and the orientation inventory: A review. *Psychological Bulletin,* 68, 260–292.

52. Podsakoff, Dorfman, Howell and Todor, Leader reward and punishment behaviors: a preliminary test of a culture-free style of leadership effectiveness.

53. Howell, Dorfman, Hibino, Lee and Tate, Commonalities and differences in effective leadership processes and substitutes across cultures.

54. Podsakoff, Dorfman, Howell and Todor, Leader reward and punishment behaviors: A preliminary test of a culture-free style of leadership effectiveness.

55. Howell, Dorfman, Hibino, Lee and Tate, Leadership in western and Asian countries: Commonalities and differences in effective leadership processes and substitutes across cultures.

CHAPTER 12 Charismatic Leadership Behavior

Learning Objectives
After reading this chapter you should be able to do the following:

1. Describe the behaviors that charismatic leaders use to influence followers.

2. Explain why charismatic leaders can have such strong effects on followers.

3. Discuss how charismatic leadership can be beneficial or destructive to followers' welfare.

4. Describe examples of effective and ineffective charismatic leadership.

5. Describe several personal traits and skills of effective charismatic leaders.

6. Describe the types of power most often used by charismatic leaders.

7. Describe the major favorable effects of charismatic leadership.

8. Explain the risks that some charismatic leaders can create for followers.

◆ EXAMPLES OF EFFECTIVE CHARISMATIC LEADERSHIP

• A leader viewed her job as transferring a dream to others in the organization so they would value the dream as she did. She used emotional terms in describing the dream, to excite her followers and get them to "buy into" it with all their creative energies.

• A new company president talked personally with every company employee in every branch during his first year as president. He told them of his vision for the company, but avoided trying to get them to adopt his vision. Instead, he encouraged them to develop a vision for their group or department. He was amazed to see how his vision stimulated harmony among the resulting department and branch visions.

• Mahatma Ghandi showed how symbols and role modeling by a leader provide a simplified message that can inspire charismatic effects in followers. The spinning wheel that Ghandi often used, for example, symbolized self-reliance, the value of cottage industries, and the demand for Indian independence. Cleaning his own toilet modeled self-reliance and humility as important values in the passive resistance action plan he advocated against the British.

• Franklin Delano Roosevelt demonstrated how charismatic leaders often project an image of unusual mental abilities. He developed an excellent memory and seized information from many sources, thus conveying the impression that he had a powerful mind and a wide range of knowledge. Roosevelt kept material ready to impress listeners whether they were business people or coal miners. This practice increased his perceived competence and insight in followers' eyes and thereby raised their faith and confidence in him.

• The company credo at Johnson and Johnson demonstrates how charismatic leadership can become a permanent part of an organization. Created by Robert Wood Johnson nearly 50 years ago, the credo emphasizes honesty, integrity, and respect for people. Senior managers still emphasize these values when they gather to discuss the credo every few years, to keep its ideas current. They also spend considerable time ensuring that employees live by the credo. The CEO stated, "If we keep trying to do what is right, at the end of the day we believe the marketplace will reward us."

These examples demonstrate effective behaviors used by charismatic leaders to influence their followers.

◆ DEFINITION, BACKGROUND, AND IMPORTANCE OF CHARISMATIC LEADERSHIP BEHAVIORS

Charisma is a Greek word meaning divine gift of grace. It is found in Biblical references to the Holy Spirit and was also used to describe the roles of specific members of the early Christian church. Max Weber, a famous German sociologist, expanded the meaning of charisma to apply to a type of authority or influence based on exceptional characteristics of an individual person (1). Weber believed these exceptional characteristics were often shown by heroic acts and/or by advocating a revolutionary mission or program of action to resolve some crisis. These exceptional characteristics were further demonstrated by repeated successes in carrying out the mission.

Weber's interpretation of charisma as an important type of social influence is consistent with the way most people use this term today. Leaders are described as charismatic when they are perceived as having exceptional (almost magical) qualities that inspire extreme devotion, commitment, and trust; when followers identify themselves with the leader and become emotionally involved in the leader's mission; and when followers feel increased self-esteem due to their association with the leader (2). The meaning of charisma has thus changed from being an endowment of divine grace from God to an endowment of exceptional qualities, high esteem, and referent power from followers (3).

Some experts believe it is primarily a leader's personal characteristics and behaviors (such as self-confidence, rhetorical skills, or expressed vision of the future) which cause the leader to be perceived as charismatic. Others believe the situational context surrounding the leader (such as the existence of a crisis) or characteristics of followers (such as low self-esteem or low self-confidence) cause people to perceive charismatic qualities in a leader. But most recent scholars believe that the leader's characteristics and behavior, the followers' characteristics, and situational factors combine to cause a leader to be viewed as charismatic. When followers view a leader as charismatic, they ascribe or attribute charismatic qualities to the leader. We therefore define charismatic leadership as an attribution made by followers about leaders who exhibit certain personal traits, abilities, and behaviors and who have unusually strong influence on followers' emotions, values, beliefs, attitudes, and behaviors. In all walks of life and throughout organizations we find gifted charismatic leaders who advocate radical solutions to critical problems and followers who are unquestioningly and magnetically attracted to these leaders (4).

Most of the leader behaviors described thus far in this book are considered transactional because they involve an informal exchange or transaction of some sort between leaders and followers. An example of this transaction occurs when followers provide competence and effort in exchange for useful direction and rewards provided by the leader. These leader activities usually appeal to followers' existing needs and values. In contrast, some experts believe that charismatic leaders raise followers' needs and values and therefore promote dramatic changes (often called transformations) in individual followers, groups, and organizations. Followers are apparently motivated by their emotional involvement with a charismatic leader and their commitment to the leader's mission, which is satisfying in itself. This distinction between transactional and charismatic leaders is especially important in descriptions of transformational and visionary leadership, which include charisma and are popular with many managers.

Some scholars have emphasized the impacts of charismatic leaders on group motivation, cohesion, and collective inspiration (5), and de-emphasized the effects on individuals. Others have noted that charisma is in the eye of the beholder, and different persons perceive it differently. One follower may perceive a leader's speech as inspirational and moving, whereas another may see it as trite, flowery, and the work of a charlatan. Recent research shows that charismatic leaders have stronger impacts on individuals than on groups (6,7). It seems that individuals are more likely than an entire group to attribute special charismatic qualities and high esteem to a leader. We will see, however, that very successful charismatics can sometimes have significant influence over large groups of people.

Charismatic leadership involves describing a desirable mission or vision of the future with goals, opportunities, and roles for followers that have a moral dimension and appeal to followers' needs and values. Charismatic leaders also make inspirational speeches that are emotionally expressive, intolerant of the status quo, and are motivational with regard to the mission. They use impression-management techniques (displaying extreme confidence in themselves, focusing on progress and success, not mentioning failures) in order to appear competent and trustworthy. They role model their own behavior for followers to emulate by setting high performance standards for themselves, having high expectations for followers, showing confidence in followers' abilities to meet these standards, and showing determination, optimism, and self-confidence. They also demonstrate creative innovative behavior, risk taking, and self-sacrifices to show their courage and convictions about achieving the mission. And they engage in frame alignment, which involves describing events and the environment in ways that make them organized, interpretable, meaningful, and understandable for followers to help guide their actions vis-à-vis these events.

These behaviors tend to produce loyalty, dedication, trust, and commitment to the leader, emotional involvement in the leader's mission, increased self-esteem, and belief in the leader's values and moral correctness. These impacts are most likely when the leader also exhibits certain personal characteristics often associated with charismatic leadership—such as self-confidence, belief in the moral rightness of her position, and outstanding speaking ability. Specific follower and situational characteristics may also contribute to these effects, with the results that followers view their leader as charismatic. Figure 12–1 summarizes the major charismatic leader behaviors.

FIGURE 12–1 Important Leader Behaviors of Charismatic Leaders

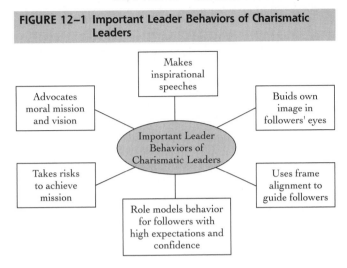

Many people believe that only a small number of individuals can successfully carry out these leader behaviors and be viewed as charismatic by their followers. However, two recent research studies showed that people can learn to carry out charismatic behaviors and have predictable charismatic effects on followers (8,9). Although these studies were conducted in a research laboratory, they involved highly realistic organizational work tasks and imply that many individuals in real organizations may learn to demonstrate charismatic behaviors and have charismatic effects on followers. The Leadership in Action box on Anita Roddick describes a current charismatic leader.

◆ CHARISMATIC LEADERSHIP HAS STRONG EFFECTS

Over seventy years ago, Sigmund Freud (10) described a major reason why charismatic leaders have such strong effects on followers. Freud believed that followers resolve inner conflicts between their self-image and what they think they should be by making the charismatic leader a representative of their ideal self. To followers, the leader becomes an ideal person whose behavior is a model they can emulate. By totally accepting a leader and her revolutionary ideas, followers fulfill the human desire to go beyond their self-interests and become more noble and worthy. By emulating this leader/ideal person, followers can become their ideal self.

Some writers believe this process is most common for followers who lack a strong sense of personal identity (11)—that is, people who are unsure of who they are, where they are going in life, and what basic values and beliefs they wish to live by. When these individuals are on their own, they often feel uneasy and have a sense of drifting through life. Charismatic leaders provide these followers with a strong identity, including important goals, beliefs, and values, and thus enhance followers' self-esteem and sense of purpose (12). This process by which followers connect with charismatic leaders is called personal identification, and it helps explain why they will actively defend the leader against critics or other attackers. They are really defending their own ideal self, which they are striving to become.

LEADERSHIP IN ACTION: ANITA RODDICK—FOUNDER AND CEO OF THE BODY SHOP

In 1976 in Brighton, England, a school teacher named Anita Roddick took an idea from her kitchen table and built it into an empire with over 1,400 shops in 46 countries and an estimated worth of $650 million by 1995. How did she do it? Roddick did it with her charismatic style encompassing a vision of global leadership, indomitable courage and passion, and a developmental attitude toward followers.

Roddick's vision of global leadership began with a desire to supply women around the world with cosmetics, soaps, and lotions made from all natural products which have not been tested on animals. Her commitment to running a socially and environmentally responsible company is symbolized in her ideology and message to other corporations to charge their leaders to be "true planetary citizens." To this end, Roddick has advocated reductions in world poverty, violence against women, and nuclear testing. Roddick models her socially active role by sacrificing profits, that is, she will not do business in countries she believes are not attempting to address her social and environmental causes.

"Anita," as she insists on being called by her employees at every level, is considered an inspirational leader who generates passion among Body Shop employees. She emphasizes strong personal relationships with her employees and tries to spend as much time with them as possible. Roddick insists that every Body Shop store is equipped with a VCR so she can send employees messages regarding her latest advances in social causes and remind employees that their work efforts are making an important contribution to larger social and environmental issues. Roddick also engages in frame alignment, as she promotes an image of female beauty that runs contrary to the one fostered by the media. As employees learn the Body Shop philosophy, they are encouraged to view women of every shape, size, and ethnicity as completely beautiful.

Another aspect of Roddick's charismatic style of leadership is signified by heavy doses of futuristic thinking and dissatisfaction with the status quo. Over her office reads a sign that says "Welcome to the Department of the Future." Roddick refers to her style of leadership as "benevolent anarchism." She inspires creativity by encouraging employees to question what they are doing and how they are doing it, in the hope of finding better working methods. Above all, Roddick tells her employees "to have fun, put love where labor is, and go in the opposite direction to everyone else." Anita Roddick's passion for social and environmental causes, her personal acceptance and belief that all women are beautiful, and her style of forward-thinking inspirational leadership have contributed to the Body Shop's overwhelming success.

Source: N. J. Adler, "Global leadership: Women leaders," *Management International Review,* 37(1) (1997): 171–196; N. Kochran, "Anita Roddick: Soap and social action," *World Business,* 3(1) (1997): 46–47; C. P. Wallace, "Can the Body Shop shape up?" *Fortune,* 133(7) (1996): 188.

Several scholars have noticed that charismatic leaders often surface during crises (13). Here the leader is viewed as a savior who will fulfill unmet needs. A similar situation occurs when followers are undergoing a major transition. In these situations, traditional methods are not working and the charismatic leader's radical ideas represent a break from the old ways that created the need for change. The crisis or the major transition creates a sense of drifting, uncertainty, and anxiety, which the leader resolves through vast knowledge, moral authority, and embodiment of follower ideals and values. When followers personally identify with a charismatic leader in this manner, they often experience euphoria. This is because the leader's perceived omnipotence and moral authority overshadow the internal guilt and hostility that often accompany an individual's conflicts between the real self and the ideal self. The charismatic leader overcomes their internal conflicts, and they are "free at last" to be the person they have dreamed they could be.

Another process that helps explain the extreme effects of charismatic leadership is known as internalization. In this case, followers adopt the leader's ideals and goals and become inspired to attain them because the goals are inherently satisfying. It is the leader's goals that inspire followers, not the leader as an individual. Through careful rhetoric, the leader causes followers to believe their own values will be achieved by carrying out the leader's objectives. This is often done by articulating a vision with ideals that include followers' values and self-concepts. Attaining this vision is a way to realize followers' values as well as their ideal self-concept. The leader describes followers' tasks as meaningful, noble, morally correct, and even heroic. This gives a moral quality to followers' task performance and makes their actions inherently satisfying. It "feels right" to actively pursue the leader's goals because they are worthwhile and necessary to attain important values shared by the leader and followers.

The two psychological processes of identification and internalization often occur together as the charismatic leader weaves a spell over followers. Followers of Mahatma Ghandi and Martin Luther King Jr. undoubtedly believed strongly in their leader's goals and values (internalization) and also saw their leader as a model of their ideal person at the time and in the situations they faced (identification). Followers of Adolph Hitler and Jim Jones undoubtedly identified with their leaders and internalized many goals and values contained in their mission. Although some charismatic leaders exploit their followers and others benefit them, the psychological processes involved in influencing followers are quite similar.

Another process that helps explain the strong impacts of charismatic leaders is closely related to followers' personal identification with the leader. Called social identification, it means that followers define themselves in terms of membership in a group or organization. In these situations, charismatic leaders create a connection in followers' minds between their self-concepts and the shared values and identities of their group (14). The leaders provide the group with a unique identity through their rhetorical skills and the vision they describe of the group's past and future accomplishments. They emphasize the group identity via group slogans, symbols (flags, emblems, uniforms), rituals (singing the organizational song, saluting the flag, reciting the company creed), and ceremonies (initiation of new members, giving awards to outstanding members) (15).

Both identification and internalization are involved in social identification, but the focus of social identification is the group rather than the leader. The leader describes the group's past, present, and future in the form of a collective mission that provides followers with a sense of continuity and order, and helps them interpret their experiences. Followers develop the feeling that they are part of something very meaningful and their motives are aroused to help carry out the collective mission.

Another social process has been described recently that may strengthen the impacts of identification and internalization. This process, called social contagion, is based on findings from social psychology. The concept assumes that most people share a heroic image as part of their self-concept. When a crisis or period of extreme change occurs, causing followers to feel anxious or frustrated, a skilled charismatic leader can activate this heroic aspect of followers' identities and cause them to behave with unusual devotion to a great cause. When other followers observe this devotion, their heroic self-images may also be activated, causing them to lose their inhibitions and replicate the observed behavior. In other words, extreme devotion to leaders and their cause becomes contagious and spreads throughout a group via social influence of one member on another.

Charismatic leaders probably cause all these processes to occur with their followers. They encourage personal and social identification through their value-laden speeches and their emphasis on a righteous mission and vision of the future. They cause followers to internalize their goals, values, and beliefs about the future and to obtain intrinsic satisfaction from the pursuit of those goals. Their influence is also heightened by social influence processes that cause followers to give themselves over to the collective spirit and enthusiasm of their fellow group members. As you can see, charismatic leadership is a complex process, and charismatic leaders make use of numerous social and psychological processes to exert strong effects on followers. The box on ethical and unethical charismatic leaders shows how these influence processes can be used for moral or immoral purposes.

LEADERSHIP IN PERSPECTIVE: ETHICAL AND UNETHICAL CHARISMATIC LEADERSHIP

Charismatic leaders often produce results, but they also create risks for followers. Well-known charismatics like Adolph Hitler, Jim Jones, and Charles Manson have carried out evil or immoral missions and brought death and destruction on their followers. Jane Howell and Bruce Avolio describe what they believe to be the qualities of ethical and unethical charismatic leaders and their effects on followers.

Ethical Charismatic Leaders	*Unethical Charismatic Leaders*
Key Characteristics and Behaviors	
* Uses power to serve others	* Uses power for personal gain or impact
* Aligns vision with followers' needs and aspirations	* Promotes own personal vision
* Considers and learns from criticism	* Censures critical or opposing views
* Stimulates followers to think independently and to question the leader's views	* Demands own decisions be accepted without question
* Uses open, two-way communication	* Uses one-way communication
* Coaches and develops followers; shares recognition with followers	* Is insensitive to followers' needs
* Relies on internal moral standards to satisfy organizational and societal interests	* Relies on convenient external moral standards to satisfy self-interests

Major Impacts on Followers

* Develops followers' ability to lead themselves	* Selects and produces obedient, dependent, and compliant followers
* Uses crises as learning experiences, to develop a sense of purpose in the mission and vision, and to emphasize the leader's intention to do right	* Uses crises to solidify their own power base, to minimize dissent, and to increase dependence of followers
* Avoids the trappings of success, rather shares credit with followers and stays humble	* Success brings delusions of invincibility, greatness, and extreme emphasis on image management

Based on their research, Howell and Avolio suggest that the following organizational practices can create and sustain ethical charismatic leaders:

- Top management commitment and enforcement of a clear code of ethical conduct
- Recruiting, selecting, and promoting managers with high moral standards
- Developing performance standards and rewards that emphasize respect for people
- Providing leaders with education and training that teaches them how to integrate new and old perspectives and diverse points of view
- Training individuals who have the necessary personality characteristics, social skills, and motivations to acquire ethical charismatic leader behaviors
- Identifying and celebrating heroes and heroines who exemplify high moral conduct

These practices should lead to a culture of ethical responsibility that promotes moral development, acceptable standards for leaders' conduct, and long-term success for the organization.

―――
Based on J.M. Howell and B.J. Avolio, "The ethics of charismatic leadership: Submission or liberation?" *Academy of Management Executive,* 6(2) (1992): 43–54.

◆ EXAMPLES OF INEFFECTIVE CHARISMATIC LEADERSHIP

Charismatic leadership is not always an effective influence strategy. The following examples demonstrate how charismatic leadership can sometimes result in unpleasant consequences.

1. One charismatic leader took advantage of a crisis situation to solidify his power base. Followers hungered for a resolution to the crisis and looked to the leader for a magical solution. The leader used his power base to minimize follower dissent and to help attain his personal vision. Followers became dependent on the leader for guidance and lost their self-confidence to think on their own. When the crisis ended and the leader was unable to adapt his vision to the changed environment, followers were unable to be self-guiding. The leader blamed the followers for his and their inadequacies.

2. A leader described a vision of the future and energized followers to strive for that vision, but in doing this she created expectations in followers which were unrealistic and unattainable. When the results were far short of what was envisioned, followers felt the

leader had misled them. They became frustrated and angry with the leader who created their unrealistic expectations.

3. A previously successful charismatic leader became trapped by followers' expectations that the leader's magic would continue indefinitely. This caused the leader to take high risks when the situation no longer warranted it. When the leader's risky actions were not successful, he suffered a "loss of magic" in followers' eyes, and a crisis in leadership resulted.

4. Leadership in an organization was focused on a single charismatic individual. Thus, the time, energy, expertise, and interests of that leader limited the organization's ability to deal with various issues. During a time of extreme change, when different issues required different types of competencies, these limits became problematic because the single leader did not possess expertise in all the needed areas.

In all these situations, followers developed an overreliance on a single charismatic leader. Either the leader was unable to meet their expectations, or the followers lacked the training and development needed to meet the demands of the mission and the environment. A slower leadership approach which focused on solidifying gains and developing expertise throughout the organization may have been more effective in these situations. The boxed self-assessment describes some personal tendencies of charismatic leaders.

◆ HOW TO USE CHARISMATIC LEADER BEHAVIORS

Charismatic leaders work hard at developing critical skills so they can have extraordinary effects on followers. For one thing, charismatic leaders develop outstanding communication and rhetorical skills (16). They can provide emotionally stimulating descriptions of an ideal future, and they can outline a mission to achieve their vision that generates excitement and commitment by followers. They relate follower values, aspirations, and beliefs to their vision and incorporate moral dimensions to bind followers together with them in carrying out the mission. They often relate followers' historical roots to their mission and provide a broad picture of the importance of followers' collective roles in a historical context. They may relate their mission to wider social movements such as environmentalism, religious purity, or political equality and freedom. These activities clearly require considerable verbal skills, and successful charismatic leaders develop these skills.

Next, charismatic leaders often develop personal characteristics that support and enhance their verbal skills. They are usually assertive, dynamic, outgoing, and often forceful. They are not shy or timid in dealing with others. They are verbally and nonverbally expressive of their ideas and feelings. When holding public office, they seem to enjoy interacting with the press and other members of the public. As they gain experience and achieve short-term goals, their self-confidence and self-assurance usually increase. This, in turn, increases the strength of their conviction in their ideas, mission, and goals. This strong conviction is needed to convince followers the mission and goals are achievable (17,18).

Furthermore, charismatic leaders usually have or develop a high need for power. This refers to leaders' desire to influence and sometimes control their environment,

LEADERSHIP SELF-ASSESSMENT: DO YOU HAVE CHARISMATIC TENDENCIES?

To investigate your charismatic tendencies, answer the questions below. *Fortune* devised this quiz with the help of Jay Conger, a leadership expert at the University of Southern California school of business. If your present situation does not apply to the questions, imagine how you would react if placed in the situation.

1. I worry most about
   a. my current competitors
   b. my future competitors

2. I'm most at ease thinking in
   a. generalities
   b. specifics

3. I tend to focus on
   a. our missed opportunities
   b. opportunities we've seized

4. I prefer to
   a. promote traditions that made us great
   b. create new traditions

5. I like to communicate an idea via
   a. a written report
   b. a one-page chart

6. I tend to ask
   a. "How can we do this better?"
   b. "Why are we doing this?"

7. I believe
   a. there's always a way to minimize risk
   b. some risks are too great

8. When I disagree with my boss, I typically
   a. coax him or her nicely to alter his or her view
   b. bluntly tell him or her, "You're wrong."

9. I tend to sway people by using
   a. emotion
   b. logic

10. I think this quiz is
    a. ridiculous
    b. fascinating

Source: Adapted from Patricia Sellers, "What Exactly is Charisma?" *Fortune,* January 15, 1996. Copyright Time Inc. All rights reserved.

often including other people. This characteristic is sometimes complemented by a low degree of authoritarianism. Individuals who are low in authoritarianism do not require absolute obedience to authority, they show restraint in using their power and do not dominate or manipulate others exclusively for their own ends (19). This is opposed to highly authoritarian leaders with high need for power who often dominate and use followers for their own ends and have a grand sense of self-importance (20). The pattern of high power need and low authoritarianism is particularly effective for high-level leadership positions in large formal organizations (21). It may be that low authoritarianism tempers a leader's power needs, making these leaders more concerned with their followers' welfare and causing them to demonstrate more "caring" behaviors.

Effective charismatic leaders often develop two types of power to help them exert extraordinary influence on followers. They develop referent power from their achievements and personality, their strongly held beliefs and values that support the vision, and their willingness to take personal risks to carry out the mission. Referent power causes followers to feel affection for the leader, to identify with the leader and her vision, to emulate the leader's behavior, and to adapt their beliefs and values to fit the leader's (22). Followers exhibit these feelings and behaviors because they want to be like the leader, whom they admire and look up to for guidance and inspiration.

Charismatic leaders also develop expert power by accumulating extensive knowledge and understanding of problems facing followers and the means to overcome those problems. They work diligently to simplify and interpret a complex environment to help followers understand key issues that concern them. They become skilled at designing and communicating a strategic mission to achieve the shared vision and serve as role models for important behaviors to carry out that mission. Because of these factors, followers view the leader as having a high degree of expertise, so they trust her, willingly obey her requests, and accept her directives without question (23).

Some charismatic leaders make use of the legitimate power of their high-level position in an organization. By controlling many resources and having extensive staff help, they give the impression of having vast amounts of personal knowledge and understanding of situations. They build on this perceived expert power by emphasizing their own past successes and de-emphasizing failures, and by being forceful in proposing and implementing strategies for followers to carry out. Historians have noted that Franklin Delano Roosevelt, our 32nd president, was particularly adept at building his expert and

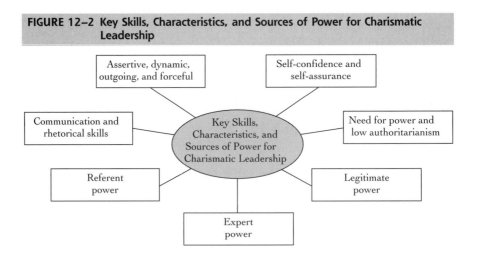

FIGURE 12–2 Key Skills, Characteristics, and Sources of Power for Charismatic Leadership

---

ANSWERS TO: DO YOU HAVE CHARISMATIC TENDENCIES?

Charismatic types tend to give the following answers: 1.b; 2.a; 3.a; 4.b; 5.b; 6.b; 7.a; 8.b; 9.a; 10.b. If you respond to seven or more of these questions in this way, you have strong charismatic tendencies.

referent power with the public. Figure 12–2 summarizes key power sources, skills, and characteristics for charismatic leadership.

Several organizational characteristics may predispose leaders to use charismatic leader behaviors and followers to view their leaders as charismatic. The number of studies of these factors is quite small, however, so much of the literature on organizational factors that precipitate charismatic leadership is still at the theoretical stage.

Max Weber believed that a crisis was essential for charismatic leadership to emerge. Followers experience anxiety and distress during crises, and they yearn for a way out of their predicament. A leader who confidently explains the reasons for the crisis and advocates a radical mission which involves followers in resolving the crisis is often seen as a savior with exceptional powers of understanding, foresight, and vision (charisma). Recent studies show that a crisis is not essential for charismatic leadership to occur, but followers' anxiety or distress can create an opportunity for charismatic leaders to emerge. Many organizational factors can create anxiety and stress in followers. Periods of radical social change such as political revolution or disrupted family patterns, the impending financial failure of an organization, the stress of starting a new business, or severe competition that threatens followers' livelihood can all cause followers to feel inadequate, fearful, or alienated and to hunger for an all-encompassing solution to their problems (24,25,26,27). In some cases, leaders have precipitated crises through enflamed rhetoric or other actions, resulting in anxiety, distress, and fear, which causes followers to seek a charismatic savior.

Some evidence indicates that groups with a history of charismatic leaders are more likely to attribute charismatic qualities to their leaders. In these situations, the followers have mental images of an effective leader who possesses many charismatic qualities, and as a result, followers tend to look to leaders who have these qualities. It may also be helpful for a leader to hold a high-level office (such as president), to have a history of success as a leader, and/or to be physically distant from followers in order to be viewed as a charismatic leader (28,29). These factors likely combine with a leader's characteristics, skills, and behavior to produce the image followers identify as a charismatic.

Little has been written and almost no research has been conducted on factors that prevent or limit charismatic leadership from occurring. Several writers have noted that charisma is transitory in nature, occurring as long as the factors causing followers' anxiety, fear, and distress are present (30). When these factors are removed, followers may prefer to maintain the status quo and thus seek other leaders with a less revolutionary vision. The political fate of Winston Churchill after the end of World War II is a case in point. Churchill was ousted as prime minister of Britain when his arrogant and combative leadership style no longer fit with the new peacetime attitudes of British voters. Some have suggested that charisma can be prolonged through institutionalization of the leader's mission in an organization's processes, but this appears to be difficult. Others have noticed that followers who work closely with a charismatic leader often perceive fewer charismatic qualities than those who are physically distant (31). Followers who are highly educated and/or professional may also attribute fewer charismatic qualities to a leader (32). These possible constraints on the emergence of charismatic leadership will likely receive attention by researchers in the future. The Leadership in Perspective box on spirituality and charismatic leadership describes the extreme power and danger of some charismatic leaders.

LEADERSHIP IN PERSPECTIVE: SPIRITUALITY AND CHARISMATIC LEADERSHIP

Several writers have emphasized that charismatic leadership emerges from a leader's spirituality, personal philosophy, and inner vision. James Kouzes and Barry Posner described Major General John Stanford as an example. Stanford was a charismatic leader who commanded the U.S. Army's Military Traffic Management Command and later became an inspirational superintendent of public schools in Seattle, Washington. Stanford firmly believed he knew the secret of success in life: "The secret of success is to stay in love." He explained this to mean that leadership is an affair of the heart. Loyal followers must be convinced that the leader passionately believes in his or her vision of the future and believes in each of them. Anita Roddick, Nelson Mandela, Mahatma Ghandi and Martin Luther King Jr. are examples of passionate charismatic leaders who also demonstrated this process.

However, other writers point out that leaders who are viewed in spiritual terms often evoke strong personal identification in followers who suffer from fear, guilt, or alienation. Gary Yukl gave an example of a young man experiencing an identity crisis because he had no clear concept of an ideal self due to weak or abusive parents. This individual could develop a strong emotional attachment to a charismatic gang leader who symbolizes an ideal self. Another individual who has caused great harm to others may experience extreme guilt. He could identify with a charismatic religious leader who represents strong moral values, vicariously experience this leader's moral superiority, and overcome his guilt. When followers attribute intense spirituality and inner vision to charismatic leaders, this may reflect a weakness in followers' psychological or social condition or character. This can be a dangerous situation for followers, as shown by charismatics like David Koresh, Adolph Hitler, and Charles Manson. Followers must be sure that their spiritual charismatic leaders also have the qualities of an ethical charismatic described earlier in this chapter.

Based on J. Kouzes and B. Posner, *The Leadership Challenge: How to Keep Getting Extraordinary Things Done in Organizations.* (San Francisco: Jossey-Bass, 1995); G. Yukl, *Leadership in Organizations* (4th ed.). (Upper Saddle River, NJ: Prentice Hall, 1998).

◆ EFFECTS OF CHARISMATIC LEADER BEHAVIORS

Charismatic leadership has the most immediate effects on followers' emotional attachment to the leader, their emotional arousal (excitement), and their motivation regarding the leader's mission (33,34). These emotional effects are often very strong. When followers have a leader who skillfully demonstrates charismatic behaviors, they often feel inspired and exhilarated and they attribute charismatic traits to that leader.

EFFECTS ON FOLLOWER/GROUP PSYCHOLOGICAL REACTIONS

When followers view a leader as charismatic, they place a high degree of respect, trust, loyalty, and acceptance in the leader and her judgment, and are loyal to her mission (35,36,37,38). Followers may also experience increased self-esteem, self-assurance, and belief that their work for the leader is highly meaningful and important (39,40). Because these psychological reactions all contain a large emotional component, followers often experience the effects of charismatic leaders as unusually strong and memorable.

These positive emotional reactions explain the most frequently repeated finding from research on charismatic leader behavior. Followers of charismatic leaders are usually more satisfied with the leader, their work, and their overall job and organization. These effects of charismatic leaders on followers' satisfaction are often quite strong (41,42,43,44,45,46). Followers' positive emotional states and high satisfaction levels help explain the high levels of organizational commitment and low levels of stress and low job burnout reported by followers in studies of charismatic leaders (47,48).

When followers become emotionally attached to a leader, when they are excited and internally motivated by a vision and rhetoric, and when their own self-esteem and self-assurance are heightened, they respond positively to a leader's requests for extreme effort, self-sacrifice, perseverance, and commitment. These responses explain how charismatic leadership can sometimes inspire high performance in followers.

EFFECTS ON FOLLOWERS' PERFORMANCE AND BEHAVIOR

A growing volume of research explores the effects of charismatic leadership on follower and group performance, using performance ratings of the charismatic leader as their outcome variable, rather than more direct quantitative measures of follower performance or productivity. In these studies, followers and superiors have rated their charismatic leaders as highly effective in diverse groups and organizations (49,50,51,52,53,54).

These findings support the strong emotional effects of charismatic leaders. However, because the performance measures are based on perceptions of those who work with the charismatic leader, the overall positive impression of the leader could result in both the charismatic attributions and the positive performance perceptions. In other words, if followers are impressed with a leader's behavior, skills, and past achievements, they may assume the leader is charismatic and evaluate the leader as highly effective regardless of her actual performance in her current position. If this occurs, then the charismatic leader's behavior has not caused the positive performance perceptions. Instead, the general positive impression of the leader has only made her appear effective.

When people believe that charismatic leaders are effective, these positive impressions can impose an important bias on their ratings of the leader's effectiveness. Researchers recently adjusted for this bias by having one follower rate a leader's charisma and a second follower rate the leader's effectiveness. With this more careful approach, charismatic leader behavior was not related to perceived effectiveness. Only when the same followers rated the leader's behavior and effectiveness was there a relationship between charisma and effectiveness. Clearly, few solid conclusions can be drawn from research on perceived effectiveness of charismatic leaders.

Some researchers have carefully measured one or more aspects of follower or group performance under a charismatic leader. One experimental study of business students doing a business simulation with trained leaders showed that charismatic leaders produced high-quality performance among followers (higher than supportive leaders and about the same level as directive leaders). Followers of charismatic leaders also generated more possible courses of action in the simulation than did followers of directive or supportive leaders (55). Also, a study of church ministers found that when church members saw their minister as charismatic, they attended church more often and church membership increased (56). Another study of managers and supervisors in a distributing company showed that charismatic leaders had higher-performing followers than noncharismatic leaders (57).

Charismatic leadership also improved follower performance among petrochemical workers and U.S. Army commissioned and noncommissioned officers. In these situations, charismatic leaders created positive psychological reactions in their followers (especially trust in the leader and commitment to the organization), and these improved psychological reactions resulted in better performance on the job (58,59). Finally, a few researchers have measured some aspect of group, department, or division performance in relation to charismatic leadership. Business-unit performance in a financial institution and in an audit committee have improved under charismatic leaders, and so has technological innovation (60,61,62).

It seems safe to conclude that charismatic leadership can improve follower and group performance. Because this research is still accumulating, and widely different methods have been used by researchers, it is difficult to estimate the size of this effect. It appears from the research thus far, however, that the effects of charismatic leadership on followers' attitudes and emotional reactions are considerably stronger than the effects on their performance (63,64). The situations where these impacts are most likely to occur will be addressed in the next chapter. Because charismatic leadership has the most immediate effects on followers' psychological reactions, such as emotional attachment to the leader, motivation, and arousal, these are likely the factors that transmit the leader's effects onto follower or group performance.

With all this said, however, charismatic leaders do not always create positive follower reactions. For example, charismatics sometimes inspire strong opposition and hatred in individuals who favor the old order of things (65). This finding is consistent with the conclusion of one writer, that charismatic leaders who transform followers, organizations, and governments are either loved or hated by their constituency. It is also supported by an historical study that found that charismatic U.S. presidents experienced ei-

FIGURE 12–3 Effects of Charismatic Leadership on Followers

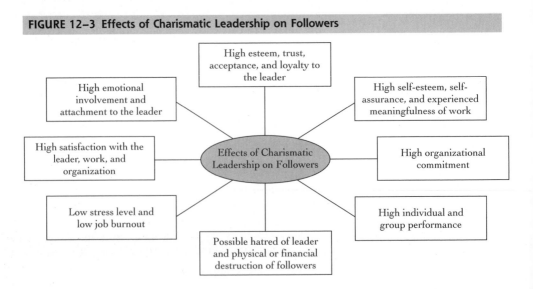

LEADERSHIP IN PERSPECTIVE: CHARISMATIC LEADERSHIP IN OTHER COUNTRIES

Several examples of charismatic leaders from outside the United States have been given in this chapter. These examples demonstrate that followers respond favorably to these leaders in other countries. This conclusion is supported by research showing that charismatic leader behaviors improve followers' attitudes and perceptions in Mexico and several Asian countries. However, there is little research evidence at this time that charisma improves follower or group performance outside the United States. One ongoing international study has shown that individuals believe charismatic leadership is effective in their culture, but this research has yet to relate charismatic behaviors to actual measures of follower performance in these countries.

Some have suggested that charismatic leaders need to adapt their behavior to the culture. They might be more participative in India and Japan than in Pakistan or Taiwan because workers expect participation in the former countries. We suspect future international research will show that charismatic leadership improves followers' performance outside the United States. However, the actual behavior of charismatic leaders may vary to fit the followers' cultural expectations.

Based on P. W. Dorfman and J. P. Howell, Managerial leadership in the United States and Mexico: Distant neighbors or close cousins? (1997). In C. K. Granrose and S. Oskamp (Eds.), *Cross-Cultural Work Groups,* 234–264. Thousand Oaks, CA: Sage; P. W. Dorfman, International and cross-cultural leadership research (1996). In P. J. Punnett and O. Shenker (Eds.), *Handbook for International Management Research,* 267–348. Cambridge, MA: Blackwell.

ther an assassination attempt during their first term, were reelected, or both (66). Martin Luther King Jr., Malcolm X, and Mahatma Ghandi are other examples who all faced attacks by individuals who violently opposed their missions. Both charismatic leaders and their followers can face large risks. Figure 12–3 summarizes the effects of charismatic leadership. The Leadership in Perspective box on charismatic leadership in other countries describes recent findings and ongoing studies outside the United States.

Summary ▪

Charismatic leadership is an attribution (causal explanation) followers make about a leader who exhibits certain personal characteristics, abilities, and behaviors and has unusually strong influence on followers' emotions, values, beliefs, attitudes, and behaviors. Charismatic leaders are found in many organizational contexts, where they often advocate radical solutions to critical problems and reflect a personal magnetism that inspires unquestioning loyalty, esteem, and emotional attachment in their followers. Their effects on followers appear to result from a combination of leader characteristics and behaviors, follower characteristics, and situational factors.

The key behaviors of charismatic leaders include describing a mission or vision of the future that appeals to followers' moral values and growth needs, making inspirational speeches, using impression management to enhance their image in followers' eyes, modeling behavior that reflects high expectations and confidence in followers, demonstrating creative risky behavior for the sake of the mission, and frame alignment to help followers develop shared perspectives that guide their behavior.

The strong effects of charismatic leaders on followers often occur because followers identify with the leader and his lofty goals, beliefs, and values. This identification, in turn, enhances followers' self-esteem and sense of purpose. Followers may also view the leader's mission and ideals as inherently satisfying because the leader convincingly describes their achievement as a way to realize followers' values and self-concepts. Here followers internalize the leader's goals because they "feel right." Some charismatic leaders convince followers to invest their identities in a group.

Charismatic leadership inspires followers' emotional involvement and attachment to the leader. Followers hold charismatic leaders in high esteem and show trust, acceptance, and loyalty to them. They often experience increased self-esteem and self-assurance and view their work with the leader as meaningful and important. Followers of charismatics are very highly satisfied with their leader, their work, and their overall job and organization. Their organizational commitment can be high, whereas stress levels and rate of job burnout are often low. For followers who do not "buy in" to the leader's mission, however, charisma may inspire strong opposition.

Although followers of charismatic leaders consistently rate their leaders as highly effective, few studies have measured actual follower or group performance under charismatics. The evidence is slowly accumulating, however, that the favorable effects of charismatic leadership on followers' emotional and psychological reactions often create improvements in follower and group performance. Charismatic leadership is also risky though—attacks on the leader and follower destruction are both possible outcomes.

Figure 12–4 summarizes most of the findings on charismatic leadership reported in this chapter. This figure shows charismatic leader behaviors affecting follower and group psychological reactions, which in turn affect followers' behavior. Chapter 13 includes a more complete model, illustrating the effects of situational factors on charismatic leadership.

Key Terms and Concepts in This Chapter ▪ ▪ ▪ ▪ ▪ ▪ ▪ ▪ ▪ ▪ ▪ ▪ ▪ ▪ ▪ ▪ ▪ ▪ ▪

- charismatic leadership
- emotional involvement
- frame alignment
- internalization
- personal identification
- social contagion
- social identification

Review and Discussion Questions ▪

1. Which charismatic leader behaviors described in this chapter do you believe are most important in influencing followers? Why?

2. Think of a charismatic leader you have known, read about, or seen on film. Describe how that leader used one or two of the leader behaviors described in this chapter.

3. Do you think the followers of the charismatic leader described in question 2 were influenced through personal identification, social identification, internalization, or social contagion? If these leaders used some other influence

FIGURE 12–4 Partial Model of Charismatic Leadership

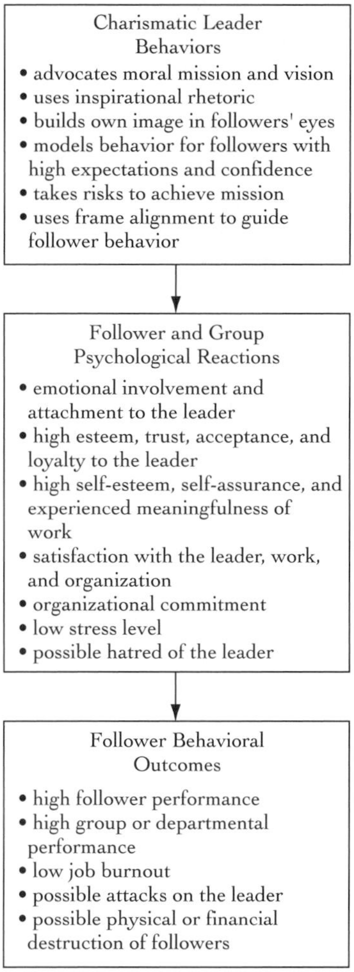

Charismatic Leader
Behaviors

- advocates moral mission and vision
- uses inspirational rhetoric
- builds own image in followers' eyes
- models behavior for followers with high expectations and confidence
- takes risks to achieve mission
- uses frame alignment to guide follower behavior

Follower and Group
Psychological Reactions

- emotional involvement and attachment to the leader
- high esteem, trust, acceptance, and loyalty to the leader
- high self-esteem, self-assurance, and experienced meaningfulness of work
- satisfaction with the leader, work, and organization
- organizational commitment
- low stress level
- possible hatred of the leader

Follower Behavioral
Outcomes

- high follower performance
- high group or departmental performance
- low job burnout
- possible attacks on the leader
- possible physical or financial destruction of followers

strategy with followers, describe this strategy and how it differs from those described here.

4. Explain how a charismatic leader can use expert and referent power to influence followers. If you can, describe a specific charismatic leader who has used these types of power.

5. If you have ever worked with or observed a charismatic leader, describe the effects the leader had on you. Are these effects consistent with those described in this chapter?

6. Why do you think charismatic leaders have stronger effects on followers' attitudes and emotions than on follower and group performance?

Exercise: Analyzing Charismatic Leader Communication ∎ ∎ ∎ ∎ ∎ ∎ ∎ ∎ ∎ ∎ ∎

After reading Dr. King's speech, analyze the charismatic communication characteristics by answering the questions that follow the speech.

"I Have a Dream"

Martin Luther King Jr. delivered the following address on the steps of the Lincoln Memorial in Washington, D.C. on August 29, 1963.

I say to you, my friends, that in spite of the difficulties and frustrations of the moment I still have a dream. It is a dream deeply rooted in the American Dream.

I have a dream that one day this nation will rise up and live out the true meaning of its creed: "We hold these truths to be self-evident; that all men are created equal."

I have a dream that one day on the red hills of Georgia the sons of former slaves and the sons of former slave owners will be able to sit down together at the table of brotherhood.

I have a dream that one day even the state of Mississippi, a desert state sweating in the heat of injustice and oppression, will be transformed into an oasis of freedom and justice.

I have a dream that my four little children will one day live in a nation where they will not be judged by the color of their skin but the content of their character.

I have a dream today.

I have a dream that one day the state of Alabama, whose governor's lips are presently dripping with the words of interposition and nullification, will be transformed into a situation where little black boys and girls will be able to join hands with little white boys and white girls and walk together as sisters and brothers.

I have a dream today.

I have a dream that one day every valley shall be exhalted, every hill and mountain shall be made low, the rough places will be made plains, and the crooked places will be made straight, and the glory of the Lord shall be revealed, and all flesh shall see it together.

This is our hope. This is the faith with which I return to the South. With this faith we will be able to transform the jangling discords of our nation into a beautiful symphony of brotherhood. With this faith we will be able to work together, to pray together, to struggle together, to go to jail together, to stand up for freedom together, knowing that we will be free one day.

This will be the day when all of God's children will be able to sing with new meaning, "My country 'tis of thee, sweet land of liberty, of thee I sing. Land where my fathers died, land of the pilgrim's pride, from every mountainside, let freedom ring."

And if America is to be a great nation this must become true. So let freedom ring from the prodigious hilltops of New Hampshire. Let freedom ring from the mighty mountains of New York. Let freedom ring from the heightening Alleghenies of Pennsylvania!

Let freedom ring from the snowcapped Rockies of Colorado!

Let freedom ring from the curvaceous peaks of California!

But not only that; let freedom ring from the Stone Mountains of Georgia.

Let freedom ring from every hill and molehill of Mississippi. From every mountainside, let freedom ring.

When we let freedom ring, when we let it ring from every village and every hamlet, from every state and every city, we will be able to speed up that day when all of God's children, black men and white men, Jews and Gentiles, Protestants and Catholics, will be able to join hands and sing in the words of that old Negro spiritual, "Free at last! Thank God almighty, we are free at last!"

1. How would you rate the charismatic appeal of King's speech? (If feasible, listen to the speech on tape to better comprehend the nonverbal aspects of the speech.)

2. What specific charismatic elements can you identify in this famous speech?

3. Would a speech of this emotional intensity be appropriate in a work setting? Explain your reasoning.

Source: Andrew J. Dubrin. *Leadership: Research Findings, Practices, and Skills.* (Boston: Houghton Mifflin Company, 1998), 78–79. The reprint of Dr. King's speech is used by arrangement with The Heirs to the Estate of Martin Luther King Jr., c/o Writers House, Inc. as agents of the proprietor. Copyright 1963 by Martin Luther King, copyright renewed 1991 by Coretta Scott King.

Endnotes ■■

1. Weber, Max (1947). *The theory of social and economic organization* (T. Parsons, translator). New York: The Free Press.

2. House, R. J. (1977). A 1976 theory of charismatic leadership. In J. G. Hunt and L. L. Larson (Eds.), *Leadership: The cutting edge.* Carbondale: Southern Illinois University Press.

3. Bass, B. M. (1990). *Bass & Stogdill's Handbook of Leadership.* (3rd ed.). New York: The Free Press.

4. Ibid.

5. House, R. J. and Shamir, B. (1993). Toward the integration of transformational, charismatic and visionary theories. In M. M. Chemers and R. Aymon (Eds.), *Leadership theory and research: Perspectives and directions.* New York: Academic Press.

6. Yammarino, F. J. and Bass, B. M. (1990). Transformational leadership and multiple levels of analysis. *Human Relations, 43,* 975–995.

7. Avolio, B. J. and Yammarino, F. J. (1990). Operationalizing charismatic leadership using a levels-of-analysis framework. *Leadership Quarterly,* 1(3), 193–208.

8. Howell, J. M. and Frost, P. J. (1989). A laboratory study of charismatic leadership. *Organizational Behavior and Human Decision Processes,* 43, 243–269.

9. Kirkpatrick, S. A. and Locke, E. A. (1996). Direct and indirect effects of three core charismatic leadership components on performance and attitudes. *Journal of Applied Psychology,* 81(1), 36–61.

10. Freud, S. (1922). *Group psychology and the analysis of ego.* London: International Psychoanalytic Press.

11. Downton, J. V. (1973). *Rebel Leadership: Commitment and Charisma in the Revolutionary Process.* New York: The Free Press.

12. Freemesser, G. F. and Kaplan, H. B. (1976). Self-attitudes and deviant behavior: The case of the charismatic religious movement. *Journal of Youth and Adolescence,* 5(1), 1–9.

13. Bass, *Bass and Stogdill's Handbook of Leadership.*

14. Shamir, B., Zakay, E., Breinin, E. and Popper, M. (1998). Correlates of charismatic leader behavior in military units:

Subordinates' attitudes, unit characteristics, and superiors' appraisals of leader performance. *Academy of Management Journal,* 41(4), 387–409.

15. Yukl, G. (1998). *Leadership in Organizations* (4th ed.). Upper Saddle River, NJ: Prentice Hall.

16. Shamir, B., Arthur, B. B. and House, R. (1994). The rhetoric of charismatic leadership: A theoretical extension, a case study, and implications for research. *Leadership Quarterly,* 5(1), 25–42.

17. Simonton, D. K. (1988). Presidential style: Personality, biography, and performance. *Journal of Personality and Social Psychology,* 55(6), 928–936.

18. House, A 1976 theory of charismatic leadership.

19. House, R. J., Spangler, W. D. and Woycke, J. (1991). Personality and charisma in the U.S. presidency: A psychological theory of leader effectiveness. *Administrative Science Quarterly,* 36, 364–396.

20. Post, J. M. (1993). Current concepts of the narcissistic personality: Implications for political psychology. *Political Psychology,* 14(1), 99–121.

21. Dubrin, A. J. (1998). *Leadership: Research Findings, Practice, and Skills.* Boston: Houghton Mifflin Company.

22. Halpert, J. A. (1990). The dimensionality of charisma. *Journal of Business Psychology,* Summer 1990, 401.

23. Ibid.

24. Cell, C. P. (1974). Charismatic heads of state: The social context. *Behavioral Science Research,* 4, 255–304.

25. Trice, H. M. and Beyer, J. M. (1986). Charisma and its routinization in two social movement organizations. *Research in Organizational Behavior,* 8, 113–164.

26. Roberts, N. C. (1984). Transforming leadership: Sources, processes, consequences. Paper, Academy of Management, Boston.

27. Kets de Vries, M. F. R. (1988). Origins of charisma: Ties that bind the leader and the led. In J. A. Conger and R. N. Kanungo (Eds.), *Charismatic leadership: The elusive factor in organizational effectiveness.* San Francisco: Jossey-Bass.

28. Bass, *Bass & Stogdill's Handbook of Leadership.*

29. Puffer, S. M. (1990). Attributions of charismatic leadership: The impact of decision style, outcome and observer characteristics. *Leadership Quarterly,* 13, 177–192.

30. Bass, *Bass & Stogdill's Handbook of Leadership.*

31. Conger, J. A. and Kanungo, R. N. (1987). Toward a behavioral theory of charismatic leadership in organizational settings. *Academy of Management Review,* 12(4), 637–647.

32. Bass, B. M. (1985). Leadership: Good, better, best. *Organizational Dynamics,* 13(3), 26–40.

33. House and Shamir, Toward the integration of transformational, charismatic and visionary theories.

34. Bass, Leadership: Good, better, best.

35. Maranell, G. M. (1970). The evaluation of presidents: An extension of the Schlesinger polls. *Journal of American History,* 57, 104–113.

36. Smith, B. J. (1983). An initial test of a theory of charismatic leadership based on responses of subordinates. Doctoral dissertation, University of Toronto, Toronto.

37. Podsakoff, P. M., MacKenzie, S. B., Moorman, R. H. and Fetter, R. (1990). Transformational leader behaviors and their effects on followers' trust in leader, satisfaction, and organizational citizenship behaviors. *Leadership Quarterly,* 1(2), 107–142.

38. Willner, A. R. (1984). *The spellbinders: Charismatic political leadership.* New Haven, CT: Yale University Press.

39. Carlton-Ford, S. L. (1992). Charisma, ritual, effervescence, and self-esteem. *Sociological Quarterly,* 33(3), 365–387.

40. House and Shamir, Toward the integration of transformational, charismatic and visionary theories.

41. Deluga, R. J. (1991). The relationship of leader and subordinate influencing activity in naval environments. *Military Psychology,* 3(1), 25–39.

42. Yammarino, F. J. and Bass, B. M. (1990). Transformational leadership and multiple

levels of analysis. *Human Relations,* 43(10), 975–995.

43. Kirby, P. C., Paradise, L. V. and King, M. I. (1992). Extraordinary leaders in education: Understanding transformational leadership. *Journal of Educational Research,* 85(5), 303–311.

44. Podsakoff, MacKenzie, Moorman and Fetter, Transformational leader behaviors and their effects on followers' trust in leader, satisfaction, and organizational citizenship behaviors.

45. House, R. J., Woycke, J. and Fodor, E. M. (1988). Charismatic and noncharismatic leaders: Differences in behavior and effectiveness. In J. A. Conger and R. N. Kanungo (Eds.), *Charismatic leadership: The elusive factor in organizational effectiveness.* San Francisco: Jossey-Bass.

46. Howell and Frost, A laboratory study of charismatic leadership.

47. Peterson, M. F., Phillips, R. L. and Duran, C. A. (1989). A comparison of Japanese performance-maintenance measures with U.S. leadership scales. *Psychologia–An International Journal of Psychology in the Orient,* 32, 58–70.

48. Seltzer, J., Numerof, R. E. and Bass, B. M. (1987). Transformational leadership: Is it a source of more or less burnout or stress? Paper, Academy of Management, New Orleans.

49. Hater, J. J. and Bass, B. M. (1988). Superiors' evaluations and subordinates' perceptions of transformational and transactional leadership. *Journal of Applied Psychology,* 73, 695–702.

50. House, Woycke and Foder, Charismatic and noncharismatic leaders: Differences in behavior and effectiveness.

51. Yammarino, F. J., Spangler, W. D. and Bass, B. M. (1993). Transformational leadership and performance: A longitudinal investigation. *Leadership Quarterly,* 4(1), 81–102.

52. Deluga, R. J. (1992). The relationship of leader and subordinate influencing activity in Naval Environments. *Military Psychology,* 3(1), 25–39.

53. Waldeman, D. A., Bass, B. M. and Yammarino, F. J. (1990). Adding to

contingent reward behavior: The augmenting effect of charismatic leadership. *Group and Organizational Studies,* 15(4), 381–394.

54. Kirby, Paradise and King, Extraordinary leaders in education: Understanding transformational leadership.

55. Howell and Frost, A laboratory study of charismatic leadership.

56. Onnen, M. K. (1987). The relationship of clergy leadership characteristics to growing or declining churches. Doctoral dissertation, University of Louisville, Louisville, Kentucky.

57. Waldeman, D. A., Bass, B. M. and Einstein, W. O. (1987). Leadership and outcomes of performance appraisal processes. *Journal of Occupational Psychology,* 60, 177–186.

58. Podsakoff, MacKenzie, Moorman and Fetter, Transformational leader behaviors and their effects on followers' trust in leader, satisfaction, and organizational citizenship behaviors.

59. Dorfman, P. W., Howell, J. P., Cotton, B. C. G. and Tate, U. (1992). Leadership within the discontinuous hierarchy's structure of the military: Are effective leadership behaviors similar within and across command structures? In K. E. Clark, M. B. Clark and D. P. Campbell (Eds.), *Impact of Leadership.* Greensboro, NC: Center for Creative Leadership.

60. Howell, J. M. and Avolio, B. J. (1993). Transformational leadership, transactional leadership, locus of control, and support for innovation: Key predictors of consolidated-business-unit performance. *Journal of Applied Psychology,* 78(6), 891–902.

61. Howell, J. M. and Higgins, C. A. (1990). Champions of technological innovation. *Administrative Science Quarterly,* 35(2), 317–341.

62. Spangler, W. D. and Braiotta, L. (1990). Leadership and corporate audit committee effectiveness. *Group and Organization Studies,* 15(2), 134–157.

63. Lowe, K. B., Kroeck, K. G. and Sivasubramaniam, N. (1996). Effectiveness of correlates of transformational and transactional leadership: A meta-analytic

review of the MLQ literature. *Leadership Quarterly,* 7, 489–508.

64. Fuller, J. B., Patterson, C. E. P., Hester, K. and Stringer, D. Y. (1996). A quantitative review of research on charismatic leadership. *Psychological Reports,* 78, 271–287.

65. Tucker, R. G. (1970). The theory of charismatic leadership. In D. A. Rustow (Ed.), *Philosophers and Kings: Studies in leadership.* New York: Braziller.

66. House, Woycke and Fodor, Charismatic and noncharismatic leaders: Differences in behavior and effectiveness.

CHAPTER 13

Situational Dynamics of Charismatic Leadership Behavior

Learning Objectives
After reading this chapter, you should be able to do the following:

1. Identify situations in which charismatic leadership is especially effective.

2. Identify situations in which charismatic leadership may not be needed.

3. Explain how leaders can modify situations to make charismatic leadership more effective.

4. Explain how leaders can modify situations to replace the need for charismatic leadership and still maintain favorable follower attitudes, motivation, and performance.

5. Describe how followers, situations, and charismatic leaders affect each other.

6. Describe how to apply the information contained in Chapters 12 and 13 to diagnose situations, provide charismatic leadership behaviors, and modify situations in a continuous dynamic process.

Chapter 12 described charismatic leadership behaviors as well as the overall effects of these behaviors on followers and groups. Chapter 13 addresses the situational dynamics of charismatic leadership. That is, it describes the situational and follower characteristics that may make charismatic leadership more or less effective. Strategies are also discussed for influencing situational and follower characteristics to improve the effectiveness of charismatic leadership. The continual interaction between charismatic leaders, their followers, and environmental factors are emphasized. Because only a small portion of the research on charismatic leadership has dealt with situational and follower characteristics, some of the findings described in this chapter are still tentative.

Charismatic leadership behaviors may or may not be effective in the following situations. Place an X next to those situations where you believe charismatic leadership is appropriate.

1. _____ Followers work in an industry that is extremely competitive, with rapid technological change and constant threats of mergers and takeovers by other companies.
2. _____ Followers work in an organization that emphasizes peer reviews of their performance, collegial decision making, and a culture of self-management.
3. _____ There is a long history of charismatic leaders in the organization.
4. _____ Followers' work involves providing social services to low-income recipients.
5. _____ Followers are highly experienced, educated, older employees who hold high-level positions in the organization and work at tasks that they find interesting and enjoyable.
6. _____ Followers are voluntary members of a "self-help" organization designed to assist its members in overcoming alcohol and drug addiction.

Charismatic leadership has been found to be highly effective in four of these situations. Items 1, 3, 4, and 6 describe situations where followers usually respond positively to a charismatic leader. In these situations, followers may be highly stressed and anxious about the future, expect their leader to be charismatic due to a history of charismatic leaders in their organization, or work at tasks that are morally gratifying but probably under-rewarded. These situations often enhance the effectiveness of charismatic leadership. The situations described in items 2 and 5 may have the opposite effect. Here followers may be highly trained and experienced, enjoy their work and have considerable status in their organization, and/or their organization emphasizes independence, self-control, and equality of power and influence. In any of these situations, followers may not feel the need for an inspirational and dynamic charismatic leader. They are probably accustomed to charting their own course in carrying out job duties, and their organization has rewarded their independence and self-management in the past. This chapter explains how these and other situational and follower characteristics influence effective charismatic leadership.

◆ SITUATIONAL FACTORS THAT INCREASE EFFECTIVENESS OF CHARISMATIC LEADERSHIP

Few studies have been conducted on situational factors that increase (enhance) the effectiveness of charismatic leadership. Empirical research on this topic is probably limited because researchers have focused instead on simply understanding the behaviors and characteristics of charismatic leaders. Nevertheless, the findings on situational enhancers are described here, followed by several conclusions made by leadership experts based on historical descriptions of charismatic leaders. Each of these sources provides evidence about when charismatic leaders should be most effective.

ORGANIZATIONAL AND ENVIRONMENTAL CHARACTERISTICS

Researchers found that charismatic leaders had stronger positive effects on project quality in research groups that worked on new concepts and ideas than in groups that developed existing products and technology (1). This finding is consistent with the tendency of charismatic leaders to describe a vision and mission that includes a major change from the status quo. The new research group projects involved more uncertainty and had more potential for ground-breaking advancements than did the development of existing products. In groups, researching new projects as well as in high technology industries and new business start-ups, major changes can happen quickly in new materials, processes, technology, or markets. Charismatic leaders who envision these changes can inspire followers to persist with excitement and vigor, and to change the current ways of thinking and doing things in their field. In situations where rapid change is likely, charismatic leadership may be highly effective.

In a study of managers and professional workers in Asia, researchers found that a leader's expertise and rank as well as the existence of extensive formal plans, goals, and procedures all enhanced the effects of charismatic leadership on followers' satisfaction and commitment to the organization (2). When followers viewed their leaders as high in rank or as experts in followers' tasks, or when there was considerable documentation to guide followers in their activities and to support the leader's mission, charismatic leadership tended to be more effective at improving followers' attitudes. Leaders who are experts and hold a high status or rank can intensify the "superhuman" image of a charismatic leader and therefore enhance their effects on followers (3). Extensive plans, goals, and procedures that support the leader's vision may help clarify how followers can carry out the leader's mission to achieve the vision. Each of these situational factors has been found in previous studies to enhance other leadership behaviors, but this is the first time they have been studied in conjunction with charismatic leadership.

Based on historical analyses of charismatic leaders, several writers have suggested that environmental conditions or events can enhance the impacts of charismatic leadership (4,5). Culture shocks, a general decline in cultural values, absence of behavioral norms, or extreme crises that threaten the life or well-being of followers may turn a charismatic leader into a savior in followers' eyes. Here there is a lack of clarity regarding appropriate goals, and few environmental cues are available to guide behavior. Followers have no structure or guidance other than the leader and may be grateful for a mission and role model to guide them in a constructive manner (6). Conditions like these were faced by Ghandi in India before its independence, Hitler in post-World War I Germany, Martin Luther King Jr. in the United States during the 1950s and 1960s, and Lee Iacocca with Chrysler Corporation in the 1980s. In each of these situations, followers faced extremely difficult existing conditions or possible disaster, causing them to look to a charismatic leader to save them from their intolerable situation.

The culture of the leader's organization or group may enhance the impacts of charismatic leadership in at least two ways. First, an organization, group, or society may have a history of charismatic leadership that causes followers to attribute charisma to their leaders and to respond favorably to charismatic behaviors. In Jewish and Muslim cultures, there is a strong history of having charismatic prophets as leaders of the people; in Japan, leaders have traditionally been viewed as men of exemplary courage and self-sacrifice; and in the United States, leaders are historically seen as strong, outspoken individuals with a vision of the future (7). Alcoholics Anonymous was started by a charismatic individual and has maintained the culture of divine inspiration to help lead individuals out of their difficulties with alcohol.

A second way in which culture may enhance charismatic leadership is through its relationship with followers' tasks (8). For example, if a task reflects the dominant social values of a culture, followers can become "morally involved" in pursuing these values through their task. Such conditions occur for military leaders during wartime and when workers of Alcoholics Anonymous try to save alcoholics from their addiction. They were also in place when Lee Iacocca saved tens of thousands of Chrysler employees from losing their jobs. In these situations, a charismatic leader's vision, inspirational speeches, and innovative behavior may instill followers with a feeling of "correctness" and moral striving that can result in persistent, high-energy devotion.

Followers who have feelings of self-doubt, helplessness, anxiety, cynicism, insecurity, isolation, distress, and/or low self-esteem are particularly susceptible to the influence of charismatic leaders (9,10,11,12). These conditions may accompany a loss of control over one's environment, perhaps due to social crises. Individuals in these situations respond to a confident, persuasive charismatic leader who resolves their feelings of anxiety, isolation, and distress by directing their efforts toward a morally worthwhile goal. Charismatic leaders also involve these followers in meaningful, self-fulfilling activities that increase their self-esteem.

International researchers identified several other follower characteristics that increased the effects of charismatic leadership on follower satisfaction and commitment. Followers' number of years of schooling was an enhancer in Korea and Mexico; followers' high rank was an enhancer in Taiwan and Mexico; and followers' professionalism enhanced in Korea (13). These factors are related—followers with more years of schooling will typically have higher rank and a more professional attitude toward their work, organization, and leaders. It appears that workers in these countries who progress in organizations and have professional attitudes see much value in charismatic leadership. Each of these countries has a predominantly collectivist orientation toward life and work. Collectivism implies sacrifice for the good of the group or organization and responsiveness to leaders, who are often viewed as highly charismatic. It may be that followers who are trained, competent, and successful adhere very closely to the collectivist cultural patterns that are approved in their country. This may be less true in individualistic countries such as the United States. These cultural patterns may be key factors affecting enhancers of charismatic leadership.

Several writers have suggested that when followers' needs, values, and identities are congruent with a charismatic leader's vision, they will likely respond with very positive attitudes and commitment to carry out that vision (14,15). Others believe that followers who have an expressive orientation to their work life and a principled orientation to social relations may be more susceptible to the influence of charismatic leaders (16). Expressively oriented individuals view work as more than just an exchange of their time for money and other extrinsic rewards; they see it as a means of expressing who they are. Principle-oriented people try to maintain a clear code of conduct in dealings with others, as opposed to letting the situation entirely dictate their behavior. Because charismatic leaders usually have a moral element to their mission, followers with these characteristics are likely to identify with these leaders.

Empirical and historical research indicates that situational and follower characteristics may enhance charismatic leadership. It is still premature to suggest definite conclusions about which situational enhancers are most important.

INFLUENCING SITUATIONS TO MAKE CHARISMATIC LEADERSHIP MORE EFFECTIVE

Figure 13–1 summarizes the findings from research on enhancers of charismatic leadership. Many of these enhancers refer to some type of follower distress, anxiety, isolation, or extreme uncertainty. We do *not* advocate that leaders or organizations create these difficulties for organizational members simply to make charismatic leader behaviors more impactful (although some leaders have actually resorted to this strategy). It seems clear, however, that organizations should be alert to the presence of these follower conditions and equip their leaders with charismatic behavioral skills. When coached, leaders can learn to identify and define a mission with a moral dimension, make emotionally expressive speeches to arouse followers to support the mission, manage followers' impressions, and model desired behaviors for followers. These charismatic behaviors should allow leaders to respond to enhancing conditions when they exist among followers.

Because building a leader's status, rank, and expertise may enhance the impacts of charismatic leadership, organizations can provide champions, mentoring, and training programs to help leaders build their reputation, status, technical skills, and eventually, to

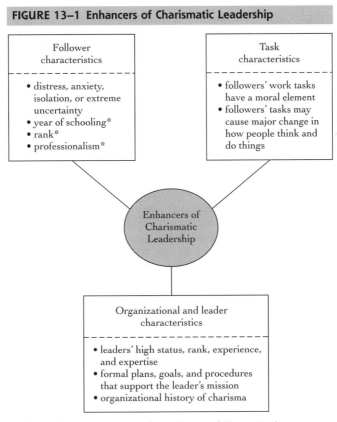

FIGURE 13–1 Enhancers of Charismatic Leadership

Follower characteristics
- distress, anxiety, isolation, or extreme uncertainty
- year of schooling*
- rank*
- professionalism*

Task characteristics
- followers' work tasks have a moral element
- followers' tasks may cause major change in how people think and do things

Enhancers of Charismatic Leadership

Organizational and leader characteristics
- leaders' high status, rank, experience, and expertise
- formal plans, goals, and procedures that support the leader's mission
- organizational history of charisma

*These enhancers may vary depending on followers' culture.

increase their rank in the organization. Providing staff assistance to help leaders develop plans, goals, and procedures (organizational formalization) consistent with the mission should also enhance a charismatic leader's impact. Internal communications can emphasize charismatic characteristics and accomplishments of past leaders in the organization, which can create a history of charisma in the organization. It may also cause current and future leaders to emulate charismatic behaviors, and followers to respond positively to the leader's behavior.

One recent study on follower characteristics that enhance charismatic leadership occurred primarily in organizations outside the United States (17). Each follower characteristic identified in that study reflects some aspect of follower empowerment—years of schooling, rank, or degree of professionalism. Although certain cultural characteristics of these countries may have caused employees to become highly responsive to charismatic leadership, programs in these organizations that provide education and

LEADERSHIP IN ACTION: ORIT GADIESH— A CHARISMATIC LEADER

"True North!" This refers to the set of principles that Orit Gadiesh has used to lead consulting firm Bain & Co. to expand operations and increase revenues by 25 percent a year. "True North," defined by Gadiesh as that which is virtuous and right, has made Gadiesh one of the most powerful women in business.

Her looks and nervy style get her noticed. Her skirts start eight inches above the knee and her hair is magenta. It is not unusual to see Orit Gadiesh sit down at a serious meeting and throw her high-heeled feet on the table. However, it is her "intense passion" about being true to herself and her clients that makes Orit so charismatic, according to Tom Tierney who is managing director at Bain. "She is complex, intense, driven, painfully direct, sometimes ribald, and a lot of fun."

Her father was a commander in the Israeli army. She served two years in army intelligence before enrolling in the Harvard business school, where she graduated in the top 5 percent of her class. She was hired by Bain & Co. right out of Harvard as one of their first female consultants. She impresses people with her high energy level and her ability to pull "emotional levers" of others.

She leads an organization of consultants who are frequently instrumental in making major changes in their clients' organizations. The individuals in these organizations are often experiencing anxiety and distress from problems when the consultants arrive. Gadiesh's expertise and position inspire respect and admiration in her firm's consultants and clients. Her success as a charismatic leader stems from these factors as well as being a brilliant consultant who can inspire and empathize with clients and her staff.

Though chair of one of the most secretive firms in the industry, Gadiesh still manages to spend 70 percent of her time with clients. This is the type of role modeling she provides for Bain & Co. members, where she is seen as a generous mentor for junior consultants. She constantly reminds herself, "If I were the client, how would I feel about this?" It is this empathy, intense passion, and her energetic style that creates the "Orit Mystique," making her an impressive charismatic leader.

Source: P. Sellers, What exactly is charisma? *Fortune,* January 15, 1996, 68–75.

training, promote professional affiliations, and encourage company loyalty and promotion from within may also increase the impacts of charismatic leadership. The Leadership in Action box on Orit Gadiesh describes how her charismatic style is especially effective for dealing with clients of the consulting firm that she leads.

SITUATIONAL FACTORS THAT DECREASE EFFECTIVENESS OF CHARISMATIC LEADERSHIP

Little research exists on factors that decrease (neutralize) the effects of charismatic leadership. Leadership experts have suggested, however, that in organizational situations that call for routine reliable performance in pursuit of pragmatic goals (such as a post office), charismatic leadership would not likely be effective (18). These situations normally lack the crises or unusual opportunities that make extraordinary inspiration and effort particularly helpful. Although this prediction has not been tested directly, two recent empirical studies may contradict it. In a laboratory study involving a business simulation, researchers found that a low productivity norm did not neutralize the effect of charismatic leadership on follower performance or satisfaction (19). A study of real business managers later confirmed this lack of neutralizing effect (20).

When followers and leaders are equal in power, another expert predicted charismatic leadership would have little effect on followers. Although equality of power between leaders and followers might seem highly unusual in most organizations, it can happen. One situation where this could occur is in a high-technology organization where technical personnel have information, knowledge, and expertise that are equal to or greater than their hierarchical leader. This also may occur in universities or health service organizations, where highly trained professionals report to administrators whose knowledge base in certain areas is less extensive than that of the followers. To date, no studies have tested this prediction, so we do not know if this factor can actually neutralize the effects of charismatic leadership.

In summary, although several writers have made interesting predictions, the research is very sparse on possible neutralizers of charismatic leadership. At this time, no research supports the suggestion that situational or follower characteristics can neutralize the impacts of charismatic leadership.

SITUATIONAL FACTORS THAT REPLACE THE NEED FOR CHARISMATIC LEADERSHIP

Several types of formal organizational procedures have been described as replacing the need for charismatic leadership. These factors may make charismatic leadership unnecessary.

TASK, ORGANIZATIONAL, AND FOLLOWER CHARACTERISTICS

Group bonus-pay plans may induce group motivation and commitment to goal achievement in lieu of charismatic leadership. As another example, organizational requirements for peer review committees, tenure regulations, and consensus decision making may inhibit and replace the possible influence of charismatic leaders in universities and colleges (21).

Similar requirements also apply in many health service organizations. Federal and state regulators as well as funding and accrediting agencies often specify policies and procedures for these organizations in great detail. This structured atmosphere can inhibit the flexibility and creativity needed for charismatic leaders to influence organizational members.

Charisma may not be needed in organizations that value independence and self-management among employees, commonly found in universities or Theory Z-type business organizations. Theory Z organizations emphasize clear, detailed goal statements and supportive policies that encourage individuals to transcend self-interest and focus on the good of the organization. Hewlett Packard, a highly successful manufacturer of computers and information systems equipment, is one example. This type of organization may inspire high motivation without a charismatic leader.

One recent empirical study identified two other situational replacements for charismatic leadership (22). First, formal organizational plans, goals, and procedures replaced charismatic leadership in Mexico. There, the mere existence of formal plans and procedures seemed adequate to obtain follower satisfaction and commitment and actually alleviated the need for charismatic leadership. Second, a high level of task expertise by the leader also alleviated the need for charismatic leadership behaviors in both the United States and Mexico. Although these factors can also be enhancers, they sometimes replace specific leader behaviors by encouraging task expertise and autonomy among followers or by providing formal goals and guidance. It appears that situational factors may replace the impacts of charismatic leadership, at least in the United States and Mexico. However, several of the Mexican organizations in this research were affiliated with U.S. corporations, and this connection may explain why the replacement effects were similar in both countries. More research is needed on these replacement effects.

Some researchers have suggested that certain follower characteristics may replace the need for charismatic leadership. They proposed that followers will resist charismatic leadership if they are self-confident, highly educated, and have a strong belief in human equality (23). Such individuals are expected to be more careful, discerning, and independent in making decisions about their own behavior and in their judgments of others (including leaders) and to be less likely to surrender their judgment to a charismatic leader. They also often perform well on job tasks. These follower characteristics may be most effective as replacements for charisma in individualistic cultures like the United States. Followers who were older, had many years of work experience, and worked at tasks they found enjoyable and satisfying also demonstrated positive attitudes without the need for charismatic leadership (24). These individuals are usually highly confident, knowledgeable, and high in status, causing them to be independent thinkers. Although a single study cannot confirm a certain replacement effect, these findings support the idea that specific follower characteristics may make charismatic leadership unnecessary. Figure 13–2 summarizes findings on replacements for charismatic leadership.

CREATING FACTORS THAT REPLACE THE NEED FOR CHARISMATIC LEADERSHIP

Several organizational actions may create replacements for charismatic leadership. Selection programs that induct older employees with considerable work experience into the organization and on-the-job training programs that build more work experience

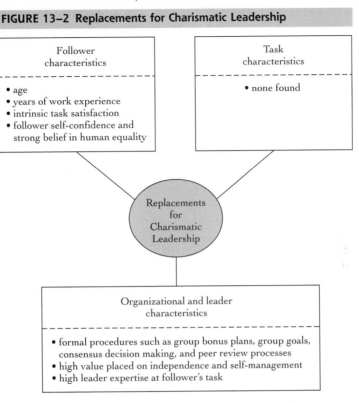

FIGURE 13–2 Replacements for Charismatic Leadership

Follower characteristics
- age
- years of work experience
- intrinsic task satisfaction
- follower self-confidence and strong belief in human equality

Task characteristics
- none found

Replacements for Charismatic Leadership

Organizational and leader characteristics
- formal procedures such as group bonus plans, group goals, consensus decision making, and peer review processes
- high value placed on independence and self-management
- high leader expertise at follower's task

may result in a more independent workforce that has less need for a charismatic leader. In addition, job design programs that make jobs inherently satisfying will cause employees to derive positive attitudes and feelings from their work rather than from a charismatic leader. Also, creation of formal plans, goals, and procedures can provide guidance and direction for employees in place of the mission and role modeling provided by a charismatic leader. Finally, programs that develop leaders' competence and expertise and eventually result in their promotion to higher levels may encourage followers to emulate these leaders and themselves become more independent. All of these programs may make followers less dependent on a charismatic leader for motivation, inspiration, and guidance.

The Leadership in Perspective box on Nelson Mandela describes how his charismatic leadership effectively addressed the difficult political and social situation of South Africa. Table 13–1 summarizes the situational and follower characteristics that affect the impact of charismatic leadership. Figure 13–3 describes the influence of situational factors on the impact of charismatic leadership by a public school principal.

◆ ASSESSING THE DYNAMICS OF CHARISMATIC LEADERSHIP

Effective charismatic leaders are especially sensitive to followers and situations. As they carry out the three key leadership tasks of diagnosing situations, behaving appropriately, and modifying situations, charismatic leaders shape their vision, mission, and

TABLE 13–1 Situational and Follower Characteristics that Affect the Impact of Charismatic Leadership

Factors that Increase the Effectiveness of Charismatic Leadership	*Factors that Decrease the Effectiveness of Charismatic Leadership*	*Factors that Replace the Need for Charismatic Leadership*
• crisis or major social change • follower distress, anxiety, isolation, helplessness, low self-esteem, or extreme uncertainty • organizational history of charisma • creative and/or inherently satisfying work task • high leader rank, status, or expertise • educated and professional followers • formal plans, goals, and procedures that support leader's mission	• none found	• high leader expertise • older experienced followers who are self-confident and enjoy their work • group bonus plans, group goals, and peer review processes • consensus decision making or self-management

FIGURE 13–3 Influence of Situational Factors on the Charismatic Leadership Behaviors of Public School Principals

Situational factors that could increase effectiveness of a principal's charismatic leadership

- The board of education institutes formal plans, goals, and procedures that support the mission communicated by the principal.
- The teachers obtain satisfaction from their students' performance and positive feedback from students and parents.
- The board of education introduces major changes in curriculum and teacher evaluation.

How Situational Factors can Affect the Impact of Charismatic Leadership by a Public School Principal

Situational factors that could decrease the effectiveness of a principal's charismatic leadership

- None have been identified in research to this point.

Situational factors that could replace the need for a principal's charismatic leadership

- The school board institutes extensive plans, goals, and procedures to guide teachers' behavior independently of the principal.
- The teachers are highly experienced and have been doing their jobs for a long period of time.

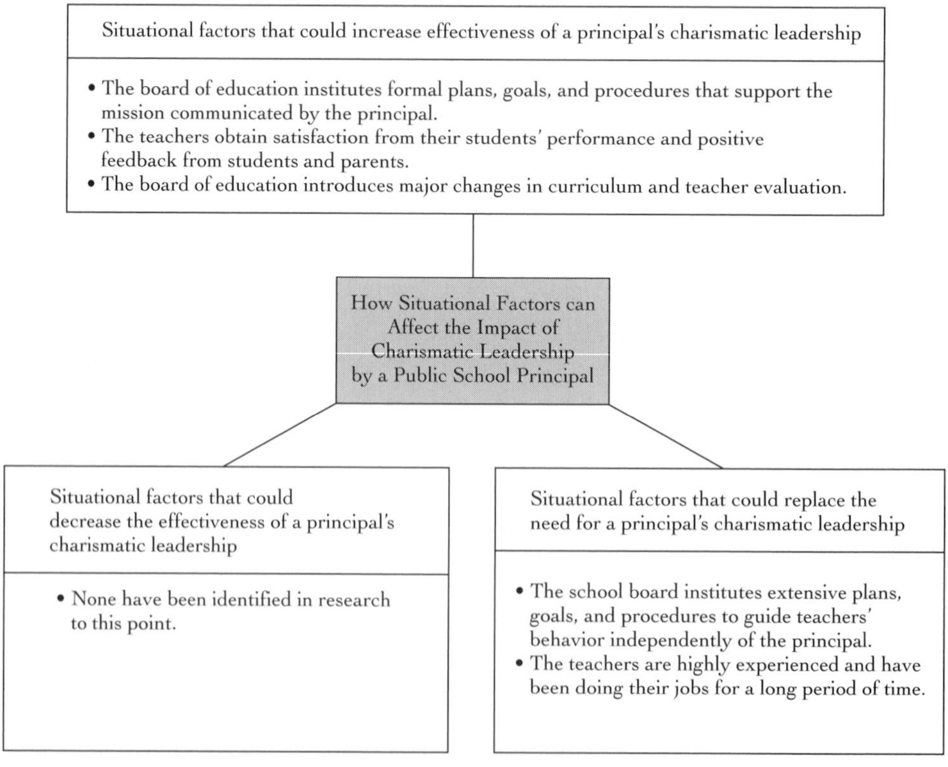

LEADERSHIP IN PERSPECTIVE: NELSON MANDELA

Nelson Mandela, the past president of South Africa and a 1993 Nobel peace prize winner, was born in the rural village of Qunu, in what is now the black homeland of Transkei. After a brutal and harsh 27 years of imprisonment on charges of treason and sabotage, Mandela then led his country with his unique charismatic style.

South Africa has a long history of poverty and apartheid. Apartheid is the oppressive system of laws and regulations that kept Africans in an inferior position to whites for centuries. It is easy to imagine that isolated, anxious, and helpless South Africans longed for a leader with the courage and principle to free them from apartheid, just as Moses freed the children of Israel from Egypt.

Twenty-seven years of harsh prison life certainly steeled Mandela. During the period in prison, he talked about politics, developed his vision of a nonracist society in which white and black would live together in harmony, and even strengthened his courage and principles. Soon, the prison became known as Mandela University. His strong beliefs and courage allowed him to speak clearly to white audiences and convince them that they must take responsibility for the past and act according to democratic principles. He also spoke realistically to black audiences, telling them that material needs would not be satisfied immediately.

His charismatic behaviors included providing a clear vision of a nonracist society, making the personal sacrifice of 27 years in prison for his beliefs, and speaking his beliefs to anyone who would listen. Two critical situational factors made Mandela's charisma especially effective: (1) the feelings of anxiety and helplessness of black South Africans due to apartheid and extreme poverty, and (2) a tremendous expectation among South Africans and the world community that South Africa must change from a white-dominated society to a democratic one. A Harvard professor once described Mandela as "a small man who has taken on the giant forces of evil, and it looks like he is going to win. All of us, black and white, need to know that David can still beat Goliath."

Source: N. Mandela, *Long Walk to Freedom.* (Boston: Little, Brown and Company, 1994).

---

communications to fit followers' perceptions of themselves and the environment. In this way they inspire followers to persist with unusually high effort to reach their goals.

In diagnosing situations, charismatic leaders look for current and future culture shocks or crises that create anxiety and distress in followers. They also engage followers by identifying tasks that have a moral component and a high potential for major change. They build their own status and expertise, develop organizational procedures, and describe historical charismatic leaders to give followers a sense of continuity and respect for their own charismatic efforts. They also may include followers in their mission who are highly educated, professional, and hold a high rank to add to the legitimacy of the mission. When these follower and environmental factors are present, a leader should use the charismatic behaviors described in figure 12–1 to influence followers.

If none of these factors are present, effective charismatic leaders consider modifying environmental or follower characteristics to improve the situation. They may create enhancers by redefining followers' tasks to contain a new moral component or more potential for major change, increase their own status by having their supporters tell stories of the leaders' past successes, build their expertise through continuous training, or promote and develop competent followers who support the leader's mission. Each of these actions can enhance the effects of charismatic leader behaviors.

Charismatic leaders who are concerned with their followers' development may also consider modifying environmental and follower characteristics to create factors that replace the need for charismatic leadership. Leaders can do this by (1) providing followers with valuable work experiences that are inherently interesting and satisfying and (2) helping followers succeed at their tasks to build their self-confidence. Leaders can also develop standard procedures for group bonuses or tenure that do not depend on the leader, or peer review committees that develop and evaluate followers. They can encourage consensus decision making or self-management to make followers less dependent on the leader. This type of situational modification can cause followers to look more to themselves and peers in decision making and problem solving and to be less reliant on a charismatic leader for guidance and inspiration. This may free up the leader to do other needed activities that have received little attention in the past.

When a leader correctly diagnoses important enhancers and provides charismatic leadership behaviors, the effects on followers are usually favorable. Then the leader will continue this successful strategy, at least until follower or situational factors change significantly. If the leader misdiagnoses the situation, and the effects of charismatic leader behaviors are disappointing, then the leader considers other behaviors or perhaps modifies other situational and follower characteristics. Leaders may create enhancers to increase their effect on followers or replacements to make followers more capable, confident, and independent of the leader. Either strategy can result in improved attitudes and performance by followers. Effective charismatic leaders thus adapt their behaviors and strategies to fit both the situation and followers' reactions and performance. Charismatic leader behaviors may be needed when followers face threatening and highly uncertain situations. As the environment changes and followers experience success at overcoming their problems, they probably have less need for a charismatic inspirational leader and can operate on their own as independent and competent groups of individuals.

Summary ▪▪

Most recent research on charismatic leadership has dealt with the behaviors these leaders demonstrate. In this concluding section, we will summarize when these charismatic leader behaviors are most effective and when they are likely to be ineffective. Of course, specific situations and leader characteristics can predispose leaders to show these behaviors. However, effective leaders should think about their behavior before they act, and attempt to behave in ways that suit the situation.

Charismatic behaviors are most likely to have positive effects on followers' psychological reactions and behaviors when important enhancers are present. These organizational and follower conditions (described in figure 13–1) tend to make charismatic leader behaviors highly effective with followers. When a leader finds these conditions, the use of charismatic behaviors described in chapter 12 and summarized in figure 13–4 is recommended.

When replacements for charismatic leadership behaviors are present (described in figure 13–2), these situational and follower characteristics may provide followers with motiva-

FIGURE 13–4 Process Model of Charismatic Leadership

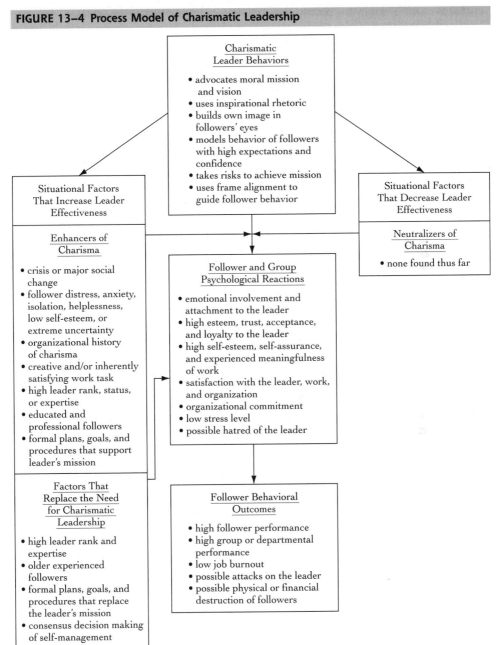

tion or positive attitudes without charismatic leadership. This leadership pattern is therefore less necessary, and the leader should choose a different set of behaviors in order to influence followers. Very little empirical research has been conducted to identify replacements for charismatic leadership, although writers have proposed replacements based on theoretical and historical research.

There is some evidence that cultural differences may cause several factors to emerge as enhancers in one country and as replacements in another country. It does seem clear that the effects of charismatic leadership depend on the situation in different countries, and leaders should probably use their understanding of the culture they work in to help diagnose the need for this leadership behavior pattern. Regardless of whether situational and follower characteristics operate as enhancers or as replacements in a given culture, they have been shown to have favorable effects on followers. If further research supports the replacements and enhancers described in this chapter, leaders should foster and develop them in order to improve followers' psychological reactions and behaviors.

Figure 13–4 summarizes material from Chapters 12 and 13 on the behaviors, effects, and important situational factors affecting charismatic leadership. Figure 13–4 shows charismatic leadership behaviors at the top with arrows pointing downward to show that these behaviors affect follower and group psychological reactions. These psychological reactions result in spe-

FIGURE 13–5 Applying the Model of Charismatic Leadership

1. Diagnosing the Situation

- Do followers face a crisis or major change causing them distress, anxiety, isolation, helplessness, low self-esteem, or extreme uncertainty?
- Are followers' tasks creative or inherently satisfying?
- Is there a history of charisma in the organization?
- Does the leader have a high-level position, status, or expertise?
- Are there formal plans, goals, and procedures that support the leader's mission?
- Are there educated and professional followers who support the leader's mission?

If "yes" to one or more of these questions, then followers will probably respond favorably to charismatic leadership.

3. Modifying Followers and Situations

Leaders act to:
- alleviate crisis, distress, anxiety, isolation, low self-esteem, or extreme uncertainty
- make followers' tasks more creative and satisfying
- increase their own rank, status, and expertise
- create plans, goals, and procedures that support or replace the leader's mission
- develop educated or professional followers

2. Providing Charismatic Leadership

Leader demonstrate charismatic behaviors like the following:
- advocating a moral mission and vision
- using inspirational rhetoric
- building own image in followers' eyes
- modeling behavior for followers with high expectations and confidence
- taking risks to achieve mission
- frame alignment to guide follower behavior

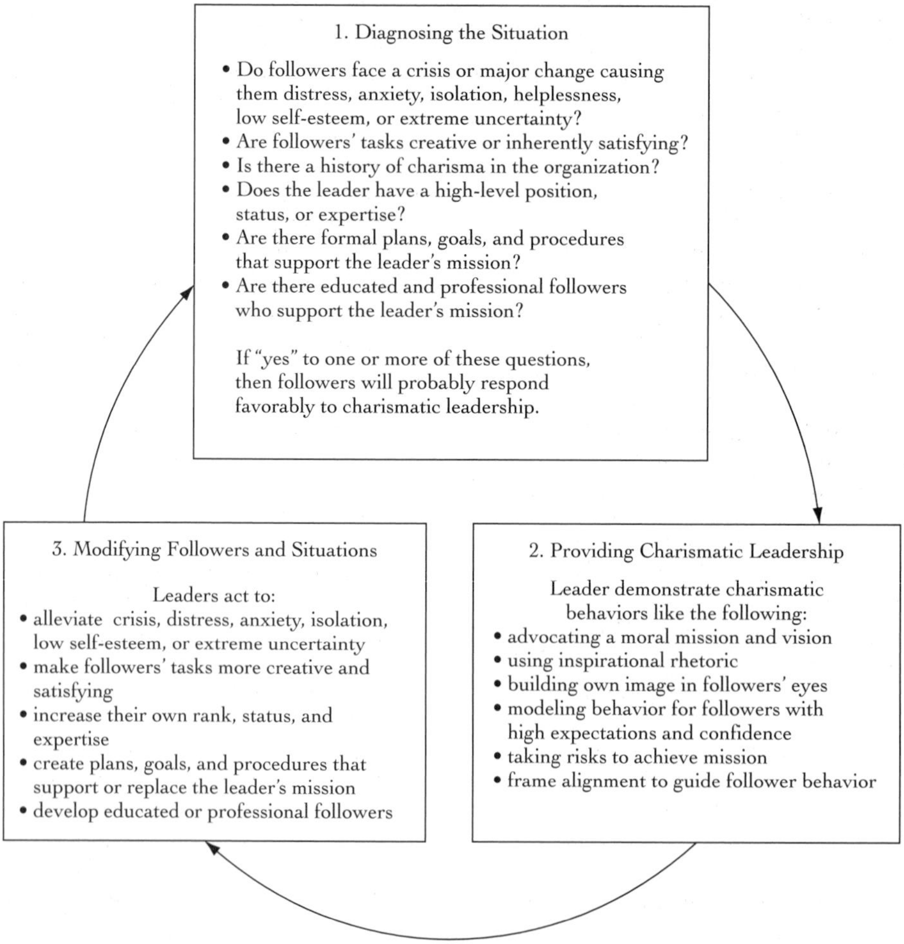

cific follower behaviors and performance. Situational factors that may increase or replace the effects of charismatic leadership are shown on the left side of figure 13–4. No factors have yet been found that neutralize the effects of charismatic leadership. Arrows from the leader behaviors to the situational factors show that leaders can modify situations to enhance or replace the effects of charismatic leadership. Arrows from situational factors that intersect the leader behavior-psychological reaction arrow show how situational factors can increase or replace the effects of charismatic behaviors by leaders.

Figure 13–5 shows how a leader can apply the information in figure 13–4 to a real leadership situation. The leader diagnoses the situation by answering the questions at the top of figure 13–5. These questions help identify enhancers that will probably cause followers to respond favorably to charismatic leadership. If the answer is "yes" to one or more of these questions, the leader should provide this type of leader behavior and monitor the results. These behaviors are shown by the items listed on the right of figure 13–5. The leader can then try to modify situational factors to make the charismatic behaviors more effective. Leaders may also consider creating factors that can replace the effects of charismatic leadership, to make followers less dependent. These actions are shown on the left of figure 13–5. The leader then rediagnoses the situation to determine if charismatic behaviors are still needed and the dynamic cycle of situational diagnosis, providing charismatic leadership, and situational modification begins again.

Key Terms and Concepts in this Chapter ■ ■ ■ ■ ■ ■ ■ ■ ■ ■ ■ ■ ■ ■ ■ ■ ■ ■

- charismatic leadership
- consensus decision making
- culture shocks
- extreme crisis
- expressive orientation
- principled orientation
- professionalism
- self-management
- theory Z organizations

Review and Discussion Questions ■

1. Think of an effective charismatic leader you have known, observed, or heard about. What situational or follower characteristics were present that made this leader effective?

2. Can you think of a situation you have experienced, observed, or heard about where charismatic leadership was not needed? If so, describe this situation.

3. Think of your current job situation or a job you would like to have. Do you believe charismatic leadership would be effective in this situation? Why or why not?

4. Describe an organizational situation where it would be desirable to create a replacement for charismatic leadership. What type of replacement would be desirable?

5. Do you believe charismatic leadership would be effective for a group of maintenance personnel in an office building? Why or why not?

6. Do you believe charismatic leadership would be effective for the captain of a football team? Why or why not?

EXERCISE: The Reverend Jesse Jackson ▪▪▪▪▪▪▪▪▪▪▪▪▪▪▪▪▪▪▪▪▪▪▪▪▪

The Reverend Jesse Jackson addressed the National Convention of the Democratic Party on July 19, 1988. *The New York Times* stated that "Jesse Jackson moved friend and former foe alike tonight with his revival-style speech. By the time he was finished . . . there were tears and cheers of passion flowing through the hall. . . ." Supporters and critics of Mr. Jackson may disagree on much of what Jesse Jackson represents, but most agree he possesses the personal traits, abilities, and behaviors of a charismatic leader. In his address to the Convention, Jesse Jackson soundly modeled the behavior that is indicative of a charismatic leader. He advocated a moral mission or vision through the use of inspirational rhetoric, producing a common theme throughout his speech. "America" he stated, "must never surrender to a high moral challenge." Advocating what is morally right or just, he tried to raise his followers to more principled levels of judgment. As exhibited here in an excerpt from his address to the National Convention:

> Leadership cannot just go along and get along . . . Leadership must meet the moral challenge of the day . . . I'm often asked "Jesse, why do you take on these tough issues? They're not very political. We can't win that way." If an issue is morally right, it will eventually become political . . . Dr. King didn't have the most votes about the Vietnam War, but he was morally right. If we're principled first, our politics will fall into place.

The Reverend Jackson created an image in the eyes of his followers that transcends the charisma he built based on his black identity, instead emphasizing a shared identity with Americans regardless of race. "When I look out at this convention, I see the face of America, red, yellow, brown, black and white . . . The real rainbow coalition . . . We sit here together, a rainbow, a coalition . . . " He also went on to say "America's not a blanket woven from one thread, one color, one cloth." He shared a story of his grandmother who used rags to create a quilt that was both strong and warm. He used this metaphor to join democrats together to "build such a quilt," to join forces and work together.

Jackson is masterful at role modeling. He shared his personal history with followers, that he was not born with a silver spoon in his mouth. Instead, he was born to a teenage mother and lived his early life in poverty. Reverend Jackson's ability to overcome life's obstacles provides a lesson to followers and helps them to build self-esteem and confidence, holding them to the same high standards that he requires of himself.

> . . . America, hold your head high now. We can win. We must not lose you to drugs and violence, premature pregnancy, suicide, cynicism, pessimism, and despair. We can win . . . Wherever you are tonight you can make it. Hold your head high, stick your chest out. You can make it. It gets dark sometimes but the morning comes. Don't you surrender. Suffering breeds character. Character breeds faith. In the end faith will not disappoint.

By associating himself with the late Dr. Martin Luther King Jr., Jesse Jackson created the image that he is a risk taker. Reverend Jackson alluded to the fact that his leadership springs from the "blood and sweat of the innocent" and that he will not fail those who struggled. He stated, "As a testament to the struggles of those who have gone before; as a legacy for those who will come after, as a tribute to the endurance, the patience, the courage of our forefathers and mothers; as an assurance that their prayers are being answered, their work has not been in vain, and hope is eternal; tomorrow my name will go into the nomination for the presidency of the United States of America."

By drawing a parallel between himself and Dr. Martin Luther King Jr., Jesse Jackson also demonstrated the ability to unite past, present, and future events and create a shared frame of reference, which creates continuity. His speech contained several references to collective history and traditions and emphasized that his leadership is a continuance of a historical tradition. Such statements give followers a feeling of security, a sense of 'evolving' that contributes to the meaningfulness of actions and goals.

Jesse Jackson's speech was an extraordinary performance, and it provides an example of the charismatic use of rhetoric. He encouraged personal and social identification through a value-laden speech, and caused followers to identify and internalize goals, values, and beliefs about the future and obtain intrinsic satisfaction from the pursuit of these goals.

Source: B. Shamir, B. B. Arthur, and R. House. "The rhetoric of charismatic leadership: A theoretical expansion, a case study, and implications for research," *Leadership Quarterly,* 5(1) (1994): 25–42.

Discuss Jesse Jackson's speech in groups and answer the following questions:

1. What situational or follower characteristics did Jackson appeal to in this speech?
2. If this speech were to be given today, do you believe the audience would have the same emotional reactions? Why or why not?

◆◆◆ **Case Incident**

Charismatic Leadership: A Follower's Perspective

Deborah Layton grew up in a house of secrets. She was 16 before her parents told her she was Jewish. Later they informed her that the grandmother, who supposedly had died of a heart attack, had actually committed suicide and that her mother had fled Nazi Germany. After these revelations, she was sent to a British boarding school to curb her adolescent rebellion. These early experiences resulted in lack of trust and extreme feelings of insecurity in Deborah.

When she was 17 and on summer vacation, her brother Larry introduced her to Jim Jones at the first People's Temple in northern California. Larry was already a member of the Temple, and he believed it would help him survive the atomic war he expected. Jones frequently wore dark glasses indoors and out, his hair was glossy black, he wore sweeping robes, and liked to be called Father of his flock.

Deborah describes herself at this time as "young and unanchored." She was charmed when Jones fixed his penetrating brown eyes on her and

warmly invited her to "join me and my family of all races." He claimed to have "hundreds of followers working to feed the hungry, house the homeless, and help addicts get clean." She further states, "The people that joined the People's Temple were really good people. They were innocent. They were naïve. . . . They were looking for something larger than themselves to be involved in."

Deborah joined the People's Temple and became a trusted financial officer for Jones. He later told her, "You are the only one I can really trust." But she began to learn about another side of Jim Jones and the People's Temple. Beatings of members who disagreed with Jones and fake healings were increasingly common. When the Temple was moved to Jonestown, a jungle encampment 250 miles from the capital of Guyana, she knew she had entered a prison. In Jonestown, the residents who were able worked the fields and the population subsisted on rice. "Dissent was unthinkable. Offenders sweltered in "The Box," a 6-by-4-foot underground enclosure. Misbehaving children were dangled head-first into the well late at night. . . . Loudspeakers broadcast Jones' voice at all hours. Once he barked out the warning, "White night!" This meant they were about to be attacked and everyone was to take poison punch. At this time Jones was only testing their devotion.

Deborah escaped in May, 1978 when she was chaperoning a youth group in the capital city. She spread the alarm that Jones was planning a mass suicide, but few listened. Finally on November 17, a group of reporters and concerned family members arrived, led by U.S. Representative Leo Ryan. They toured Jonestown and spent the night. The next day, as they were about to board their plane to leave with about 20 defectors, they were ambushed. Ryan and four others were killed. Deborah's brother, Larry Layton, was posing as a defector and was one of the shooters. He is now serving a life sentence in federal prison.

In Jonestown, Jim Jones was orchestrating the mass suicide of all its residents. Poison punch was squirted into babies' mouths. Then adults were instructed to drink the poison. Some were shot by security guards. Jones was shot through the head. In all, over 900 of Jones' followers died.

Source: Las Cruces Sun News, November 15, 1998.

Discuss this incident in groups and answer the following questions:

QUESTIONS

1. Describe the elements of Jim Jones' charismatic leadership.
2. What situational and/or personal characteristics might have caused Deborah Layton to become a follower of Jim Jones' charismatic leadership?

3. Why would so many residents of Jonestown choose to stay when their lives there were so harsh and punishing?

Endnotes

1. Keller, R. T. (1992). Transformational leadership and the performance of research and development project groups. *Journal of Management,* 18(3), 489–501.
2. Howell, J. P., Dorfman, P. W., Hibino, S., Lee, J. K. and Tate, U. (1994). Leadership in western and Asian countries: Commonalities and differences in effective leadership processes and substitutes across cultures. Bureau of Business Research, New Mexico State University.
3. Hollander, E. P. *Leadership Dynamics: A Practical Guide to Effective Relationships.* New York: The Free Press, 1978.
4. Conger, J. A. and Kanungo, R. N. *Charismatic Leadership: The Elusive Factor in Organizational Effectiveness.* San Francisco: Jossey-Bass, 1988.
5. Bass, B. M. (1985). Leadership: Good, better, best. *Organizational Dynamics,* 13(3), 26–40.
6. Shamir, B., House, R. J. and Arthur, M. B. (1993). The motivational effects of charismatic leadership: A self-concept based theory. *Organizational Science,* 4, 1–17.
7. Bass, B. M. *Bass and Stogdill's Handbook of Leadership* (3rd ed.). New York: The Free Press, 1990.
8. House, R. J., Woycke, J. and Fodor, E. M. (1988). Charismatic and noncharismatic leaders: Differences in behavior and effectiveness. In J. A. Conger and R. N. Kanungo (Eds.), *Charismatic leadership: The elusive factor in organizational effectiveness.* San Francisco: Jossey-Bass.
9. Madsen, D. and Snow, P. G. (1983). The dispersion of charisma. *Comparative Political Studies,* 16, 337–362.
10. Newman, R. G. (1983). Thoughts on superstars of charisma: Pipers in our midst. *American Journal of Orthopsychiatry,* 53(2), 201–208.

11. Freemesser, G. F. and Kaplan, H. B. (1976). Self-attitudes and deviant behavior: The case of the charismatic religious movement. *Journal of Youth and Adolescence,* 5(1), 1–9.

12. Bass, *Bass and Stogdill's Handbook of Leadership.*

13. Howell, Dorfman, Hibino, Lee and Tate, Leadership in western and Asian countries: Commonalities and differences in effective leadership processes and substitutes across cultures.

14. Shamir, House and Arthur, The motivational effects of charismatic leadership: A self-concept based theory.

15. Yukl, G. (1998). *Leadership in Organizations* (4th ed.). Upper Saddle River, NJ: Prentice Hall.

16. Shamir, House and Arthur, The motivational effects of charismatic leadership: A self-concept based theory.

17. Howell, Dorfman, Hibino, Lee and Tate, Leadership in western and Asian countries: Commonalities and differences in effective leadership processes and substitutes across cultures.

18. House, Woycke and Fodor, Charismatic and noncharismatic leaders: Differences in behavior and effectiveness.

19. Howell, J. M. and Frost, P. J. (1989). A laboratory study of charismatic leadership. *Organizational Behavior and Human Decision Processes,* 43, 243–269.

20. Howell, J. M. and Avolio, B. J. (1993). Transformational leadership, transactional leadership, locus of control, and support for innovation: Key predictors of consolidated-business-unit performance. *Journal of Applied Psychology,* 78(6), 891–902.

21. Bass, Leadership: Good, better, best.

22. Howell, Dorfman, Hibino, Lee and Tate, Leadership in western and Asian countries: Commonalities and differences in effective leadership processes and substitutes across cultures.

23. Bass, Leadership: Good, better, best.

24. Howell, Dorfman, Hibino, Lee and Tate, Leadership in western and Asian countries: Commonalities and differences in effective leadership processes and substitutes across cultures.

PART III

Current Leadership Issues in Organizations

CHAPTER 14

Boundary Spanning and Team Leadership

Learning Objectives
After reading this chapter you should be able to do the following:

1. Describe boundary-spanning leader behaviors and provide specific examples of these behaviors.
2. Explain why boundary-spanning behaviors can have positive effects on followers.
3. Describe skills and abilities leaders need to be effective at boundary spanning.
4. Identify how a leader can use sources of power to increase the effectiveness of boundary-spanning behaviors.
5. Describe the individual and organizational benefits that can result from effective boundary-spanning behaviors.
6. Identify follower characteristics for which boundary-spanning behaviors would be highly effective.
7. Identify organizational and task characteristics for which boundary-spanning leader behaviors would be highly effective.
8. Describe how followers, situations, and boundary-spanning behaviors interact to affect each other in a dynamic process.

◆ EXAMPLES OF EFFECTIVE BOUNDARY SPANNING

• The new superintendent of a manufacturing plant successfully convinced his autocratic boss to purchase a new piece of material-processing equipment that was badly needed but had been vetoed by the boss when proposed by the previous superintendent. The new superintendent carefully prepared his boss by making an appointment with him to tour the plant, where the conditions spoke for themselves. The superintendent added to the visual clues with a description of how the old equipment hampered the plant. The boss had no option but to agree about the problem, and he asked

"What do you propose?" The superintendent responded with a carefully worked out proposal that the boss approved almost immediately (1).

• A manager at Data General protected and facilitated a group of young, creative, and motivated computer design engineers to help them design a faster computer than the competition. Data General at this time was internally competitive, highly political, and resource poor. The leader obtained work space that was isolated—encouraging considerable interaction among the team members and discouraging interaction outside the team. He articulated overall project requirements and negotiated deadlines, stayed out of internal disputes, obtained required resources wherever he could, and buffered the team from organization politics. The team developed a high degree of camaraderie during the project and completed the project successfully in record time (2).

• The manager of a staff department demonstrated effective negotiation skills when asked by a production manager about getting assistance from one of his key staff members. "There is no way I can get Harry to work on that, even though he is the one you want and could do it best. But I could get Harry to look over Bill and Jane's work, to be sure it's consistent with the way you like things done." The production manager agreed, the work was successfully completed, and the working relationship between production and the staff department was strengthened (3).

All organizations and groups have boundaries of some type that determine who is and who is not a member. Leaders have much of the responsibility for establishing and maintaining these boundaries. The incidents described above demonstrate effective boundary-spanning leadership. Boundary-spanning leadership is defined as leader actions that establish and maintain a group's integrity through negotiating with nongroup members, resolving disputes among followers and subgroups, obtaining resources, establishing influence networks, and helping followers deal with the external environment.

Boundary-spanning activities may include interacting with superiors on behalf of the group to obtain resources or approval for changes or buffering the group from unreasonable demands. They can also include lateral interactions with other individuals and groups to obtain and provide information, coordinate activities, and resolve disputes. Internal boundary spanning is similar to lateral interactions, except the focus is on providing information, coordinating, and resolving disputes among subgroups and members within the leader's immediate group. One study found that 70 percent to 80 percent of the boundary-spanning activities in a large formal organization were carried out by leaders (4).

As organizations and their environments have increased in complexity, these boundary-spanning activities have become more important and time consuming. Several developments inside modern organizations contribute to this trend, including more worker participation in decision making, more autonomous or self-managed work groups, advances in information technology, and specialized staff units (5). All of these increase the needs for resources, information, and coordination. Boundary-spanning interactions can be complicated because several groups are often involved, each with its own norms, values, goals, and loyalties. These interactions also occur sporadically and are difficult for leaders to predict. They therefore interrupt other important leadership activities and may interfere with departmental procedures. Boundary spanning can also be time consuming for the leader, especially when negotiating with another group or persuading a superior to approve a major change in departmental plans, procedures, or objectives.

The following are examples of boundary spanning leadership behaviors:

1. Defining and modifying organizational or unit boundaries so members know who is and who is not a member
2. Protecting and representing the group while resisting unreasonable demands and responding to outside influence
3. Managing interactions between leaders and followers, among followers themselves, and among subgroups within the leader's unit, including helping to resolve stalemates and conflicts
4. Negotiating with upper management and other outsiders to obtain resources for the unit and to arrange for distribution of the unit's output
5. Identifying and describing for group members what they should attend to in the environment and what they should ignore to help them make sense of developments that may affect them (otherwise known as frame alignment)
6. Developing and maintaining networks inside and outside the leader's own organization, and using these networks to describe the unit's activities, accomplishments, and capabilities in order to increase its legitimacy, image, and power
7. Obtaining, filtering, and storing valuable information from the unit's environment, putting the information into a useful form, and disseminating it to unit members

By defining and protecting the group boundaries and mission, the leader establishes and maintains a shared identity that builds cohesion and cooperation among members. Managing interactions among various follower and subgroup roles within the unit helps maintain this shared identity and prevents the unit from fracturing into combative subgroups. Obtaining resources and building influence networks increases the potential performance and reputation of the group, which increases future support and further builds cohesion. Identifying key dimensions of the environment, regularly scanning these environmental dimensions, and conveying information to members in a useful form helps make members sensitive to the unit's welfare. These activities also allow the group to adapt to new technical developments, innovations in organizational design, legal issues, trends in related fields, interest groups, and other external issues to keep the unit "in sync" with its environment. Figure 14–1 summarizes major boundary-spanning behaviors by leaders.

◆ EXAMPLES OF INEFFECTIVE BOUNDARY SPANNING

Some leaders recognize the importance of boundary-spanning activities but they are unsuccessful at carrying them out. The following incidents describe examples of ineffective boundary-spanning activities by leaders.

• A new departmental manager was faced with an urgent request from his boss that required critical input from another department. When contacted by the new manager, the other department head said he could not provide the needed input in the near future, if at all. The new manager became indignant and saw the other manager as inefficient and an obstacle. Since he was new in the organization, he decided against trying to bully or

FIGURE 14–1 Boundary-Spanning Leader Behaviors

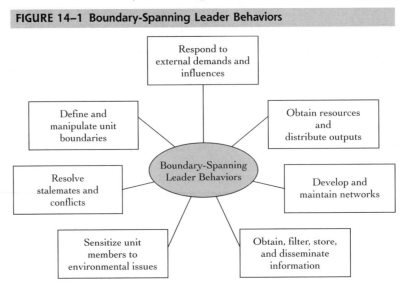

threaten the other manager. He opted instead for a strategy of trying to "fool" the manager into believing he would share credit for meeting the boss's request. The other department manager saw through this and the new manager lost credibility in the organization. He did not realize that effective managers must build long-term relationships and count on friendship and respect to obtain the cooperation they need.

• A young supervisor with a recent college degree described his inability to obtain needed resources from another department as "just a misunderstanding, a communication problem. When the situation is 'clarified', they will cooperate and come through for us." However, the supervisor did not get the resources to the extent he wanted, regardless of his repeated efforts to "get them to listen." His mistaken assumption was that the organization was one big happy family in which everyone had the same interests and goals. Other departments had different interests and were often rewarded for things that were not consistent with the new supervisor's needs.

• A new manager of a highly professional group of research and development workers was anxious to please her superior. She saw her job as representing upper-level management to the R & D workers. She became a "mouthpiece" for upper management, conveying all their concerns and requests directly to the employees. The R & D personnel began to see her as not standing up for them in maintaining the independence they needed to pursue new ideas for products and as passing down unreasonable management requests with deadlines that were not realistic. They wanted a manager to buffer them from unreasonable requests and to serve as an advocate in obtaining flexibility and resources to pursue projects they believed were potentially valuable to the company. The new manager lost their respect because she did not realize that she was responsible to her people as well as to upper management.

Each leader in these incidents failed to realistically assess some aspect of their group or its environment. Accurate perceptions of the group's needs as well as important environmental factors are essential for effective boundary-spanning leadership.

◆ IMPORTANCE OF BOUNDARY SPANNING

Organizations have traditionally been viewed as having relatively fixed boundaries, and the leader's job included focusing on exchanges of resources and information between the organization and its environment. Early experts described a key leadership function as the defense of organizational integrity. They pointed out that a leader's influence with higher-ups affected the leader's influence on followers and unit performance (6).

One organizational expert, writing in 1961, distinguished between representative functions and linking pin functions of leaders. He described representatives as spokespersons for their own group, and their loyalties were entirely to that group. Linking pins were viewed as members of two or more interacting groups with loyalties to both; they fulfill a liaison role, helping to coordinate and resolve conflicts among groups (7). Today, boundary spanners are seen as playing both representative and linking pin roles, depending on the situation. Organizational boundaries are no longer fixed, but are constantly changing. The leader's job frequently includes engaging in boundary modification and redefinition as work teams, departments, and organizations are divided, merge, or acquire one another.

Another writer described ten key leadership roles that managers play, seven involve some sort of boundary spanning:

1. **Figurehead**—performing symbolic acts such as representing the organization at social gatherings
2. **Liaison**—forming and maintaining networks outside the unit including making new contacts, keeping in touch with important outsiders, and doing favors
3. **Monitoring**—obtaining information from outside the leader's unit that may help the overall unit's performance
4. **Disseminator**—Passing information on to insiders or to subunits about other subunits
5. **Spokesperson**—Transmitting information and expressing value statements to outsiders
6. **Disturbance handler**—dealing with conflicts among subordinates or subunits, loss of subordinates, strikes, and other "crisis situations"
7. **Negotiator**—Bargaining for the unit in dealing with others over resources and constraints; buffering the unit and its members from higher-ups and outsiders (8)

In this era of rapid change, increasing interdependence, and networking between and within organizations, boundary-spanning activities require increasing amounts of a leader's time and effort. The flexible nature of boundaries, complex environments, and increasing importance of networks also mean that boundaries offer less protection than before. Advocacy groups, government regulators, courts, and professional standards committees all penetrate today's organizations, and their view of appropriate procedures may differ markedly from the leader. One researcher noted that 93 outsiders entered an inner-city school during one week to perform some type of service (9). These outsiders are not socialized into the organization's norms and practices in the way of employees. Consequently, leaders have little control over them. They create both learning opportunities and risks of subversion. Leaders are usually responsible for dealing with these outsiders and the impacts of their activities on the organization.

Organizations today are composed of increasingly diverse groups of people. Employees identify with ethnic groups, age groups, gender groups, religious groups, and many others. For many people, their personal lives are no longer distinct from their work lives. They often work at home and on weekends, they rely on their employers for child care, elder care, and health care, and their friendships are work related. These factors continually change employees' expectations of organizations, requiring leaders to actively manage evolving boundaries among followers and between followers and the organization. One result of these changes is that followers often view leaders as more powerful than leaders view themselves. So leaders must continually clarify their role, including powers and limitations in dealing with follower roles.

In organizations of the year 2000 and beyond, information will increasingly be viewed as the major resource. The information-processing function of leaders is especially important because they convert raw data to summaries, conclusions, and inferences. Information that is thus converted is difficult for other organizational or group members to verify, but it slowly becomes part of an organization's collective intelligence—that is, once created, it tends to be well accepted. Thus, the information-processing aspects of leaders' boundary spanning have long-term implications for the organization's strategies and actions.

The following leadership assessment provides specific examples of boundary-spanning behaviors.

LEADERSHIP SELF ASSESSMENT: BOUNDARY-SPANNING LEADERSHIP

Think of a team, committee, or other group you have participated in that had an identifiable leader. If you have trouble thinking of a group of your own, then think of a leader you have observed, read, or heard about. Describe the leader's boundary-spanning behaviors using the rating scale for the items below.

	Hardly Ever					Almost Always	
	1	2	3	4	5	6	7

My leader...

1. Establishes procedures that shield employees from unnecessary interference so that they can perform their jobs effectively and productively
       1 2 3 4 5 6 7

2. Resists unrealistic demands on the work group from outsiders (customers, vendors, other departments)
       1 2 3 4 5 6 7

3. Filters out irrelevant material while keeping the team supplied with information important to the work group
       1 2 3 4 5 6 7

4. Persuades upper management and outsiders to appreciate and support the work group by telling them about its abilities, activities, and accomplishments
       1 2 3 4 5 6 7

5. Coordinates activities with other groups	1	2	3	4	5	6	7
6. Actively seeks out any additional resources (extra supplies, materials, tools, or equipment) needed to complete the team's work	1	2	3	4	5	6	7
7. Forms contacts with people outside the work group who can provide useful information	1	2	3	4	5	6	7
8. Attends social events to develop contacts and find out what is happening in other parts of the organization	1	2	3	4	5	6	7
9. Collects relevant information and verifies its accuracy before confronting employees about interpersonal conflicts	1	2	3	4	5	6	7
10. Encourages members to resolve conflicts in a constructive manner	1	2	3	4	5	6	7
11. Promptly addresses employee concerns about poor treatment by coworkers (for example, sexual harassment, racial slurs, etc.)	1	2	3	4	5	6	7
12. Introduces new employees to everyone in the department	1	2	3	4	5	6	7
13. Provides accurate information directly to employees about past and/or future events in order to prevent or dispel rumors	1	2	3	4	5	6	7

Those items that you rated as 6 or 7 indicate a high level of boundary-spanning behavior by this leader. Why do you think this leader was so active in using these behaviors? Describe any environmental or group characteristics that made these boundary-spanning behaviors especially important.

◆ HOW LEADERS SPAN BOUNDARIES

Leadership researchers have not carefully studied the personal characteristics of boundary spanners. It appears, however, that effective boundary spanners should have a high internal locus of control. That is, they should believe in their own abilities to influence environmental factors. Having confidence in one's abilities is essential for success in dealing with environmental demands and constraints.

Descriptions of boundary spanning also imply other skills that leaders should develop to effectively carry out these behaviors. For example, many boundary-spanning activities require effective communication skills. Such skills are critical to advocating for the group, persuading outsiders to support the group, and influencing individuals and subgroups to look beyond turf battles and to cooperate for the sake of the unit. Communication skills also include telling stories about past successes (such as when a coach describes how a team rallied to win an important game) or creating slogans (such as an automobile-leasing firm proclaiming "We try harder!"). These activities help establish a "we feeling" among unit members and consequently shape the unit or organization's boundaries. Political and negotiation skills are also critical for boundary spanning in order to place the unit in a favorable position to influence its environment. Conflict-management skills are key to overcoming internal and external disputes that can threaten the unit's supply of resources and freedom of action. Leaders can develop these boundary-spanning skills through formal education and training experiences (such as membership in a Toastmaster's club), relevant work experiences, and coaching or mentoring programs. These skills should enable leaders to effectively represent their people, buffer them from environmental jolts, and obtain the resources and cooperation needed to facilitate their group and organization's performance. The boxed example provides guidelines for negotiations that can be an important part of a leader's boundary spanning.

In nearly any organizational situation, leaders who are recognized as experts in their group or organizational tasks are highly respected. They convey an image of competence to group members and outsiders alike. This competence or expert power causes others to listen carefully and often to react favorably to what the expert leader says (10). This tendency to elicit positive reactions from others is extremely helpful to leaders' boundary-spanning efforts. When leaders possess expert power, outsiders and group members hesitate to question or challenge their arguments, and they are more likely to go along with the leader's requests. This ability to influence others can result in adequate resources, cooperative agreements, and favorable relationships with outsiders who can help the group achieve its goals. Leaders often develop expert power through continuous learning and training programs, formal education, as well as meaningful work experiences.

In addition to task expertise, when leaders are highly respected or admired for other reasons, their boundary-spanning behaviors are probably more effective. This referent power may result from the leader's past accomplishments, high status, or a magnetic personality. It often complements expert power in helping the leader represent the group effectively. Others in the organization can help build a leader's referent power by emphasizing the leader's achievements and potential for future accomplishments.

Effective boundary spanners usually develop networks of relationships with important individuals and groups outside the leader's group or organization. These networks help build the leader's connection/resource power, which is critical to keeping the leader's group well supplied with the resources needed to accomplish its goals. The

---

LEADERSHIP IN PERSPECTIVE: GUIDELINES FOR NEGOTIATING

- Begin with a plausible demand or offer. Remember that reasonableness promotes effective negotiation.
- Keep the people and the problem separate. Avoid blaming individuals.
- Focus on the parties' interests, not their positions on the topic; on end results, not "means." What would satisfy the individuals' needs?
- Seek win-win outcomes, where all parties obtain desired results.
- Be sensitive to individual differences in negotiating style.

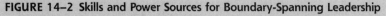
FIGURE 14–2 Skills and Power Sources for Boundary-Spanning Leadership

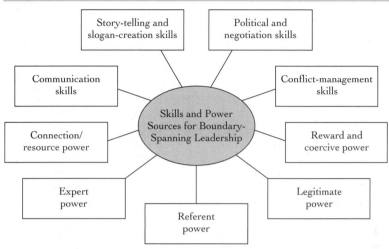

leader's connections also help obtain cooperation with other groups that interact with the leader's group. In organizations working with sophisticated technology, such as those conducting complex medical procedures or complicated manufacturing operations, willing cooperation from other departments can be essential to effective performance.

Two other sources of power can help leaders especially with boundary spanning inside their own group. Leaders who hold a high-level position in the organization are likely to be respected due to their position. In other words, the leader's efforts to resolve disputes among subgroups or members of the leader's group will likely be influential due to the leader's legitimate power of position. Followers will probably assume that high-level leaders also possess reward and coercive power due to their position, and may be anxious to keep on these leaders' "good side." Although many leaders do not emphasize their formal position or control over rewards and punishments, these power sources are implied when a high-level leader offers to help two followers work out a disagreement that is interfering with the group's performance (11). Although legitimate power is usually bestowed on a leader by the organization, all leaders control some types of rewards and punishments—either tangible (such as a bonus or a demotion) or intangible (a compliment or a reprimand). Effective leaders typically make use of several of these power sources when carrying out boundary-spanning activities. Figure 14–2 summarizes important skills and power sources for boundary-spanning leadership.

◆ EFFECTS OF BOUNDARY SPANNING

Leaders' boundary-spanning activities have produced favorable results in many organizational situations. For example, coordination problems were almost completely eliminated among legal, judicial, and mental health departments in a city government when managers of these units engaged in extensive external boundary-spanning activities (12). In business organizations, when leaders "went to bat" to defend followers and kept their superiors informed regarding group activities, these leaders received higher performance evaluations (13). High performance evaluations were also given to school principals by superintendents and teachers when principals were active in boundary spanning by obtaining resources for their schools and disseminating information to outsiders (14).

Boundary spanning is also important for project managers in research and development departments. These managers often obtain important technical and career information from external sources and then convey it to personnel in their departments. This activity can result in improved staff development and socialization, especially among younger personnel. These improvements produce lower turnover and higher promotion rates for these personnel than those who have managers who are less active in boundary spanning (15). Other studies show that followers' satisfaction, morale, and confidence in the leader are increased by effective boundary spanning (16).

Leaders can also experience negative consequences from their boundary-spanning activities however. For example, managers in research and development organizations reported a high level of role conflict when they were heavily involved in boundary spanning. The requirements of their different roles created varying demands and multiple loyalties that were difficult for these managers to juggle. Leaders in human service organizations also report high levels of stress and job burnout associated with their boundary-spanning duties (17). Although leaders' boundary-spanning activities have favorable effects on their organizations and followers, the negotiations and haggling that may accompany these activities can clearly take their toll on leaders.

◆ SITUATIONAL FACTORS AND BOUNDARY SPANNING

The amount of boundary-spanning activities required of a leader is often related to factors in the organization's environment (18). A highly uncertain environment often requires more boundary spanning. Here the leaders need to monitor the environment in order to gather information and adapt to unforeseen changes that might affect the organization. But researchers have also found that predictable and controllable environments encouraged boundary spanning by company managers to influence that environment (19). Here the boundary spanners were able to create and exploit opportunities for their organization as they interacted with outside individuals and organizations. In both situations the organizational environment stimulated the need for external boundary spanning, but the objectives of the boundary spanners differed depending on the nature of the environment and the organization's position.

Internal organizational factors can also create a need for boundary-spanning activities by leaders. When followers' tasks are uncertain and difficult (such as designing new computer software or hardware), leaders spend much time in boundary-spanning activities (20). Here the group members often need information and guidance from other sources in order to complete their tasks, and boundary spanners are active in obtaining this information. If the leader's group is central to the organization's activities and engages in highly interdependent operations with other organizational groups, then boundary-spanning activities are needed (21). Much coordination with other groups is needed in these situations, and boundary spanners provide this coordination by anticipating and solving problems before they get out of hand.

A leader is likely to be highly effective when she responds to these environmental, task, and organizational situations with boundary-spanning behaviors. Leaders are also most likely to be successful in boundary-spanning efforts when they are familiar with the organization's operations and have extensive leadership experience (22). These factors increase respect for the leader by followers and others who interact with her, thereby enhancing the effectiveness of the leader's boundary-spanning behaviors. When the leader is responsible for one or more self-managed work teams, boundary-spanning activities are also especially important. These teams are increasingly common in organizations and are described in the following section.

On the other hand, research indicates that boundary-spanning activities are less important in certain settings. For example, numerous formal policies, procedures, and written guidelines replaced the need for many boundary-spanning activities among noncommissioned U.S. Army officers (23). Formalized procedures are very prevalent in military organizations. These procedures may assure that certain needs of followers are met, and they need not rely on the leader's boundary-spanning activities to provide for them.

Also, some studies have reported that older followers or those with higher rank and years of service are less affected by boundary-spanning activities of their leaders (24). These individuals may be in a position to satisfy their own needs without the leader's help, whereas younger, less experienced followers may depend on the leader's boundary spanning. Followers' age, rank, and years of experience may thus neutralize the effects of the leader's boundary spanning. Although the information is sparse, it does appear that the leader must consider situational and follower characteristics in order to assess the need for the boundary-spanning function. The three types of situational and follower characteristics that affect boundary-spanning leadership are summarized in Table 14–1. The Leadership in Action box on Bill Gates describes a current example of boundary spanning.

TABLE 14–1 Situational and Follower Characteristics that Affect the Impact of Boundary-Spanning Leadership

Factors that Increase the Effectiveness of Boundary Spanning	*Factors that Decrease the Effectiveness of Boundary Spanning*	*Factors that Replace the Need for Boundary Spanning*
• environmental uncertainty versus predictability • task uncertainty and difficulty • centrality of leader's unit • leader's experience and familiarity with organizational operations • leader's extensive internal and external networks • team-based organization structure	• older followers with many years of service • followers with high rank	• numerous formal organizational procedures

LEADERSHIP IN ACTION:
BILL GATES—BOUNDARY SPANNER

Bill Gates is chairman and cofounder of Microsoft and the world's richest man. He has created the dominant computer software company by staying abreast of rapid technological developments in the computer industry and negotiating agreements with other companies that have potentially valuable products. Microsoft then modifies, repackages, and markets these products to the expanding market for computer software. Gates' boundary-spanning activities of obtaining information and negotiating agreements have allowed Microsoft to achieve its position in the software market.

Gates dropped out of Harvard in 1975 to found Microsoft. Its first product was an adapted version of the programming language BASIC for the first personal computer—the Altair 8800 (both were invented by other people). In 1980, Gates made a deal with IBM to build operating systems for their personal computers. Microsoft bought Q-DOS from another company and revised it for IBM's PCs. Microsoft created its famous Windows operating system based on a window-mouse system pioneered years earlier by Xerox Corporation. Most of Microsoft's products were made possible through agreements that Gates negotiated with other companies.

In the early 1990s, e-mail and the Internet were becoming popular, and the worldwide Web emerged in 1994. Gates negotiated a licensing agreement with another company to provide a Web browser called Internet Explorer. In the late 1990s, the U.S. Justice Department brought suit against Microsoft for exerting monopoly power in the computer software industry. Gates became active in representing and defending his company against these charges. Most observers believe that whatever the outcome, he will still be the number one man in the computer software industry.

Gates has used boundary-spanning behaviors in gathering and disseminating information to Microsoft employees (he is an avid e-mail user), negotiating with other companies for new products and markets, and in buffering Microsoft from charges of monopoly power. In the fast-changing and uncertain computer software industry, Gates' boundary-spanning skills have produced incredible success for Microsoft.

Source: D. Galernter, "Bill Gates—Software strongman," *Time,* December 7, 1998, 201–205.

◆ TEAM LEADERSHIP—A KEY SITUATIONAL FACTOR

Organizations today face tremendous competitive pressures from international firms for marketing their products and services. They also face competition for raw materials as growing populations worldwide make more demands on our planet's limited natural resources. They face demands from investors, consumer groups, and government regulators to be more efficient and profitable, more socially responsible, and more proactive on environmental and employee issues. In response to these pressures, leaders in these organizations are making major changes in the way work processes are organized and new technology is implemented. Many organizations are implementing team-based structures in which groups of operating personnel are involved in tasks previously done by management. In these situations, boundary spanning is becoming a large part of the leader's role for team leadership.

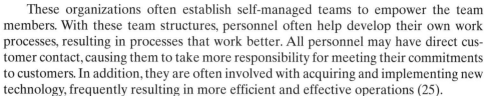

These organizations often establish self-managed teams to empower the team members. With these team structures, personnel often help develop their own work processes, resulting in processes that work better. All personnel may have direct customer contact, causing them to take more responsibility for meeting their commitments to customers. In addition, they are often involved with acquiring and implementing new technology, frequently resulting in more efficient and effective operations (25).

Team-based structures require leaders to obtain and distribute up-to-date information, providing employees with increased knowledge about organizational and technical processes and increased quality of information for decision making. This information is essential for team members to effectively use their increased authority and responsibility to implement their ideas. With team structures, employees also rely more on their coworkers for guidance and support than on their formal superior. These changes require a shift in leadership strategy from that used in traditional organizations.

The leadership of work teams, often called team leadership, is a popular topic in organizations because of the widespread use of team structures. Some surveys indicate that up to 40 percent of the U.S. workforce will function in teams in the near future (26). Although some organizations have shown significant improvements with a team structure, other team approaches have failed. One major reason for this failure is poor team leadership (27). This section focuses on teams and the behaviors needed to lead them effectively.

WHAT ARE WORK TEAMS?

A work team is a group of individuals (often from a single work unit) who have a common purpose that helps them develop mutually helpful relationships for accomplishing tasks and goals. The existence of the team implies that members work together in a coordinated and cooperative effort to achieve their common purpose. Teams that are popular in organizations today include cross-functional teams, product development teams, process improvement teams, and quality circles. Each type has similar properties, issues, and problems that the leader and team members must address. A popular structure in manufacturing and many other organizations is the self-managed team.

Self-managed teams are usually composed of six to ten workers who are responsible for some aspect of producing a product or delivering a service. They have the authority to plan, schedule, and assign work to members and to make and implement decisions related to production and personnel (28). Variations of self-managed teams are sometimes called self-directed, self-governing or self-led teams. These types are closely related and differ primarily in their authority to carry out tasks previously done by their manager. Since self-managed teams are so popular, most of the recent research on work teams has focused on them.

The activities and responsibilities of self-managed teams vary considerably, partly due to the experience and developmental level of the teams themselves. Early in its life, a team will begin to regulate its own members' task assignments, vacation and training schedules, and attendance; monitor team performance; and do some problem solving regarding quality or interpersonal issues. As a team matures and gains confidence, its members often contact suppliers and customers directly regarding the team's product or service. Team members become involved in their own planning, goal setting, hiring, equipment acquisition, and budgeting decisions. Very mature teams may make many of these decisions on their own and also manage their own overtime needs, conduct performance appraisals, or discipline members regarding performance problems (29).

Members of these teams are usually multiskilled, in fact the pay system normally encourages employees to master all the tasks carried out by their team. Members are also often assigned team roles in addition to their job tasks. These team roles are usually rotated and may include recognizer, innovator, monitor, communicator, task master, and internal leader. The team usually reports to a formally designated leader, often called a team coach or facilitator. The team coach or facilitator is in the formal position of a first-line supervisor, but the coach's functions under the self-managed team structure differ significantly from those of the traditional foreman (30).

EFFECTIVE LEADER BEHAVIORS FOR TEAM LEADERS

The most important leadership behaviors for a team leader/coach vary with the experience and level of development of a team. From the beginning, however, a self-managed team needs a leader who can effectively perform the boundary-spanning activities described earlier in this chapter. These teams are especially in need of the buffering, linking, communicating, resource acquisition, and mediating efforts of leaders if they are to maintain their autonomy and self-control and still deal effectively with their environment. One recent study of creative teams found boundary spanning to be the most important role of the team leader (31). Specifically, leaders of self-managed teams reduce uncertainty for the team by finding and sharing information on team performance, new technology, performance of competitors, pay levels, goals of the organization and other departments, and sources of raw materials. Negotiating implicit or explicit contracts and agreements with outsiders is also important. Team boundary spanning also involves advocacy for the team, such as making the team's case to managers who are skeptical, indifferent, or opposed to the self-management concept. Publicizing team successes, rebutting arguments or proposals that could harm the team, being vigilant for other forces that could unintentionally damage team independence or performance, and working to prevent mistakes from destroying the team are all part of the team leader's advocacy activities. Taking over functions from upper management, negotiating increased autonomy for the team, and opening doors for the team and its members are also important. The leader often encourages joint training and decision making with other teams when issues concern both teams.

One particularly challenging boundary-spanning role involves mediating conflicts within the team and with other teams. Experienced team leaders try to avoid giving advice or offering to solve a conflict themselves; rather, they concentrate on asking questions to help guide the teams to their own solutions. As team members become comfortable with their roles and participation, they begin to assert themselves, and conflict usually occurs within the team. The effective team leader usually acknowledges the frustration of members and asks questions such as "Have you talked with this individual about that?" or "Have you looked at it from his viewpoint?" The leader may help the team develop objective feedback for a problem member and rehearse with them what they will say when they discuss the issue with that member. When conflict occurs with other teams, the leader urges the team to acknowledge unproductive behavior by both teams and to define the issues as shared needs rather than opposing views. The team is urged to stay focused on problem solving and look for points of agreement. It is often wise not to stifle occasional outbursts of anger, but to follow up on them with a restatement of the issues.

Much research on team leadership emphasizes the importance of the leader's supportive behaviors to encourage team members and help them treat mistakes as learning opportunities. Active listening, which is empathetic and respectful without passing judgment, which validates and alleviates member concerns, and which mirrors back to the team what the leader hears, is an important skill for the supportive team leader. The supportive team leader also arranges for or conducts training in communication and interaction skills to help team members communicate more openly and honestly, to keep communication focused on work issues and behaviors rather than individuals, and to gauge team expectations and reactions (32). The supportive leader also provides mentoring by giving informal guidance and career counseling. The supportive team leader facilitates team development by identifying needed skills, providing training in these skills, and helping the team address problems as they work through the early stages of team development.

Good team leaders also provide subtle direction for new teams, while gradually increasing the amount of participation and consultation. Perhaps surprisingly, two researchers reported that the most advanced self-managing teams had supervisors who were highly directive in the early stages (33). These leaders clarified the meaning and boundaries of self-management for the team, delegated management tasks to the team, and provided benchmarks for the team to gauge its own progress. These leaders were also active in providing and helping their teams shape their visions or mission statements and goals, as well as strategies to achieve them. Newcomers to these teams often sought information and feedback from the team leader, who shaped their perceptions of the team (34).

Effective team leaders allow teams to make decisions and mistakes, as long as they are not devastating to the team. If the leader sees the team about to make a serious error, she will often ask key questions such as, "Why do you think that is right?" or "Have you viewed it from this perspective?" Asking questions of the team is an important skill that establishes the leader as a resource but encourages the team members to handle their own problems. A major goal of the team leader is to assure that every member knows the team's goals and how to perform to achieve them. The leader does, however, help the team handle production problems that are beyond their experience or expertise, such as managing raw materials with unusual properties. And the leader provides rewards and recognition to the team through positive feedback when the team performs well and through a policy of skill-based pay that encourages members to master all the tasks facing the work team.

CREATING TEAM-BASED REPLACEMENTS FOR LEADERSHIP

Throughout the process of developing a self-managed team, the leader works steadily to create team-based leadership that can replace many behaviors previously performed by the first-line supervisor. For example, the leader's negotiations with upper management, delegation of administrative tasks, and team development efforts are all designed to encourage the team to control its own behavior for high performance. Continuous training is conducted to increase the knowledge and skills of team members, which can alleviate much of the need for direction by the team leader. Delegation with coaching is designed to increase members' abilities, experience, and confidence so leader direction and support are less necessary. Team development, which increases cohesion and encourages positive performance norms, can help maintain the morale of the team and improve member attitudes and motivation with less need for leader supportiveness or charismatic behaviors. The philosophy of empowering the team to take over management activities encourages a strong need for independence within the team, which, in turn, increases members' desire to act without the leader's guidance.

Developing these leadership replacements also involves teaching and coaching the team and its members in several skills of self-leadership (35). First, self-observation involves gathering information on team behavior and performance, as well as on the factors that affect performance, and comparing this information with team goals. Second, self-goal setting involves setting shared team goals. Third, antecedent modification involves actively influencing the task environment by removing environmental stimuli that encourage undesirable behavior (such as removing pictures of vacation spots to stop daydreaming), and increasing exposure to stimuli that encourage desirable behavior (such as changing the team's work space to improve interactions among members). Fourth, self-reward and punishment means that team members learn to reinforce desirable performance by providing tangible and/or intangible rewards for members and the team in return for important behaviors. It also involves learning to accept punishment for behaviors that do not help the team (such as agreeing to work overtime for too much socializing). Fifth, rehearsal involves practicing a key performance activity. Sixth, strategic planning involves examining team standards of performance as well as goals and tactics and interactively creating a shared team vision of goals and strategies to accomplish them. And finally, learning to avoid groupthink tendencies means not assuming that the group is inherently more moral or less vulnerable than other groups, not pressuring dissenters to keep quiet, and avoiding retreat from difficult problems the group faces. Leader comments like "We can do this!" are often helpful in difficult situations to avoid this retreat mentality. The team leaders who can teach these skills help the team operate more independently and with flexibility and creativity.

EFFECTS OF TEAM LEADERSHIP

Increasing evidence indicates that when leaders carry out the behaviors described here, the results are favorable. Research and case studies credit well-led teams with increased productivity, improved quality of work, more positive attitudes, less member absenteeism, and a desire by members to stay in the team (36). Company reports also point to major cost savings, improved work quality and attitudes, some productivity improvements, and reduced need for supervisors (37).

The movement toward work teams appears to be a major trend in organizations. Increasingly, effective team leaders will be required to make these teams successful. Boundary-spanning activities as well as the other leader behaviors described in this section will be essential for team leaders.

Summary ■

Boundary spanning with the organization's environment appears to be particularly needed when a team or organization faces a rapidly changing, complex, resource poor, or threatening environment, or when the environment presents unique information or opportunities for the organization to exploit. Boundary spanning inside the organization and/or team is especially needed when conflict exists between teams or team members or the leader's unit and other units are highly specialized, interdependent, or use complex technology requiring extensive coordination and cooperation. Finally, when an organization is composed of work teams that operate with some independence from higher management, boundary spanning will be especially important. These situational factors are very common in today's organizations, making boundary spanning an important type of leader behavior. Leaders may be especially effective at boundary spanning when they are good communicators, assertive, knowledgeable, and experienced in organizational operations, and have many connections outside their group or department.

Figure 14–3 describes a process model of boundary-spanning leadership. It summarizes the major boundary-spanning leadership behaviors and how they affect follower reactions, which in turn affect followers' behaviors and outcomes. Boxes at each side of figure 14–3 show how situational factors influence the effectiveness of the leader's boundary spanning.

Figure 14–4 describes how leaders can use the process model of boundary-spanning leadership. Box 1 at the top of figure 14–4 describes diagnostic questions leaders can ask to determine if boundary-spanning leadership is needed. If the answer is "yes" to one or more of these questions, then the leader should carry out boundary-spanning behaviors like those described in box 2. The leader should then assess the situation to determine if it can be modified to make followers more independent of the leader's boundary-spanning activities (box 3). After taking feasible action to modify the followers' situation, the leader then returns to box 1 and rediagnoses the situation to determine if boundary spanning is still needed. The leader thus carries out the three key leadership tasks of (1) diagnosing situations, (2) providing boundary-spanning leadership, (3) modifying the situation, and so on in a continuous and dynamic process.

Key Terms and Concepts in this Chapter ▪

- antecedent modification
- active listening
- boundary-spanning behaviors
- communication skills
- conflict-management skills
- delegation

- environmental uncertainty
- groupthink
- leadership roles
- linking pin functions
- locus of control
- negotiation skills

- political skills
- rehearsal
- representative functions
- team development
- self-managed teams
- work teams

Review and Discussion Questions ▪

1. Describe boundary-spanning behaviors you have engaged in or observed. Which of these boundary-spanning behaviors were effective and which were ineffective? Why?

2. How can you improve your skills and abilities necessary for effective boundary spanning?

3. Describe situational factors you have observed or heard about that show a need for boundary-spanning behaviors?

FIGURE 14–3 Process Model of Boundary-Spanning Leadership

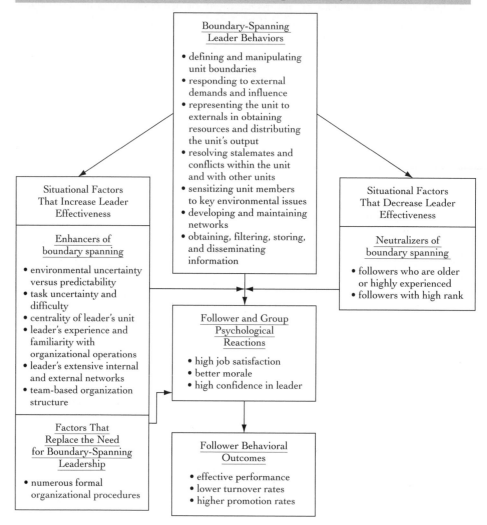

4. Describe a conflict situation you have observed in a group. What did the leader do to resolve the conflict? Could the conflict have been resolved more effectively? How?

5. Describe an organization where you think a leader's boundary spanning would be especially needed. Why is it needed?

6. How could effective boundary spanning improve effectiveness of a student group working on a class project?

7. Think of an effective team and an ineffective team you have belonged to. What were the differences in the effective team and the ineffective team? What could have been done to make the ineffective team effective?

FIGURE 14-4 Applying the Model of Boundary-Spanning Leadership

1. Diagnosing the Situation

- Is the leader's environment uncertain or can it be manipulated?
- Are followers' work tasks highly uncertain, difficult, or conflict prone?
- Is the leader's group central to the overall organization's success?
- Is leader responsible for one or more self-managed teams?
- Does the leader have important connections that can benefit the group?

If "yes" to one or more of these questions, then followers will probably respond favorably to boundary-spanning leadership.

3. Modifying Followers and Situations

Leaders act to:
- build procedures that allow followers to obtain resources and solve problems on their own
- place followers who are older, experienced, and high status into boundary-spanning positions
- create self-leadership capabilities in the leader's group through training and development

2. Providing Boundary-Spanning Leadership

Leaders demonstrate boundary-spanning by:
- manipulating and protecting group boundaries to resist jolts from the environment
- interacting with outsiders to obtain resources and develop agreements that help the group
- managing interactions among followers to resolve conflicts and overcome difficulties
- obtaining, filtering, storing, and disseminating valuable information for the group's benefit

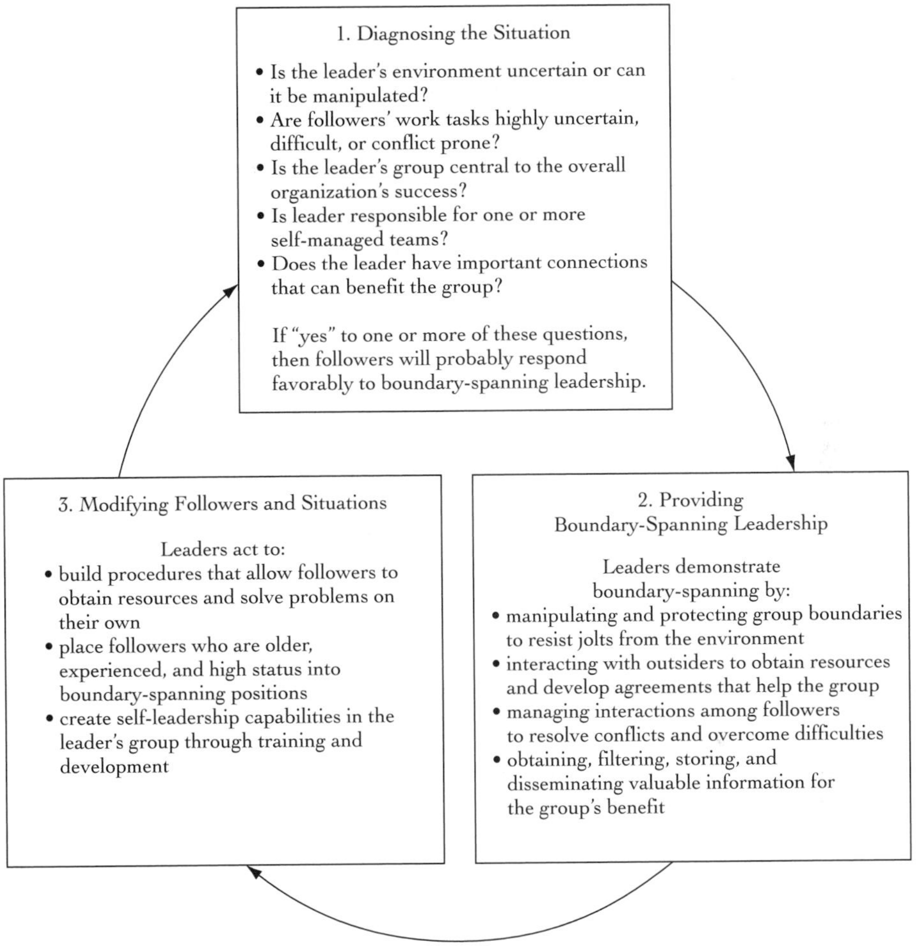

EXERCISE: Boundary-Spanning with the Boss ▪▪▪▪▪▪▪▪▪▪▪▪▪▪▪▪▪▪▪

Leonard Sayles described an effective boundary-spanning strategy middle managers can use to influence a boss. First, managers must accept the fact that their boss has a different perspective than they do. The boss may be viewing things with a longer term perspective, maintaining a "larger picture" than the manager's own department. Second, managers must realize that their job involves built-in role conflict. They will always be "in the middle" between upper management's concerns and followers' concerns. However, managers must not be a sieve, passing down everything that comes from above. Nor can they simply immerse themselves in the work group and pretend to be "just one of the gang." Third, managers must learn to be persuasive with their boss by developing strong presentation skills, assembling convincing information, designing tables and graphs, and articulating an appealing line of argument. Sayles adds that when attempting to persuade the boss to approve a big decision, the manager should present the problem in stages so no solution will be immediately apparent. This will keep the boss from forming a conclusion before you have presented your entire case. The example of a new superintendent of a manufacturing plant on the first page of this chapter demonstrates this approach. Once a boss has made a decision, it is next to impossible to get that decision reversed. Bringing the boss through each phase of the problem with the solution still unclear increases the chances of getting your solution accepted.

After reading the description of boundary spanning with the boss, meet with two or three students and develop responses to the following questions.

1. How could a leader develop the presentation skills mentioned by Sayles in this description of influencing a boss?
2. Why can't managers be "just one of the gang?"
3. Why does Sayles believe a supervisor should present a problem in stages to her boss, rather than proposing a final solution at the beginning? Do you agree with this approach? Why or why not?

Source: L. R. Sayles, *Leadership: Managing in Real Organizations* (2nd ed.) (New York: McGraw-Hill, 1989).

◆◆◆ **Case Incident**

Can the Conflict be Resolved?

You supervise the shipping department for a tool manufacturing company. There are seven packers who put tools in individual boxes and place them in cartons for shipment. Each packer works alone to box his or her share of the tools each day. Rebecca Garcia finishes her work in about half the time required by the other packers. Because she finishes faster, Rebecca takes longer breaks and has more time for lunch than the other packers. On breaks and after she has completed her work for the day, Rebecca usually works on assignments for college courses she is taking. Rebecca does not seem to have much in common with the other packers and spends little time talking with them. All the packers receive the same hourly pay and there is no extra pay for greater output.

The other packers frequently complain about Rebecca's longer breaks and her studying. You have encouraged Rebecca to work toward a degree and approved her studying during breaks as long as she does her share of the work. Even though the other packers agree that Rebecca gets her share of the work done, they have requested that you assign her more work. You know that if you don't take action, you will have continuing conflict between Rebecca and the other packers.

QUESTIONS

1. As supervisor, should you continue to allow Rebecca to take longer breaks and study on the job? If you do, how will you explain your action to the other packers?

2. How can you maintain productivity and resolve the conflict between Rebecca and the other packers? What boundary-spanning behaviors would be involved in your proposed solution?

Endnotes ▪▪▪

1. Sayles, L. R. (1989). *Leadership: Managing in Real Organizations* (2nd ed.). New York: McGraw-Hill.

2. Kidder, T. (1981). *The Soul of a New Machine.* New York: Little Brown.

3. Sayles, L. R. (1989). *Leadership: Managing in Real Organizations.*

4. Katz, R. and Tushman, M. L. (1983). A longitudinal study of boundary spanning supervision on turnover and promotion in research and development. *Academy of Management Journal,* 26(3), 437–456.

5. Kerr, S., Hill, K. and Broedling, L. (1986). The first-line supervisor: Phasing out or here to stay. *Academy of Management Review* 11(1), 103–117.

6. Selznick, P. (1957). *Leadership in Administration,* Evanston, IL: Row Peterson; Pelz, D. (1958). Influence: A key to effective leadership in the first line supervisor. *Personnel,* 29, 209–217; Hills, R. J. (1963). The representative function: Neglected dimension of leadership behavior. *Administrative Science Quarterly,* 8, 83–101.

7. Likert, R. (1961) *New Patterns of Management.* New York: McGraw-Hill.

8. Mintzberg, H. (1973). *The Nature of Managerial Work.* New York: Harper & Row.

9. Gilmore, T. N. (1982). Leadership and boundary management. *Journal of Applied Behavioral Science,* 18, 343–356.

10. Dorfman, P. W., Howell, J. P., Cotton, B. C. G. and Tate, U. (1992). Leadership within the "discontinuous hierarchy" structure of the military: Are effective leadership behaviors similar within and across command structures? In K. E. Clark, M. B. Clark and D. P. Campbell, *Impact of Leadership.* Center for Creative Leadership, Greensboro, North Carolina, 399–416.

11. Yukl, G. (1998). *Leadership in Organizations* (4th ed.). Upper Saddle River, NJ: Prentice Hall.

12. Steadman, H. J. (1992). Boundary spanners—a key component for the effective interactions of the justice and mental health systems. *Law and Human Behavior,* 16(1), 75–87.

13. Kerr, S., Hill, K. and Broedling, L. (1986). The first-line supervisor: Phasing out or here to stay.

14. Hills, R. J. (1963). The representative function: Neglected dimension of leadership behavior.

15. Katz, R. and Tushman, M. L. (1983). A longitudinal study of boundary spanning supervision on turnover and promotion in research and development.

16. Dorfman, P. W., Howell, J. P., Cotton, B. C. G. and Tate, U. (1992). Leadership within the "discontinuous hierarchy" structure of the military: Are effective leadership behaviors similar within and across command structures?; Hills, R. J. (1963). The representative function: Neglected dimension of leadership behavior.

17. Steadman, H. J. (1992). Boundary spanners—a key component for the effective interactions of the justice and mental health systems.

18. Louis, M. R. and Yan, A. (1996). The migration of organizational functions to the work unit level: Buffering, spanning and bringing up boundaries. Working paper, Boston University.

19. Schwab, R. C., Ungson, G. R. and Brown, W. B. (1985). Redefining the boundary spanning-environment relationship. *Journal of Management,* 11(1), 75–86.

20. Ito, J. K. and Peterson, R. B. (1986). Effects of task difficulty and interunit interdependence on information processing systems. *Academy of Management Journal,* 29(1), 139–149.

21. Friedman, R. A. and Podolny, J. (1992). Differentiation of boundary spanning roles: Labor negotiations and implications for role conflict. *Administrative Science Quarterly,* 37(1), 28–47.

22. Steadman, H. J. (1992). Boundary spanners—a key component for the effective interactions of the justice and mental health systems.

23. Dorfman, P. W., Howell, J. P., Cotton, B. C. G. and Tate, U. (1992). Leadership within the "discontinuous hierarchy" structure of the military: Are effective leadership behaviors

similar within and across command structures?

24. Dorfman, P. W., Howell, J. P., Cotton, B. C. G. and Tate, U. (1992). Leadership within the "discontinuous hierarchy" structure of the military: Are effective leadership behaviors similar within and across command structures?; Katz, R. and Tushman, M. L. (1983). A longitudinal study of boundary spanning supervision on turnover and promotion in research and development.

25. Deeprose, D. (1995). *The Team Coach.* AMACOM–American Management Association, New York.

26. Stewart, G. L. and Manz, C. C. (1995). Leadership of self-managed work teams: A typology and integrative model. *Human Relations,* 48(7), 747–770.

27. Ibid.

28. Deeprose, D. (1995). *The Team Coach.*

29. Ibid.

30. Manz, C. C. and Sims, H. P. (1987). Leading workers to lead themselves: The external leadership of self-managing teams. *Administrative Science Quarterly,* 32, 106–139.

31. Kolb, J. A. (1992). Leadership of creative teams. *The Journal of Creative Behavior,* 26(1), 1–9.

32. Versteeg, A. (1990). Self-directed work teams yield long-term benefits. *Journal of Business Strategy,* November–December, 9–12.

33. Walton, R. E. and Schlesinger, L. A. (1979). Do supervisors thrive in participative work systems? *Organizational Dynamics,* Winter, 25–38.

34. Major, D. A., Kozlowski, S. W. J., Chao, G. T. and Gardner, P. D. (1995). A longitudinal investigation of newcomer expectations, early socialization outcomes, and the moderating effects of role development factors. *Journal of Applied Psychology,* 80(3), 418–431.

35. Neck, C. P., Stewart, G. and Manz, C. C. (1996). Self-leaders within self-leading teams: Toward an optimal equilibrium. In *Advances in Interdisciplinary Studies of Work Teams,* JAI Press, 3, 43–65.

36. Cohen, S. G. and Baily, D. E. (1997). What makes teams work: Group effectiveness research from the shop floor to the executive suite. *Journal of Management,* 23, 239–290; Huselid, M. A. (1995). The impact of human resource management practices on turnover, productivity, and corporate financial performance. *Academy of Management Journal,* 38, 635–672; MacDuffie, J. P. (1995). Human resource bundles and manufacturing performance: Organizational logic and flexible production systems in the world auto industry. *Industry and Labor Relations Review,* 48, 197–221; Stewart, G. L. and Manz, C. C. (1995). Leadership of self-managed work teams: A typology and integrative model.

37. Smith, P. B., Peterson, M. F. and Misumi, J. (1994). Event management and work team effectiveness in Japan, Britain and USA. *Journal of Occupational and Organizational Psychology,* 67, 33–43.

Building Social Exchanges, Fairness, and Ethics

Learning Objectives
After reading this chapter you should be able to do the following:

1. Describe the nature and importance of social exchanges between leaders and followers.

2. Describe and provide examples of leader behaviors that build social exchanges with followers.

3. Explain why a leader's social exchange behaviors can have a positive influence on individual and group performance.

4. Describe how to develop and maintain effective exchanges between leaders and members.

5. Describe the skills, traits, and sources of power that help leaders build effective social exchanges with followers.

6. Give examples of the effects of leader social exchange behaviors.

7. Identify situational factors that increase, decrease, or replace the effects of leader exchange behaviors.

8. Describe and give examples of three types of leader fairness that are important to followers.

9. Identify behaviors leaders use to assure followers of their fairness and ethics.

10. Describe the impacts of perceived leader fairness and unfairness.

◆ EXAMPLES OF BUILDING SOCIAL EXCHANGES

• The new manager asked about and discussed each group member's job expectations, as well as each member's concerns and expectations of the manager. He also used "active listening" skills to decipher important issues. The manager also shared some of his own expectations about his new job, the members' jobs, and their working relationship.

• Noting which group members responded well to early task assignments, the leader carefully selected increasingly complex tasks for them, with longer time horizons, and eventually began to delegate administrative duties to these group members.

• With group members who continued to perform well and expressed positive attitudes toward their task assignments and the leader, the leader began to allow more freedom in the choice of approaches to tasks with statements like, "I'll support you in whatever you decide."

• The leader expressed understanding and some agreement with a follower's position on an important issue, before explaining her own position. Rather than stating outright her preferred strategy for dealing with the issue, she prefaced her strategy by saying, "I was just wondering if we might consider another approach . . . ."

The above incidents demonstrate effective leader behaviors that build social exchanges with followers. Leaders' social exchange behaviors are those that define followers' and leaders' roles and obligations in relation to one another as they work to achieve group and organizational goals.

Several types of exchange behaviors occur between leaders and followers. For example, chapter 10 described leaders' contingent reward and punishment behaviors as effective influence strategies when provided in exchange for specific follower actions such as effective performance or poor attendance. Recent studies have looked closely at how leaders solicit their followers' assistance in achieving goals and how various exchanges affect followers. Certain patterns are discernible in these exchanges, and effective leaders must be aware of these patterns, how they develop, and how they affect individual and group performance.

Early in a leader-follower relationship, an informal process occurs called role making (1). Roles are standard or repeated patterns of behavior that are expected or required of a person in a specific functional relationship. Roles in organizations are only partially specified by job descriptions and are usually more completely defined by the interactions of leaders and followers. Leaders play certain roles vis-à-vis their followers or groups, and followers play specific roles vis-à-vis their leader.

Leaders usually have a vested interest in the role performance of followers, and they therefore exert pressure on followers in the form of role expectations. For example, they expect followers to be punctual, to come to work regularly, and to give careful attention to leader requests. A leader's expectations of a given follower may be based on the follower's test scores, recommendations, interviews, or initial interactions. Over time, these role expectations help the follower define an appropriate role in the leader's group. Followers also have expectations of their leaders. Examples may be fairness in distributing rewards and punishments, creativity in problem solving, and provision of task guidance when needed. The responses of a specific leader and follower to early role expectations often define the type of exchange that will develop between them (2).

New leaders frequently find themselves short on time or energy to adequately attend to all aspects of their job. They therefore look for dependable individuals in the group for help. Leaders usually perceive some followers as more experienced and ready for added responsibility and duties than others. The leader then invests more time and energy to develop this subset of group members and maintains this disproportionate attention to preserve their contributions. This subgroup is sometimes called the leader's ingroup, and their roles involve much more than merely complying with leader requests and completing prescribed duties. They are expected to become committed to the unit's activities and goals, to be more dependable, to give more time and energy, to become more involved in administrative activities, and to be more responsive to the leader's wishes than other group members. In return, the leader offers ingroup members wider latitude in their roles; increased attention, information, and support; added influence on the unit's operation; and increased responsibility for the unit's performance (3). These added inputs and latitude help the leader obtain the extra commitment and assistance needed to run the unit effectively. These exchanges between a leader and ingroup members are sometimes called "high-quality" exchanges because they are based on a high degree of trust, reciprocity, and implicit obligations (4).

A leader's time limitations and unique personal characteristics lead to a range of exchanges—many that are less intense than ingroup exchanges. Some followers inevitably evolve a more distant relationship with their leader. These individuals are sometimes called outgroup members, and their exchange with the leader is referred to as "low quality"—reflecting lower levels of trust, interaction, support, rewards, decision influence, and little or no involvement in administrative activities. With outgroup exchanges, the job description defines the leader-follower exchange, with little need for any other social exchange.

Leaders generally devote more time and attention to developing ingroup members, and as a result, they may receive extra effort, loyalty, and support from these followers. Outgroup members receive less of the leader's time, and they usually bring less effort and commitment to their roles as group members. Once these exchanges are established, they seldom change. Given the time leaders invest in ingroup members, they usually do not wish to replace them. Ingroup and outgroup exchanges are both theoretically fair and equitable to leaders and followers. Both parties to an ingroup exchange provide a high degree of input, and both parties to an outgroup exchange provide lower inputs. In practice, however, outgroup members often report wanting more information, attention, support, and latitude from their leader. In some situations, a middle group may emerge that falls between the ingroup and outgroup in terms of effort and commitment provided and attention and support received from the leader.

Understanding social exchanges between leaders and followers is important because they affect followers' attitudes and behaviors as well as the leader's ability to carry out her responsibilities. High-quality (ingroup) exchanges allow followers to feel competent and valued by their leader. This helps satisfy their esteem and growth needs and they experience more career success (more promotions). Low-quality (outgroup) exchanges often frustrate followers, resulting in poorer attitudes and less career success in the organization. Research shows that when leaders are trained in how to develop more high-quality exchanges, the improvement in attitudes and behaviors of outgroup members are most pronounced because leaders finally acknowledge and address their previously unsatisfied needs for esteem and growth.

◆ DEVELOPING THE LEADER-FOLLOWER EXCHANGE

Leaders and followers bring their unique blends of personal characteristics to their early interactions. These include similarities or differences in race, gender, age, education, experience, aspirations, work ethic, and so on. As these personal characteristics are revealed during initial interactions, they likely affect how close a leader and member feel toward one another. Early task assignments given by the leader reflect these initial impressions. If a follower's effort, diligence, performance, and feelings expressed are consistent with the leader's positive impressions of the follower, then a basis for an in-group exchange is established (5).

The leader then begins to engage in accommodating behaviors, which are meant to further define the follower's role in relation to the leader, by showing the leader's willingness to consider and/or adapt to the follower's ideas and concerns. The leader eventually uses aligning behaviors, which bring the leader and follower closer together by minimizing power differences between them. These accommodating and aligning behaviors are also used to maintain the leader-follower exchange as the leader and in-group members face problems as a team of colleagues rather than as a hierarchically organized group. The following leader behaviors are used in this process of building and maintaining the leader-follower exchange:

1. Delegating tasks to certain followers and monitoring their performance, effort, diligence, and feelings expressed toward the task and the leader
2. Negotiating a follower's expanded role by first politely acknowledging the follower's other duties and responsibilities, responding to that follower's concerns, and sometimes using humor to soften an additional role expectation
3. Being polite when expressing an objection or disagreement with a follower. This often takes the form of offering understanding and some agreement with the follower's position to establish a common ground before objecting, in order to avoid polarizing differences and negatively impacting the exchange
4. Framing choices for followers by describing a decision situation and often revealing the alternative the leader prefers, but letting the follower make the decision
5. Demonstrating that the leader's values and goals converge with those of the followers. This is often done through spiraling agreement patterns. For example, the leader states an opinion or describes an idea and waits to see if the follower agrees or extends the idea by building on the leader's opinion. As this convergence evolves, either party may complete the statement the other was about to make
6. Establishing a common ground with a follower through the use of "insider markers," such as informal address forms, jargon/slang, insider joking, friendly teasing, laughter, and informal discussion
7. Showing high supportiveness of followers by "standing behind" them when they take risks or try innovative approaches to complex problems. The leader is also very careful to keep promises and commitments
8. Sharing pressures, problems, and responsibilities with select followers who recognize their complexity and are able and willing to help the leader make sense of complex problems and find viable solutions (6)

In general, leaders build and sustain high-quality exchange relationships through aligning and accommodating moves that emphasize similarities between leader and follower, mutual supportiveness, membership in the ingroup, and relations that are more collegial than hierarchical. Figure 15–1 summarizes important social exchange behaviors used by leaders. The Leadership in Action box on the new department head demonstrates the use of several social exchange behaviors.

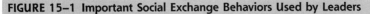

FIGURE 15–1 Important Social Exchange Behaviors Used by Leaders

LEADERSHIP IN ACTION:
THE NEW DEPARTMENT HEAD

The new department head of a university department had no management experience when he assumed the position. Thus, he carefully selected two highly experienced individuals in the department to advise and keep him informed. Both had been colleagues of the new leader for many years, and they all had high levels of trust and respect for each other. These two individuals formed the new leader's ingroup during his first two years in the position.

The new department head used accommodating behaviors such as insider joking, laughter, and friendly teasing as well as acknowledgment of the significant responsibilities and contributions of his two ingroup members. He expressed agreement with their positions on key issues and supported them when they took risks. He also used aligning behaviors such as politeness when disagreeing with them, spiraling agreement patterns, and choice framing to help assure that their values and goals would converge. These social exchange behaviors resulted in a high degree of commitment by the ingroup members to help the new leader succeed. They devoted considerable extra time to discussing strategic issues with him and reacting to his ideas prior to their implementation. They also let him know when other department members were unhappy with key decisions or practices, but were unwilling to confront the leader. The department head's social exchange behaviors created an ingroup that provided him with valuable help as he "learned the ropes" of his new position.

◆ EXAMPLES OF INEFFECTIVE SOCIAL EXCHANGE BEHAVIORS

Some leader behavior patterns cut off possible high-quality exchanges between leaders and followers. These behaviors are not effective in developing followers' capabilities and willingness to take on added responsibilities. The following are examples of these ineffective social exchange behaviors:

- In dealing with followers, the leader constantly referred to formal role prescriptions as specified in the employment contract. The leader repeatedly emphasized his formal authority and the obligations of each group member to be "bound by the contract."
- The leader's interaction with a follower was brief, with specific questions directed at the follower and little time or effort provided for exchanging ideas on issues. The questions were designed to gather information on the follower's performance on specific tasks.
- A leader showed little understanding of a follower's job problems and needs and blamed the problems on the follower's lack of effort. When the follower attempted to explain her perceptions of the problems, the leader ignored her and constantly interrupted.

Each of these examples shows a leader who has low expectations of a follower and has no apparent interest in hearing the follower's ideas. These leaders probably stifle the follower's motivation and future development.

◆ HOW TO BUILD SOCIAL EXCHANGES

Effective leaders can develop specific skills, traits, and sources of power that will help them build social exchanges with followers. As they are for many leader behaviors, communication skills are especially valuable in building social exchanges. Leaders who use verbal and nonverbal skills to acknowledge a follower's capabilities and job responsibilities, respond to followers' concerns, and use insider joking, good-natured teasing, and informal discussion can minimize the social distance between themselves and followers. Learning to build on a follower's ideas can create spiraling agreement patterns that build convergence in thoughts, values, and goals. Also, leaders who share their own pressures and responsibilities with followers encourage followers to do likewise. Finally, active listening by the leader helps to build and maintain an open dialogue with followers as they gain the necessary knowledge and confidence to interact with the leader to solve group problems.

Other skills that can help leaders build social exchanges with followers include empathy and social perceptiveness. When leaders show a genuine concern for followers' problems, feelings, and anxieties, followers often feel they have more in common with the leader. When leaders demonstrate understanding of followers' difficulties and support their efforts to solve problems creatively, they convince followers that the leader is on their side. When a leader learns to sense followers' problems as they develop and helps followers act to address these problems, the leader is viewed as a confidant and helper who the follower can trust. Flexibility by a leader in responding to followers' concerns and in allowing followers to try new approaches to problem solving can also build followers' trust in the leader. Leaders can develop each of these skills through training, practice, and coaching from other experienced leaders.

Three sources of power are also useful to leaders in building social exchanges with their followers. When leaders acquire referent and expert power, followers usually want to get to know them and to emulate their traits and behaviors. Followers are then easily influenced to take on extra tasks and responsibilities to help the leader. These leaders are also effective at "choice framing" for followers, conveying their preferred approach to a decision situation and being relatively sure that followers will implement a solution that is consistent with the leader's preferences. When followers emulate the leader's behavior and decision making, they feel "in sync" with the leader, creating the "we feeling" that characterizes ingroup/high-quality exchanges.

Effective leaders also use reward power to acknowledge extra effort, commitment, and loyalty by specific followers. When a leader praises a follower's continued efforts, shows fondness for a loyal follower, or spends extra time explaining a complex organizational issue to a committed follower, she makes that individual feel like a valued member of the group. This encourages further follower efforts to help the leader and to advance the group's goal achievement. These added efforts create more appreciative gestures by the leader, which gradually creates a higher-quality exchange with this follower.

As described in earlier chapters, leaders can develop referent and expert power through knowledge gained from continuous training and work experience and through publicizing past accomplishments and supporting statements made about the leader by higher-level leaders. Most leaders possess the power to administer intangible but significant rewards. Examples are appreciative comments and behaviors directed at followers or extra time spent with a follower who shows unusual capability and willingness to learn. When a leader selectively directs gestures of approval at individual followers, this can increase the value of this approval and build on the leader's reward power.

No research has directly addressed constraints on leaders' social exchange behaviors, but a few writers have pointed to some possible constraints. Strong union contracts may specify a violation if a leader treats some employees differently from others. Also, limitations on the leader's time and/or emotional resources may prevent her from engaging in high-quality exchange behaviors with all followers. Future research may verify if these or other organizational factors constrain leaders from developing high-quality exchanges with followers.

◆ EFFECTS OF LEADERS' SOCIAL EXCHANGE BEHAVIORS

Leaders' social exchange behaviors have a strong effect on the attitudes of followers. Group members who are the focus of leaders' high-quality exchange behaviors are highly satisfied with their leader, work, and organization. They also have favorable perceptions of their organization's climate, high commitment to the organization, fewer feelings of inequity, and perceive few social differences between themselves and the leader (7). They may have fewer thoughts about quitting and more influence on decision making with the leader, and they are more ingratiating by doing personal favors and complimenting the leader (8).

Leaders tend to reciprocate in high-quality exchanges by providing high performance ratings and faster promotions for ingroup members (9). Interestingly, ingroup members receive high performance ratings regardless of their actual performance (10). In other words, it is not clear if the actual performance of ingroup members exceeds that of other followers. However, once a leader has selected an ingroup, the leader seems to have a favorable image of these followers and to maintain this image through positive evaluations and recommendations for promotion. This tendency or bias may also be reflected in a study of nurses that showed leaders reporting more altruistic behavior by ingroup members (11). This positive image, or "halo," is also shown in the tendency of leaders to attribute good performance by ingroup members to hard work and high ability, whereas good performance by outgroup members may be attributed to luck.

It is often stated that ingroup members who are the focus of high-quality leader exchange behaviors have less turnover than other followers (12). However, summaries of studies show that the impacts of these leader behaviors on turnover are uncertain. Whereas some researchers find reduced turnover among ingroup members, others report no difference between ingroup members and other followers (13). There is also evidence that ingroup members do not necessarily spend more hours working than other followers, and they may not reduce the leader's administrative duties by taking on more of those duties themselves (14). It appears uncertain, then, whether followers who are involved in high-quality exchanges actually do more for the leader.

One group of researchers trained leaders in high-quality exchange behaviors. They found that both ingroup and outgroup members improved their performance and satisfaction under the trained leaders, but the largest improvements occurred for outgroup members (15). This may indicate that the high degree of leader trust, attention, and involvement contained in these behaviors is useful for all followers and that outgroup members may be highly responsive to the opportunities provided by these leader behaviors.

Overall, the leader behaviors designed to produce high-quality exchanges definitely improve follower attitudes, and they have the potential to improve follower performance. Leaders should, however, be careful not to be too selective about which followers are the focus of these behaviors. Followers who the leader initially views as outgroup members may have much to contribute if given the opportunity, attention, and support by their leader. Figure 15–2 summarizes the effects of a leader's social exchange behaviors.

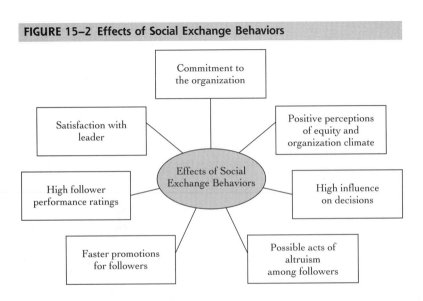

FIGURE 15–2 Effects of Social Exchange Behaviors

◆ SITUATIONAL FACTORS AFFECTING LEADERS' EXCHANGE BEHAVIORS

Although only a few studies have addressed situational factors and leader exchange be-haviors, their results point to some factors that may increase, decrease, or replace the effects of these leader behaviors. For example, when followers had highly routine or highly challenging work tasks, these factors increased the impact of high-quality leader exchange behaviors on followers' performance. For routine tasks, the added attention and high expectations by the leader probably motivated the followers. With challenging tasks, the leader's strong support and high expectations may have given followers con-fidence to meet the challenges. High-quality leader exchange behaviors were less ef-fective when followers' tasks were neither routine nor particularly challenging (these tasks possess variety but require little creativity, such as construction or retail sales jobs) (16). Also, followers who were achievement oriented and liked to be challenged re-sponded favorably to the developmental opportunities provided by greater job latitude, decision involvement, and delegation, which were part of the high-quality exchange be-havior by their leader (17). It seems possible, then, that these situational factors may en-hance the impacts of leaders' social exchange behaviors.

One situational factor, the redesign of followers' jobs, may replace leaders' ex-change behaviors in work organizations. Job redesign approaches are intended to cre-ate satisfaction, commitment, and motivation among nonmanagement employees. When these programs have been combined with goal setting, they have promoted both positive attitudes and high performance. By emphasizing increased worker autonomy and self-determination, these programs may operate in place of the intensive leader-follower interactions that characterize high-quality exchanges. These possible replace-ment effects should be tested in future research.

Researchers have identified two situational characteristics that may decrease the effects of leader exchange behaviors. These are (1) a lack of trust between a leader and followers and (2) peer group pressure to ostracize followers who do extra work. A lack of trust could interfere with the mutual confidence needed in a high-quality exchange, and peer pressure may inhibit an ingroup member from putting in the extra effort ex-pected by the leader (18). As yet, no empirical research has tested the possible neutral-izing effects of these situational factors.

◆ WHEN TO USE SOCIAL EXCHANGE BEHAVIORS

One reason that leaders develop high-quality exchanges with specific followers is to help fulfill the leader's responsibilities. When leaders have too many responsibilities and certain followers are underutilized (that is, they welcome more opportunities to achieve and challenge themselves on the job), then leaders' social exchange behaviors may create high-quality exchanges that benefit the leader and these followers. How-ever, there must be mutual trust between leaders and followers and an absence of nor-mative pressure (contractual or otherwise) that may prevent followers from accepting additional duties and responsibilities.

The reader should remember that social exchange behaviors by a leader may be most effective with followers who have previously had low-quality exchanges. The potential of these outgroup members is often underestimated, and leaders' social exchange behaviors may unleash this potential.

◆ LEADER FAIRNESS AND ETHICS

Leaders' fairness and ethics or moral character are important aspects of their leadership and are often critical to the social exchanges they develop with followers (19). Fairness is important to followers because they are concerned with resource allocation and reward distribution, job assignments, decision making, performance evaluation, and many other administrative matters. Fairness can become an ethical issue when one person is treated differently from another. One influential writer stated that leaders have a moral "duty of fair play" (20). This duty requires leaders to recognize the interests and aspirations of all parties as legitimate. This may limit leaders' ability to pursue their self-interests in a given social exchange.

High-quality exchanges between leaders and followers are usually based on assumptions of fairness and ethics by the leader and follower. These must be present in order to establish trust, which is needed for mutual cooperation. Perceived fairness, ethics, and trust go together. All three are needed to promote high-quality exchanges as well as ethical behavior by leaders and followers.

IMPORTANCE OF FAIRNESS AND ETHICS

Studies show that perceptions about a leader's fairness also shape people's judgments of her/his ethics (21). For one thing, unethical leaders often ignore unfair or questionable behavior in their organization as long as they benefit. However, this type of leadership behavior can backfire on an organization and draw government legal action, increased regulation, public criticism, customer dissatisfaction, and employee turnover or retaliation (22). Followers respond favorably to leaders who fulfill their promises and agreements, who show integrity by dealing with all individuals in a straightforward and ethical manner, and who listen with their eyes and ears to followers' concerns. When followers are treated this way, they often respond by going beyond their job requirements for the sake of their leader and group (23).

Organizations and their environments will continue to change rapidly during the twenty-first century. Organizational members will face much uncertainty about the future of their organizations and their roles in those organizations. Specifically, resources are shrinking in many organizations, organizations frequently acquire or merge with one another, and international competition as well as advancing technology threaten the future of many organizations and their members. Prior social exchanges between leaders and followers that people have relied on are uncertain, and people are increasingly concerned about their own welfare. In uncertain times, people usually look to their leader for assurances of fair and ethical treatment. Regardless of their philosophy or preferred pattern of behavior, effective leaders recognize that fair and ethical behavior is essential for successful leadership (24).

WHAT ARE LEADER FAIRNESS AND ETHICS?

Several writers have noted that a leader's fairness is in the mind of the beholder, and followers often form their perceptions of a leader's fairness quickly. A leader's truthfulness, kindness, consideration, values, ethics, and integrity are often mentioned as elements of a leader's fairness (25). Judgments of a leader's fairness and ethics are not arbitrary, but are based on moral principles that followers consider legitimate (26). What they consider legitimate depends on their culture, economic environment, history, and many other factors. Most experts indicate that moral judgments should be based on sound principles and an impartial consideration of the interests of all individuals (27). But generally speaking, when a leader breaks some mutual understanding or agreement, whether explicitly stated or implied, most followers consider this unfair and/or unethical (28).

Sometimes a group or organization establishes specific norms that govern leader decision making and behavior, and a leader must adhere to these norms to be considered fair and ethical. For example, in a large Japanese business organization the reward system was based primarily on the needs of each employee. A person's salary was primarily determined by factors such as the size of their family, whether they owned their own home, and how far they drove to work. The performance of the employee was only a minor factor. The employees in that organization considered this a fair and ethical reward system. The boxed example describes leaders' activities that can improve ethical conduct in organizations.

TYPES OF FAIRNESS

Recently, researchers have described three types of fairness as important to followers—distributive, procedural, and interactional. Distributive fairness refers to the outcomes (rewards) a follower receives in relation to his/her inputs (efforts or abilities). This is often called an equity comparison. Followers evaluate what they receive for their efforts and skills and compare it to what others like them are receiving. If the two outcomes are comparable, the leader is considered fair. Procedural fairness describes followers' assessment of the procedures used to make decisions that affect them, such as resource

---

LEADERSHIP IN PERSPECTIVE: LEADER ACTIONS TO IMPROVE ORGANIZATIONAL ETHICS

1. Increase the level of trust through fair leader-follower exchanges.
2. Develop and commit to a clearly stated code of ethics.
3. Provide education and training to support moral development.
4. Recruit, select, and promote people with high moral standards.
5. Measure and reward ethical performance.
6. Assure that leaders model ethical behaviors.
7. Identify heroes who exemplify ethical conduct.

Source: Adapted from Howell, J. M. and Avolio, B. J. (1992). The ethics of charismatic leadership: Submission or liberation. *Academy of Management Executive,* 6 (2), 43–54; and Petrick, J. A. and Manning, G. E. (1990). Developing an ethical climate for excellence, *Journal for Quality and Participation,* 13, 84–90.

allocations and reward distributions. If the procedures used are considered fair, then followers will likely accept a decision even if they are not happy with the amount of distribution. Interactional fairness refers to the quality of interpersonal treatment the follower receives from a leader. Is she honest, consistent, unbiased, informative, and careful in carrying out the organization's procedures? If so, then the leader is usually viewed as fair. All three types of fairness are important to followers, but interactional fairness may be the most important.

Interactional fairness flows from the leader's behavior with the follower and is thus under the direct control of the leader. These interactions leave a vivid impression on followers, because the leader essentially represents the organization to them. Followers assess these interactions as indicators of their standing in the organization, and this influences their self-worth. We believe leader-follower interactions exert the primary influences on followers' perceptions of a leader's fairness and ethics.

HOW DO LEADERS DEMONSTRATE FAIR AND ETHICAL BEHAVIOR?

Leaders influence the moral judgments of their followers and the ethical culture of their organization (29). Leaders also have the responsibility to lead their followers and organizations toward fair and ethical decision making and action. In this regard, supportive leadership is one of the most important behaviors leaders use to assure followers and others of their concern for fairness and ethics. Supportive leaders respect followers' views and rights as mature adults; they are honest and open with information about rewards, plans, and procedures; and they are courteous, kind, and concerned for the ethical development of followers. These supportive behaviors show leaders' respect for all individuals and their willingness to treat them fairly.

Two types of information provided by the leader are particularly helpful in assuring a fair and ethical social exchange. Providing information to followers about procedures for resource allocation, reward policies, or decision criteria shows followers that the leader has nothing to hide. Providing explanations for why policies exist or certain decisions are made provides the follower with a clearer image of the rationale behind them. These explanations are particularly effective if they address the reasoning and assumptions behind the decisions or policies, rather than blaming upper management or making excuses.

Leaders' contingent reward behavior is generally viewed as a sign of fairness in western countries. Leaders who use this behavior effectively try to assure equity among followers by basing reward allocations on follower performance. Such leaders are also consistent and unbiased in carrying out procedures and making judgments for all followers. Ethical leaders also promote and reward ethical behavior by their followers.

In some countries, it is considered morally right (fair) to distribute rewards equally among followers, regardless of their individual effort, ability, or performance. Other situational factors can also determine a leader's judgment of fairness. For example, leaders in the United States may use equality as a guideline for distributing resources or rewards when group solidarity, harmony, and follower cooperation are needed or when followers' performance is determined by factors outside their control (30).

Leaders' boundary-spanning behavior is particularly important with regard to fairness issues during times of major change in organizations and their environments. By actively and consistently representing followers' fairness concerns to higher-ups and influencing these individuals to ensure fair treatment of followers, leaders show their allegiance and concern for followers. Active boundary spanning on followers' behalf also fits most followers' normative expectations of an ethical leader.

Participative leadership is also important for fairness, as it includes encouraging followers to voice their views on issues and decisions that affect them. This allows followers to raise their concerns, and it shows the leader's respect for them. When followers are allowed to affect the outcomes of decisions, they often view their leader as very fair and ethical. When implementing decisions, directive leaders who observe followers on the job can assure followers that they base their allocation and reward decisions on accurate information. Directive leaders can also demonstrate competence at the followers' tasks, assuring followers that the leader can recognize good performance. And directive leaders can emphasize the importance of ethical considerations by insisting on ethics audits to review decisions and actions throughout the unit.

Finally, charismatic leadership often includes modeling ethical behaviors for followers, articulating a vision and mission with a moral component for the organization, and identifying ethical principles to guide followers' behavior (31). Each of these behaviors can be powerful tools for effective leaders and assure followers that ethics and fairness must be emphasized in their organization. Most leaders rely on several behavioral strategies to convey this message to followers.

ETHICAL PRINCIPLES AND SITUATIONS

Writers have suggested several theoretical principles to guide leaders in ethical behavior. First, a rigid set of rules that apply in all circumstances is often cited as the only meaningful ethical guideline. These rules usually identify important values of a society or culture, but exceptions can occur where thoughtful people might violate a rule and still be viewed as ethical. Second, politicians often advocate the greatest good for the greatest number as a guiding principle. However, in most developed countries today we believe that minorities have basic human rights and deserve equal treatment. Third, some argue that practical leaders must ignore past actions and rules and base choices of action only on the immediate situation. This procedure ignores individual and cultural values, may have undesirable long term consequences, and leaders using it can appear inconsistent and not trustworthy (32).

In most situations, ethical considerations often involve taking a long-term view of a problem (33). Although situational factors strongly influence leaders' actions and decisions, they should not completely dictate ethical or unethical behavior for every decision. Situational factors are important, but leaders must consistently model the values or ethical principles they want followers to use because this helps shape the ethical choices made by followers. Most applied approaches to ethical leadership recommend an assessment of situational and follower characteristics followed by application of the leader's code of ethical conduct.

Important situational factors for leaders to consider include characteristics of followers' tasks. Certain tasks involve significant risks to followers, such as coal mining or construction jobs on high-rise buildings. Individuals take these jobs knowing they are dangerous, and managers cannot eliminate all risks. The manager's ethical obligation is to assure that the best precautions are taken to protect the workers and to maintain an effective operation. Environmental factors are also important issues for leaders to

LEADERSHIP IN ACTION: THE FOUR-WAY TEST

Several public service organizations in the United States have emphasized the following code of ethical conduct for many years. It is short and simple, but has broad application to all types of organizations. Labor and contract negotiators have found the Four-Way Test especially useful as a set of overall guiding principles.

The Four-Way Test

1. Is it the truth?
2. Is it fair to all concerned?
3. Is it profitable or beneficial to all concerned?
4. Will it build friendship among all concerned?

The four points can be followed and used as an ethical test for any decision or action. Individuals may not be able to answer yes to each question in every situation, but they do provide a set of useful criteria that are easily remembered. The more an individual strives to use these guidelines, the more salient they become.

consider in choosing ethical actions. For example, legal requirements, possible pollution, and resource conservation are often viewed as moral issues and they affect leaders' decisions. Different expectations of individuals and groups may cause ethical dilemmas for leaders. Examples are employees, stockholders, labor unions, churches, and ethnic groups who expect leaders and organizations to fit their views of ethical behavior. These views differ from one another and the leader must consider them in making ethical decisions.

After evaluating these situational factors, ethical leaders apply their own principles or code of ethical conduct to decide a course of action. The Leadership in Action box describes a code of conduct used by many ethical leaders.

Leaders who seriously consider the situational factors relevant to an ethical decision problem and who try to apply a reasonable code of conduct to their behavior, will be respected by followers and others as a person of integrity. If they carefully consider the interests of followers and others when they choose their behavior, they will be trusted by followers to fulfill their needs and expectations whenever possible. A simple rule is that an action that does not promote trust may not be ethical.

EFFECTS OF LEADER FAIRNESS AND ETHICS

Research evidence and common sense both indicate that a leader who is seen as fair and ethical is likely to have followers who are satisfied and committed. These followers are also likely to have more trust in the leader, and to be more helpful and responsible for their own performance than followers who see their leader as unfair or unethical (34). Findings also indicate that fair and ethical leaders encourage followers to go beyond their normal job descriptions and engage in organizational citizenship behaviors. This behavior includes going out of their way to help coworkers, showing excellent attendance and low tardiness, and participating actively in departmental meetings (35). Such behavior clearly helps the organization and its members do their jobs. Thus, ethi-

LEADERSHIP IN ACTION: HIGHLY UNETHICAL LEADERS

John W. Gardner (36) identified five types of unethical leaders. The first type is cruel to followers. They emphasize coercive processes that include psychological intimidation, overt commands for obedience based on legitimate authority, and threats of physical force if followers do not comply (37). An example is Idi Amin, past ruler of Uganda, who tortured, mutilated, and killed over 100,000 of his subjects from 1971 to 1979. Leaders of the Ku Klux Klan and other extremist groups comprise the second type of unethical leader, who treat followers well but encourage them to do evil to others. The third type of unethical leader uses hate, fear, revenge, and paranoia to motivate followers. An example is the Ayatollah Khomeini of Iran, who used hatred and revenge to motivate his followers. The fourth type of unethical leader diminishes followers, creating dependency and obliterating adult judgment. In Guyana, Jim Jones isolated his followers from the outside world and broke up their families to set the stage for the mass suicide of 911 men, women, and children. Several writers have warned that charismatic leaders can be highly unethical, as Jim Jones and Adolf Hitler were. Because of their effectiveness in influencing followers, unethical charismatic leaders are particularly dangerous. The final type of unethical leader destroys processes that civilized people have created to preserve freedom, justice, and dignity. Mussolini's end of parliamentary government in Italy in the 1930s is an example of this type of unethical leadership.

cal and fair leaders simply make their organization a nicer place, and they probably make it more effective and efficient.

When leaders are seen as unfair or unethical, the effects are quite different. Followers often become jealous, feel vulnerable to the leader's capriciousness, form cohesive groups with strong norms to oppose the leader, and exclude those whom they view as unfairly favored by the leader (38). These leaders also prompt followers to satisfy their own needs by any means possible. Follower loyalty suffers, and unethical behavior becomes more likely (39).

The Leadership in Action box shows possible extreme effects on followers of unethical leaders. Followers may react with hatred, fear, paranoia, and diminished judgment. Under the most extreme conditions, followers may be willing to engage in torture, mutilation, destruction of organizations, and murder. Unethical leaders present a clear danger to all followers, groups, and organizations.

Summary

Figure 15–3 summarizes much of the information about leaders' social exchange behaviors, including fairness and ethics. These behaviors are shown at the top of figure 15–3, affecting follower reactions, which, in turn, influence follower outcomes and behaviors. Situational factors on the left of figure 15–3 may enhance or replace the effects of social exchange behaviors. Situational factors on the right may decrease the effectiveness of social exchange behaviors. The situational factors shown are tentative until further research is carried out on the effects of these organizational characteristics.

FIGURE 15–3 Tentative Process Model of Leaders' Social Exchange Behaviors

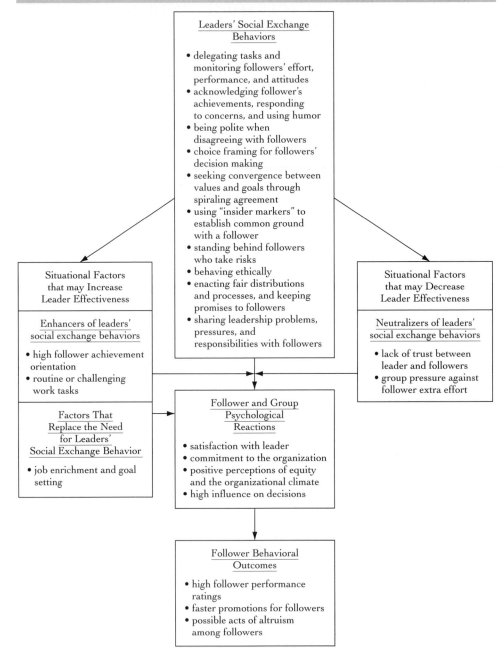

FIGURE 15–4 Applying the Tentative Process Model of Leaders' Social Exchange Behaviors

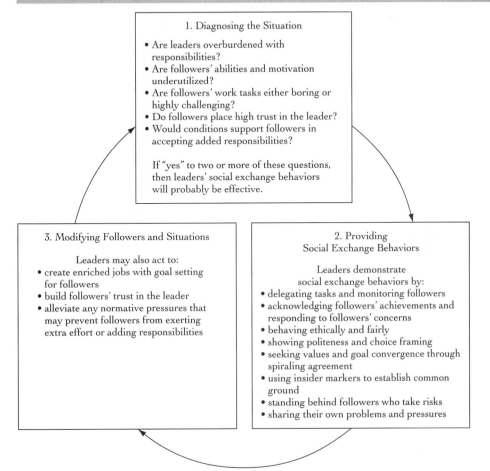

1. Diagnosing the Situation

- Are leaders overburdened with responsibilities?
- Are followers' abilities and motivation underutilized?
- Are followers' work tasks either boring or highly challenging?
- Do followers place high trust in the leader?
- Would conditions support followers in accepting added responsibilities?

If "yes" to two or more of these questions, then leaders' social exchange behaviors will probably be effective.

3. Modifying Followers and Situations

Leaders may also act to:
- create enriched jobs with goal setting for followers
- build followers' trust in the leader
- alleviate any normative pressures that may prevent followers from exerting extra effort or adding responsibilities

2. Providing Social Exchange Behaviors

Leaders demonstrate social exchange behaviors by:
- delegating tasks and monitoring followers
- acknowledging followers' achievements and responding to followers' concerns
- behaving ethically and fairly
- showing politeness and choice framing
- seeking values and goal convergence through spiraling agreement
- using insider markers to establish common ground
- standing behind followers who take risks
- sharing their own problems and pressures

Figure 15–4 describes how leaders can use the tentative process model of leaders' social exchange behaviors. Box 1 describes several questions that determine the need and appropriateness of leaders' social exchange behaviors. If the leader answers "yes" to two or more of these questions, then the leader should probably provide social exchange behaviors. Box 2 shows several social exchange behaviors that can be used to create high-quality exchanges with followers. Recall that followers whom the leader may have viewed as outgroup members may benefit from these behaviors as well or more than followers the leader viewed more favorably. Once the leader has enacted these social exchange behaviors, she assesses the followers' situation to determine if it can be modified to improve follower and group effectiveness. This situational modification can either make the exchanges more effective (create enhancers) or alleviate the need for social exchange behaviors by the leader (create replacements). In either case, any modifications carried out should help followers work more effectively on their own or in close cooperation with their leader. Once any modifications are implemented, the leader rediagnoses the situation, provides needed exchange behaviors, and so on in a dynamic process.

Key Terms and Concepts in This Chapter ▪ ▪ ▪ ▪ ▪ ▪ ▪ ▪ ▪ ▪ ▪ ▪ ▪ ▪ ▪ ▪ ▪ ▪ ▪

- accommodating behaviors
- achievement oriented
- aligning behaviors
- boundary spanning
- choice framing
- distributive fairness

- empathy
- equity comparison
- ethics
- fairness
- goal setting
- interactional fairness

- normative pressures
- procedural fairness
- social exchange behaviors
- social perceptiveness
- spiraling agreements

Review and Discussion Questions ▪

1. Describe a situation you have experienced or heard about where leader-member exchange behaviors were effective. Why did these leader-member exchange behaviors have a positive effect?

2. Describe a situation you have experienced or heard about in which leader-member exchange behaviors were ineffective or produced undesirable effects. Why were these leader-member exchange behaviors ineffective?

3. What can a leader do to develop the skills and abilities necessary to build effective social exchanges with followers?

4. When you are in a leadership position, what are specific leader behaviors you could use to show supportiveness of followers when they take risks or try innovative approaches to problem solving?

5. Describe how as a leader you would use reward power to create positive social exchanges that would result in extra effort and high commitment by followers.

6. What leader behaviors make you feel that you are being treated fairly or unfairly by the leader? Why do you feel some leader behaviors are fair and others unfair?

7. How do you define ethical and unethical leader behavior? Describe the criteria you use to make decisions about whether a leader's behavior is ethical or unethical?

EXERCISE: Assessing your Social Exchange ▪

Think of a leader you now have or have had in the past. You can use any type of leader such as an employer, supervisor, coach, military officer, committee chair, or manager. Use the scale below to describe your relationship with your leader.

1. Do you know where you stand with your leader? That is, do you usually know how satisfied your leader is with what you do?

1	2	3	4	5
Rarely	Occasionally	Sometimes	Fairly often	Very often

2. How well does your leader understand your job problems and needs?

1	2	3	4	5
Not at all	A little	A fair amount	Quite a bit	A great deal

3. How well does your leader recognize your potential?

1	2	3	4	5
Not at all	A little	Moderately	Mostly	Fully

4. What are the chances that your leader would use his/her power to help you solve problems in your work?

1	2	3	4	5
None	Small	Moderate	High	Very high

5. What are the chances that he/she would "bail you out" at his/her expense?

1	2	3	4	5
None	Small	Moderate	High	Very high

6. I have enough confidence in my leader that I would defend and justify his/her decision if he/she were not present to do so.

1	2	3	4	5
Strongly disagree	Disagree	Neutral	Agree	Strongly agree

7. How would you characterize your working relationship with your leader?

1	2	3	4	5
Extremely ineffective	Worse than average	Average	Better than average	Extremely effective

If you rated five of the items above with a 4 or 5, then you probably have a high-quality (ingroup) social exchange with this leader. Describe any behaviors the leader has demonstrated that led (or could have led) to a high-quality social exchange.

If you rated five of the items with a 1 or 2, then you probably have a low-quality (outgroup) social exchange with this leader. Describe any behaviors the leader has demonstrated that led (or could have led) to a low-quality social exchange.

Meet with three to five other members of your class. Share your responses with other members of your group. Compile a list of leader behaviors that led to high-quality social exchanges. Then compile a list of behaviors that led to low-quality social exchanges. Compare your lists with the leader behaviors described in this chapter.

Source: Adapted from Graen, G. B. and Uhl-Bien, M. (1995). Relationship-based approach to leadership: Development of leader-member exchange (LMX) theory of leadership over 25 years: Applying a multi-level multi-domain perspective. *Leadership Quarterly,* 6 (2), 219–247.

◆◆◆ **Case Incident**

The Improvement Suggestion

Brian James is the team leader of a production team that manufactures furniture. Part of the manufacturing process includes gluing and nailing the components that make up the frame of furniture pieces.

Richard Marks, a member of the production team, learned from a friend of a new type of wood adhesive. Richard conducted tests with the new adhesive and determined it formed a stronger bond than the adhesive currently being used. Richard obtained cost data that indicated the new adhesive would be half the cost of the current adhesive. Richard's tests also indicated that the new adhesive alone would produce a stronger bond than the old process of both gluing and nailing.

Richard suggested the change in adhesives to Mr. James who then sold the idea to top management. Mr. James never told management it was Richard's suggestion. Mr. James received all the credit for the process improvement and was awarded a cash bonus for the suggestion.

QUESTIONS

1. How do you think Mr. James's actions will affect his future social exchanges with the team?
2. What fairness and ethics issues are raised by the leader's behavior in this situation?
3. If team members think Mr. James's behavior was unfair and unethical, what should he do to create positive reactions from the team?

- -

Endnotes -

1. Dienesch, R. M. and Liden, R. C. (1986). Leader-member exchange model of leadership: A critique and further development. *Academy of Management Review,* 11(3), 618–634; Wayne, S. J. and Greene, S. A. (1993). The effects of leader-member exchange on employee citizenship and impression management behavior. *Human Relations,* 46(12), 1431–1440.

2. Dansereau, F., Graen, G. and Haga, W. J. (1975). A vertical dyad linkage approach to leadership within formal organizations. *Organizational Behavior and Human Performance,* 13(1), 46–78.

3. Liden, R. C., Wayne, S. J. and Stilwell, D. (1993). A longitudinal study on the early development of leader-member exchanges. *Journal of Applied Psychology,* 78(4), 662–674.

4. Graen, G. B. and Scandura, T. A. (1986). Toward a psychology of dyadic organizing. In B. M. Staw and L. L. Cummings (Eds.), *Research in Organizational Behavior,* volume 9. Greenwich, CT: JAI Press.

5. Dienesch, R. M. and Liden, R. C. (1986). Leader-member exchange model of leadership: A critique and further development.

6. Fairhurst, G. T. (1993). The leader-member exchange patterns of women leaders in industry: A discourse analysis. *Communication Monographs,* 60(4), 321–351.

7. Wayne, S. J., Liden, R. C. and Sparrowe, R. T. (1994). Developing leader-member exchange: The influence of gender and ingratiation. *American Behavioral Scientist,* 37(5), 694–714; Wilhelm, C. C., Herd, A. M. and Steiner, D. D. (1993). An investigation of leader-member exchange effects. *Journal of Organizational Behavior,* 14(6), 531–544.

8. Scandura, T. A., Graen, G. B. and Novak, M. A. (1986). When managers decide not to decide autocratically: An investigation of leader-member exchange and decision influence. *Journal of Applied Psychology,* 71(4), 579–584; Dockery, T. M. and Steiner, D. D. (1990). The role of initial interaction in leader-member exchange. *Group and Organization Studies,* 15(4), 395–413; Wayne, S. J. and Ferris, G. R. (1990). Influence tactics, affect, and exchange quality in supervisor-subordinate interactions: A laboratory experiment and field study. *Journal of Applied Psychology,* 75, 487–499.

9. Graen, G. B. and Scandura, T. A. (1986). Toward a psychology of dyadic organizing.

10. Duarte, N. T., Goodson, J. R. and Klich, N. R. (1993). How do I like thee? Let me appraise the ways. *Journal of Organizational Behavior,* 14(3), 239–249; Rosse, J. G. and Kraut, A. T. (1983). Reconsidering the vertical dyad linkage model of leadership. *Journal of Applied Psychology,* 56(1), 63–71.

11. Wayne, S. J. and Greene, S. A. (1993). The effects of leader-member exchange on employee citizenship and impression management behavior.

12. Rosse, J. G. and Kraut, A. T. (1983). Reconsidering the vertical dyad linkage model of leadership.

13. Vecchio, R. P. (1985). Predicting employee turnover from leader-member exchange: A failure to replicate. *Academy of Management Journal,* 28(2), 478–485; Graen, G. B., Liden, R. C. and Hoel, W. (1982). Role of leadership in the employee withdrawal

process. *Journal of Applied Psychology,* 67: 868–872; Ferris, G. (1985). Role of leadership in the employee withdrawal process: A constructive replication. *Journal of Applied Psychology,* 70(4), 777–781.

14. Rosse, J. G. and Kraut, A. T. (1983). Reconsidering the vertical dyad linkage model of leadership.

15. Graen, G. B., Wakabayashi, M., Graen, M. R. and Graen, M. G. (1990). International generalizability of American hypotheses about Japanese management progress: A strong inference investigation. *Leadership Quarterly,* 1(1), 1–24.

16. Dunegan, K. J., Duchon, D. and Uhl-Bien, M. (1992). Examining the link between leader-member exchange and subordinate performance: The role of task analyzability and variety as moderators. *Journal of Management,* 18(1), 59–76.

17. Graen, G. B., Scandura, T. A. and Graen, M. R. (1986). A field experimental test of the moderating effects of growth need strength on productivity. *Journal of Applied Psychology,* 71(3), 484–491.

18. Ibid.

19. Jones, H. B. Jr. (1995). The ethical leader: An ascetic construct. *Journal of Business Ethics,* 14 (10), 867–874; Gini, A. (1997). Moral leadership: An overview. *Journal of Business Ethics,* 16, 323–330.

20. Rawls, J. (1958). Justice as fairness. *Philosophical Review,* 67, 164–194.

21. Singer, M. S. (1996). The role of moral intensity and fairness perception in judgments of ethicality: A comparison of managerial professionals and the general public. *Journal of Business Ethics,* 15, 469–474.

22. Groner, D. M. (1996). Ethical leadership: The missing ingredient. *National Underwriter,* 100(51), 41–43.

23. Deluga, R. J. (1995). The relation between trust in the supervisor and subordinate organizational citizenship behavior. *Military Psychology,* 7(1), 1–16.

24. Meindl, J. R. (1989). Managing to be fair: An exploration of values, motives, and leadership. *Administrative Science Quarterly,* 34, 252–276.

25. Bobocel, D. R. and Farrell, A. S. (1996). Sex based promotion decisions and interactional fairness: Investigating the influence of managerial accounts. *Journal of Applied Psychology,* 8(1), 22–35; Sashkin, M. and Williams, R. L. (1990). Does fairness make a difference? *Organizational Dynamics,* 19(2), 56–71.

26. Zajac, E. E. (1995). *Political Economy of Fairness,* Cambridge, MA: MIT Press; Rachels, J. (1993). *The elements of moral philosophy* (2nd ed.). New York: McGraw-Hill.

27. Rachels, J. (1993). *The elements of moral philosophy* (2nd ed.).

28. Zajac, E. E. (1995). *Political Economy of Fairness.*

29. Dukerich, J. M., Nichols, M. L., Elm, D. R. and Vollrath, D. A. (1990). Moral reasoning in groups: Leaders make a difference. *Human Relations,* 43, 473–493.

30. Meindl, J. R. (1989). Managing to be fair: An exploration of values, motives, and leadership; Wagstaff, G. F. (1994). Equity, equality and need: Three principles of justice or one? An analysis of "equity as desert." *Current psychology: Developmental, Learning, Personality, Social,* 13(2), 138–152.

31. Bobocel, D. R. and Farrell, A. S. (1996). Sex based promotion decisions and interactional fairness: Investigating the influence of managerial accounts; Enderle, G. (1987). Some perspectives of managerial ethical leadership. *Journal of Business Ethics,* 6, 657–663.

32. Costley, D. L., Santana-Melgoza, C. and Todd, R. (1994). *Human Relations in Organizations* (5th ed.). St. Paul, MN: West.

33. Ciulla, J. B. (Ed.) (1998). *Ethics: The Heart of Leadership.* Westport, CT: Praeger.

34. Hegtvedt, K. S., Thompson, E. A. and Cook, K. S. (1993). Power and equity: What counts in attributions for exchange outcomes? *Social Psychology Quarterly,* 56(2), 100–119; Sias, P. M. and Jablin, F. M. (1995). Differential superior-subordinate relations, perceptions of fairness, and coworker communication. *Human Communication Research,* 22(1), 5–33; Schappe, S. E. (1996). Bridging the gap between procedural knowledge and positive employee attitudes. *Group and Organizational Management,* 21(3), 337–364.

35. Deluga, R. J. (1995). The relation between trust in the supervisor and subordinate organizational citizenship behavior; Konovsky, M. A. and Pugh, S. D. (1994). Citizenship behavior and social exchange. *Academy of Management Journal,* 37 (3), 656–669; Niehoff, B. P. and Moorman, R. H. (1993). Justice as a mediator of the relationship between methods of monitoring and organizational citizenship behaviors. *Academy of Management Journal,* 36(3), 527–556.

36. Gardner, J. W. (1990). *On leadership.* New York: The Free Press.

37. Rost, J. C. (1991). *Leadership for the twenty-first century.* New York: Praeger.

38. Sias, P. M. and Jablin, F. M. (1995). Differential superior-subordinate relations, perceptions of fairness, and coworker communication.

39. Tyler, T. R. and Bies, R. J. (1990). Beyond formal procedures: The interpersonal context of procedural justice. In J. S. Carroll (Ed.) *Applied Social Psychology and Organizational Settings,* 77–98, Hillsdale, NJ: Lawrence Erlbaum Associates, Publishers.

CHAPTER 16

Followership

Learning Objectives
After reading this chapter you should be able to do the following:

1. Describe followership behaviors and provide specific examples of them.

2. Explain why effective followership behaviors can have positive influences on group and organizational performance.

3. Describe ineffective followership behaviors and the negative influences they can have on group and organizational performance.

4. Identify how group members can become more effective in followership behaviors by increasing their technical competence and developing social skills.

6. Identify helpful follower characteristics.

7. Identify organizational and task characteristics where followership behaviors would be highly needed and effective.

◆ EXAMPLES OF EFFECTIVE FOLLOWERSHIP

• A member of a new-product development team found out that no one was taking responsibility for coordinating engineering, marketing, and manufacturing. "She worked out an interdepartmental review schedule that identified the people who should be involved at each stage of development. Instead of burdening her boss with yet another problem, this woman took the initiative to present the issue along with a solution" (1).

• A welder in a large railroad car assembly plant liked being a welder but avoided being a boss. "Although he stood on the lowest rung of the hierarchy in the plant, everyone knew Joe, and everyone agreed that he was the most important person in the entire factory. . . . The reason for his fame was simple: Joe had apparently mastered every phase of the plant's operation, and he was now able to take anyone's place if the necessity arose. Moreover, he could fix any broken-down piece of machinery, ranging from huge mechanical cranes to tiny electronic monitors. . . . Joe not only could perform these tasks, but actually enjoyed it when he was called upon to do them" (2).

• Michael Eisner, CEO of Walt Disney Company, described one of his best followers. "[He] is a great devil's advocate. . . . He will ask the questions nobody ever thought of, and he will take the opposite side of everything. But he is a deal maker, not a deal breaker and that's very unique" (3).

- A leader described an effective follower as someone who was continuously mastering organizationally useful skills. Her personal standards for her own performance were generally higher than the organization required, and she continuously updated her skills in any way she could.

These incidents are examples of effective followership, which is an essential role in all leadership situations. The American Heritage Dictionary defines a follower as "one who subscribes to the teachings of another; an attendant, servant or subordinate; one who emulates . . . or agrees with another; one who accepts guidance or leadership of another"(4). As these examples demonstrate, the behavior of effective followers today is often more proactive than implied by these definitions.

A leader who embodies all the best traits and behaviors of classical and current theories of leadership probably does not exist. All leaders, successful or not, have weaknesses and gaps in their leadership styles. Effective followers fill in for these gaps and weaknesses. One researcher pointed out that followers contribute a lion's share of the effort that goes into achieving organizational goals (5).

Leadership cannot exist without followers. Leadership takes place within the context of a specific group of followers (6) and leadership and followership are interdependent (7). Leaders regularly adjust their own behavior to fit followers' characteristics and behaviors. Followers forgo rewards like money, status, and fame that go with leadership and instead find meaning in working with their leader and coworkers. In Japan, the follower role is a highly valued tradition. Bushido is a traditional Japanese term for a faithful follower of one's lord. Although the lord has been replaced by the modern corporation, this traditional follower role is still associated with high social standing in Japan.

However, effective followers today are not "yes men" or "sheep" who do whatever the leader desires. Numerous factors influence the roles of followers in organizations. Today, these factors include scarce resources, increased foreign competition, higher operating costs, increasing education of the work force, changing attitudes toward formal authority, increased technology in the workplace, and reductions in the number of middle-management positions in large organizations. All these developments are causing followers to take on more responsibilities than in the past. Proactive followers who take responsibility for organizational tasks and improvements, who demonstrate self-management individually and in groups, and who carry out activities previously performed by leaders are increasingly common in many organizations (8).

In today's organizations, followership is defined as an interactive role individuals play that complements the leadership role and is equivalent to it in importance for achieving group and organizational performance. The followership role includes the degree of enthusiasm, cooperation, effort, active participation, task competence, and critical thinking an individual exhibits in support of group or organizational objectives without the need for "star billing."

In formal organizations, most individuals (including leaders) spend much of their time as followers. No matter how many subordinates one has, she usually also has one or more bosses. Many military experts believe the first step in developing leadership potential is teaching individuals how to be good followers. Research shows that the same individuals who are nominated as most desired leaders are also nominated as most desired followers (9). The characteristics of good leaders are also characteristics of good followers, and one of the important skills of followers may be the ability to shift easily between leadership and followership roles (10).

The following are effective followership behaviors:

1. Demonstrating job knowledge and competence while working without close supervision and completing work tasks on time
2. Demonstrating independent critical thinking by developing one's own opinions and ideas that show inventiveness and creativity
3. Showing initiative in taking on responsibilities, participating actively, seeing tasks through to completion, and taking responsibility for one's own career development
4. Speaking up frequently to offer information, share viewpoints, or take issue with decisions or actions that may be unethical or ill-advised
5. Building collaborative and supportive relationships with coworkers and the leader that result in partnerships for achieving organizational goals
6. Exerting influence on the leader in a confident and unemotional manner to help the leader avoid costly mistakes. Effective influence tactics often include logical persuasion, mobilizing coalitions, and being persistent and assertive. Flattery and praise of the leader are used sparingly
7. Showing up consistently when needed and accurately representing the leader's interests and views
8. Competently spanning group or organizational boundaries when needed to acquire resources, export products, manipulate or interpret the environment, and provide key information for the organization
9. Setting work goals that are action oriented, challenging, measurable, and aligned with group and organizational goals
10. Demonstrating proper comportment for the organization. This may include manner of speech, dress, grammar, and etiquette
11. Demonstrating a concern for performance as well as a supportive and friendly atmosphere within the work group (11)

The followership role fulfills important personal needs for individuals. It provides for comradeship with valued others and thus helps satisfy one's social needs. It allows individuals to serve others and thus confirms a favorable self-concept and personal identity for many people. In addition, effective followers often identify with the leader and her mission. This identification with a respected leader and a worthwhile mission can enhance followers' self-concepts. By helping to reinforce one's self-concept, the followership role can also satisfy the needs for self-esteem and self-actualization. Finally, followership roles can provide for personal growth of individuals by helping them become more mature and effective performers or even future leaders, thus helping to satisfy human needs for competence and self-determination. Figure 16–1 summarizes the major followership behaviors.

◆ EXAMPLES OF INEFFECTIVE FOLLOWERSHIP

Some follower behaviors are very common but ineffective. Here are some examples:

- Hawkeye Pierce, in the TV series MASH, was a capable cynic who sarcastically criticized the leader's actions, often withheld his own efforts, and gradually sunk into disgruntled acquiescence (12).

FIGURE 16–1 Followership Behaviors

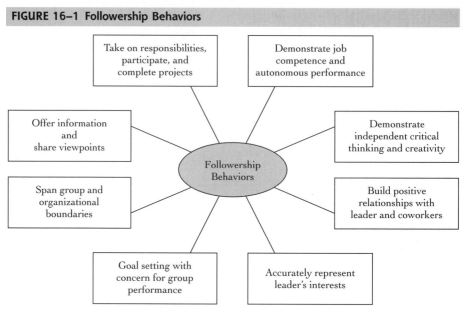

FOLLOWERSHIP IN ACTION: TAKING RESPONSIBILITY IN A DIFFICULT SITUATION

Pilots of passenger airlines are operational leader-managers and their decisions have major impacts on cost and safety of the passengers. A major pilot error can cost tens of millions of dollars as well as hundreds of lives. Pilots must have the ability to rapidly evaluate complex situations and arrive at effective decisions. A case occurred where the captain on an international flight arrived for the preflight check in a drunken condition. The ground staff carefully ignored his condition and said nothing. When the first officer arrived, however, things were different. Drawing the older captain aside, the first officer asked him in a firm tone, "Captain, will you turn yourself in, or will I have to turn you in?" The captain went immediately to the chief pilot's office and voluntarily grounded himself. Getting control of his drinking problem took the captain six months, but he returned to flying without any further problems with alcohol. The effective followership behavior of the first officer demonstrated concern for the organization and the captain. The first officer demonstrated both job competence and autonomy. He took responsibility even though the captain was his superior in rank. After the captain got control of his alcohol problem, positive relations developed between the two pilots that lasted for years and contributed to organizational effectiveness. In this situation the followership behavior of the first officer was clearly in the best interest of the airline, the customers, and the two individuals involved.

- Conformist followers are intellectually lazy because they "allow the leader to make the moral decisions for which they are responsible and . . . readily do what they are told" (13).
- Passive followers "act morally only under someone else's prodding" (14).
- Pragmatic followers "avert their eyes from wrongdoing rather than stop it or . . . are unwilling to disturb the status quo to do something worthwhile" (15).
- Apathetic, passive, or cynical followers exhibit a spectator-like noninvolvement that invites abuse by unethical leaders (16).
- Ineffective followers expect training and development to be served to them. These individuals attend seminars and training experiences only if their organization sends them. They require a parental leader to care and feed their development or they become obsolete.

These followers are ineffective because they are not actively participating with the leader in individual and group development and performance. In contrast, the Followership in Action box shows an effective follower.

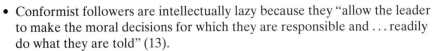

◆ IMPORTANCE OF FOLLOWERSHIP

Followers have historically been thought of as dependent individuals who need to be told what to do. Followership was therefore viewed as a passive role like clay awaiting the leader's creative force. Organizations have emphasized leadership initiatives with rewards for outstanding leadership performance. Organizational researchers, university faculties, and management trainers have produced leadership programs, books, articles, and seminars offering leadership prescriptions to help guide groups and organizations toward higher performance.

But in the 1990s, many organizational members came to resent leaders with ridiculously high salaries and bonuses, extreme status symbols, and golden parachutes. Followers now want a larger role in making organizational decisions, in carrying out those decisions, and in reaping the benefits. In the next decades we will see followership roles being emphasized in organizations. The popularity of work teams, productivity improvement groups, employee ownership programs, and gainsharing all point to a larger role for followers in organizations of the future.

Followership roles provide growth and development experiences for individuals to prepare them for greater responsibilities. As individuals develop, they typically contribute more to group or organizational performance. They also increase their self-confidence and become more willing to make moral judgments about possible unethical actions contemplated or taken by their leaders. By becoming proactive regarding ethical issues, they may prevent major mistakes that could cause serious damage to their organization. As noted earlier, followership roles can satisfy psychological needs for comradeship, service to others, identification with a valued cause, self-determination, and self-esteem. Followership roles help organizations address increased competition, high costs of operation, and organizational downsizing (by taking over some management functions) that characterize many major industries today (17). They also help their organizations by increasing their technical competence, as detailed in the box on how to increase your technical competence.

FOLLOWERSHIP IN PERSPECTIVE: HOW TO INCREASE YOUR TECHNICAL COMPETENCE

1. Assess how your job contributes to organizational success.
2. Evaluate your current technical skills by seeking feedback from superiors and peers and reviewing past appraisals.
3. Seek out and attend formal education and training programs.
4. Observe others who handle work problems effectively and follow their examples.
5. Visit other parts of the organization and volunteer for different positions or roles to gain experience.
6. Work on team projects and volunteer for projects that expand relevant skills.

Source: Adapted from Kelley, R. E. (1992). *The Power of Followership.* New York: Doubleday.

◆ HOW TO BE AN EFFECTIVE FOLLOWER

Although the research on followership is sparse, a few writers have suggested traits and skills that should help fulfill the followership role in formal organizations. When a follower develops a high degree of expertise or technical competence, often resulting from extensive education and/or relevant work experience, the follower is usually more capable of self-management and less reliant on a leader for direct guidance on the job. When followers develop good social skills, they can build cooperative relationships with leaders and coworkers. Cooperation builds cohesion and avoids cliques that subvert the group's objectives. Followers who are friendly and agreeable may also help the unit by building effective relationships with important outsiders (18). Followers who share attitudes and values with their leader and coworkers are also likely to build effective relationships (19).

Flexible followers can adapt to changing demands and environments without being paralyzed by the stressful ambiguity that accompanies rapid change. Leaders usually appreciate a sense of humor and they rate this quality highly in followers.

Followers provide an audience for leaders. As such, a requirement for effective followership is a readiness to accept the leader's influence without being "yes men." This involves listening and learning without feeling threatened or sensing any loss of status. This readiness may result from the followers' maturity, including a sense of confidence and self-esteem. With charismatic leadership, however, the readiness may reflect followers' feelings of helplessness due to a perception that the situation is more than they can handle on their own. For whatever reason, effective followers must address the leader with a willingness to engage in a dynamic interaction of followership vis-à-vis leadership.

When followers are intelligent, competent, and possess critical thinking skills, others will probably view them as having expert power. If a follower's expertise is complemented with sociability, flexibility, and ability to handle stress, the follower will likely possess referent power. Both these sources of power can make followers more effective and influential with the leader and coworkers.

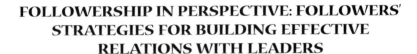

FOLLOWERSHIP IN PERSPECTIVE: FOLLOWERS' STRATEGIES FOR BUILDING EFFECTIVE RELATIONS WITH LEADERS

1. View your own and the leader's success as interdependent.
2. Try to understand the leader's personal and organizational objectives.
3. Recognize and complement the leader's weaknesses and limitations.
4. Keep the leader informed about activities, developments, and changes in the group.
5. Clarify your own role with the leader.
6. Adapt to the leader's style of leadership.
7. Show up prepared to perform.

Source: Adapted from Kelley, R. E. (1992). *The Power of Followership.* New York: Doubleday.

A leader's expectations and perceptions of the follower may influence the follower's willingness to engage in certain followership behaviors. For example, if a leader has high expectations for a follower, this can result in constructive follower behaviors, such as speaking up and exerting influence on the leader. By the same token, low expectations and perceptions can cause followers to be overly tentative, afraid to speak up, and unwilling to take unpopular (but needed) positions on important issues (20). A similar result may occur when a leader's beliefs, philosophy, or style are not compatible with those of followers. In this case, followers may not be willing to carry out the active followership behaviors needed to help the leader meet objectives. Certain leaders simply rub followers the wrong way. When this occurs, the follower should consider the followers' strategies for building effective relations with leaders, described in the box on followers' strategies for building effective relations with leaders. If the follower is unable or unwilling to attempt these strategies, then she had best seek another position with a leader who is more compatible.

◆ EFFECTS OF FOLLOWERSHIP

A limited number of research studies have been carried out on the effectiveness of followership behaviors and skills described here. These studies show that followership behaviors resulted in higher performance ratings by superiors (21). We believe that these followership behaviors will also result in increased motivation, satisfaction, feelings of empowerment, and group cohesion. Much more research is needed to verify whether objective performance and productivity measures or other follower reactions are related to these followership behaviors.

◆ SITUATIONAL FACTORS AND FOLLOWERSHIP

We believe that the active followership behaviors described in this chapter are valuable in virtually any leader-follower relationship. There are probably specific situations, however, in which the followership behaviors are especially needed and effective.

Enhancers of followership may be common in many organizations today. When the leader is frequently absent or distant from followers, the followership behaviors involving task competence, taking initiative, actively participating, and thinking independently may be especially critical for team performance. When followers' work tasks are highly complex or interdependent, then followers' task competence and activities that build cooperation with coworkers are probably especially important for group performance. When the followers' group faces frequent emergencies, high risk situations, or rapid change, then followership behaviors of speaking up, task competence, proactive initiative, and concern for performance are probably especially important.

Because it is an essential role in the leadership process, there can be no complete replacement for followership. However, there may be replacements for specific followership behaviors. This might occur when the leader is very active in external boundary spanning by gaining resources for the unit, building and maintaining networks with key outsiders, and facilitating important exchanges for the group. Here, the followers' external boundary-spanning behaviors may be unnecessary. When the leader is unusually adept at critical thinking, creativity, and inventiveness, this may at least partially alleviate the need for followers to demonstrate these characteristics. We have difficulty imagining, however, any replacements for followers' task competence, active participation, taking responsibility, building positive relations with coworkers, and several other followership behaviors.

One situational factor might possibly decrease (neutralize) the favorable effects of followership behaviors. A domineering, autocratic, and self-centered leader may want nothing but "yes men" as followers, who flatter the leader and do not think for themselves. This type of leader may not value competent followers who show initiative and speak their mind. In these situations, the competent follower should work on building better relations with the leader or seek another position.

Although there is no research data, we suspect that neutralizers and replacements of followership behaviors are quite rare. Future research is clearly needed to better understand how followership behaviors interact with situational characteristics. The fol-

---

FOLLOWERSHIP IN PERSPECTIVE: FOLLOWERS' STRATEGIES FOR BUILDING COOPERATIVE RELATIONSHIPS WITH COWORKERS

1. Lend a hand to help others with problems.
2. Acknowledge shared interests, values, goals, and expectations.
3. Establish informal communication links with others.
4. Show a willingness to listen.
5. Think the best of others.

Source: Adapted from Kelley, R. E. (1992). *The Power of Followership.* New York: Doubleday.

lowership in perspective box below offers suggestions for building cooperative relationships with coworkers. These strategies may help create a cohesive group of followers, which can be an effective replacement for other leader behaviors described in this book.

Summary ■

Followership is a necessary element in the leadership process. Most followership behaviors described in this chapter are needed to achieve group goals. However, certain followership behaviors may be especially important in specific situations. For example, when leaders are frequently distant from followers, when followers' tasks are complex or interdependent, or when followers face frequent high risks, emergency situations, or rapid change, the followership behaviors of speaking up, taking initiative, acting competently, building relationships with coworkers, and thinking independently can be especially important. Although research on these behaviors is sparse, we believe that nearly all leaders prefer this type of followership to having "yes men" or "sheep" who simply do as they are told. The changes occurring in organizations in the year 2000 and beyond will make these followership behaviors increasingly important. Because nearly all leaders in organizations report to higher-level leaders, these followership behaviors are useful for virtually all organizational members.

Figure 16–2 depicts a tentative process model of followership that summarizes much of the information in this chapter. Followership behaviors are shown at the top of figure 16–2 as affecting group and follower reactions, which in turn affect follower outcomes. Boxes at either side of figure 16–2 show how certain situational factors can increase or decrease the effectiveness of followership behaviors. Although the relationships shown in figure 16–2 are based on sparse research, we believe they will be strongly confirmed in the future.

Figure 16–3 shows how followers can apply the information contained in figure 16–2. The questions contained in box 1 at the top of figure 16–3 help identify situations where effective followership behaviors will be especially needed and effective. If the answer is "yes" to one or more of these questions, then the active followership behaviors shown in box 2 are needed, and followers should carry them out. The follower can then assess the situation to determine if modifications can be made to make the followership behaviors more effective (box 3). Enterprising followers can sometimes increase the distance from their leader, or identify rapidly changing environmental factors that will increase the leader's appreciation for their active followership. Once these situational factors are addressed, the follower then reevaluates the questions in box 1, provides the needed followership behaviors in box 2, and so on in a dynamic fashion.

Key Terms and Concepts in This Chapter ■

- boundary spanning
- comportment
- empowerment
- followership
- goal setting
- group cohesion
- leader expectations
- leader perceptions
- social skills
- technical competence

FIGURE 16–2 Tentative Process Model of Followership

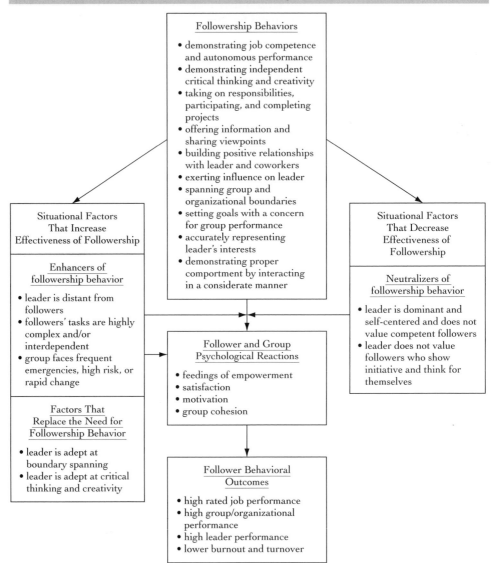

Followership Behaviors

- demonstrating job competence and autonomous performance
- demonstrating independent critical thinking and creativity
- taking on responsibilities, participating, and completing projects
- offering information and sharing viewpoints
- building positive relationships with leader and coworkers
- exerting influence on leader
- spanning group and organizational boundaries
- setting goals with a concern for group performance
- accurately representing leader's interests
- demonstrating proper comportment by interacting in a considerate manner

Situational Factors That Increase Effectiveness of Followership

Enhancers of followership behavior

- leader is distant from followers
- followers' tasks are highly complex and/or interdependent
- group faces frequent emergencies, high risk, or rapid change

Factors That Replace the Need for Followership Behavior

- leader is adept at boundary spanning
- leader is adept at critical thinking and creativity

Situational Factors That Decrease Effectiveness of Followership

Neutralizers of followership behavior

- leader is dominant and self-centered and does not value competent followers
- leader does not value followers who show initiative and think for themselves

Follower and Group Psychological Reactions

- feedings of empowerment
- satisfaction
- motivation
- group cohesion

Follower Behavioral Outcomes

- high rated job performance
- high group/organizational performance
- high leader performance
- lower burnout and turnover

Review and Discussion Questions ■

1. Describe a situation you have experienced or heard about where one or more of the followership behaviors positively contributed to group performance. Why was the followership effective in this situation?

FIGURE 16–3 Applying the Tentative Model of Followership

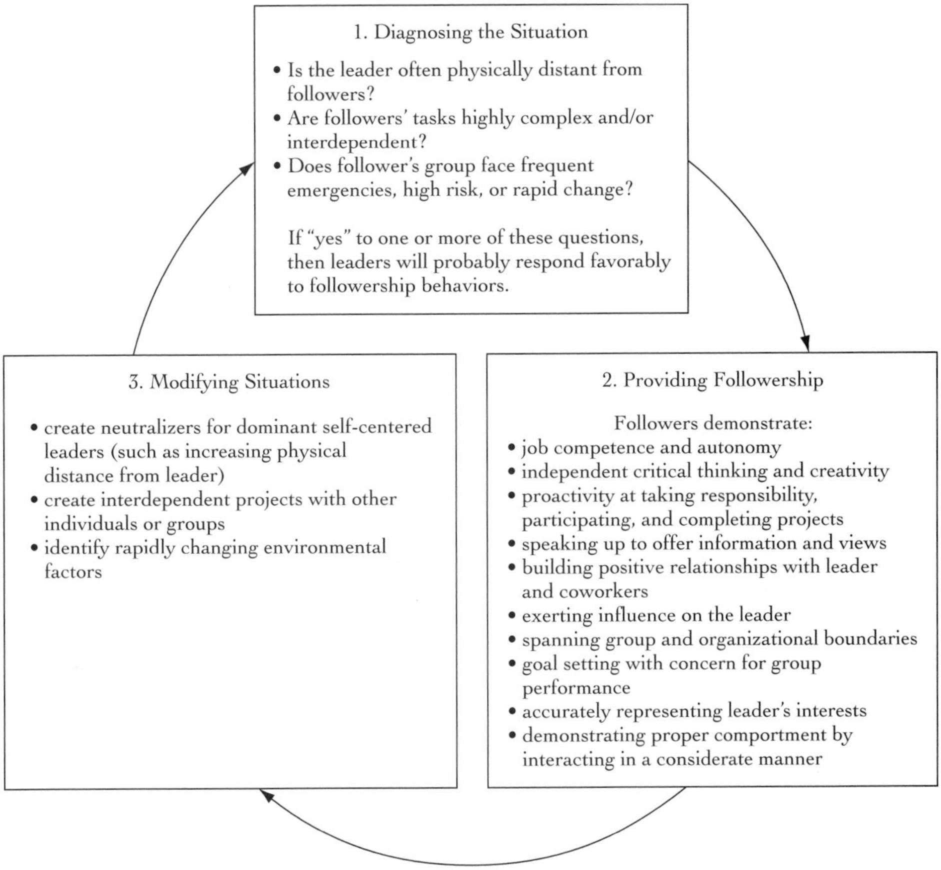

1. Diagnosing the Situation

- Is the leader often physically distant from followers?
- Are followers' tasks highly complex and/or interdependent?
- Does follower's group face frequent emergencies, high risk, or rapid change?

If "yes" to one or more of these questions, then leaders will probably respond favorably to followership behaviors.

3. Modifying Situations

- create neutralizers for dominant self-centered leaders (such as increasing physical distance from leader)
- create interdependent projects with other individuals or groups
- identify rapidly changing environmental factors

2. Providing Followership

Followers demonstrate:
- job competence and autonomy
- independent critical thinking and creativity
- proactivity at taking responsibility, participating, and completing projects
- speaking up to offer information and views
- building positive relationships with leader and coworkers
- exerting influence on the leader
- spanning group and organizational boundaries
- goal setting with concern for group performance
- accurately representing leader's interests
- demonstrating proper comportment by interacting in a considerate manner

2. Describe a situation you have experienced or heard about where certain followership behaviors decreased the effectiveness of a group. Why was followership not effective in this situation?

3. As a follower, which situational characteristics described in this chapter have had the most impact on your desire to engage in followership behaviors? How could a leader create these characteristics that encouraged you to engage in followership behaviors?

4. Think of your current job or a job you would like to have. What skills or abilities could you develop to become a more effective follower in this situation?

5. Do you think followership behaviors would contribute to improving patient care in a hospital? Explain why they would or would not?

6. How could followership behaviors improve customer service in a fast-food restaurant?

Followership Self-Assessment: Effective Followership Behaviors ▪ ▪ ▪ ▪ ▪

Instructions: Indicate the extent to which you engage in the following followership behaviors when you are a member of a group or team, using a scale of:
(5) almost always; (4) usually; (3) occasionally; (2) seldom; (1) almost never.

1. I work at improving my knowledge, skill, and ability in ways that will improve group performance.   1   2   3   4   5
2. I contribute to solving problems faced by the group with independent thinking and creativity.   1   2   3   4   5
3. I take responsibility and actively participate to help achieve group objectives.   1   2   3   4   5
4. I support group members and try to help them improve their contribution to the group.   1   2   3   4   5
5. I set personal goals that are action oriented, challenging, measurable, and supportive of group goals.   1   2   3   4   5
6. I behave in ways that are considered acceptable by the group and interact in a considerate manner.   1   2   3   4   5
7. I show up when the group needs me and accurately represent the leader's interests and views.   1   2   3   4   5
8. I try to obtain resources and information needed by the group from sources outside the group.   1   2   3   4   5
9. I try to influence the leader in a confident and unemotional manner to avoid costly mistakes.   1   2   3   4   5
10. I try to build positive working relationships with group members and the leader that are cooperative and supportive.   1   2   3   4   5

Tentative Interpretation: Total the numbers you circled for the 10 items. The following scores indicate the extent of your engagement in followership behaviors.

    40–50 highly engaged in followership behaviors
    30–39 moderately engaged in followership behaviors
    20–29 occasionally engaged in followership behaviors
      0–19 seldom engaged in followership behaviors

Source: Items adapted from material presented by Kelley, R.E. (1992). *The Power of Followership.* New York: Doubleday; and Hollander, E.P. (1992). The essential interdependence of leadership and followership. *Current Directions in Psychological Science,* 1(2), 71–75.

◆◆◆ **Case Incident**

How Can Ralph's Followership Be Improved?

You work as a programmer in the computer center of a service organization. As a member of a programming and systems design team, you work with six other professionals. With the exception of Ralph Hughes, the members of the team get along very well together. If Ralph was not on your team, you could be more productive and jobs would be more enjoyable.

Ralph repeatedly resists the ideas of other team members and thereby blocks progress at improving the system. He is very aggressive in finding fault with suggestions from others. In attacking one of your ideas he said, "Why do you keep coming up with these bright ideas to make more work? Why don't you try selling them to IBM?" On another occasion, Ralph responded to your idea with, "That's what I would expect from someone who knew nothing about this system." He often prevents team members from making suggestions by interrupting them with comments like, " I have something important to say."

As a result of Ralph's uncooperative behavior, discussions often turn into arguments with people shouting at him. You have never worked with anyone who is as hard to get along with as Ralph. You often leave work angry with Ralph and wish he would get fired.

QUESTIONS

1. How can you respond to Ralph to encourage him to develop positive followership behaviors?

2. What could the team members do to change Ralph's followership behaviors?

Endnotes

1. Kelley, R. E. (1988). In praise of followers. *Harvard Business Review,* November-December, 142–148.
2. Kelley, R. E. (1992). *The Power of Followership.* New York: Doubleday.
3. Ibid.
4. *The American Heritage Dictionary* (2nd college ed.) (1985). Boston, MA: Houghton-Mifflin.
5. Kelley, R. E. (1992). *The Power of Followership.*
6. Hughes, R. L., Ginnett, R. C. and Curphy, G. J. (1996). *Leadership: Enhancing the Lessons of Experience* (2nd ed.). Chicago: Irwin.
7. Heller, T. and Van Til, J. (1982). Leadership and followership: Some summary propositions. *Journal of Applied Behavioral Science,* 18(3), 405–414; Hollander, E. P. (1992). Leadership, followership, self, and others. *Leadership Quarterly,* 3(1) 43–54.
8. Lee, C. (1991). Followership: The essence of leadership. *Training,* 28(1), 27–35; Kelley, R. E. (1992). *The Power of Followership.*
9. Bass, B. (1990). *Bass and Stogdill's Handbook of leadership* (3rd ed.). New York: The Free Press.
10. Hollander, E. P. (1992). The essential interdependence of leadership and followership. *Current Directions in Psychological Science,* 1(2), 71–75; Hollander, E. P. (1993). Legitimacy, power, and influence: A perspective on relational features of leadership. In M. M. Chemers and R. Ayman (Eds.), *Leadership Theory and Research: Perspectives and Directions.* New York: Academic Press.
11. Gilbert, G. R. and Hyde, A. C. (1988). Followership and the federal worker. *Public Administration Review,* 48(5), 962–968; Kelley, R. E. (1992). *The Power of*

Followership; Gilbert, G. R. and Whiteside, C. W. (1988). Performance appraisal and followership: An analysis of the officer in the boss/subordinate team. *Journal of Police Science and Administration,* 16(1), 39–43; Hafsi, M. and Misumi, J. (1992). The leader-follower's mutual effect: Developing a performance-maintenance interactional model. *Psychologia: An International Journal of Psychology in the Orient,* 35(4), 201–212.

12. Kelley, R. E. (1992). *The Power of Followership.*

13. Ibid.

14. Ibid.

15. Ibid.

16. Gardner, J. (1990). *On Leadership.* New York: The Free Press.

17. Flower, J. (1991). The art and craft of followership: A conversation with Robert Kelley. *Healthcare Forum,* January/February, 56–60; Buhler, P. (1993). Managing in the 90s: The flipside of leadership—cultivating followers. *Supervision,* March, 17–19.

18. Kelley, R. E. (1992). *The Power of Followership;* Hughes, R. L., Ginnett, R. C. and Curphy, G. J. (1996). *Leadership: Enhancing the Lessons of Experience.*

19. Shamir, B., House, R. J. and Arthur, M. B. (1993). The motivational effects of charismatic leadership: A self-concept based theory. *Organizational Science,* 4, 1–17.

20. Lippitt, R. (1982). The changing leader-follower relationships of the 1980s. *Journal of Applied Behavioral Science,* 18(3), 395–403.

21. Gardner, J. (1990). *On Leadership;* Gilbert, G. R. and Hyde, A. C. (1988). Followership and the federal worker.

CHAPTER 17

Conclusions and Issues for 2000 and Beyond

Learning Objectives
After reading this chapter you should be able to do the following:

1. Summarize the general effects of leaders' behavior on followers' reactions and outcomes.

2. Identify leader behaviors that most consistently increase quantity or quality of performance by individuals and groups.

3. Describe the leadership styles that result from various combinations of leader behaviors.

4. Identify the combinations of leader characteristics and skills that complement the different leadership styles.

5. Identify follower and situational characteristics that impact the effectiveness of different leadership styles.

6. Describe two general strategies leaders can use to influence the attitudes and performance of individuals and groups.

7. Explain the concept of equifinality in leadership and how it can be applied to increase leadership effectiveness.

◆ GENERAL EFFECTS OF LEADER BEHAVIORS

All the leader behaviors described in this book have some effects on followers and their groups. Most of these effects are favorable, though as we have noted, many situational and follower characteristics influence the direction and strength of these effects. Table 17–1 summarizes the general effects of the leader behaviors on follower reactions and outcomes. Although the effects described in table 17–1 depend somewhat on situational and follower characteristics facing the leader, they are usually as specified in the table.

As shown in table 17–1, directive, supportive, and contingent reward leader behaviors have been most consistent at increasing the quantity or quality of performance by followers and groups. The other leader behaviors may improve the quantity or quality

317

TABLE 17–1 General Effects of Leader Behaviors on Followers (a)

Leader Behaviors	Quantity or Quality of Individual/Group Performance	Supervisor Ratings of Individual/Group Performance	Individual Role Clarity or Development	Individual Satisfaction, Commitment or Motivation	Group Cohesion	Individual Turnover, Burnout, or Intent to Quit
Directive(b)	Positive	Positive	Strongly Positive	Strongly Positive	Positive	Negative
Supportive(b)	Positive	Positive	Positive	Strongly Positive	Positive	Negative
Participative	Small Positive	Probably Positive	Probably Positive	Positive	Probably Positive	Probably Negative
Contingent Reward	Positive	Positive	Positive	Positive	Probably Positive	?
Contingent Punishment	Probably Positive(c)	?	?	?	?	?
Charismatic	Probably Positive	Strongly Positive	?	Strongly Positive(d)	?	Negative
Building Social Exchanges	?	Strongly Positive	Probably Positive	Strongly Positive	?	?
Boundary Spanning	Probably Positive	Positive	?	Probably Positive	?	Probably Negative
Followership	Probably Positive	Probably Positive	?	Probably Positive	Probably Positive	?

a - A positive effect means a leader's behavior results in an increase in followers' performance, attitudes, role clarity, or group cohesion. A strongly positive effect means the leader behavior results in a large improvement in these follower outcomes. Probably positive means that the results are not certain, but indications point to a positive effect. A negative effect means a leader's behavior resulted in a decrease in followers' burnout, turnover, or intent to quit. Question mark (?) means research results are either contradictory or there are too few studies to draw a conclusion.

b - Positive effects of directive and supportive leadership were often found when both leader behaviors were provided together by the leader.

c - When used in conjunction with contingent reward behavior.

d - Most followers react very positively to charismatic leadership, although some individuals can react very negatively.

of followers' performance, but the effects are either small or require further research for complete verification. Charismatic and social exchange behaviors by leaders strongly increased the performance ratings they received from their supervisors. Directive, supportive, contingent reward, and boundary-spanning behaviors also produced favorable ratings of leaders by their supervisor. Directive leadership produced the strongest improvements in followers' role clarity, although supportive and contingent reward leader behaviors also improved this follower reaction.

Supportive, directive, charismatic, and social exchange behaviors produced the strongest improvements in followers' attitudes, such as satisfaction and commitment to the organization, as well as motivation. Recall, however, that charismatic leader behavior can also produce strong negative reactions from followers. Participative and contingent reward leader behaviors also improved followers' attitudes, but not as strongly as the other leadership behaviors. Directive and supportive leader behaviors improved group cohesion, whereas directive, supportive, and charismatic leadership all decreased followers' turnover, burnout, and intentions to quit. Notice that contingent punishment behavior resulted in a "probably positive" effect on followers' performance only when used along with contingent reward behavior. There were no other reliable affects of contingent punishment on followers' reactions or outcomes.

◆ TYPICAL LEADERSHIP STYLES

The leader behaviors described in this book are usually used in combination with one another. These combinations often result in several typical leadership styles found in many organizations. Some of these styles are described in this section. In the real world, many leaders do not fit precisely into any of these types. Some leaders combine several of these styles. We believe, however, that readers with experience in real organizations will recognize some of these styles. The description of each is followed by a figure summarizing when the style could be effective and how the leader might enact the style and modify the situation as needed.

THE COACH

A leader with this style places maximum importance on developing followers' potential to perform well (1). Coaches are usually highly directive with followers, spending considerable time explaining expectations about quantity, quality, and rules and procedures; outlining useful methods to complete tasks; and clarifying task assignments. At the same time, they are supportive by showing concern and consideration for followers as individuals and expressing confidence in them as they develop. Coaches may slowly increase the amount of participation they use with followers as they develop. That is, as followers' knowledge and ability increase, coaches increase the amount they involve them in decision making and the scope of tasks delegated to them.

Coaches probably use contingent (intangible) reward behavior to reinforce followers' development and good performance, showing appreciation for their efforts through compliments and recognition. They most likely use very little contingent punishment behavior; rather, they allow followers' performance to speak for itself. Coaches may not reprimand followers solely for low performance, but they would do so for extreme cases of disruptive follower behavior.

Coaches spend considerable time with their followers, and they generally have good interpersonal and communication skills. Most coaches have a fairly high socialized need for power, which is a strong desire to build influence through others. In the process, they help the followers to become independent performers to support their goals. Many coaches also may have a high need for affiliation, which is a need to spend time interacting with others and a desire to feel valuable and accepted by them.

Coaching is often an effective leadership style for followers who are "learning the ropes" of the organization and are still developing their job skills. The directive and supportive aspects of this style may be less effective for followers who are highly trained and experienced at their job tasks or who have other sources of guidance and encouragement readily available, such as helpful and proficient coworkers or specialized training personnel. In these situations, the coach's participation and reward behaviors should be emphasized.

Tommy LaSorta was described earlier as past coach and manager of the Los Angeles Dodgers. LaSorta's coaching style of leadership combined directive leadership with much supportiveness for young players, followed by compliments and recognition as players became more proficient. He eventually used participation by consulting with veteran players on key decisions. He is well known for his success in developing young players. Figure 17–1 summarizes the coaching leadership style.

THE HUMAN RELATIONS SPECIALIST

Leaders with this style emphasize keeping followers happy and comfortable, apparently assuming they will respond with effective performance (2). These leaders are highly supportive by showing concern for followers' welfare, happiness, and comfort. They are often also highly participative, especially when followers have the desire to be involved in management decision making. They consult often with followers and delegate frequently. These leaders often use boundary spanning to represent their people to those outside, obtaining resources needed for their comfort. They are usually not directive with followers, spending little time defining management expectations. They seem to assume that followers know best what to do. If performance problems occur, they often appeal to followers to get together and figure out what to do. They may modify situations to make the followers' work more comfortable and pleasing to them.

Human relations specialists have good interpersonal skills in order to interact in a pleasant manner with followers. They likely have a high need for affiliation and nurturance, and they enjoy seeing followers happy and comfortable in the work situation. This type of leadership style is useful when followers are recovering from some traumatic event, such as a disaster or perhaps a merger or major downsizing that involved layoffs and/or a reorganization of work. It can be used effectively as a short-term strategy to restore equilibrium among followers so they can settle into their new routines. It is not usually an effective leadership style for achieving high levels of performance, unless the leader's followers are unusually competent, highly trained individuals who rely on one another for any needed job guidance.

The human relations specialist style was shown by an interim coach of a youth swimming team. This coach filled the position after the previous coach was asked to leave for mistreating the swimmers and driving kids away from the sport. The interim coach showed concern and supportiveness for the remaining swimmers and solicited in-

FIGURE 17–1 Applying the Coaching Leadership Style

1. Diagnosing the Situation

- Are followers "learning the ropes" of the organization?
- Are followers still developing their job skills?
- Are followers faced with high job stress or insecurity?
- Do followers have a high need for clarity and guidance in their work roles?
- Does the leader have good interpersonal and communication skills?

If "yes" to one or more of these questions, then followers will probably respond favorably to coaching leadership.

3. Modifying Followers and Situations

Leaders act to:
- alleviate stressors, insecurities, and conflicts facing followers
- modify followers' situations to increase intrinsic satisfaction and task feedback
- build procedures that allow followers to obtain resources and solve problems on their own
- encourage reliance on other followers with high levels of competence and experience

2. Providing a Coaching Leadership Style

Leaders demonstrate coaching behaviors by:
- explaining what is expected in terms of goals for quantity, quality, and timeliness of performance
- outlining useful methods to complete tasks
- increasing the amount of participation as followers' development progresses
- showing concern and consideration for followers as individuals and expressing confidence in followers' potential
- showing appreciation for followers' efforts through compliments and recognition

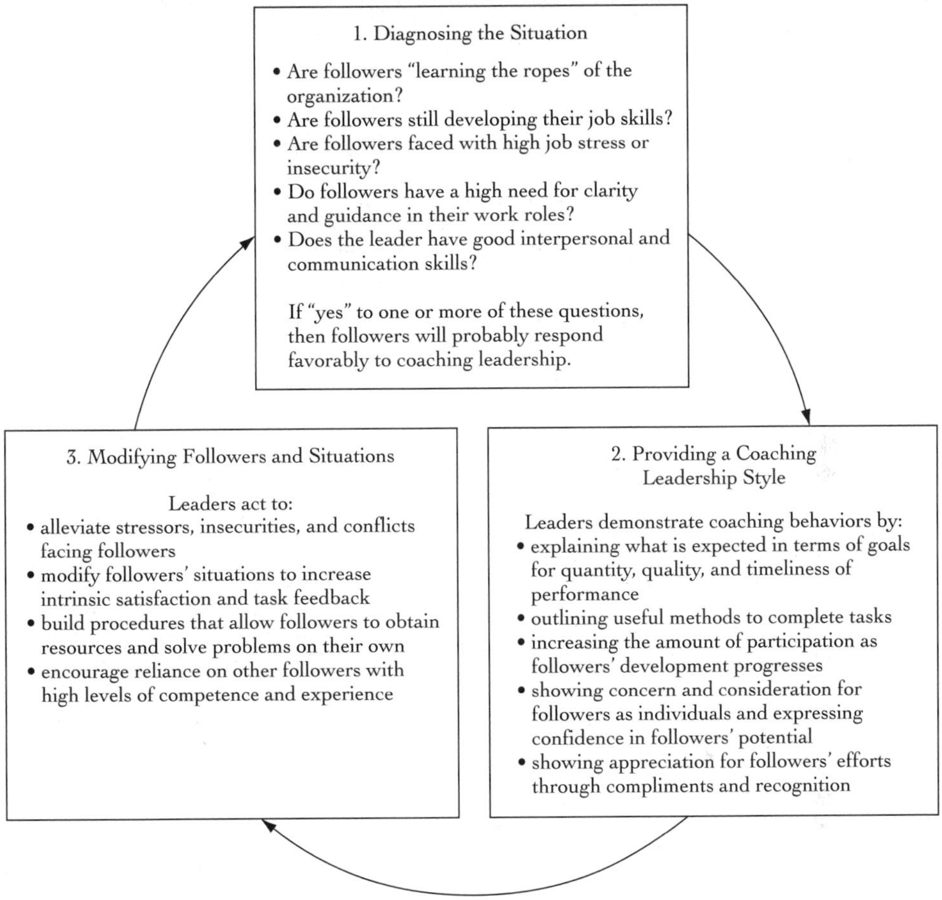

put from their parents on how to rebuild team morale. She did not direct any major changes in team procedures or swimming techniques and did not differentiate rewards among team members. Instead, she treated all members equally with the same caring attitude. She was effective at providing stability and kept the team together until the new coach was hired. Figure 17–2 summarizes the human relations specialist style of leadership.

THE CONTROLLING AUTOCRAT

Individuals using this leadership style are often obsessed with controlling the actions of those around them (3). They are highly directive with followers, giving detailed instructions regarding work methods, output expected, quality standards, rules, and regulations. They use contingent and noncontingent punishment extensively. Followers often see these leaders as arbitrary and unfair. They usually do not use much participative, supportive, rewarding, or boundary spanning leader behaviors in dealing with followers.

FIGURE 17–2 Applying the Human Relations Leadership Style

1. Diagnosing the Situation

- Is the organization undergoing a major change such as a merger or downsizing?
- Has there been some environmental or economic event that has damaged the organization's or follower's group?

If "yes" to one or both of these questions, then followers will probably respond favorably to human relations leadership.

3. Modifying Followers and Situations

Leaders act to:
- alleviate uncertainty and ambiguity for followers
- affirm the importance of followers' roles to the organization
- create policies and procedures to guide followers through organizational changes
- assure followers have the physical and human resources to do their job

2. Providing a Human Relations Leadership Style

Leaders demonstrate human relations behaviors by:
- showing concern for followers' welfare and comfort
- keeping followers informed about important issues
- listening actively to followers' ideas and concerns
- including followers in decision making and problem solving
- interacting frequently with outsiders to obtain needed information and other resources

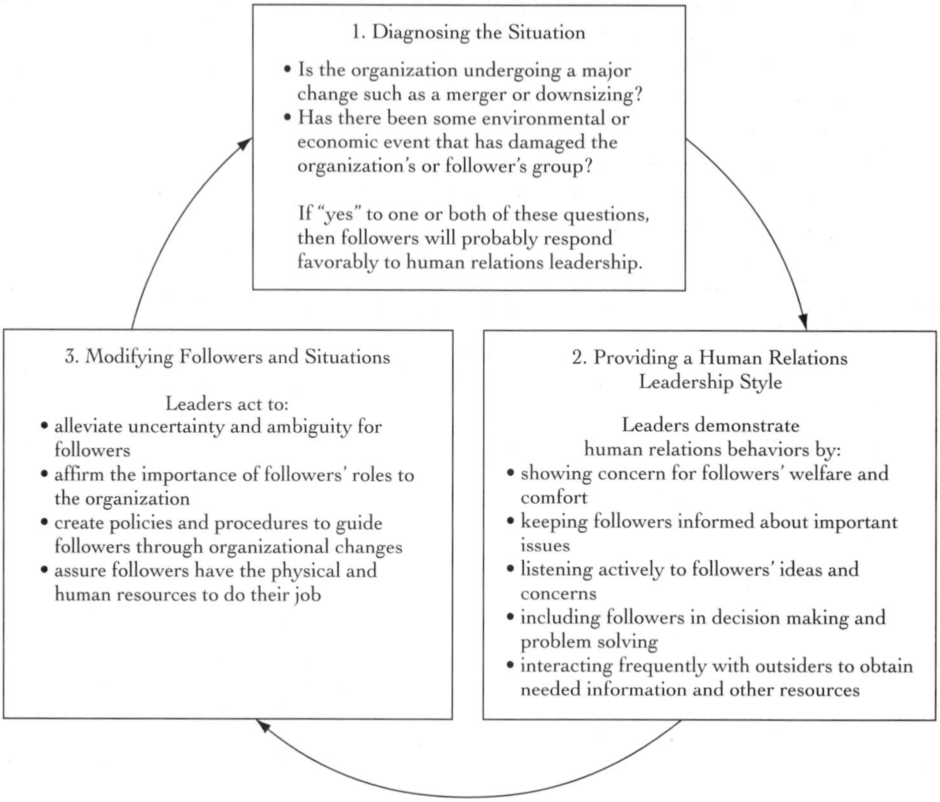

Controlling autocrats have a high personal need for power, meaning they constantly desire to control their environment and other people around them. They often have poor interpersonal skills and dominate followers with authoritarian demands. They are frequently dogmatic in their beliefs and do not value new input or criticism from others. This leadership style may achieve results under emergency conditions, when time is short and the stakes are high. In most organizational situations, however, this style produces so much resentment among followers that they do not willingly cooperate with the leader and usually seek other positions as soon as possible.

A supervisor who worked for a government contractor on a construction project used the controlling autocratic style to enforce government specifications and meet a short project deadline. When the project was later extended to include another phase with no specific deadline, the supervisor continued using the same controlling autocratic style. Followers who cooperated to meet the earlier deadline saw no reason for this close direction and control during the new phase. They began to resent the supervisor when he gave them no freedom to determine how they did their work and he threatened to lower their pay or fire them if they did not follow his detailed directions. Their dissatisfaction was shown by increased absenteeism and turnover among the workers. Figure 17–3 summarizes the controlling autocratic style of leadership.

FIGURE 17–3 Applying the Controlling Autocratic Leadership Style

1. Diagnosing the Situation

- Are followers facing s situation that is an immediate threat to their welfare?
- Are followers facing an emergency requiring quick action?
- Do followers' clients or customers require immediate action to save them from great loss or damage?

If "yes" to one or more of these questions, then followers will probably respond favorably to the controlling autocrat in this situation.

3. Modifying Followers and Situations

Leaders act to:
- better define procedures to deal with threatening situations
- provide training to prepare followers for emergencies
- improve the group's ability to predict threats or emergencies before they occur

2. Providing a Controlling Autocratic Leadership Style

Leaders demonstrate autocratic behaviors by:
- giving detailed no-nonsense instructions regarding work methods
- clearly stating quantity and quality standards for performance
- clarifying rules and regulations for the group
- explaining to followers the consequences of nonperformance
- punishing followers who do not follow instructions, rules, or regulations

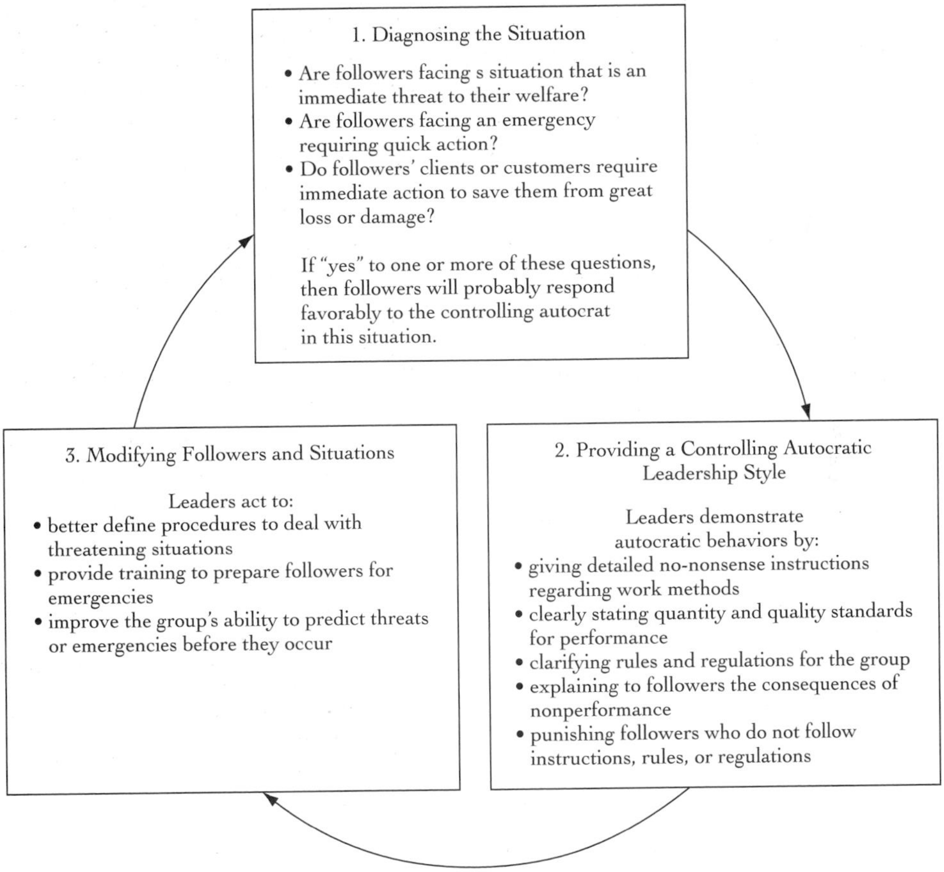

THE TRANSFORMATIONAL VISIONARY

This style is currently very popular in the management literature and is thought to create extreme devotion and extraordinary effort among followers (4). This type of leader uses charismatic behaviors extensively, giving inspirational speeches using metaphorical language, often describing current conditions as immoral and intolerable, and outlining a future vision that is radically different from the status quo. These leaders are also highly supportive of followers, showing concern and consideration for them as individuals. They may try to develop followers' leadership skills through mentoring relationships in which they demonstrate and encourage followers to try new and challenging tasks. They use boundary-spanning behaviors to represent followers and groups effectively to outsiders and to gain acceptance, resources, and cooperation needed to carry out the mission. Perhaps surprisingly, these leaders are often not participative with followers. That is, they do not necessarily consult with followers or solicit their input for decision making. They are usually very self-confident and although they may occasionally consult with a few key advisors, they consciously project an image of assuredness and certainty in the mission and strategy they outline for followers.

Transformational visionaries have excellent communication skills that they use to convey their mission and vision in a convincing manner. They also have a high socialized need for power, desiring to build their influence and move the group or organization toward their vision. They use impression management skills to create a positive image, which further enhances their confidence and the confidence of followers in their leadership. Transformational visionary leaders may also be highly intelligent and creative in defining a vision and mission for followers, in cleverly relating that mission to strong follower desires and needs, and in communicating that mission through emotional speech patterns and their own behavior.

This leadership style is highly effective when followers are frustrated, stressed, or unhappy with their current situation. This may occur because of an intolerable political or organizational administration, a dangerous emergency, rapid change, or prolonged discrimination, economic hardship, or other personal factors that have weakened followers. It is not clear whether transformational visionary leaders are effective when followers are not experiencing stress and frustration.

Lawrence A. Bossidy used the transformational leadership style to stop the decline of Allied Signal in the early 1990s. When Bossidy took over as CEO, Allied was overextended with too many operations, too much debt, and was rapidly losing cash. He first focused on selling certain divisions, cutting staff, and combining operations. He then developed a company vision and mission for the future, with goals that people found attractive. He visited workers at all levels to describe the mission and encouraged and supported their efforts to contribute toward the goals. He focused on teamwork to pull employees together to save the company and to help it prosper. Today, Allied is a successful defense and auto parts conglomerate, its stock has soared, and employees take pride in the fact that they saved the company (5). Figure 17–4 summarizes the transformational visionary leadership style.

THE TRANSACTIONAL EXCHANGE STYLE

This leadership style is based on exchanges between the leader and followers (6). The leader provides guidance, attention, and benefits to particular followers based on their inputs to the group. Directive leader behavior is one major element of this style. Leaders tell followers their expectations and clarify the procedures and work methods needed to complete tasks. They also make extensive use of contingent reward behavior, providing compliments and recognition as well as extra time, attention, and other rewards for followers when they perform well. They also use contingent punishment behavior by letting followers know when they have not performed well. Transactional leaders may reprimand followers for repeated rule violations and low effort leading to poor performance. These leaders also build close social exchanges (create in-groups) with selected followers whom they view as effective or potentially effective performers. They often exclude others from close social exchanges.

Transactional exchange leaders often have high achievement motivation, setting high goals for themselves and their groups and focusing their intense effort on achieving those goals. They are sometimes described as single minded in their pursuit of these goals. They also often have good interpersonal and communication skills, which they concentrate on their highest performing followers. These leaders can be effective with followers who are very rational in their approach to tasks and who view their time with

FIGURE 17–4 Applying the Transformational Visionary Leadership Style

1. Diagnosing the Situation

- Are followers extremely frustrated or unhappy with their current situation?
- Are followers highly stressed due to strong competition, government action, or economic developments?
- Is followers' welfare endangered due to technological, political, or other environmental changes?
- Are followers psychologically weakened due to discrimination, economic hardship, or other personal factors?

If "yes" to one or more of these questions, then followers will probably respond favorably to the transformational visionary style of leadership

3. Modifying Followers and Situations

Leaders act to:
- decrease stress in followers' environment
- provide education and training to develop followers' abilities to respond to change
- provide counseling services to help followers with personal problems
- develop plans and procedures for responding to changes that may affect the followers' group

2. Providing a Transformational Visionary Leadership Style

Leaders demonstrate transformational behaviors by:
- giving inspirational speeches that describe the current situation as intolerable
- outlining a mission and favorable vision of the future
- demonstrating self-confidence and confidence in followers to carry out the mission
- showing concern and consideration for followers and encouraging their development
- representing followers to outsiders to gain resources, cooperation, and support

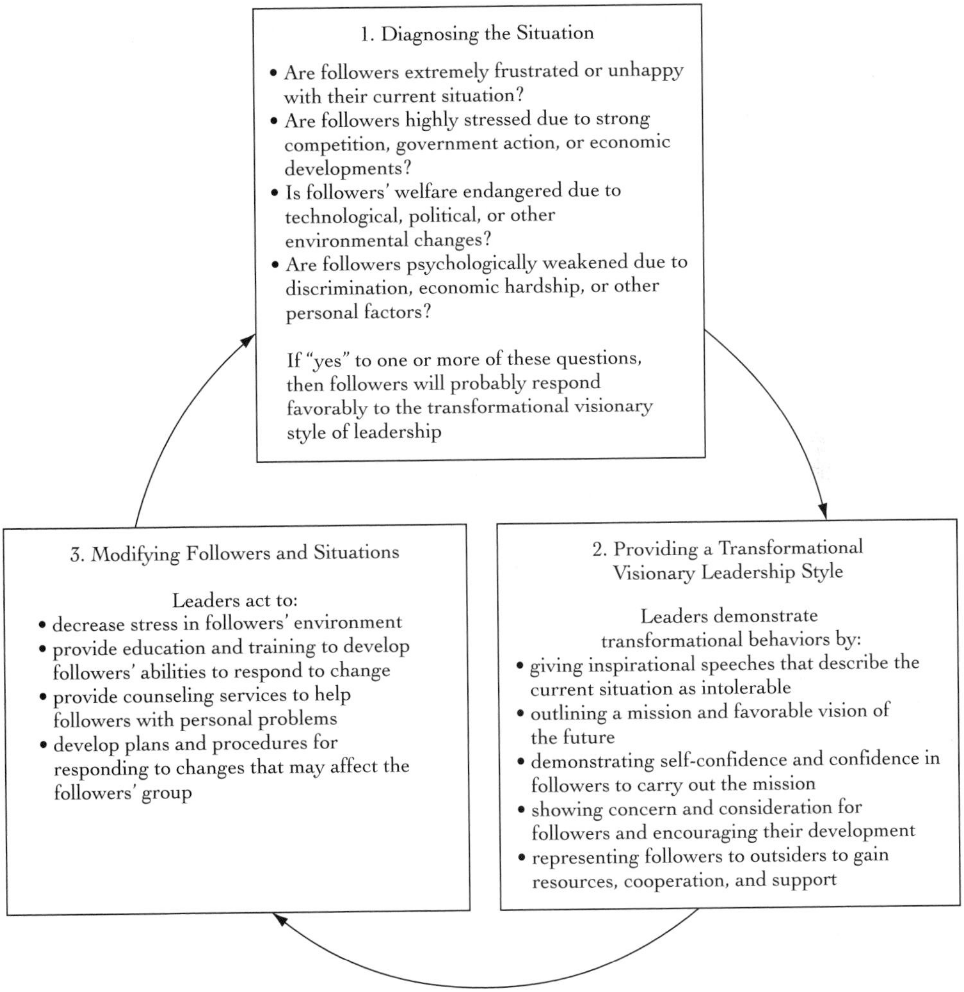

the leader as an opportunity to benefit themselves professionally. This style may be less effective in situations where the leader has few rewards at her disposal or where methods are unclear and extensive creativity is required.

The transactional exchange style was used when the trans-Alaska oil pipeline was under construction. The contractors hired skilled and unskilled labor to work in isolated areas and under severe weather conditions for very high wages. Supervisors expected workers to put in 10- to 12-hour days and work six or seven days per week. All their living needs were provided for by the company when they were on the job, so many workers saved substantial amounts of money. The supervisors were highly directive and rewarded good performance by rehiring workers who went south every few weeks for rest and relaxation. They enforced strict rules of conduct when workers were on the job or in the enclosed living facilities the companies provided. They also expected employees to show up for work on time. Supervisors made these expectations clear to employees when they first arrived, and when employees complied with expectations, the monetary rewards were very significant. Figure 17–5 summarizes the transactional exchange style of leadership.

THE SERVANT LEADER

The term servant leader has recently appeared in the popular management literature to describe a variation on the coach and the transformational visionary styles. Like coaches, servant leaders' primary concern is for their followers. They view their leadership position as most useful when they are meeting followers' needs. This means assuring that followers are growing as persons, becoming healthier, freer, morally mature, and autonomous in their work and life. In this sense, the servant leader is a servant first and leader second.

FIGURE 17–5 Applying the Transactional Exchange Leadership Style

1. Diagnosing the Situation

- Do followers view their role primarily as trading their time for tangible rewards?
- Are followers seriously considering other positions outside the group?
- Does the leader have significant resources available to reward followers?
- Do followers' job tasks involve work methods that are clearly learnable and require little inventiveness and creativity?

If "yes" to one or more of these questions, then followers will probably respond favorably to the transactional exchange style of leadership.

3. Modifying Followers and Situations

Leaders act to:
- create programs that increase followers' commitment to the organization
- create organization-wide reward systems that operate independently of the leader
- create procedures that invite follower participation in creatively solving organizational problems

2. Providing a Transactional Exchange Leadership Style

Leaders demonstrate transactional behaviors by:
- defining what is expected of followers
- clarifying procedures and work methods
- rewarding, complimenting, and recognizing followers
- letting followers know when they have not performed well
- reprimanding followers for repeated rule violations and low effort
- building close social exchanges with followers the leader believes have high potential

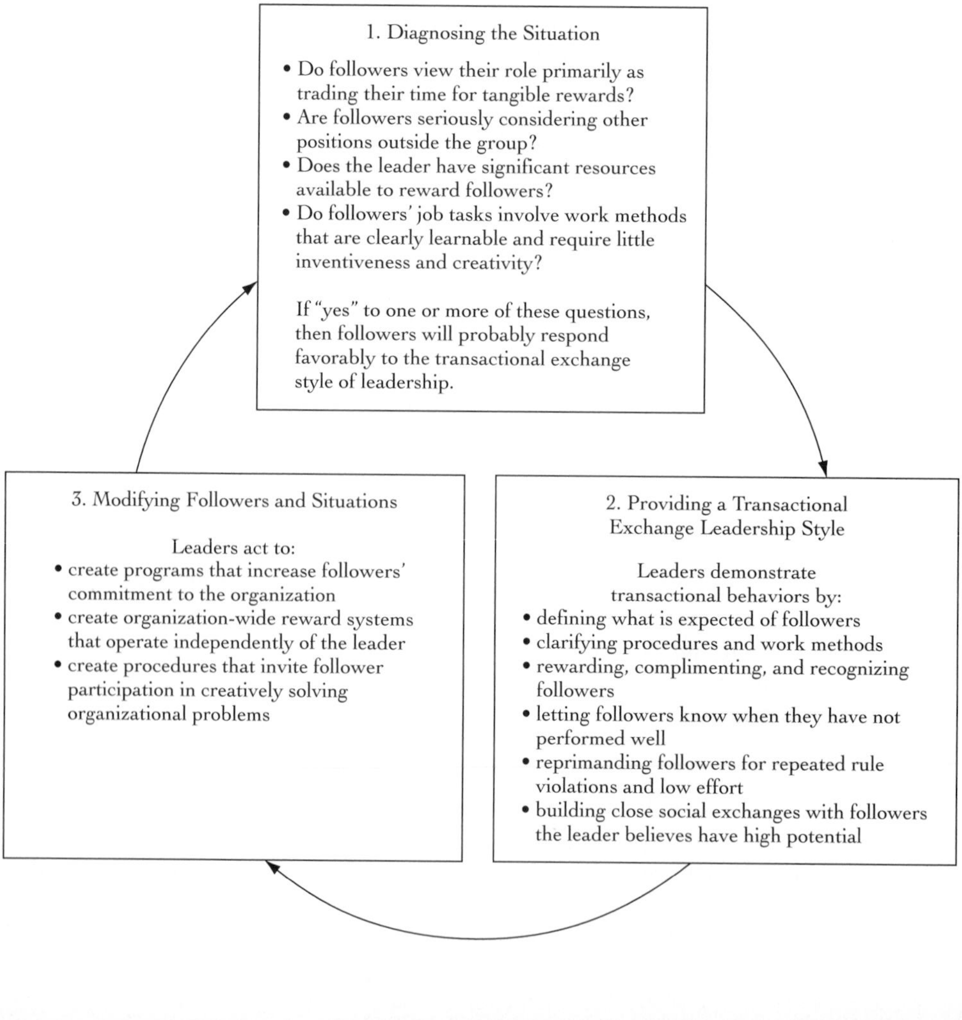

Some writers describe a spiritual element as part of servant leadership (7). These leaders urge followers to seek the power of their human spirit and to let their conscience guide them as they accept their responsibilities. This can mean that servant leaders are extremely open and willing to share their own pain and frustrations with followers.

Servant leaders are often supportive and participative, as well as charismatic with their followers. They are excellent listeners, they seek to fully understand the problems followers face and to affirm their confidence in followers. They try to provide followers with whatever they need to do their jobs and grow as individuals. They engage with followers in problem solving. They think the best of others and strive for moral excellence. They effectively communicate a vision and mission that is exciting and challenging. Servant leaders are also competent at followers' tasks and often challenge the status quo. They emphasize and model ethical behavior for followers and oppose injustice in the organization. These characteristics evoke a high level of trust in the servant leader by followers.

The servant leadership style is probably most effective when followers are discouraged or face a long difficult task. Their discouragement may come from past leaders who have made unrealistic promises or have exploited followers, or from a lack of confidence in their own ability. They need a leader who is trustworthy, supports their development, and provides encouragement and confidence in their abilities.

Mother Theresa is an example of a highly committed servant leader. She devoted her life to serving the sick and poor population of India and she inspired hundreds of followers and millions of dollars in donations. On a smaller scale, in one manufacturing plant, managers give assembly-line workers time off to read thought-provoking books to help develop their minds (8). Figure 17–6 summarizes the servant leader style of leadership.

◆ MODIFYING SITUATIONS AND FOLLOWERS

In addition to describing effective leader behaviors in this book, we have also emphasized how follower characteristics and situational factors affect the attitudes and performance of individuals and groups. Incompetent leaders have often been saved by followers who "knew the ropes" and ignored the leader's directives while relying on their own job knowledge and experience to complete their tasks in a competent manner. Experienced leaders know that environmental factors can play a key role in many group performance situations. Plentiful supplies may allow a group to easily recover from early mistakes; technological breakthroughs or market shifts can give an organization a sudden competitive advantage; or an act of God may destroy an important competitor and give an organization a virtual monopoly. Internal organizational factors such as company programs for job redesign, gainsharing, goal setting, empowerment, autonomous work groups, and self-management can significantly affect employee attitudes and performance. These programs are all created, controlled, and influenced by leaders in organizations.

Leaders therefore have two general strategies of influence on followers. First, they can use the behaviors described in this book, which have direct effects on followers' reactions and behaviors. Second, they can modify or develop organizational programs and environmental factors that guide and shape followers' behavior and performance. Many organizational programs have the potential to foster increased ability, motivation, and performance among followers. For example, reward systems or goal-setting programs may enhance a leader's effectiveness by making followers

FIGURE 17–6 Applying the Servant Leadership Style

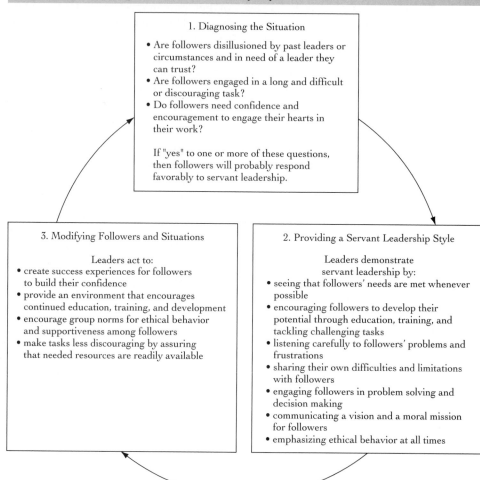

1. Diagnosing the Situation

- Are followers disillusioned by past leaders or circumstances and in need of a leader they can trust?
- Are followers engaged in a long and difficult or discouraging task?
- Do followers need confidence and encouragement to engage their hearts in their work?

If "yes" to one or more of these questions, then followers will probably respond favorably to servant leadership.

3. Modifying Followers and Situations

Leaders act to:
- create success experiences for followers to build their confidence
- provide an environment that encourages continued education, training, and development
- encourage group norms for ethical behavior and supportiveness among followers
- make tasks less discouraging by assuring that needed resources are readily available

2. Providing a Servant Leadership Style

Leaders demonstrate servant leadership by:
- seeing that followers' needs are met whenever possible
- encouraging followers to develop their potential through education, training, and tackling challenging tasks
- listening carefully to followers' problems and frustrations
- sharing their own difficulties and limitations with followers
- engaging followers in problem solving and decision making
- communicating a vision and a moral mission for followers
- emphasizing ethical behavior at all times

increasingly responsive to leaders. Other programs that emphasize job redesign, empowerment, autonomous work groups, or self-management can allow followers to govern their own work behavior more effectively and actually replace certain behaviors leaders have often provided in the past.

We wish to emphasize one last time that leadership replacements *do not* eliminate the need for leadership in organizations. They can, however, reduce or eliminate the need for leaders to do certain things that have occupied much of their time. The time a leader devotes to supervising operations, providing interpersonal "strokes" to bolster follower confidence, or monitoring performance of individuals and groups can all be drastically reduced by creatively modifying situations and followers. Replacements can have enduring effects, as when a challenging job becomes a lasting source of motivation for an employee or when a gainsharing program engages all employees in actively achieving organizational goals. The evidence from research shows that organizational programs that create these leadership replacements can foster increased productivity and improve employee attitudes and behaviors.

One expert recently described how replacements for leadership can be developed in schools as a strategy to foster morality and virtue as well as high-quality performance among teachers, students, administrators, and involved community members (9). At an early stage of a school's development, the leader provides the behaviors described in this book to guide and motivate staff members to work on tasks that are needed for goal accomplishment and to create satisfying experiences in the process. At this early stage, the leader's behavior directly affects followers' actions, attitudes, and performance.

At a more evolved stage of a school's development, the leader encourages a sense of community, with norms and goals for excellence and achievement. All staff share values, commitments, and obligations to work professionally and collegially to carry out those norms and goals. These norms, shared values, professionalism, and collegiality represent replacements for leadership that "glue" the school together by governing and guiding members' behavior and engaging them in intrinsically satisfying work as an organizational community. These replacements thus provide much of what school leaders have traditionally provided through directive, reward and punishment, or even charismatic leader behaviors. Guidance, motivation, and satisfaction come from increasingly self-managed members of the school community, who rely on each other to obtain help, advice, ideas, encouragement, and feedback to carry out their shared values, norms, and goals.

Such replacements for leadership may be the only strategy that adequately addresses the complex and changing demands that now face organizations. These replacements empower individuals to develop their own problem solving abilities, to communicate and cooperate with their colleagues, and to develop and enforce codes of ethics that define individual duties and moral responsibilities. By creating more self-management, organizational leaders are freed up for needed boundary-spanning activities—for example, to obtain the political, resource, moral, and administrative support needed to foster organizational performance and development.

This work on replacements for leadership in schools represents one application of the situational modification strategy for leadership. In the long run, this approach is designed to help organizational leaders, members, and clients achieve human and organizational goals with efficiency and integrity.

◆ LEADERSHIP AND DIVERSITY

The U. S. population, the workforce, and the buying public are all changing. The age, race, gender, ethnic heritage, mental and physical abilities, and sexual orientation of organizational members and customers are becoming the bases for identifiable groups that demand respect and equal treatment. The U. S. population and the workforce are not a "melting pot" where all groups blend together, but a "salad" of diverse groups of people who want to maintain their own beliefs and customs and still participate fully in organizations (10). Leaders in the new millennium face the difficult task of integrating these diverse groups of individuals into a unified effort to achieve organizational goals efficiently and effectively.

In a broad sense, diversity is anything that makes people different, not just racial and ethnic differences. The average organizational member is now older, and more people of color, women, and immigrants are entering the workforce (11). Between now and the year 2015, only 15 percent of the individuals entering the workforce will be white males. People of color represent the majority population in 16 of the top 25 urban markets in the United States. Increasing numbers of organizations are involved in operations in other countries. Organizations must draw their members and customers from this changing population and leaders must acknowledge and value these differences to improve organizational operations and outcomes.

Leaders of a diverse workforce face many obstacles, including stereotypes, fear by the majority of losing their advantage status, and lack of understanding of other cultures. But leaders can create and direct certain programs that are helpful in overcoming these obstacles. Research shows that three types of programs are helpful in leading a diverse workforce. One program exposes personnel to individuals with different backgrounds, characteristics, and cultures. This exposure may open peoples' eyes to ideas and perspectives of different groups and can be done through diversity training, mentoring, and networks with other organizations. A second program involves educating organizational members to overcome their stereotypes and prejudice in interacting with people different from themselves. This educational program also includes helping minorities prepare for increasingly responsible positions. The third program involves enforcing fair treatment and nondiscrimination for all individuals in the leader's organization or group. This can be done by establishing and enforcing company policies, establishing advocacy groups, and internal audits of the organization's performance on diversity issues (12). The end product of these programs is hopefully a true appreciation of the value of diversity in organizations for solving societal and organizational problems. This appreciation is necessary to effectively address diverse markets, to manage diverse groups of followers, and to attract competent employees of all types. These programs also reflect society's sense of fairness and moral behavior and help organizations meet legislative requirements for equal treatment of all individuals.

Leaders use directive leadership in establishing and carrying out these diversity programs. They also use supportive behaviors such as mentoring to help minority individuals adapt to organizational conditions that are new to them. Leaders listen to followers' frustrations and concerns, and help them work through needed adjustments on the job. And they help followers build networks and support groups with others who have had similar experiences. Leaders use participative leadership to obtain input and feedback from followers on diversity programs. This keeps the programs relevant and oriented to followers' problems and concerns. Leaders recognize and compliment followers for success in completing diversity training and development programs, and for applying the training to their work situation. And they celebrate the promotion of nontraditional minorities into positions of increasing responsibility. When these leader behaviors are used in concert with the diversity programs described earlier, the leader's organization should be prepared to effectively utilize the rich and diverse workforce of the new millennium.

◆ EQUIFINALITY IN LEADERSHIP

The systems concept of equifinality refers to the fact that a final goal can be achieved from many starting points and via numerous means. Viewing organizations as systems, the final goal is usually a state of high productivity and positive follower attitudes. Many suggestions have been given in this book regarding how leaders can demonstrate spe-

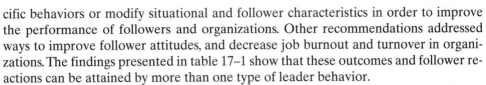

cific behaviors or modify situational and follower characteristics in order to improve the performance of followers and organizations. Other recommendations addressed ways to improve follower attitudes, and decrease job burnout and turnover in organizations. The findings presented in table 17–1 show that these outcomes and follower reactions can be attained by more than one type of leader behavior.

For example, table 17–1 indicates that followers' individual performance can be significantly improved by directive, supportive, and contingent reward leader behaviors. Also, follower satisfaction and commitment are improved by most of the core leader behaviors, while group cohesion, role clarity, and turnover can be improved by a smaller number of leader behaviors. Of course, any leader behavior is most effective when provided in the correct situations. But more than one type of leader behavior can produce favorable results. This demonstrates the equifinality of the different behaviors available to leaders. Some leader behaviors may have stronger effects on a given outcome than others, but leaders usually have behavioral choices regarding how to influence followers.

High-level organizational leaders can also use various approaches to overcome leadership problems experienced by lower-level leaders. For example, problem leaders can be trained to use a specific leader behavior more effectively or to use a different leader behavior to achieve a desired outcome. When training is not a viable option due to a leaders' stubbornness or some other factor, problem leaders can also be replaced or transferred to different duties. Finally, if replacement is difficult due to seniority, tenure, or other constraints, a higher-level leader can modify situational or follower characteristics to enhance the problem leader's effects on followers. Alternatively, leadership replacements can be created to fill in for weaknesses in the leader's behavioral skills. Since replacements are often durable, this approach can allow the problem leader to concentrate on those aspects of leadership that match her skills (13). These approaches demonstrate equifinality for high-level leaders in solving leadership problems in their organizations.

Both approaches to situational modification can improve leadership effectiveness. Creating enhancers often increases a leader's control of the situation and increases the direct effects of a leader's behavior on followers. Followers who lack competence, self-confidence, or self-esteem; are insecure; or have a high fear of failure may need regular interaction with the leader to maintain their sense of well-being and focus on the job. Enhancers facilitate followers' interactions with and responsiveness to the leader, usually making their reactions and performance more favorable.

Leadership replacements, the other situational modifier, often increase followers' control of the situation. For followers who are highly trained and/or educated, professionally oriented, and independent in their work, replacements are useful. They can make such employees even more capable of performing well on their own and even less reliant on their leader. A leader's interpersonal guidance, support, personal recognition, and/or inspirational speeches are then less necessary in achieving favorable follower reactions and performance.

Thus, both approaches to situational modification can result in improved follower reactions and performance (14). The correct approach often depends on the type of followers. Replacements for leadership are appropriate to many current workforce and organizational trends, such as increasing levels of formal education and professionalism, networked computer systems, computer integrated manufacturing, and telecommuting. These trends emphasize worker competence and autonomy without the leader's frequent input, and they are common in highly developed countries. If leadership replacements are implemented carefully, they will allow more freedom and independence for organizational employees in the year 2000 and beyond. They will also allow leaders to spend more time on increasingly important boundary issues, building productive exchanges with all employees, and developing followers' abilities to perform on their own.

Key Terms and Concepts in this Chapter ■ ■ ■ ■ ■ ■ ■ ■ ■ ■ ■ ■ ■ ■ ■ ■ ■ ■

- boundary spanning
- coaching leadership style
- commitment
- controlling autocratic leadership style
- diversity
- equifinality
- followership

- group cohesion
- human relations leadership style
- impression management skills
- leadership styles
- need for affiliation
- personal need for power

- role clarity
- servant leadership style
- social exchanges
- socialized need for power
- transactional exchange leadership style
- transformational visionary leadership style

Review and Discussion Questions ■

1. What three leader behaviors have been most consistent at increasing the quality or quantity of performance by followers and groups? Why do you think these three leader behaviors consistently increase performance?

2. Describe specific situations where charismatic or social exchange behaviors improved your opinion of a leader's performance. Why did these behaviors work so well?

3. Describe a leader you have observed or heard about who used a coaching leadership style. What situational characteristics contributed to the effectiveness of this leader's coaching?

4. Identify situations you have observed or heard about where human-relations-style leaders were effective or ineffective in achieving high levels of performance. What situational factors made the human relations style effective or ineffective?

5. Think of a controlling autocratic leader you have observed or heard about. What behaviors did the leader use to influence followers? Was the controlling autocratic leader effective? How did followers react to the controlling autocratic leader?

6. Why do you think that the transformational visionary leadership style is currently very popular? How effective would transformational visionary leaders be in influencing your behavior?

7. Of the leadership styles presented in this chapter, which is the closest to your "preferred" style as a leader? How would you modify the style to better fit your preferred leadership style?

8. Explain the concept of equifinality in leadership. How could you use this concept to be a more effective leader?

◆◆◆ **Case Incident**

Gaining Compliance

Jim Stanley has accepted his first supervisory job after graduating in the top five percent of his college class with a degree in management. Jim's new position is supervisor of the purchasing department for a state government agency. By working hard in the agency's training program and spending considerable time studying on his own, Jim has gained an in-depth understanding of the agency's policies on how jobs are to be done. From Jim's first day on the job he has carefully explained to employees how the agency's policies and procedures are to be followed in accomplishing all work. Even after repeated explanations, some employees insist that they be allowed to do their jobs their "own way," which Jim feels is not according to agency policies.

Jim took David Murphy aside, one of the employees who continually refuses to cooperate, and said, "You are going to have to do the job according to agency procedures."

David replied, "No, sometimes you have to be practical and get around the agency's bureaucratic procedures. The way I do the job is the most effective way."

Jim responded, "I am not going to be a party to getting around agency policies and procedures. You either do it the way I told you, or I'll recommend that you be replaced."

David retaliated, "If you knew anything about management, you'd realize that you should support employees. We can do the best job when we do it our own way."

Jim is beginning to wonder if there is any way to get through to David that things must be done according to agency policies and procedures. Jim knows that David thinks that because he is a civil service employee, he cannot be fired or subjected to severe disciplinary action.

QUESTIONS

1. How would you characterize Jim Stanley's leadership style? What leader behaviors seem to dominate Jim's attempts to influence David's behavior?
2. What situational and follower factors should Jim take into account in deciding which leader behaviors would be effective?
3. What advice would you give Jim about how to effectively influence the behavior of his employees and achieve the objectives of the agency?

Endnotes

1. Hersey, P. and Blanchard, K. H. (1984). *Management of Organizational Behavior: Utilizing Human Resources* (4th ed.). Upper Saddle River, NJ: Prentice Hall; Marcic, D. and Seltzer, J. (1995). *Organizational Behavior: Experiences and Cases.* Cincinnati, OH: Southwestern College Publishing; Vecchio, R. P. (1997). Situational leadership theory: An examination of a prescriptive theory. In R. P. Vecchio (Ed.), *Leadership: Understanding the Dynamics of Power and Influence in Organizations.* Notre Dame, Indiana: University of Notre Dame Press, 318–333.
2. Lau, J. B. and Jelinek, M. (1984). *Behavior in Organizations: An Experiential Approach.* Homewood, IL: Irwin.

3. Blake, R. R. and Mouton, J. S. (1983). *Consultation: A Handbook for Industrial and Organizational Development.* Reading, MA: Addison-Wesley, 564–565; Costley, D., Santana-Melgoza, C. and Todd, R. (1994). *Human Relations in Organizations* (5th ed.). St. Paul, MN: West.

4. Bass, B. M. (1997). Does the transactional-transformational leadership paradigm transcend organizational and national boundaries? *American Psychologist, 52,* 130–139; Bass, B. M. (1997). From transactional leadership to transformational leadership: Learning to share the vision. In R. P. Vecchio (Ed.), *Leadership: Understanding the Dynamics of Power and Influence in Organizations.* Notre Dame, Indiana: University of Notre Dame Press, 318–333.

5. Daft, R. L. (1999). *Leadership: Theory and Practice.* New York: Dryden.

6. Hollander, E. P. (1978). *Leadership Dynamics: A Practical Guide to Effective Relationships.* New York: The Free Press; Hollander, E. P. (1993). Legitimacy, power, and influence: A perspective on relational features of leadership. In M. M. Chemers and R. Ayman (Eds.), *Leadership Theory and Research: Perspectives and Directions.* New York: Academic Press; Jacobs, T. O. (1970). *Leadership and Exchange in Formal Organizations.* Alexandria, VA: Human Resources Research Organization.

7. Daft, *Leadership: Theory and Practice.*

8. Ibid.

9. Sergiovani, T. J. (1992). *Moral Leadership: Getting to the Heart of School Improvement.* San Francisco: Jossey-Bass.

10. Daft, *Leadership: Theory and Practice.*

11. Ibid.

12. Morrison, A. (1992). *The New Leaders: Guidelines for Leadership Diversity in America.* San Francisco: Jossey-Bass.

13. Howell, J. P., Bowen, D. E., Dorfman, P. W., Kerr, S. and Podsakoff, P. M. (1990). Substitutes for leadership: Effective alternatives for ineffective leadership. *Organizational Dynamics, 19,* 21–38.

14. Podsakoff, P. M., MacKenzie, S. B. and Bommer, W. H. (1996). Meta-analysis of the relationships between Kerr and Jermier's substitutes for leadership and employee attitudes, role perceptions and performance. *Journal of Applied Psychology,* 8(4), 380–399.

Name Index

Subject Index